Oman

the Bradt Travel Guide

Diana Darke
Sandra Shields

edition
I

www.bradtguides.com

Bradt Travel Guides Ltd, UK
The Globe Pequot Press Inc, USA

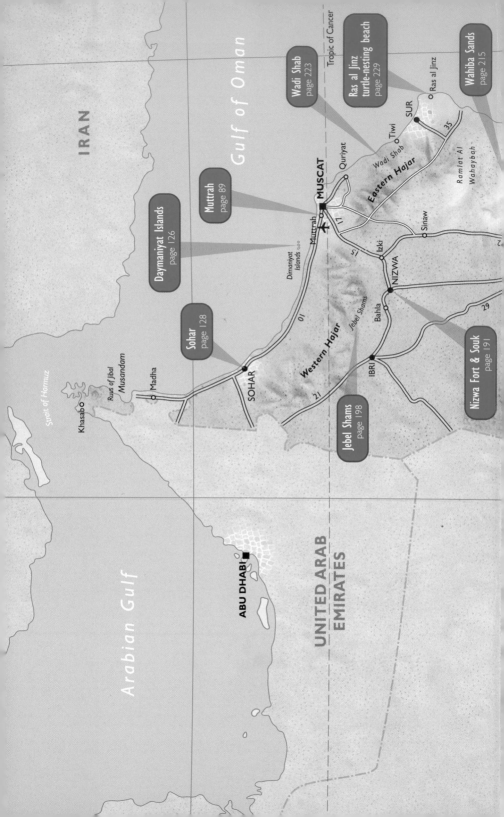

IRAN

Gulf of Oman

Arabian Gulf

Strait of Hormuz

Khasabo

Ruus of Jibal Musandam

Madha

Wadi Shab page 223

Tropic of Cancer

Ras al Jinz turtle-nesting beach page 229

Ras al Jinz

Wahiba Sands page 215

SUR

Tiwi

Muttrah page 89

Quriyat

Wadi Shab

Eastern Hajar

35

Ramlat Al Wahaybah

Daymaniyat Islands page 126

MUSCAT

Muttrah

Dimaniyat Islands

17

Sinaw

Z

15

Izki

NIZWA

Sohar page 128

01

Western Hajar

Jebel Shams

Bahla

29

SOHAR

21

IBRI

Nizwa Fort & Souk page 191

Jebel Shams page 198

ABU DHABI

UNITED ARAB EMIRATES

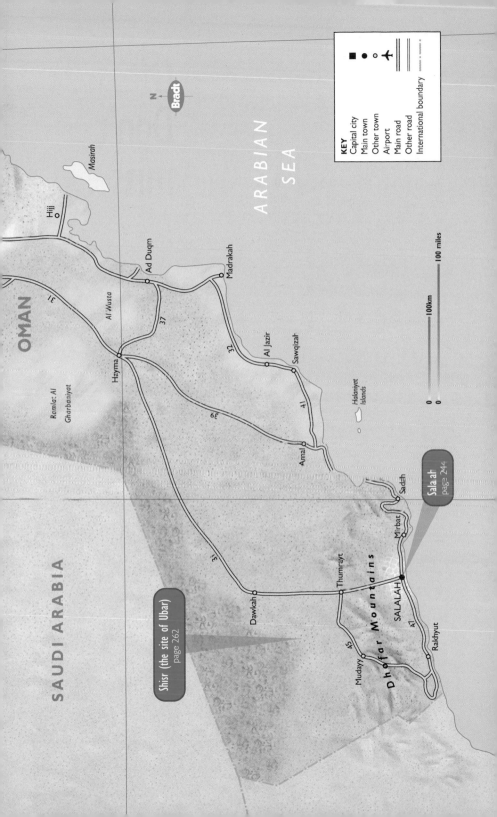

Oman
Don't
miss...

Wadis
Lush oases in the desert —
'bash' the dry ones in a 4x4
(PS) page 122

Jebel Akhdar
Mountain villages, wild goats
and natural springs
(DB) page 185

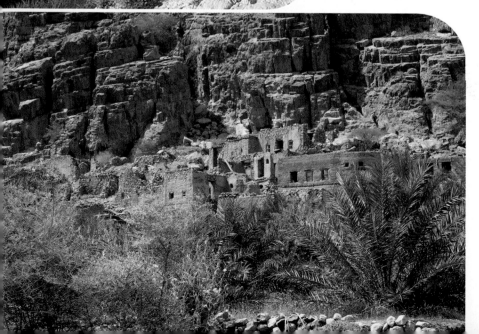

Souks
Spices, ornaments,
fruits and perfumes
(DB) page 90

Muscat
The bustling
Omani capital
(DB) page 42

Wahiba Sands
Take a desert safari
trip to remember
(DB) page 215

top	Interior walls, Nizwa Fort (DB) page 191
above left	Lookout tower in fishing village of Ayega, near Sur (DS) page 224
above right	Gravestone, Masirah Island (SS) page 230
below	Restored Portuguese fort, Sohar (PS) page 131

Authors

Diana Darke first lived in the Sultanate of Oman in 1980 when she worked for a year in a government department. At that time foreigners were few and far between and it was a rare opportunity to see an entirely unspoilt country through the eyes of Omani colleagues. The chance to write this book presented itself nearly 20 years later during a three-year spell in neighbouring Dubai, when she was able to re-explore Oman, travelling regularly throughout the country, and seeing the changes and progress the intervening years had brought.

Sandra Shields resided in Oman from 2000 to 2002 in association with a construction project for the BBC World Service at A'Seela, to the east of the country. She successfully completed her BA (Hons) degree in literature while resident overseas, and has a keen interest in writing, travel and photography. She revisited Oman in 2005 and 2006, driving herself from one end of the country to the other. She has a deep love of the country and the relaxed nature of the Omani people.

FEEDBACK REQUEST

Oman is a fast-changing society, so events may in some instances overtake what is described. Your help in enabling future editions to be as accurate as possible will be all the more appreciated, as will any suggestions you have for additional content. Please write or email via the publishers at: Bradt Travel Guides, 23 High Street, Chalfont St Peter, Bucks SL9 9QE; e info@bradtguides.com.

PUBLISHER'S FOREWORD

Hilary Bradt

The first Bradt travel guide was written in 1974 by George and Hilary Bradt on a river barge floating down a tributary of the Amazon. In the 1980s and '90s the focus shifted away from hiking to broader-based guides covering new destinations – usually the first to be published about these places. In the 21st century Bradt continues to publish such ground-breaking guides, as well as others to established holiday destinations, incorporating in-depth information on culture and natural history with the nuts and bolts of where to stay and what to see.

Bradt authors support responsible travel, and provide advice not only on minimum impact but also on how to give something back through local charities. In this way a true synergy is achieved between the traveller and local communities.

* * *

Oman came to my attention when we first published *Zanzibar*, many years ago. I learned about the historic links between the two countries – going back to the 1800s when, bizarrely, Zanzibar was the capital of Oman – and thought that any country in the Middle East that was once governed from east Africa would be a perfect addition to our list. It's taken a few years to bring this about, but the timing is perfect. Oman is on the ascendancy as a holiday destination and Diana Darke and Sandra Shields have unearthed a range of attractions and hotels to satisfy the visitors who do not have to rely on the trade winds to reach this exotic destination.

First published October 2006
Reprinted March 2007

Bradt Travel Guides Ltd
23 High Street, Chalfont St Peter, Bucks SL9 9QE, England; www.bradtguides.com
Published in the USA by The Globe Pequot Press Inc, 246 Goose Lane,
PO Box 480, Guilford, Connecticut 06475-0480

British Library Cataloguing in Publication Data
A catalogue record for this book is available from the British Library
ISBN-10: 1 84162 168 4   ISBN-13: 978 1 84162 168 5

Photographs Derek Brown (DB), Patrick Syder Images (PS), Dave Saunders (DS), Sandra Shields (SS), Ulana Switucha/Alamy (US)
Front cover Rooftops of Nizwa Mosque in the Dakhiliyah region (US)
Back cover Bedu and camel, Rub'al Khali (PS), Man reducing air pressure in tyres, Wahiba Sands (DS)
Title page Necklaces and *khanjar* at Old Muttrah Souk, Muscat (DB), Al Zawawi Mosque, Ghubra (SS), Dates, Batinah region (SS)
Illustrations Carole Vincer   **Maps** Dave Priestley

Typeset from the authors' disc by Wakewing
Printed and bound in Italy by Legoprint SpA, Trento

Acknowledgements

Diana Darke would like to acknowledge the help of Omani friends and colleagues too numerous to mention, but especially the late Sheikh Sair Al Harithy; also to Mike and Barbara Baddeley, Paul Flaherty and Andy Coulson.

Sandra Shields would like to thank all the people who assisted her on this project. They are Asma Alhajry of the Ministry of Tourism, Oman; Sharon Bernstein and Rabia Charkaoui of Representation Plus, London; Mahmood al Ghafri of the Ministry of Tourism; Lakshmy Narayanan of Bahwan Tours; Nizar Ahmed of Mark Tours; Antonio Rodrigues of Corniche Hotel; Charryce Nixon-Luke of Treasure Tours; John Wilson and Tom Hunter of the BBC World Service; Emad Alnadhif of Zahara Tours, Salalah; Stefanie of the Oman Dive Centre; Vidhyadharan of Dolphin Tourism, Khasab; Mohan of Dolphin Tourism; Tomy of Khasab Travel & Tours; Sulieman al Rahbi; Kate Jones of the Shangri-La Group; Azzan al Jabri; Zahid Mohamed Sheikh of Mezoon Travel LLC; Kevin Maguire of Oman Aviation Services; Manoj Dass of Mezoon Travel; G Ragan of Oriental Nights Rest House; Moktil Louis of Al Sharqiya Sands Hotel; Mathew Kuriakose of Ras al Hadd Beach Hotel; Pius Borges of the Crowne Plaza Hotel, Salalah; Yousuf al Mahrooqi of Sumharam Watersports and Dive Centre, Salalah; Rosemary Hector of the Ministry of Information; Talal al Rawahi of Oman Beach Hotel; Michael Murray in London; Len Hobbs, former language lecturer of the Sultan Qaboos University; Sarah White of the Bait al Zubair Foundation, Professor Reginald Victor of the Sultan Qaboos University.

I would also like to give special thanks to the following people. Hilary Bradt for giving new writers with a love for a country the chance to demonstrate it, and especially Tricia Hayne for reading my initial letter and offering this opportunity. John Wilson, for showing me all the countries he did, and for bringing out within me the huge love and appreciation of travel, and other ways of seeing. Thanks also to Lorraine Shields and Michael Hayes; Hayley Browne, Steve Browne, Sophie Browne and Alex Browne; Chris Shields and Heather Shields; Dal and Nee Shields; Terriejane Snell; and Brian Shields.

A final thanks to Geoff Major for astounding kindness and care since our meeting in May. What luck!

DEDICATION

Dedicated to the memory of Albert Snell (1912–97), Alice Snell (1913–99) and Barry Snell (1939–99).

Contents

LIST OF MAPS

Introduction

In a region notorious for religious extremism, turbulence and unrest, it is a relief to find a country characterised by calm and composure. Amid uneasy Middle Eastern neighbours, Oman and the Omani people sit peaceably – strong and silent. Geographically, it is a place of awe-inspiring natural landscapes: mountains, ravines, cliffs, canyons, desert and coastline endure, unchanged, under an incessant Middle Eastern sun. Politically, Oman is stable and so offers a safe environment – as safe as any can be anywhere today. Financially it is strong with oil, agriculture and fisheries industries, and now its emerging tourism sector.

Considering that when Sultan Qaboos took over in 1970 there were only 5km of surfaced roads, three schools (all primary, and for boys only), one hospital (run by American missionaries), no police force, newspapers, radio or television stations, the scene today is incredible. The advances in all aspects of society are astounding.

Oman's modern mindset has facilitated its entrance on the global scene ensuring its future prosperity, while simultaneously improving the lives of its people. Witnessing today's juxtaposition of old and new in the country, Oman serves to endow us with an appreciation of the qualities of both ways of life. Although the modern way may be anathema to the late British writer and explorer Wilfred Thesiger, who valued the trials and rewards of life as the Bedu lived it in the Omani desert, it cannot be denied that the Omanis today at the very least have a fundamentally improved lot. Indeed the reason why the country has been slow to embrace tourism is because of concerns to preserve the old ways of life – the culture and the heritage. This is demonstrated today in the restoration projects of historic sites, aimed at keeping Oman's history intact and its story alive. Four areas are now UNESCO World Heritage Sites. The Omani people too are keen, proud and enthusiastic in showing and sharing their country's fruits (both literally and figuratively) with you.

With a varied wilderness terrain of desert, wadi, mountain and ocean, there is huge scope for adventure, eco- and cultural tourism. From the fjords and barrenness of Musandam, to the sand deserts of the Wahiba and Empty Quarter, from the Hajar mountain range, to the green monsoon area of Dhofar in the south, the draw of Oman lies in the outdoors – in its nature.

There are figures in history, myth and legend who have travelled, lived and explored Oman. The Queen of Sheba, Alexander the Great, Pliny the Elder, Vasco da Gama, Marco Polo, Freya Stark, Ibn Battutah, Lawrence of Arabia, H St J B Philby, Wilfred Thesiger and Ranulph Fiennes have all passed through, leaving invaluable writings behind. They provide a fascinating link to the past, illuminating the country for us today.

For the future there is The Wave, the Journey of Light and the Blue City – three enormous construction projects which will incorporate international-class hotels, residential villages, restaurants and retail and leisure facilities, including 18-hole green international-standard golf courses. And this comes at the same time as the opening of the property market to foreign ownership.

Although it is considered an upscale destination for the discerning traveller, it is possible to tour the country keeping an eye on the financial outlay. If this is not a concern, the ultra-modern and busy Dubai makes a perfect contrasting partner for a twin-centre getaway, something which the Omani government is now keen to promote.

If you are from the West, and still in a fast-paced Western mode, the heat is soon likely to change that, and slow you to a more leisurely pace. After any extended length of time here, you may even find yourself developing the *inshallah* mentality, meaning 'if God wills it, it will happen'; and *bukra*, 'sometime after tomorrow'.

Thankfully, the Oman of old remains intact; and thanks to a liberal-minded, peace-loving, democratic sultan, we now have been invited in.

Blanford's fox

Part One

GENERAL INFORMATION

Location Southeastern edge of Arabian peninsula at 21°N, 57°E

Neighbouring countries United Arab Emirates, Saudi Arabia, Yemen

Size 309,500km² approx

Population 2,415,576 (Ministry of National Economy, 2004)

Capital Muscat; population 664,826 (Ministry of National Economy, 2004)

Other main towns Salalah, Nizwa, Sohar, Sur

Ports Mina Qaboos, Mina Raysut, Muttrah, Sohar

Climate Predominantly arid, with regional variations. Summer (April–September) coastal regions hot and humid with the interior hot and dry (average 40°C); winter (October–March) warm and dry throughout, with high mountain areas becoming cold, sometimes with snow. Rainfall is rare and irregular.

Status Monarchy

Sultan and head of state Qaboos Bin Said (from 1970)

Ethnic divisions Arab, Baluchi, south Asian (Indian, Pakistani, Sri Lankan, Bangladeshi) and Zanzibari

Languages Arabic (official), English (widely spoken), Baluchi, Urdu, Swahili, Hindi, Indian dialects. German and French spoken in larger hotels.

Religion Predominantly Muslim: Ibadhi Muslim (75%), Sunni Muslim and Shi'a Muslim (12.4%), Hindu (5.7%), Christian (4.9%), Buddhist (0.8%), other (1.2%)

Chief exports Oil, dates, copper, silverware, fish

GDP US$40.14 billion

Currency Omani rial (OMR/RO)

Exchange rate £1 = RO0.73, US$1 = RO0.38, €1 = RO0.50 (September 2006)

National airline Oman Air, Gulf Air (of which the Omani sultanate owns one third)

International telephone code +968

Time GMT+4

Electrical voltage 220–240v AC; British three-pin plugs widely used

Flag Three equal horizontal bands of white, red, and green with a broad, vertical, red band on the hoist side; the national emblem (a *khanjar* dagger in its sheath superimposed on two crossed swords in scabbards) in white is centred at the top of the vertical band

National emblem The *khanjar* (a silver-sheathed curved dagger)

National holidays Non-religious: New Year's Day (1 January), National Day (18 November), Sultan's Birthday (19 November); religious (dates alter each year according to the Islamic Lunar Calendar): *Eid al Fitr* (at the end of Ramadan), *Eid al Adha* (during the Hajj), *Mawlid al Nabi* (Prophet's Birthday), *Muharram* (Islamic New Year). See page 52 for dates.

Background Information

GEOGRAPHY

Oman is located on the southeastern edge of the Arabian peninsula and is bordered by Yemen (in the southwest), Saudi Arabia (in the west) and the United Arab Emirates (in the northwest). The second-largest country in the peninsula, after Saudi Arabia, it covers an area of around 309,500km², and is roughly the same size as the UK; it is bigger than Syria, Jordan and Lebanon put together.

The coastline extends to a total of some 1,700km. The northern coastline sits on the Gulf of Oman and constitutes about a third of its total length. The remaining two-thirds sit on the Arabian Sea, which is the portion of the Indian Ocean between the Arabian peninsula on the west and the Indian subcontinent on the east. The Gulf of Oman is one of the world's most important strategic waterways, providing a shipping lane for oil from the Gulf States. Tankers pass through the Strait of Hormuz – a narrow waterway linking the Persian Gulf (or Arabian Gulf) with the Gulf of Oman – that lap the northernmost part of Oman, Musandam.

The country's topography is varied, with mountains in the north and south, sand desert and gravel desert in the central plain, with areas of oases, and coastal plains. Roughly 82% of the land is made up of sand and gravel desert and valleys, about 15% is mountainous and the remaining 3% is coastal plain. The Hajar mountain range rises up out of the Strait of Hormuz at the northernmost tip of the country and continues southward, like a spine, for approximately 600km.

The name Oman is thought to mean 'the abode' or 'the land', though other local traditions hold that it was named after 'Uman Ibn Qahtan, Oman's legendary first inhabitant. Its formal name is the Sultanate of Oman or Saltanat 'Uman, but it is simply known as Oman in everyday speech.

Despite the potential for trade links beyond its shores Oman is insular in character, cut off from its neighbours by deserts, mountains or sea. Its own terrain is varied and striking, its geographic mix of mountain, desert and coast leading to different lifestyles and occasionally conflicting values. The scarcity of essential natural resources such as water and fertile land meant that it was only with a great deal of sustained effort that any people, city or district could rise above bare subsistence level.

CLIMATE

Oman is predominantly arid but, because of its size and topography, the climate tends to vary from one region to another. It is perhaps easiest to split the country into four when thinking of climatic variations: the coastal regions, the interior, the mountains and the Dhofar coast, and then consider the two Omani seasons of winter and summer.

The coastal regions are very hot and humid in the summer, while the interior is very hot and dry. In the winter months both the coastal areas and the interior are

Background Information CLIMATE |

3

pleasantly warm and dry. There is little rainfall in the country and this is always irregular. However, when the occasional localised storms do occur (any time between October and March, with a tendency towards December and January, and largely in northern Oman), it is not unusual for them to be so heavy that wadis (watercourses) are in flood, causing havoc on the roads, especially the Muscat–Nizwa road, which is crossed by many wadis running off Jebel Akhdar, and the Muscat–Sur road, crossed by the wadis running off the eastern Hajar mountain range. Hailstorms are another winter phenomenon, sometimes falling so hard that people are injured and taken to hospital, livestock killed and crops damaged.

Temperatures in Muscat (northern coastal) can range from 32–48°C in the summer (April to September) and 25–36°C in the winter (October to March), making winter the best time to visit. January and February are the coolest months with average temperatures of 25°C. From March onwards temperatures begin to climb, reaching the 40s, together with high humidity. June and July are the hottest months and so the outdoors can become off-limits. Temperatures can also vary enormously: in July it can reach 48°C in the northern oil-producing desert areas round Fahud, but reach only 13°C on Jebel Shams. Hotels, restaurants, shopping malls and cars are well air conditioned and provide essential respite.

The high mountain areas enjoy a fairly moderate climate throughout the year although in the winter, the areas of high altitude can get cold. Night-time temperatures on Jebel Shams, Oman's highest mountain, at 3,048m (10,000ft) can reach below freezing point, and there is occasional snow.

In the south, the small band of land (roughly 240km long by 3–30km wide) between the Dhofar Mountains and the coast has its own microclimate. The temperature stays around a constant 26°C, with the phenomenon of the southwesterly monsoon rains – the *khareef* – running from around mid June till mid September. Dense fog and rains revive the parched flora, and give rise to a lush, green landscape, and so the Dhofar region is at its most beautiful in September and early October, making it the best time to visit. Visitors from other GCC (Gulf Co-operation Council) countries, as well as Omanis from the north, take advantage of this Dhofar spectacle, the temperature being moderate here by Middle Eastern standards. By November the greenery has vanished.

HISTORICAL OVERVIEW

Archaeological evidence and historical writings enable us to track Oman's history over a 5,000-year period. Sohar is believed to be the ancient 'Majan' referred to in Mesopotamian texts of the 3rd millennium BC. Majan means 'Copper Mountain' and it is the copper industry that is known to have sustained Oman for over 4,000 years.

Oman's people have historically been astro-navigators, sailors and merchant traders, occupying, as they did, a prime geographical position on the sea trading route between eastern and western continents. The indigenous natural resources of copper and frankincense (both extremely important commodities in the past), transformed the country's prosperity in ancient times through trade with ancient Egypt, Greece, Rome and China, to where these goods were shipped. Evidence of Oman's prosperous seafaring history can be found in ancient texts.

Islam did not arrive in the region until AD630. There was a short rule by the Portuguese in the 16th century, who were expelled in 1650 by Sultan bin Saif al Yarubi. The Ya'arubi dynasty continued to rule until the Persians invaded in 1741. They were expelled in 1749 by the founder of the present-day dynasty, Imam Ahmed bin Said. The presence of numerous castles and forts in virtually every village is testament to Oman's uneasy warring past – serving as protection from both outside invaders and neighbouring tribes.

Historic figures have passed through. The legend of Sindbad the Sailor, of *Arabian Nights* fame, is believed to originate from here from around the 10th century AD. T E Lawrence (or Lawrence of Arabia) was a British soldier and author famed for *Seven Pillars of Wisdom*, an account of his desert campaigns with the Arabs. The Land of Frankincense (a UNESCO World Heritage Site) links the Queen of Sheba to the region. Wilfred Thesiger, an explorer and writer, lived and travelled with the Bedu of southern Arabia in the 1940s. His writings illuminate the traditional way of life in Oman, which he deeply cherished. Oman is home to the famed 'Atlantis of the Sands' (the lost city of Ubar), alluded to in the Koran, the Bible and *Arabian Nights*.

Since 1975, immense changes to the country's prosperity and outlook under the leadership of the well-respected Sultan Qaboos have been achieved, made possible by the country's oil reserves. Oman has been carefully modernised and now sits as a newly opened destination for the discerning traveller, offering top-class international hotels. For the near future, new top-end leisure resorts will continue to augment Oman's prosperity through tourism, offering international-standard golf courses, spas, shops and restaurants, as well as property for sale on the international market.

CHRONOLOGY There is no specific historical section in this guide, since historical background is woven into the text as and when relevant. For an overview therefore, the following detailed chronology is provided as a handy reference and summary.

c3000BC	Earliest-known references to Oman as Magan found at Ur in Sumeria, confirming it as a thriving and wealthy seafaring state, the source of Mesopotamian (the Tigris and Euphrates region of Iraq) copper. Settlement and graves at Bat established.
2500–2000BC	Umm Al Nar period of rich trade between Oman and Mesopotamia, mainly in copper. Camels domesticated for transportation. Wadi Jizzi sites founded.

2000BC	Rise of Dilmun (Bahrain) eclipses Oman's trading power.
2000–1300BC	Wadi Suq period where Oman's main trading partner is Dilmun. Sites at Samad and Ras Al Jinz established.
1300–300BC	Iron Age. Frankincense trade using caravan routes through Arabia to the north. Sites of Ubar, Khor Rori, Lizq and Bowshar established.
c1000BC	*Falaj* system of irrigation introduced to Oman, probably by the Persians.
24BC	Roman army attempts to reach frankincense lands of southern Arabia but is defeated by climate and disease.
AD130	Yemeni Adnani (Ghafiri) tribes settle in Oman after years of wandering in the Nejd of Saudi Arabia.
AD200	Yemeni Azdite (Hinawi) tribes migrate to Oman after the bursting of the Maarib Dam.
AD200–400	Sassanians in power, having moved from Iran down the Gulf. Sassanian governors in Sohar and Rustaq.
AD400	Persians ransack Sumharam.
AD400–500	Christianity arrives in Oman with suggestions of an early Nestorian church in Sohar and an Omani bishop.
AD630	Amr Ibn Al As, Muhammad's general, arrives in Oman to convert the country to Islam. Oman is one of the first lands to embrace Islam fully and abandon Arabian paganism. Hinawis, after Muhammad's death, follow Ibadhi puritanical Islam, while Ghafiris follow Sunni orthodox Islam.
AD633	Battle of Dibba. Arab tribes of Oman defeat the Sassanians.
AD750	Julanda Bin Masud elected first imam (spiritual leader) of Oman. Oman remains under imam rule until 1154.
8th–10th centuries	Oman is a rich country and Baghdad (capital of Abbasid Caliphate) sends expeditions to obtain large tribute from it. Nizwa becomes the Omani capital.
9th–10th centuries	Extensive trade with the Far East and India, en route to the wealthy Abbasid court of Baghdad. Sohar enjoys great wealth and takes over from Nizwa as the capital. Interior of Oman deteriorates, attacks by Qarmathians, but Sohar is unaffected on the coast as trade routes flourish.
1151	Dynasty established by Banu Nabhan.
13th century	Hormuz, island settlement in the strait of the same name, becomes the region's most important trade centre, despite no water supply on the barren rocky island. It becomes independent of the mainland and remains unchallenged until the arrival of the Portuguese in the 16th century. Qalhat becomes the Omani capital.
1330	Ibn Battuta, north African traveller and geographer, visits and describes Nizwa.
1428	Dynastic rule challenged by the imams.
1507	The first Europeans, the Portuguese under Albuquerque, reach Oman. They burn Oman's fishing fleets and pillage the towns of Qalhat, Quriyat and Muscat, followed by Sohar. Their commercial success is based on supply of spices (pepper, cinnamon, camphor, nutmeg and cloves) to European markets. The coastal area and city and port of Muscat under Portuguese control.

The golden age of the Persian Gulf under the Hormuz princes ended with the arrival of the Portuguese in the Indian Ocean. The beginning of the end was when Vasco da Gama reached India in 1498, guided by an Omani navigator. In the following 30 or so years the Portuguese carried out a series of devastating attacks on key strategic points and secured maritime domination of the Arabian seas. The Portuguese were able to achieve this through great organisational skills, benefiting from strong political and economic direction from their homeland, and inspired by religious crusading zeal. On a more down to earth level they also had new and faster ships and superior arms. Their aim was to monopolise trade, in particular the long-distance luxury trade of the Indian seas. They took Hormuz in 1507, but though they built some forts and bases in the region, their practice was to leave power in the hands of local governments as much as possible and to rule indirectly. This avoided the manpower demands, expense and trouble of a direct European administration. The Portuguese were repulsed from the Gulf in the mid 17th century by the combined forces of the Iranian Safavids and the English, leaving Oman and its chief port city Muscat to dominate the Gulf until the British again established European supremacy in the 19th century. Their rule was too loose rather than too harsh, and it was remarkable that such a small country as Portugal was able to retain control of an area as vast as the Indian Ocean for as long as it did. In the period from the end of the Portuguese domination in the mid 17th century until the 19th century, the English, Dutch and French all sailed the Gulf, but their interests were commercial rather than political. Gradually over the course of the 19th century, the British increasingly allied themselves with the Omanis against the Arab 'pirate' sheikhdoms.

1527	Forts of Jalali and Merani built by the Portuguese in Muscat harbour.
1624	First imam of the Ya'arubi dynasty begins with Sultan ibn Saif.
1649–68	The navy is built up and expeditions undertaken to liberate Omani settlements.
1650	The Portuguese evicted from Oman after 150 years of coastal domination by Sultan ibn Saif, the powerful Ya'arubi leader. Oman is independent from this point on.
17th–18th centuries	Oman under Ya'arubi rulers dominates the Gulf and trade routes to east Africa. By the end of the 18th century the Omanis controlled an extensive empire, ruling Mombasa and Zanzibar.
1698	The east African coast from Mogadishu to Cape Delgado controlled by Oman, beginning a period of great Omani wealth.
1724–1739	Hinawi ('northern' faction and descendants of the Qahtan) – Ghafiri ('southern' faction and descendants of the Nizar) civil war results in virtual anarchy.
1741	End of Ya'arubi dynasty.
1743	Persian invasion of Batinah coast. Persians retained control until 1749.
1749	Founding of the Al Bu Said dynasty by Ahmed bin Said from his capital in Rustaq. (Today's Sultan Qaboos is the current representative of the Al Bu Saids.)

Background Information **HISTORICAL OVERVIEW**

In the early 19th century Britain's main concern in the Gulf was to secure its imperial communications to India. When some of its ships got caught up in the Gulf in the war that had been ongoing for some years between the Omanis and the Arab sheikhs of the Gulf coast, they viewed it as simple piracy. They had no understanding of the cause of such attacks, no realisation that they were casualties of a local naval and trade war. Instead, they accused the Wahhabis (a highly conservative Islamic group) of initiating attacks on British shipping and talked of the 'predatory habits' of the maritime Arabs. With Omani support the British attacked 'the pirates' three times between 1805 and 1820 and then imposed a maritime peace, which had the effect of forbidding the Arab states of the Gulf to fight one another at sea without British permission.

Over the next few decades a series of other treaties followed, some formal, some informal, for establishing a set of special privileges for those who co-operated with the Western powers and restricted their participation in the slave trade. In this way insidiously and over a long period, Britain's policy of 'non-interference' in the Gulf States' internal affairs in practice radically altered the tribal status quo, and removed the method by which Gulf principalities and city-states used to dominate each other and vie for position in the Gulf. Britain saw itself as a benevolent policeman in the Gulf, preventing piracy, slave trading and maritime war. It also saw itself as gradually introducing, true to the imperial philosophy of the time, progress and civilisation to the Arab Gulf States. As a result of these truces, the Arab side of the Gulf became known as the 'Trucial coast'.

1786	Oman's capital formally moves to Muscat from the interior.
1750–1800	Oman is wooed by Britain and France, both seeking political alliance and favour. French influence dwindles, weakened by the Napoleonic Wars. Napoleon lands in Egypt en route to India. Muscat would have been on his route, but he never got that far, having been forced to retreat from Egypt. Conservative tribes in the interior elect their own imam, feeling that the sultan in Muscat has grown too liberal.
1798	Treaty of friendship with Great Britain signed.
1800	Muscat is threatened by Wahhabi invasions from Saudi Arabia, so now it seeks alliance and support from Britain.
1804	Sultan Al Bu Said is killed by pirates, and Said Bin Sultan comes to power at 18, after killing his cousin to make way. His 50-year reign brings Oman the greatest prosperity it has known since Ya'arubi days, principally from Zanzibar and Arab east Africa in the form of slaves.
1820	General treaty of peace signed between Britain and the main sheikhs of the region. The British East India Company, whose concerns in the Gulf had begun for purely commercial considerations, became gradually more political as first the company, then the British government, took on itself the business of 'preserving peace at sea'. Throughout the first half of the 19th century, Muscat and Oman was the most powerful state in Arabia, ruling Zanzibar until 1861, and coastal parts of Persia, Kenya and Pakistan.

1822, 1839, 1845, 1873	Anti-slavery treaties established with Britain.
1839, 1846, 1891	Treaties signed with Britain for friendship, commerce and navigation.
1840	Sultan Said moves to Zanzibar and visits Oman less and less frequently. The elected imams in the interior become more and more powerful and remain very separate from Muscat and the coast.
1856	Said dies, leaving one son to rule in Muscat, another in Zanzibar.
1861	Split between Muscat and Zanzibar formalised when Zanzibar agrees to pay an annual amount to Muscat, not by way of tribute, but by way of compensation for Muscat renouncing all claims on Zanzibar, and as an adjustment to the inequality of the two sons' inheritances from their father Said.
1890	Zanzibar is parcelled out to Britain as a protectorate.
1860–95	Oman is weakened by Wahhabi incursions from the north and the west, and by dissension within the ruling family. Its economy is weakened by Britain's pressure to suppress slaving activities.
1890–1910	Rivalries between Britain and France for influence in Muscat. Sultan Faisal Bin Turki dies and the tribes of the interior refuse to recognise his son Taimur as imam.
1920	Treaty of Seeb to bring peace between the people of Muscat and the tribes of the interior, confirming that each will respect the other, with the sultan recognising the imam as a spiritual leader and allowing him limited jurisdiction over the interior. The treaty is mediated by the British to avert the possibility of civil war. Omani naval power declines with the advent of steam vessels.

FINANCIAL ORTHODOXY

Said bin Taimur had a horror of debt and strove never to become dependent on creditors. In his only public statement made in January 1958 he wrote: 'Doubtless it would have been easy to obtain money in various ways, but this could only have been by a loan with interest at a set percentage rate. This amounts to usury, with which I completely disagree, and the religious prohibition of which is not unknown.' Having seen the mistakes of his predecessors he also decided it was dangerous to delegate – better to do everything oneself to be sure it was done as you wanted. The sultan followed these principles utterly consistently, controlling every issue in his country in minute detail, leading alas to a rigid form of centralised administration which became increasingly inappropriate in the 1960s though it may have been suitable in the 1940s and 1950s. When PDO (Petrol Development Oman) announced in 1964 that it had found oil in commercial quantities and would start exporting in 1967, the sultan could have easily obtained credit, but he never took a penny because of his debt principle. He continued to sit, apart from it all, mistrusting all, unapproachable except by those who had obtained special permission to visit Salalah and who had arranged a prior appointment. Those who were fortunate enough to meet him were generally won over by his charm and powers of persuasion.

1924	Exploration for oil begins.
1932	Oman's total budget is £50,000, made up of a few fish and date exports, customs' receipts, the Zanzibar subsidy and the oil concession rental.
1932	Taimur resigns as sultan and retires to Bombay where he dies in 1965.
1938	Said bin Taimur, his 22-year-old son, takes over, having been educated at a British school in India. Oman has been on the verge of bankruptcy since the Zanzibar split of 1857. Said bin Taimur balances the books, never going into debt, believing this is the best course of action for the country. He wrote: 'From 1933 to this present day there has been no financial deficit in the government's budget.'
1950s	Said bin Taimur attempts to regain total control of the interior, backed by the British because they want to prospect for oil and therefore requiring the sultan's authority to be absolute, and in addition, for Oman's borders with Saudi Arabia and Abu Dhabi to be clearly defined. Saudi Arabia ousted from Buraimi oasis by Said, the imam and the British in a rare show of unity. Said occupies the imamate dual capitals of Nizwa and Rustaq and annexes the interior.
1951	The Sultanate of Muscat and Oman achieves full independence from Britain.
1954	A serious search for oil commences.
1957–59	Rebel war between interior tribes who elect a puppet imam (Ghalib) supported by Saudi and Egyptian aid, and the sultan in Muscat with his army and British support. After the war Said retreats to Salalah and rarely leaves the city.

THE MILITARY

The SAF (Sultan's Armed Forces) was formed in 1958 from various loosely organised groups with military assistance and a subsidy from the British government. It initially had a British colonel as its commander, but by the mid 1970s it had grown to include over 13,000 personnel, an expansion forced on it by the bitterly fought Dhofar War against Marxist-led guerrillas from south Yemen. It used to be top-heavy with British officers on secondment and many of these stayed as contract officers on leaving the British army. In recent years though strenuous efforts have been made towards Omanisation, with Omanis increasingly taking the place of senior British officers. The subsidy Britain paid to SAF stopped in 1967 when the sultan was thought to have enough money from oil revenues to pay for it himself. In the Gulf wars, the 2001 US invasion of Afghanistan and the 2003 invasion of Iraq, Oman (Masirah Island) acted as a base and staging post for both Britain and the US. In 2001, Oman hosted the British army in exercise Saif Sareea II (which translates as 'Swift Sword'), in which 12,500 members of the SAF also participated. It was an exercise to practise rapid deployment and test equipment in severe conditions, but it so transpired that the Afghan invasion intervened. Today the SAF consists of the Royal Guard, land forces, the Royal Navy of Oman (RNO) and Royal Air Force of Oman (RAFO). The RNO is thought to be one of the most modern in the region, and RAFO is highly respected. It acts more as a para-police force than a military machine, entirely appropriate for a country like Oman.

1959	Development department is set up to administer the subsidy provided by Britain after the Jebel War. It has three divisions: health, agriculture and public works. Health comprises a few underfunded clinics. Agriculture is two experimental farms in Nizwa and Sohar completely unsupported by the sultan, and public works is road building and repair, a division which took six years to complete the 150-mile graded track from Azaiba to Sohar. No piece of machinery can be purchased without the sultan's authorisation.
1964	Shell discovers oil in commercial quantities at Fahud, which later provides the finance for the transformation of the undeveloped kingdom to a modern state. Smaller oilfields are established at Natih and Yibal.
1967	First oil exports from the fields of Fahud, Natih and Yibal, yielding revenues small by Middle Eastern standards, but of enormous importance to Oman. Oman now has an oil-based economy for the first time. Said refuses to spend any money on development projects, opposes any change and seeks to keep Oman isolated from the modern world. Britain withdraws from Aden. Russian and Chinese imperialists fill the vacuum left. The Marxist-led Dhofar War begins with the aim of overthrowing the sultan and taking control of Oman and the Strait of Hormuz.
1970	Qaboos (aged 30) stages a non-violent coup against his father Said with British support. Said bin Taimur goes to London in exile. Sultan Qaboos takes over power. Name changed to 'Sultanate of Oman' as opposed to 'Muscat and Oman' and a modernisation programme is launched, financed by income from oil.
1970–75	Qaboos begins the task of building up Omani infrastructure, Mina Qaboos Port in Muttrah, health care and schooling in a series of five-year development plans. The Omani rial is established to replace the Indian rupee and the Maria Teresa dollar. End of the Dhofar War, with British military assistance, including elite SAS units.
1976	Qaboos marries but later divorces. He has no children.
1981	Oman plays a key role in establishment of six-member Gulf Co-operation Council.
1982	Memorandum of understanding with UK signed, providing for regular consultation on international issues.
1986	Oman's first university opens.
1990	Majlis Ash Shura created, comprising 82 elected members from the *wilayats*.
1994	Women given the vote in the nomination process for the *Majlis Ash Shura*.
1998	Port of Raysut opens with world-class container terminal facilities.
1999	Oman's oil reserves are estimated at five billion barrels; gas reserves are estimated at 900,000 barrels a day. Tourism is estimated to contribute a mere 1% to gross national product.

2001	The Sultan Qaboos Grand Mosque opens at Bowshar.
2002	The new world-class Sohar Industrial Port project gets under way, managed by the Sohar Industrial Port Company (SIPC), which is a joint venture between Oman and the Netherlands. It will be a major hub in the upper Gulf and Indian Ocean region.
2004	The Ministry of Tourism established, tourism being a major component of the government's economic diversification plan to move away from its reliance on oil.
2006	Productive activities in the Port of Sohar commence. Royal decree announces a new property law, which will enable foreign freehold ownership of real estate on designated up-and-coming major tourist developments.

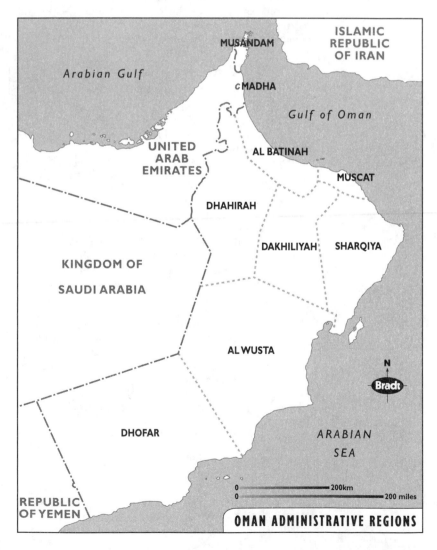

Outside of Muscat, Oman is administered by *walis* (local governors). The sultan appoints them himself, and they then report back to him via the Ministry of the Interior. The wali is responsible for all civil matters in his district *(wilayat)* and there are 59 wilayats in the country. This has been the system for many centuries, throughout the sultanate, and before that the imamate, except that at times, especially in the 19th century, they evolved into near independent city-states, defying any attempts at centralisation. Before oil the wali might, if he was lucky, have an old Land Rover or even an old wireless link to Muscat. Some places, like Izki, had neither. The wali in Sur had a wireless but no Land Rover and was once on tour on his donkey when the wireless operator received an urgent message that he should report to Muscat. The wali was fetched and given the message, whereupon he caught a dhow and was in Muscat 12 hours later. There, he was made to wait three days for an audience with the minister of the interior on a matter that was trivial. The Wali of Buraimi was once likewise summoned and kept waiting for four months until he was allowed to return. Such treatment was not regarded as unusual.

GOVERNMENT AND POLITICS

Prior to 1970, Al Said leaders assumed the political title of 'Sultan of Muscat and Oman', which implied the existence of two separate and irreconcilable political sectors. Indeed, coastal Muscat was more cosmopolitan and secular, largely because of its international trading history, whereas the interior was more insular, tribal and religious, ruled by an imam with traditional Ibadist ideologies. Under Sultan Qaboos's leadership (since 1970) the country was reconciled under the title the 'Sultanate of Oman', and has carefully and cautiously recognised its position within the global scheme, and embraced an international, diplomatic mindset.

Administratively, Oman today is divided into eight regions (or five regions and three governorates) and these regions are in turn divided into administrative areas or *wilayats*, of which there are 59, each overseen by its own chief governor or *wali*. Under Sultan Qaboos, as head of state, the government remains essentially autocratic: there is no prime minister and the sultan can accept or reject any

Islamic or Shari'a law applies to all members of the community and a *qadi* (Arabic judge) serves alongside the wali in every wilayat to administer justice according to this law. There is then a chief Qadi's court in Muscat. In all Arab countries where Shari'a law applies it is interpreted more or less strictly in accordance with the outlook prevalent in that country. For Oman this is an Ibadhi interpretation of Islamic law, which aligns it closely to the teaching of the Koran and the *Hadith* (traditions) of the Prophet, right up to the 1970s when Sultan Qaboos's father, Said bin Taimur, saw no reason to alter matters. Since Qaboos's accession in 1970 however, there has been a modernising shift towards adapting Shari'a law to cope with situations of the 20th and 21st centuries whilst still adhering to Shari'a principles. Most Arab countries have had to face this issue of how to modernise Islamic law, and most have adapted a compromise where the legal system is based either on English law or on the French Napoleonic code, depending on their historic associations. Owing to its long-standing links with Britain, and Sultan Qaboos's own ties to the British way of life, Oman favours the British legal system.

legislation. However, he has recognised that such a situation will not go on indefinitely: 'The time will come when this will have to stop and the voters' decision will be final.'

In 1970, when Qaboos came to power the sultanate had diplomatic relations with just three countries. Now it has relations with over 100, as well as the United Nations and the Gulf Co-operation Council (GCC).

The Council of Oman (Majlis Oman) is a bicameral system, comprised of the Consultative Council (Majlis al Shura) and the State Council (Majlis al Dawla). The Consultative Council was inaugurated in 1991 and was originally made up of 59 publicly elected members, representing each of the 59 *wilayats* (districts/areas) of the country. As a result of increases in the population, this has now expanded to 82, to include further representation for the *wilayats* with a population in excess of 30,000. This council acts as a consultative body only, proposing legislation and expressing views on laws once they are passed. It covers legal matters, the economy, health, education, and the environment, but has no say in Oman's foreign defence or security policies. The committees, of which it is comprised, have free reign to interrogate ministers. Elections are held every three years.

The State Council has 53 members who are appointed by the sultan on a three-year renewable term. Members are selected for their high status in society, their experience, reputation and expertise. The State Council acts as the upper chamber, playing a central role in the country's development. It holds four 'ordinary' sessions each year, with the option to hold further 'extraordinary' sessions. This council has the power to review and revise draft laws and submit proposals to the sultan and the Council of Ministers. Each of the councils includes female members, albeit in a marked minority.

ECONOMY

Prior to 1970, the economy was based on the export of dates, limes and skins, and otherwise the country had a subsistence economy based on agriculture and fisheries. Today, the agriculture and fishing industries still constitute the largest employers of the population, followed by government, then service industries, manufacturing and construction. Ironically oil and gas employ the lowest percentage of the population despite generating the largest income for the economy.

The Omani economy is still largely dependent on oil revenues, despite the fact that this dependency has been substantially reduced. In 1982, oil and gas provided 62% of GDP; this was reduced to 38% by 1998, and the decline continues; the aim is to reduce it to 19% by 2020 and to expand the non-oil sectors, thereby diversifying the economy.

Today, defence and security account for a large portion of government spending. The LNG (Liquefied Natural Gas) plant near Sur, the Raysut Port in Salalah, and now the Sohar Port will be critical to its economic future. So too will be the imminent tourism projects along its northern coastline, and the simultaneous opening of Oman's property market to foreign ownership.

ECONOMIC DIVERSIFICATION AND VISION 2020 Oman is a relatively small oil-producing state, and the remaining years of oil production are said to be limited. This fact, coupled with a drop in oil prices in the second half of 1997, revealed a vulnerability within the Omani economy and alerted the government to the need to diversify its economic base away from its reliance on oil. The country's focus has now shifted to other areas, such as trade and tourism, manufacturing and building, construction and real estate, the directives of which have been outlined in its Vision 2020 economic programme.

TOURISM Tourism in Oman is still in its infancy, and is one of the areas identified for expansion. Until the 1980s no-one was allowed into Oman without a No Objection Certificate (NOC) which could only be obtained through an Omani sponsor. If you simply wanted to visit the country out of curiosity, you were not allowed in. Journalists in particular were almost never allowed in and were regarded with great suspicion. This rigorous entry system was devised by the sultan's father, Said bin Taimur, and in his day his own personal permission had to be obtained for entry. The first organised group of tourists – 14 of them – visited the country in 1983, led by the wife of a former ambassador. Today, Oman is far more accessible and accommodating, and eco-tourism and adventure tourism are being actively promoted. This type of tourism is still in its infancy and so Oman offers a more peaceful travelling option than neighbouring tourist-dense Dubai.

Restoration and development plans for the tourism industry The Ministry of Tourism has instigated restoration projects to develop old stone buildings, restoring original mountain tracks, introducing *barasti* shades and toilets, and providing proper signage. There are plans to develop mountain villages as exclusive retreats to showcase Oman's distinct heritage, culture and natural attractions. Even the children can undergo a one-year programme to equip them with the tools to interact with tourists, which will include an English-language course.

The villages identified for tourism development include Wakan in Wadi Mistal in Nakhal where walking tracks, toilets, shaded seating areas, a café and a reception office will be built. The development of Al Hoqain village in Rustaq will be implemented in two stages. In the first stage, a paved road up to the pool area and Al Khabba al Zarqaa Restaurant, reflecting the local Omani architectural design, have already been built. In the second stage, in addition to general tourist facilities, a walking track to Al Hoqain waterfall will be built. A similar project will be undertaken at Al Aliya village in Wadi bani Kharous in Al Awabi. Renovation of old buildings and walking tracks in date-palm plantations in Hara al Sybani village in Birkat al Mawz will also be undertaken, with the intention of making the local practice of collecting dates and the ancient *falaj* irrigation system more accessible and appreciable to the visitor. Further similar projects will be implemented in Jebel Shams in Al Hamra, Jebel Akhdhar and Wadi Tanuf. Proper hotel facilities will be provided at these resorts. The Ministry of Tourism has appointed a professional company to undertake the development of Jebel Shams Canyon to fully accommodate tourists. By 2010, the ministry has plans to build eight new tourist information centres and develop castles and forts into museums with trained tourist guides and electronic gadgets explaining the displays in five languages. Such projects are set to be operational from 2007 in Nizwa Fort, Khasab Fort, Al Hazim, Bait al Na'man, Barka Fort and Nakhal Fort.

OPENING OF THE PROPERTY MARKET TO FOREIGN NATIONALS With an imminent new law coming into effect, foreign nationals will be permitted to purchase property on certain government-specified development areas. The Muscat Golf and Country Club, The Wave and the Blue City are three major imminent construction projects which will incorporate hotels, residential villages and 18-hole tournament-standard golf courses. In addition there is a Journey of Light project under discussion which will occupy beach frontage directly next to The Wave (a short distance from Seeb International Airport). Further projects are being considered for Ras al Hadd and Yitti Beach. By opening up the country to foreign investors while simultaneously expanding the country's tourism infrastructure, projects such as these will be crucial in offsetting the country's reliance on oil revenues for the future.

EMPLOYMENT AND OMANISATION Half a million jobs are currently filled by cheap hard-working imported labour which then sends remittances abroad. Under the government's Vision 2020 directive, the country plans to get Omanis doing this work. Omanis are more willing than most GCC nationals, but there is still a long way to go in attitudes and training. This is the country's biggest concern, as 60% of the population is under 18, which puts a huge pressure on youth employment. The government's solution, apart from encouraging Omanis to take on more lowly jobs currently occupied by expatriate subcontinentals (eg: petrol pump attendants, waiters, cleaners, tailors and shop assistants) is to try and broaden the economic base, so that secondary and tertiary businesses will be created and thus begin to absorb the growing workforce. The target for Omanisation was for 90% of all jobs to be held by Omanis by 2020, but the process of Omanisation is proving slower than the government had hoped, with institutions such as banks and oil companies finding it very difficult to place suitable Omanis in middle-management jobs held by Indian and Pakistani managers who have ten or 15 years of experience behind them.

INFRASTRUCTURE AND DEVELOPMENT Great improvements to the infrastructure have been made over the past few years. Streets that were nameless have now been identified and are clearly signed. Shell petrol stations abound, and so do Al Maha and Oman Oil. Oman Oil bought a 49% stake in BP Oman in December 2002, and the new brand Oman Oil was launched in October 2003. Therefore all the BP stations that were otherwise in existence throughout the country now appear as Oman Oil. New flyovers have been constructed, which seem to have eased the traffic flow considerably, where once it amassed at roundabouts, and consideration has been given to pedestrians, who now have walkways that pass up and bridge over the main motorway.

PEOPLE

The Omanis are a conservative people, and a respect for their privacy and their religion are courteous gestures from any visitor to their country. They are friendly and giving, and keen to communicate and demonstrate their culture and heritage to those who are interested. They are known for their hospitality and are deeply committed to a sense of family. In our experience Omanis generally fall over themselves to assist and welcome outsiders. Broadly, they have a relaxed, laid-back *bukra* mentality. 'Bukra' means 'tomorrow', which

GHAFIRI/HINAWI TRIBAL SPLIT

The major Ghafiri/Hinawi split came about in Oman following a quarrel over succession to the imamate in 1719, at which time there was one candidate from each tribe. But loosely speaking the divide went much further back to Azdite and Adnani tribal differences. Both originally of Yemeni descent, the Azdites adopted Ibadhi and Hinawi creeds, while the Adnanis, who were of Nizari (Nejdi) descent, adopted the Sunni and Ghafiri creeds. These allegiances were not always so clear cut, and just to illustrate how confusing matters can be, the Beni Ghafir have now become a Hinawi tribe, and the Beni Riyam, who under the rebel Suleyman took over leadership of the Ghafiris, are strongly Ibadhi and Yemeni. These tribal allegiances are important even today, and memories still exist of blood feuds of just a few generations ago. The rivalries occasionally flare up even now, but they only take the form of, say, rivalries between football teams.

Each main tribe has its paramount or senior sheikh who is consolidated in this position by the sultan, though not appointed by him. The sheikh acquires his position through the consensus of the tribe, not by hereditary succession. The sheikh is responsible if the tribe commits an offence, and he receives from the sultan the traditional tribal tribute. The interesting question is the relationship between the sheikh and the nearest wali (local governor), and the answer depends on the sheikh's power in relation to the wali's influence. The sheikh, like the wali, generally approaches the sultan via the minister of the interior. Oman is one of the few remaining places in the Arab world where the tribal system continues to matter and remain strong, though of course its force has inevitably waned over the last 20 years or so.

implies they'll do something 'tomorrow', but in reality means 'at some point in the infinite future'. You are likely to hear *'inshallah'* often, which means 'if God wills it, it will happen'.

THE STATUS OF WOMEN IN OMANI SOCIETY Women in Oman enjoy fair treatment and, broadly, equal opportunities in education and in the workplace. They increasingly take up careers in teaching, medicine and banking and can become members of the *Majlis al Dawla,* and occupy other senior government positions, unlike elsewhere in the Arabian peninsula. The sultan's philosophy is made clear from the following speech: 'Many years ago I said that if the energy, capability and enthusiasm of women were excluded from a country's active life, then that country would be depriving itself of 50% of its genius. I have taken very good care that this should not happen to Oman, and I look forward to the further progress of women in my country with the greatest pleasure and confidence.'

The true indigenous Omanis did not originally live on the coast but in the interior. They belong mainly to the highly conservative Ibadhi sect (see box, page 19), one of Islam's earliest sects. The merchant classes on the other hand lived on the coast, and the leading ones among them were the Baharina, originally of Persian ancestry and the Shi'ites, together with the Khojas or Hyderabadis who are Shi'ites of Indian origin. Their families often had strong trading links up and down the Gulf, with cousins and brothers running businesses in Bahrain, Kuwait, Dubai and Qatar. The other class of non-indigenous Omanis are the Beluch who also tend to live in specific quarters of the coastal towns.

POPULATION STATISTICS The total population of Oman is 2,415,576, which includes 612,645 non-nationals (based on 2004 Ministry of National Economy figures), mainly Indian and Pakistani, with a few thousand from other Arab countries, Europe and the US. Muscat is thought to be the most densely populated, with 664,826 people, but the Batinah coast in fact has a greater population with 667,159. The least-populated region is Al Wusta, with 23,553, closely followed by Musandam, with 29,247.

The fertility rate (births per woman, between 15 and 49 years old) has been brought down from 6% (1980) to 3.19% (2004), but many families, especially the men, believe that to have fewer than six children suggests unmanliness and conveys a lack of status. Families with fewer than four children are still regarded as odd, with the assumption that something is probably amiss. Infant mortality has dropped from 32.6 per 1,000 in 1980 to 10.3 per 1,000 in 2004.

Background Information PEOPLE

LANGUAGE

Despite the ethnic mix, Arabic remains overwhelmingly the spoken and official language of Oman. The larger indigenous population means that the dominance of Arabic is unchallenged, unlike in the United Arab Emirates next door, and the numbers of immigrant Indian and Pakistani workers, though increasing, are still not enough to have a significant impact on Omani culture. The Arabic spoken here is also one of the purest and most classical dialects. As a foreigner you may find yourself questioning all of this, since the bulk of the staff in hotels, restaurants, shops and businesses tend to be English-speaking Indians, whose labour is cheaper and who are in any case more prepared than Omanis to do such jobs. A serious effort is being made by the government to change these attitudes through the Omanisation programme (see above).

Spoken Arabic here is close to the classical, written Arabic, equating to the erstwhile BBC English, but you will have to be quite determined to use it in the capital area. In the interior however it is often the only language spoken.

Arabic is everywhere on street signs and adverts so there is plenty of opportunity to practise your Arabic alphabet (but don't panic, the English translation invariably accompanies it).

Arabic is, by the very nature of its structure, an extremely rich language, capable of expressing fine shades of meaning, and this is reflected in the wealth of Arabic literature, especially poetry. The average English tabloid reader is said to have a working vocabulary of 3,000 words, whereas the Arab equivalent is said to have about 10,000.

There are also many interesting features of the language which hint at the nature and attitudes of the Arab mind, notably the existence of only two tenses, perfect and imperfect: there is no future tense. In the Arabic concept of time there is only one distinction that matters: has something been finished or is it still going on? Another curiosity is that the plural of inanimate objects is treated grammatically as feminine singular, a characteristic which invites speculation.

The written Arabic language together with Islam is one of the few unifying factors in the Arab world. It means that newspapers published in Egypt can be distributed and read from Morocco to Iraq and even down to Yemen. In the spoken language however the 22 countries of the Arab League also express their individuality, to the extent that a Moroccan and an Iraqi speaking their local dialect will understand each other only with difficulty. In order to communicate therefore they have to compromise and speak a form of modem classical Arabic which is understood by educated Arabs everywhere, and it is this middle Arabic which you generally speak as a foreigner. The Arabic spoken in the Gulf is the closest to classical Arabic as you might expect, since the Arabian peninsula has been least influenced by external factors and has never been colonised by a foreign power. By contrast, the forms of spoken Arabic furthest away from the pure written classical Arabic are Lebanese and Egyptian, since these countries have been most exposed to foreign influences.

RELIGION

The official religion of Oman is Islam, and has been since the 7th century, predominantly of the Ibadhi sect which is very conservative and traditional in approach. The Indian and Pakistani expatriates are a mixture of Muslims, Hindus and Christians. Oman is tolerant of other religions and the presence of churches and temples demonstrates this.

The Islamic religion follows the five pillars of faith. These are: the professing of faith (*Shahadah*), the making of prayers (*Salat*), fasting (*Sawm*), the giving of charity

The Ibadhis, named after Abdullah Ibn Ibadhi (c AD683, the second half of the first Muslim century), were the most tolerant subdivision of the puritanical Kharijites who bitterly opposed Ali, the fourth caliph, and the right of the Quraysh tribe, the most powerful Meccan tribe, to choose the caliph. They wanted the Islamic state to return to how it had been before the power struggle of Ali and Mu'awiya, and believed the best person for the caliph should be chosen irrespective of his relationship to the Prophet's family. This disagreement played itself out in Basra (Iraq) and ended in persecution and exile for the Ibadhis. Some took refuge in Oman and some in Libya, Tunisia and Algeria where they still survive. The main doctrinal point on which they differ from Sunnis and Shi'a (the two main Islamic subdivisions), is that they do not feel it is essential that a visible leader must exist at all times. If there is no-one suitable, then they feel it is best to wait until someone suitable appears. From the 8th century onwards imams were appointed in Oman as spiritual, political and military leaders, best described as tolerant puritans. The Ibadhis were sometimes known as 'quietists' who believed in achieving things through quiet dignity and reasonableness, not through fanatical confrontations. The mosques reflect this style and tend to be simple and devoid of decoration except round the mihrab niche and the windows. Minarets were not used except on the coast, and in the interior the call to prayer was traditionally made from the roof, reached by an outside flight of steps. Ibadhism has always been tolerant of Christians and Jews, allowing them to practise their own religions in Oman. Even so, in the coffee-pouring etiquette where guests were always served in order of importance, Christians often came last, after the poorest Muslim in Ibadhi areas, while in Sunni areas, Christians sometimes even came higher than the wali in the coffee hierarchy. Singing is suppressed by Ibadhi Muslims as a frivolity, but most Arabs have a natural sense of rhythm and love of music, which tends to escape when they are happy and contented. Superstition runs deep too, and Islam has never completely wiped out old Semitic beliefs in blood sacrifice, fetishism and animism of ancient idolatry. The Ibadhi areas were firstly from Bahla to Izki, becoming increasingly diluted as you go northwards to Buraimi; secondly the whole of the Sharqiya (eastern province inland of Muscat down to Sur); and thirdly the Jebel Akhdar, which provided the refuge for Ibadhism and the imamate during periods of outside interference and dominance.

(*Zakat*) and the pilgrimage to Mecca (*Hajj*). Salat occurs five times a day at dawn, noon, mid afternoon, 1½ hours before sunset, and at sunset. Muslims are alerted to this by the *muezzin*, who chants a call to prayer from the mosque.

The Islamic calendar is calculated from the Hejira, which is the day of departure of the Prophet from Mecca to Medina. For the year 2000, the Hejira year was 1421.

RAMADAN Ramadan is the holy month, when Muslims abstain from eating, drinking and smoking between sunrise and sunset for 30 days. Non-Muslims are affected because it is considered disrespectful to be seen eating, drinking (in any form) or smoking in public places during daylight hours in Ramadan. As a result most restaurants are closed (though large hotels keep a screened-off area for non-Muslims), bars are closed and hotels are not permitted to serve alcohol publicly. Even after sunset, throughout Ramadan, alcohol is not sold in restaurants or bars, and therefore many are shut down. Consumption of alcohol is permitted only in the privacy of your home or hotel room. Working hours are shorter, with later starts and earlier finishes. Ramadan is looked forward to and enjoyed by Omanis, as it is a time for self-restraint, religious reflection, and visiting friends and family

The *khanjar* is a curved, sheathed dagger, which encapsulates and symbolises the Omani identity. In the past the *khanjar* had a utilitarian purpose, and served as an essential piece of weaponry used to protect against wild animals or the enemy. Today it is valued and respected, and proudly worn as part of a male Omani's traditional dress on special occasions and for official ceremonies. Its image is used on the Omani flag today.

The article itself can be broken down into three pieces: the knife, the sheath and the attaching belt, and different skills are required to fashion each piece. The price of such a souvenir is largely determined by the material used in its handle. This can be ivory, rhino horn or sandalwood, sandalwood being the cheapest. Although it is no longer permitted to obtain further stocks of ivory or rhino horn, the remaining stocks are reportedly still used until their eventual depletion. It is illegal to export such material though, and so you will need to opt for the sandalwood variety if taking one out of the country as a souvenir.

after dark, when social activity tends to go on into the small hours. During Ramadan, government offices and banks are open from 08.00 till noon, Saturday to Thursday. As it follows the lunar calendar, Ramadan moves forwards each year (falls earlier) by about 11 days.

EDUCATION

In 1970, prior to the current sultan coming to power, there were only three schools in the whole of Oman: one in Muscat, one in Muttrah and one in Salalah; they were for boys only. Now the situation has turned around and there are 1,038 government-run schools (2004 figures) providing equal schooling opportunities for boys and girls. Since 1986, there has also been the Sultan Qaboos University, the first university in Oman. Adult literacy centres are plentiful now throughout the country.

CULTURE

OMANI TRADITIONAL DRESS

Men The *dishdasha* is the ankle-length robe worn by Omani men. Usually white in colour for daytime wear or in the workplace, official and formal, this also comes in a variety of colours for evening and special occasions. The tassel at the neck is called the *furakha* or *farusha* and it is customary to perfume this.

The *kumah* (or *kummar*) is the small embroidered cap worn by Omani men. The embroidery comes in a variety of colours and floral or geometric designs to match the *dishdasha*. On formal occasions a *musr* (or *mussar*) (turban) is often worn. The *khanjar* (a curved sheathed dagger) is worn, attached to a belt (made from either leather or cotton fabric), also worn on special occasions (see *The khanjar* box above). The *assa* (stick) is another part of the Omani traditional costume, which used to be used for practical purposes in the past to control camels, but these days it is more of a decorative appendage. On the feet leather sandals are worn. On formal occasions, a *bisht* (cloak) may be worn which in part covers the *dishdasha*. The edges are embroidered in gold or silver threads.

Women Underneath the *abaya* (a black cover-all gown worn in public), Omani women can be found wearing brightly coloured traditional ankle-length dresses and headscarves made from a range of fabrics in a variety of styles, according to region and/or personal taste. The names of each part of the costume vary from region to region. Broadly, the woman's *jallabia* (dress) is usually worn over *sirwall* (trousers) and with a *lihaf* (head shawl). In some regions a *burka* (face mask) is worn. Some women wear Western clothes, but cover up with the *abaya* outside the home. Fabrics are embroidered with lace, sequins, jewels, beads, coins and other materials. Tailors are plentiful throughout the country and so costumes can be speedily made to order according to any personal design. It is traditional for women to have their hands and feet painted with henna at times of celebration. Traditionally, kohl was drawn on the eyes and indigo on the face on special occasions, festivals, weddings. Henna is still used today, pasted on the hands and feet in various patterns and designs which, when dried, leave an orangey-brown decorative stain.

TRADITIONAL SPORTING EVENTS

Bullfighting This takes place on Friday afternoons in the winter months at several places along the Batinah coast. Unlike Spanish bullfighting, the sport in Oman is bloodless. Two Brahmin bulls (who are pampered as pets) fight until the first is knocked down or runs away. It begins at 16.00 and lasts just a few minutes. The bulls lock horns in a test of strength, trying to push each other over into the sand or make them run away. There is no prize money, only honour and prestige for the winner, something that would render it unworkable as an activity in Dubai. In Oman, however, traditions are still valued for their own sake, thereby making this bullfighting a natural spectacle refreshingly devoid of commercialism. No harm comes to the bulls, as they are matched in age, strength and weight by a panel of judges, and a rope is tied to each bull so that they can be separated if need be. The bulls are often given heroic names from Islamic literature, like Antar, or even names of American wrestlers. It is noticeably an all-male event. The fun is in watching the crowd scramble when the bulls get too close and watching the owner try to retrieve his fleeing bull at the end. See *Chapter 4, The Batinah coast*, page 121, for further details.

Camel breeding and racing Intricately linked with Omani tradition and culture the camel is an integral part of the country's culture and history, stemming back to references in the Koran. Known as 'the ship of the desert' or 'the beast of burden', they were also traditionally sources of milk and meat. In Dhofar today, where there are about 60,000, this is still very much the case; they provide meat and milk and are considered part of the household. Indeed, a female can produce up to 20 litres of milk per day, which is low-fat and reportedly good for the stomach. Elsewhere, though, select camels have bypassed their traditional purpose and instead have been bred since birth for racing. Much like thoroughbred horses they are fed a healthy diet, groomed and trained, and can become great financial assets to their owners, differing considerably in appearance from their conventional cousins. A good racing camel can fetch a price of RO30,000 or more.

Camel racing has become a popular and commercial sport in the Arabian peninsula. In Oman camel-racing events are held at tracks in many areas throughout the country on occasions of celebration, such as National Day and other public holidays. It is most popular in the Batinah region, which is the camel-rearing hub of the country, as well as Seeb (in the Muscat region) and Al Mudaybi and Al Kamil (in the Sharqiya region). Al Abiadh camel racetrack is located about 30km from Sinaw, off the Sinaw–Mahawt road and attracts some top-quality camels. Admission is free.

Barka has several racetracks and camel pens. Racing camels are strictly bred and trained specifically for the sport, and represent big business, competing at both

Oman has a long silversmithing heritage. The material has been used for centuries, and expertly handcrafted into articles of jewellery and ornaments, perhaps the most famous of which is the *khanjar* (curved dagger, worn by men). (See box, page 20.) In the past, Omani men wore decorative silver as well as Omani women. They carried keys on fine chains, had silver money holders, tweezers in silver cases, silver toothpicks and ear cleaners on silver chains.

Most of the old silver was unfortunately melted down before traders realised the value of antique silver pieces, so there is remarkably little genuine old silver left. Experienced Omani silver dealers can tell whether a piece is from the Batinah, the Sharqiya or Dhofar.

Headpieces can be very heavy, weighing 2kg or more, and are worn on special occasions, usually when seated. Dhofari bracelets are adorned with coral beads and spiky silver washers threaded onto elastic. Women's silver necklaces often display Koranic inscriptions, and amulets, anklets and bangles are all intricately engraved. Other articles fashioned from silver include rose-water distillers, incense burners, trays, small engraved silver boxes (used for storing kohl or jewellery) and coffee pots (also made from copper).

national and international events, warranting their own Directorate-General of Camel Affairs. Omani thoroughbreds are well known in the region and in demand. The training season runs from June to October and the racing season from September to March. Races are generally run 06.00–09.30, and are announced in the local papers; alternatively, call The Directorate General of Camels on ℡ 26 893804.

Equestrian events Oman is famous for its purebred Arabian horses and has a centuries-old horse-breeding history. In 1983, the Oman Equestrian Federation was formed, promoting equestrian events. Each winter the federation organises a national show-jumping competition, attracting entries from The Royal Stables at Seeb, the Royal Oman Police, the Royal Guard of Oman, and various private stables. It takes place at the Enam Equestrian show ground in Seeb – one of the best riding arenas in the world; the Duke of Edinburgh, Prince Philip, participated in one such event in 1991. A Royal Equestrian Show is held every five years at the Royal Stables, and a Royal Meeting held annually where the Royal Stables competes with other horses bred in Oman. Oman is a member of the World Arabian Horse Organisation (WAHO, *www.waho.org/Reports/Oman*).

ARTS AND CRAFTS

Traditional crafts The craft industry was once an important part of Oman's economy, with artisanal skills handed down from generation to generation. It is artefacts such as pots from Bahla, decorative chests, silver bracelets, *khanjars* and coffee pots that most embody the spirit and identity of Oman; they are tangible samples of its ancient tradition and heritage – symbolic of place and the spirit of a people.

Jewellery Women's necklaces and bracelets, whether in silver or gold, plays an important part in marriage ceremonies in Oman – a bride's dowry is expected to contain a certain amount of jewellery. The wealth and status of a family may be judged by the jewellery worn by the women. There is a belief that its wearer will be protected from the evil eye. Silver is said to be representative of the moon and gold representative of the sun.

Pottery Bahla, in the Dakhiliyah region, is famous for its potters and potteries. Today there are two working factories there, which you can visit to watch the potters at work. Traditionally these pots were used as water containers and dispensers.

Incense burners (*majmars*), made from clay, are ubiquitous and make the perfect gift or keepsake of Oman. Salalah's frankincense souk (in Dhofar) or Muttrah souk (in the capital) are two prime locations for these items. Some are painted in bold colours.

Mandoos *Mandoos* are Omani chests which have been traditionally used to store valuables in. It is said that this stemmed from a Portuguese tradition which Oman inherited when they invaded Oman's shores in the 16th century. Today, *mandoos* can be bought in a variety of sizes (down to jewellery-box size) and are usually made from either walnut or rosewood. On the surface they are inlaid with brass, gold or silver, in Islamic and geometric designs, and sometimes decorated with precious stones. You will spot them all over Oman, in hotels, official buildings, offices and private homes as decorative furnishing.

Omani doors Intricately carved doors have been a tradition, and today you will find that their usage has been extended: the carved door – or rather a modern imitation of the traditional Omani door – is now used as a coffee-table top. These can be found for sale in many of the artisan and souvenir shops in Qurum, or in the souk at Muttrah, as well as in other artisan workshops scattered throughout the country.

NATURAL HISTORY AND CONSERVATION with Andrew Grieve

The diverse nature of Oman's climate and terrain provides the perfect habitat for thousands of species of plant, animal, bird and marine life and makes the country an ideal destination for lovers of nature and the outdoors.

Enthusiastically 'green' in its outlook, Oman has possibly the most enlightened policy on conservation in the Middle East. In addition to preserving its historical monuments and forts, it is committed to preserving and protecting the natural habitat of its unique species of flora and fauna, and has established several designated nature reserves, protected sites and research centres. Responsibility for this comes under the Ministry of Regional Municipalities, Environment and Water Resources, through its Directorate of Nature Conservation. Oman is a member of CITES (the Convention on International Trade in Endangered Species of Wild Fauna and Flora), which forbids any commercial trading in specific live or dead animals and animal parts.

The most popular of the reserves is indisputably the Daymaniyat Islands (along the Batinah coast, see page 126), which is a designated bird sanctuary, but is excellent for both its marine and birdlife. Indeed it is Oman's only marine-protected area. Nineteen species of dolphin and whale have been recorded in Oman's waters and the Daymaniyat Islands are probably one of the best locations from which to spot them. Boat trips for dolphin-, whale- and birdwatching can be easily arranged (there is a no-landing policy throughout the bird-breeding season between May and October), and the area is also a highly ranked world dive site.

The protected turtle-breeding beaches at Ras al Hadd and Ras al Jinz are popular places to visit, the turtles being another strong tourist draw. There are seven species in the world of which five occur in Oman and four breed. A visitor and research centre has been established at the turtle reserve at Ras al Jinz, where an on-site ranger leads you to the sea's edge in the dark for your night-time turtle-watching adventure.

Background Information   NATURAL HISTORY AND CONSERVATION

Other reserves have been established protecting the natural domain of mammals including the two species of gazelle, striped hyena, Arabian leopard, Arabian tahr, Arabian oryx, Blanford's fox, Nubian ibex and Gordon's wild cat. The Saleel Nature Reserve at Al Kamil and Al Wafi (in the Sharqiya region) is home to Arabian and sand gazelle and other animals, in addition to rare varieties of tree, namely *samr* (*Acacia tortilis*) and *ghaf* (*Prosopis cineraria*). A nursery has been established here to propagate and preserve Oman's endangered wild flora.

Although its central focus is on the endangered Arabian oryx, the Arabian Oryx Sanctuary in the Jiddat al Harasis (in central Oman) is also home to Arabian leopard, the two species of gazelle, Nubian ibex, red fox, Gordon's wild cat, sand cat, caracal, honey badger and others.

Jebel Samhan, in the Dhofar region, was declared a national nature reserve in 1997. The highest point in Dhofar at 1,800m, it is believed to be home to the Middle East's largest population of the endangered Arabian race of leopard, which is being continuously monitored. Research was also launched in 2006 to monitor the Arabian leopard in Musandam. Other species found in the Jebel Samhan reserve include the striped hyena, Gordon's wild cat and Blanford's fox.

The five Halaniyat Islands off the Dhofar coast are an important breeding ground for turtles and seabirds, although not yet designated a nature reserve. A turtle-counting and tagging programme (see *www.seaturtle.org/tracking/?project_id=145*) has also been set up on Masirah Island, one of the most important turtle-nesting sites in the world, with approximately 30,000 loggerhead sea turtles laying their eggs annually. The importance of Oman for sea turtles is highly significant and the opportunity for turtle viewing unrivalled.

The area from Ras al Hadd down to the southern borders of Oman and for 200 nautical miles out to sea from the coast has been declared, by the International Maritime Organisation (IMO), a protected marine area, conserving the sea's resources by regulating tourist and ship activity.

The commissioning of books and studies covering the country's wild flowers, butterflies, birds and other forms of wildlife has made Oman one of the best-documented countries of the Middle East in this field. As visitors it is important that we are aware of Oman's conservation policies and respect the habitats and environs of the wildlife of the country. Note that collecting sea shells, abalones or turtle eggs is strictly prohibited. So too is hunting or disturbing wild animals and birds. Driving over the sand is also illegal.

ECOSYSTEMS Oman can be broadly split into three ecosystems: the mountains of northern Oman, including Musandam; the desert plains or plateau of central Oman; and the escarpment woodlands and monsoon belt of Dhofar in the south. These very different environments support and sustain their own unique types of flora and fauna. Professor Reginald Victor of Sultan Qaboos University speaks of the importance of a National Biodiversity Strategy and Action Plan (NBSAP) for the country, which would aim (under the guidance of the World Zoo Organisation) to conserve these ecosystems or habitats. His interesting article on biodiversity conservation in Oman can be found at www.nizwa.net/env/biodiversity.

FLORA The northern mountains (including the Musandam Peninsula) and the Dhofar region contain 80% of Oman's 1,204 species of flora, of which about a hundred are endemic to Oman or regionally in Arabia. Nurseries (including mangrove) have been established at the Saleel Nature Reserve (in the Sharqiya region), the Qairoon Hairiti (in Dhofar), Qurum Natural Park (in Muscat), and the Botanical Gardens at Sultan Qaboos University (also in Muscat). These provide some, albeit limited, facility and potential for flora conservation, both 'in

The colour of the outer garment (*abaya*) and face mask (*burka*) worn by women throughout Arabia was always thought to be black, but in fact it was indigo – from the only natural plant that was suitable for dyeing clothes. It once grew wild over large areas, but farmers began to cultivate it and extract the natural dye and sell it in tablet form to the professional dyers of the towns. The wild plant used (*nil*), was pulled out and soaked in water for two days; the dye in the leaves would sink to the bottom and the surface water would be drained off. The pasty residue was hung out on a thick cloth to dry for two or three days, and then cut into small tablet-like segments. Before the advent of the pharmacy, the drying and healing properties of indigo were utilised to cure skin diseases and heal wounds such as the umbilical cord on a newborn baby or on a boy's penis after circumcision.

Over the last 15 years or so the industry has all but disappeared, and the dye is instead imported from India.

situ' (in its natural habitat) and 'ex-situ' (removed from its natural habitat).

Oman's most famous plant is the *Boswellia sacra*, which produces the frankincense resin. Found only in Dhofar (in the south), and parts of east Africa, it is a gnarled and unattractive-looking tree which grows only to 3–4m. One tree can produce up to 20kg of frankincense in a season, and at the height of the trade 2,000 years ago over 3,000 tonnes of the spice were exported by camel caravan or by boat to the wealthy civilisations of Egypt, Greece, Rome and India. In recent times, however, the trade in frankincense has declined to an insignificant level.

A remarkable tree to look out for in the Dhofar region, particularly between Wadi Darbat and Wadi Hinna near Mirbat, is the grotesque looking baobab *Adansonia digitata*, a species more familiar in the African savanna.

Mid 2004 saw a large coastal afforestation project take place with approximately 188,000 mangrove trees planted in the lagoons (*khors*) along Oman's coastline. A permanent mangrove nursery and research centre has also been established at Qurm Natural Park.

Rose-water, extracted from the desert rose (*Adenium obesum*) is used extensively in Oman in the preparation of *halwa* (see page 142), as well as in perfumes, in incense (especially at Eid and weddings), in *kahwa* and in traditional medicines. The roses are cooked for three hours and the water then stored for 40 days before being bottled and sold.

FAUNA

Mammals Around 76 species of mammal have been recorded in Oman of which one, the endemic Dhofarian shrew, is critically endangered. In addition to some of those detailed below, another endangered mammal in Oman is the Arabian jird, whilst other larger species include Blanford's fox, Rüppell's sand fox, red fox, honey badger, caracal, Gordon's wild cat, sand cat, Cape hare, Indian-crested porcupine, small-spotted genet, white-tailed mongoose, Arabian wolf, striped hyena, Brandt's hedgehog, Ethiopian hedgehog and rock hyrax.

Arabian leopard The critically endangered Arabian race of leopard, Arabia's largest cat, survives only in the remote mountains of southern Oman and in Musandam. Usually solitary, it comes together with other leopards only for breeding. The Nubian ibex and rock hyrax form the bulk of its diet.

An important sanctuary for the leopard is Jebel Samhan Nature Reserve. A survey into the animal is being carried out both here and, more recently, in

Musandam. Modern techniques of camera-trapping and satellite collars have meant that the ecology of this shy and very secretive animal has been studied for the first time. For details of how you can assist with the Arabian leopard conservation project in Oman see www.responsibletravel.com.

Arabian white oryx The globally endangered Arabian white oryx, which is a type of antelope, was extinct in Oman by the early 1970s due to excessive hunting. In 1975, Sultan Qaboos launched the Operation Oryx programme. This captive breeding programme was conducted at the sultan's Omani Mammal Breeding Centre, Bait al Barakah (at Seeb, near Muscat), with donated animals from London Zoo, the Hadhramaut (Yemen), Jordan, Kuwait, Saudi Arabia and Arizona, utilising the knowledge of the World Wildlife Fund, the Fauna Preservation Society and the International Union for Conservation of Nature and Natural Resources, who assisted with the project. The oryx were then reared at Jaaluni in the Jiddat al Harasis in central Oman, before being successfully reintroduced into the wild there in the early 1980s. UNESCO has since proclaimed the Jiddat al Harasis a World Natural Heritage Site. There is also the Arabian Oryx Sanctuary near Al Kamil on the edge of the Wahiba Sands.

Like camels, the timid oryx are supremely well adapted to a desert environment, conserving their water intake and requiring a drink only every few months. Their lifespan is around 19 years. It is thought that the mythical unicorn legend stemmed from the oryx, whose two horns, when viewed from the side, appear as one. For further information visit www.oryxoman.com.

Arabian and Reem gazelles The largest single population of Arabian gazelle (over 10,000 in 2003) can be found in the Arabian Oryx Sanctuary (see above). The male has thick horns while the female's horns are finer and straighter, and they feed on shrubs and grasses.

The Reem gazelle (sand gazelle) is a less common species and can be found on the sandy terrain at the edges of the Empty Quarter. In contrast to the Arabian gazelle, the Reem gazelle gives birth to twins. The Reem gazelle, like the Oryx, can cover long distances searching for new pastures.

Arabian tahr This south-Asian goat-antelope, with short curved horns, is one of the rarest animals in the world and is an endangered species. Its name means 'half-goat'. The ideal habitat for the tahr is at altitude, between 1,000m and 1,800m, and so the Wadi Sarin Tahr Reserve in the Hajar ash Shaqi (eastern Hajar) Mountains, and the mountains of northern Oman, including Musandam, are its natural home. The Arabian Tahr Project began in 1976 and continues to work for the animal's conservation.

Nubian ibex The Nubian ibex, another globally endangered species, is a wild mountain goat that lives in small groups. During the annual mating season, groups of up to 30 animals come together with the large adult males fighting for the right to breed. The Nubian ibex can be found in the Arabian Oryx Sanctuary and in the Jebel Samhan Nature Reserve. It does not occur in northern Oman.

Reptiles There are around 64 species of reptiles in Oman of which at least 21 are endemic to Arabia and seven are globally threatened. Only three species of amphibian are known from Oman with the Dhofar toad an Arabian endemic. Geckoes, agamas, lizards, skinks and snakes are well suited to survive in abundance in mountain and desert areas, but apart from the rarely seen horned viper, carpet viper, puff adder and the Arabian race of cobra, the remaining nine snake species are harmless. The mountains of northern Oman contain three nationally endemic species of geckos and five regionally endemic geckos and lizards. A common and widespread species worth looking out in the Dhofar region is the Arabian race of chameleon.

Birds *Andrew Grieve*
According to the Oman Bird Records Committee (OBRC), which publishes an official bird list, a total of 486 bird species had been recorded in Oman by 2003. Familiar widespread wintering species in Oman include cormorant, cattle egret, spoonbill, greater flamingo, shoveler, little stint, ruff, black-tailed godwit, kingfisher and stonechat. Other more sought-after wintering species in different parts of Oman include Indian pond heron, pallid harrier, steppe eagle, imperial eagle, lesser sandplover, pintail snipe, great black-headed gull, Egyptian nightjar, citrine wagtail, red-tailed wheatear, eastern pied wheatear, plain leaf warbler, Isabelline shrike and rose-coloured starling.

Many geographical influences can be detected in Oman's breeding birds with the influence of India provided by yellow bittern and pheasant-tailed jacana nesting in Dhofar and grey francolin, Indian roller, purple sunbird and Indian silverbill along the Batinah coast. The mangroves along this coast also support interesting species including red-wattled plover and the white-collared kingfisher, an endemic sub-species. Typical African species that are resident in the Dhofar region include the huge lappet-faced vulture, Verreaux's eagle, spotted thick-knee, namaqua dove, green pigeon, African scops owl, African paradise flycatcher, shining sunbird, black-crowned tchagra, Rüppell's weaver, African silverbill and African rock bunting. Some of the summer visitors to Dhofar are also typically African in distribution with the striking didric cuckoo, brightly coloured grey-headed kingfisher, Forbes-Watson swift and singing bush lark all breeding during the monsoon period.

The remaining breeding species are mainly Arabian endemics, seabirds, desert species or typical European and Mediterranean birds. The Arabian endemics include Arabian partridge, Arabian wheatear and the rather plain looking Yemen serin which all breed in Dhofar. Yellow-vented bulbul (north and south Oman) and Tristram's grackle (Dhofar only) are mainly restricted to the Middle East. The elegant and graceful sooty falcon, osprey and crab plover all breed on island groups such as Masirah, Daymaniyat and Halaniyat. Breeding seabirds and herons on these islands feature striated heron, western reef heron, red-billed tropic bird (also breeds on mainland sea cliffs), masked booby, socotra cormorant (Arabian endemic), sooty gull, swift tern, white-cheeked tern, bridled tern, common noddy and Saunder's tern. Jouanin's petrel probably breeds and is another endemic to the region.

Desert and mountain species are typified by golden eagle, striated scops owl, sand partridge, cream-coloured courser, four species of sandgrouse, black-crowned finch-lark, Dunn's lark, desert lark, hoopoe lark, long-billed pipit, Hume's wheatear, scrub warbler, trumpeter finch and house bunting. Palearctic species that breed around the Mediterranean and also in Oman include little bittern, Egyptian vulture, black-winged stilt, collared pratincole, turtle dove, blue-cheeked bee-eater and southern grey shrike.

The shy Houbara bustard is a desert bird that by 1996 was near to extinction in other parts of Arabia, where it was largely hunted out by Arab falconers. Now protected by CITES, it is also the subject of a conservation survey.in Oman, whose anti-falconry laws add further protection. Jaaluni in the Jiddat al Harasis in central Oman is a good place to look for this species.

For further information visit www.birdsoman.com.

Birdwatching Oman sits at the crossroads of three continents: Europe, Africa and Asia, and is therefore well placed along bird migratory routes, which makes it an excellent location for seeing transitory species as well as interesting resident and wintering birds. The best times to see the migrating species are from late August to November and from February to May with December through to February being the best for winter birds and also the coolest time of the year. Most of the indigenous species can be seen in the winter though some breeding species do not arrive until May, particularly in Dhofar.

There are good birding sites in every region of the country (see regional chapters for further details). The coastal *khors* (lagoons) offer perfect spots for wintering and migrating waterbirds including ducks, waders and terns. The Daymaniyat Islands hold substantial numbers of breeding bridled and white-cheeked terns with small numbers of common noddy, ospreys and western reef herons. The Sawadi Islands and Fahal Island (about 4km off Ras al Hamra, in the capital area) hold breeding sooty falcons, with the latter site also having nesting red-billed tropic-birds; boat trips around Fahal Island can easily be arranged from Muscat (see page 67). Al Ansab Lagoons (about 30km west of Muscat) and Qurum Natural Park in Muscat itself are good places to see typical Omani breeding species such as grey francolin, red-wattled plover, laughing dove, little green bee-eater, yellow-vented bulbul, Arabian babbler, purple sunbird and Indian silverbill.

Barr al Hikman and Masirah Island (the latter accessible by ferry only) hold perhaps a million wintering waterbirds, mainly herons, egrets, waders and gulls. Mouth-watering species such as crab plover and great knot are present in winter, the latter found south of the Shannah ferry terminal for Masirah Island when the tide is rising. A good area to watch at high tide is Film, 19km south of the town of Al Hij, where close views of great white egrets, greater flamingos, crab plover, terek sandpiper, broad-billed sandpiper and slender-billed gulls can be obtained.

Other locations offering good birdwatching opportunities include Musandam where breeding Litchenstein's sandgrouse, Chukar and Hume's wheatear and wintering eastern pied wheatear, red-tailed wheatear, Eversman's redstart and plain leaf warbler can be seen. The Sohar Sun Farms (Batinah coast) offer first class all-year-round birding with many passage and wintering species of note including a small number of the globally threatened sociable plover. The desert oasis and resthouse of Qitbit (page 262) on the desert road between Muscat and Salalah is an exellent place to stay over to see desert species such as crowned and spotted sandgrouse and hoopoe lark. A series of khors along the Dhofar coast each side of Salalah are also excellent sites for a range of waterbirds throughout the year, particularly Khor Taqa and Khor Rawri (sometimes spelt Rouri). For the Arabian endemics and Dhofar specialities, the wooden ravines inland of the coast are the places to visit in the spring, particularly Ayn Hamran just 22km from Salalah.

Birdwatching excursions can easily be arranged through many of the tour operators in Muscat (see page 67). Treasure Tours, for example, organises birdwatching trips in the winter migratory season between December and February to sites around Quriyat (Muscat region) and Sohar (on the Batinah) that cost RO27 for a half day and RO65 for a full day, inclusive of driver/guide (*min 2 people, dep Thu, 24hrs' notice required*). There are no organised tours as such for birdwatching in Musandam but internal flights to Khasab can be arranged as well as car hire to visit the best birdwatching areas. Several books have been published by the authors Hanne and Jens Eriksen, who are also renowned bird photographers and operate birding tours in Muscat (see page 68). Readers might like to get hold of a copy of their *Birdlife in Oman* (see *Appendix 3, Further information*, page 276) or any other of their publications.

Butterflies *Andrew Grieve*
There are around 80 classified species of butterfly in Oman, none endemic to either Oman or Arabia, and many can be seen in either Musandam or Dhofar mainly between October and May. Familiar colourful species such as swallowtail can be seen in northern Oman whilst the similar African lime butterfly can be seen in the Dhofar region. A large bright species likely to be seen in all parts is the plain tiger, a large orange butterfly with black wing tips. As with the birds, many species are typical of neighbouring continents, particularly Africa. Jebel Akhdar (in the interior) is another good area for a range of species.

Marine life The waters of the Arabian Sea and the Gulf of Oman provide diverse marine habitats, which give rise to and accommodate an abundance of sealife. At least 900 species of fish and around 85 varieties of hard and soft coral exist in Oman's waters, which firmly places the sultanate on any diver's itinerary. Rays, honeycomb moray eels, barracuda and frog fish are just some of the species of fish that inhabit these waters. Coral varieties such as table, black, whip, teddy bear and cabbage coral can all be found here, Fahal Island offering the widest variety in one location. For information on diving, see the regional chapters; for books on the subject, see *Appendix 3, Further information*, page 276.

Whales, dolphins and sharks Omani waters are home to 19 species of whale and dolphin, which include blue whale, sperm whale, humpback whale, Cuvier's beaked whale, pygmy killer whale, orca or killer whale, Bryde's whale, false killer whale, Cuvier's beaked whale, dwarf sperm whale, melon-headed whale, common bottlenose dolphin, spinner dolphin, bottlenose dolphin, Indo-Pacific humpback dolphin, long-beaked common dolphin, pan-tropical spotted dolphin, striped dolphin, spinner dolphin, rough-toothed dolphin and Risso's dolphin. Fahal Island is reportedly a good place to spot dolphins aplenty though the best whale-watching areas lie off southern Oman. Ras Janjari near Mirbat is a particularly good land-based viewing point. Oman is a member of the International Whaling Commission and follows the CITES regulations, which prevent all these species from being traded. The Whale and Dolphin Research Group (*www.whalecoastoman.com*) is a voluntary organisation which works in collaboration with the Environment Society of Oman (*www.environment.org.om*). The various sharks spotted in Omani waters include leopard sharks, whale sharks and black-tip reef sharks.

Sea turtles The other creature to merit its own sanctuary is the sea turtle, particularly the green turtle, on designated beaches at Ras al Hadd and Ras al Jinz on Oman's southeastern tip. These two sites are the main natural breeding areas for up to 13,000 green turtles each year. Permits, which used to involve a lot of rigmarole, can now easily be obtained at the entrance or arranged at your hotel in the region, and tourism is monitored to safeguard the turtles' environment. For further details see Turtle Beach Resort (*Chapter 8*, page 229) and Ras al Jinz Turtle Beach Camp (*Chapter 8*, page 230).

There are five species of turtle (out of the world's seven) that populate the coasts of Oman, four solely for the purpose of laying their eggs: the olive ridley and loggerhead, the endangered green and the critically endangered hawksbill turtle which nests in some number on the Daymaniyat Islands. The fifth species, leatherback turtle, occurs as a visitor offshore. Over 30,000 female loggerhead turtles nest on just 14km of beach on Masirah Island. The green turtle is a protected species in Oman. These marine turtles can live for up to 200 years and most only start to breed once they are between the ages of 30 and 50. Each female can lay up to 100 eggs in a clutch and several clutches in a breeding season. She spends hours covering them up in the holes she has dug for their protection. She then returns to the water (keeping close by) for a fortnight before she returns to lay another clutch, in a cycle that is repeated up to eight times in the season. It will be another two to four years (depending upon the species) before a female will lay more eggs. The eggs take around two months to hatch, and the sight of tiny baby turtles emerging from the sand is extraordinary. They struggle through the sand, making their way to the sea, but only a small proportion will make it, as many are eaten en route by seagulls and other predators.

CONSERVATION Wildlife conservation is actively carried out at the nature reserves in the country. However, for endangered species, the two principal centres are the Arabian Oryx Sanctuary at Jaaluni, in the Jiddat al Harasis (Al Wusta region) and the Oman Mammal Breeding Centre at Bait al Barakah, in Seeb (Muscat region). Mammals being bred in captivity in these locations include the Arabian oryx, the Arabian tahr, Arabian gazelle, Arabian wolf, the white-tailed mongoose, the striped hyena and Gordon's wild cat.

UNESCO World Heritage Sites Oman has four sites on the UNESCO World Heritage Site list. These include Bahla Fort (in the Dakhiliyah region); the Arabian Oryx Sanctuary (in Al Wusta region); the 'Land of Frankincense' (in the Dhofar region), which includes the archaeological sites at Shisr and Sumharam/Khor Rori and the archaeological sites at Bat, and neighbouring Al Khutm and Al Ayn (in Al Dhahirah region).

2

Practical Information

WHEN TO VISIT

The **winter season** (October to March) is the peak time to visit Oman as the temperature is broadly on a par with summer in the Mediterranean. The **summer season** (April to September) is the cheaper option, as it is generally deemed too hot for most visitors – temperatures can reach around 48°C. Hotels prices differ depending on the season.

During the winter season is the **Muscat Festival**, an annual event running from January until early February (see *Chapter 3*, page 105), when traditional Omani villages are erected at a few specific locations in the city and artisans demonstrate Oman's array of traditional crafts. Funfairs, rides and fireworks all add to the festivities of this time, when Oman promotes its culture and heritage. It is an interesting time to visit as you get a taste of Oman condensed into one area, although inevitably, early-evening traffic gets extremely busy and congested, especially going towards Qurum Natural Park and Azaiba Beach. The hotels too can become full, and some prices may even be increased a little.

During **Ramadan** (see page 52), no alcohol is served in restaurants, bars or private clubs, and minibars in hotel rooms tend to be emptied, too. You are permitted to order alcohol to your room through room service, but this must be consumed within the privacy of your room. No independent restaurants are open in the day at all, and hotel restaurants that are open have their windows draped over and obscured for discretion and in order not to offend local sensibilities. Ramadan, then, may or may not affect your choice of time to visit the country.

HIGHLIGHTS

Oman has a multitude of natural and cultural sites for the visitor to experience and explore. Some of the highlights of Oman include: the Daymaniyat Islands (off the Batinah coast); the old town of Nizwa, with its fort and souks; Jebel Shams and the Jebel Akhdar range (in the Dakhiliyah); Muttrah Souk and Muttrah and Muscat bays (in Muscat); the turtle beaches of Ras al Hadd and Ras al Jinz; the idyllic scenery of Wadi Sham and the Wahiba Sands (all in the Sharqiya); the barren fjord-like landscape of Musandam; the fort and ancient town of Sohar and the three forts and villages of the Rustaq Loop (all in the Batinah region); and the greenness of Dhofar (southern Oman) during the *khareef* season (July–September).

SUGGESTED ITINERARIES

One week is fine for a holiday here, but if you want to get a fuller taste of what Oman has to offer you will need to travel out of the capital area. Three weeks is a great amount of time which will allow for a full round trip where you will see pretty much everything. Below are itineraries that may be helpful in giving you some idea of how much time to allot to each location. Juggle these around to suit your preferences.

DAY TRIPS FROM MUSCAT
* The Rustaq Loop (see *Chapter 4, The Batinah coast*, page 136) makes a great day out. Take along a picnic and find a spot at the Nakhl Springs. A 4x4 is not necessary.
* Nizwa (see *Chapter 7, The Dakhiliyah*, page 187) can be visited as a full-day trip from Muscat. It is steeped in history and provides a real sense of the Oman of old. A 4x4 is not necessary.
* Take a wadi trip (either independently or with a tour operator) to Wadi bani Auf (see *Chapter 4, The Batinah coast*, page 119); it will give you an idea of the amazing mountain scenery of the country. You reach an incredible mountain village oasis (Bilad Sayt) at the top, which beggars belief. A 4x4 is necessary here.

OVERNIGHT TRIPS
* Visit Ras Al Hadd or Ras al Jinz to see the turtles. Stay overnight in either camp there, or in one of the Sur hotels.
* Take a boat trip to the Daymaniyat Islands, stay in Sohar, visiting the Sohar Fort and museum.
* Visit Jebel Shams, Bahla, Jabreen and Tanuf, staying at a hotel in Nizwa.

ONE WEEK
Day 1   Muscat Old Town – Al Alam Palace; Jalali and Merani forts; Bait Al Zubair; Muttrah corniche and souk; The Grand Mosque, Al Bustan Palace Hotel visit; overnight Muscat.

Day 2   Birkat Al Mawz Fort; Nizwa Fort and souk; Bin Ateeq for traditional Omani food; Tanuf ruins; overnight Nizwa.

Day 3   Hamra Old Town; Wadi Ghul, Jebel Shams; Bahla Town, fort and souk; Jabreen Castle; Wadi Dank scenery; overnight Nizwa/Bahla.

Day 4   Return towards Muscat visiting Fanja old citadel; Nakhl Fort; Ain Ath-Thowrah Hot Springs; overnight Sawadi.

Day 5   Rustaq Town and fort; Hazm Fort; Barka Fort; overnight Muscat.

Day 6   Take a cruise around the bays of Muscat (to be arranged through any tour operator). Shopping excursion to Qurum plazas or City Centre (after Seeb Airport, but before Seeb village). Visit to Qurum Natural Park.

Day 7   R&R in Muscat.

TWO WEEKS With an additional week you can add on a flight to Khasab in Musandam, where you can take a half-day dhow cruise to Telegraph Island and do a half-day mountain safari tour in a 4x4 with driver/guide. The flight timetable means that you either stay for one night or seven nights. One night is enough just to get a taste of Musandam; you will be able to fit in an afternoon tour on the day you arrive and a morning tour the following day prior to your return flight to Muscat in the afternoon. Juggle this itinerary around so that it falls in with the Thursday morning flight to Khasab, and Friday afternoon return.

Day 8   Drive the inland route to Sur, visiting en route Bidbid Fort; Samad ash Shan; Ibra ruined quarter; overnight in Sharqiya Sands Hotel.

Day 9   Collected by tour company to take a desert safari through Wahiba Sands. The dunes require a 4x4 vehicle and a skilled and experienced driver with knowledge of the terrain, and it is best to pre-arrange a trip with a tour operator in Muscat, or with one of the tour operators listed in this chapter, so you will have an accompanying driver/guide. If you choose to visit the Wahiba independently, it is strongly recommended that you follow at least one other vehicle and have at least one experienced person in the group, in the interests of your safety. Watch the sunset in the desert and stay at a desert camp.

Day 10 On towards Al Ashkhara; visit bani Bu Hassan Fort; Ras al Hadd, Ras al Jinz. Arrange evening visit to turtle beach with Ras al Hadd Beach Hotel (tours start at 21.00) or at the Ras al Jinz Turtle Beach Camp. Stay overnight at Ras al Hadd Beach Hotel or Ras al Jinz Turtle Beach Camp.

Day 11 On to Sur; tour Sur; Qalhat; with a 4x4 you can return from Sur along the coast to Muscat via Wadi Dayqah and Tiwi. Wadi Shab is a must if you do this coastal route back to Muscat. If not, then return to Muscat via the inland route (the way you came). It's quite a long drive, but once out of the way, you can relax back in the capital.

Day 12 Fly Khasab; take mountain safari tour with driver/guide (can be arranged on arrival, but you might like to pre-book); overnight Golden Tulip or your preferred choice.

Day 13 Morning dhow cruise. Fly to Muscat in the afternoon. Meal at Mumtaz Mahal (pre-book a seat by the window), Golden Oryx (the Thai Pavilion at the back is very private and intimate) or Pavo Real (buzzing Mexican with live music), to name but a few excellent restaurants. Overnight Muscat.

Day 14 Flight home.

THREE WEEKS With a third week you can fly to Salalah – the land of frankincense – and spend three days visiting the main sights (three days is really all you need). Then return to Muscat and drive up to Sohar for a couple of nights, exploring Sohar itself and its hinterland with copper mines, the Arja ziggurat and medieval stronghold of Hawra Burghah. Return to Muscat and relax until your flight home after buying your souvenirs in Muttrah souk or in the shopping complexes in Qurum.

SHORT VISIT If your time in the country is limited, here are some recommendations for sites relatively close to Muscat.

If you have time for only one old town, make it Nizwa. Located in the interior, it is truly evocative of the Oman of old. If you have time for only one wadi trip, make it Wadi bani Auf, where you can climb in your 4x4 up the mountainside, taking in spectacular gorges and ravines, and finally witness the amazing thriving village of Bilad Sayt that clings to the side of the mountain. If you can do one short trek along a ravine, go to Wadi Shab (on the coastal road to Sur), and let the boys guide you along and show you the cavernous mountain pool at the end – the peace and the colours of nature here are outstanding. If there's time for a souk, make it the historical souk at Muttrah, where you can take in the ambience of Muttrah harbour. If there's time, visit Al Bustan Palace Hotel, one of the best hotels in the world, with its awe-inspiring atrium. For a unique culinary experience, try Mumtaz Mahal Restaurant by Qurum Natural Park with excellent food and service, topped with views over the capital. Finish your meal with a *snake coffee* (a liqueur coffee where alcohol is lit and the flame poured down the long, peeled skin of an orange) and watch it being made at your table.

i TOURIST INFORMATION

In 2004, the Ministry of Tourism was founded as evidence of the sultanate's commitment to expanding and promoting its tourism sector. It is located at Azaiba

2

(before the Azaiba roundabout) on the left-hand (coastal) side of the highway (*Directorate General of Tourism, PO Box 550, Muscat, PC113;* ✆ *24 588 700;* e *dgt@ mocioman.gov.om or info@omantourism.gov.om; www.omantourism.gov.om*).

TOURIST BOARDS AND PR COMPANIES Oman now has representation in the following countries: the UK and Ireland, France, Germany, Australia and New Zealand, and Benelux.

UK and Ireland Representation Plus, 11 Blades Ct, 121 Deodar Rd, London SW15 2NU; ✆ 020 8877 4508; e oman@representationplus.co.uk
French-speaking countries Oman Tourism Office France, Embassy of Sultanate of Oman, 50 Av d'Iena, 75116 Paris; ✆ +33 1 47 20 56 06; f +33 1 47 20 55 80; e omantourism@wanadoo.fr
German-speaking countries Sultanate of Oman Representative – Germany, Interface International, GMBH Petersburger Strabe 94, 10247 Berlin; ✆ +49

30 4225 6027; f +49 30 4225 6286; e Kzwiersinterface@t-online.de
Australia and New Zealand Air Marketing Pty Ltd, Level 11, 99 York St, Sydney, NSW 2000, Australia; ✆ +61 9244 1841; f +61 9279 3786; e bill@airmaketing.com.au
Benelux BrouwerBetist, Hoge Gouwe 93, Post Bus 277, NL 2800, AG Gouda; ✆ +31 182 670244; f +31 182 526959; e rbrouwer@brouwerbetist.nl; www.brouwerbetist.nl

TOUR OPERATORS

UK Package holidays from London Heathrow start at around £650 per person for a week, including scheduled flights, airport transfers and bed-and-breakfast accommodation.

Destination2Oman ✆ 020 7720 8484; www.destination2oman.co.uk. Package holidays with Gulf Air as carrier.
Dream Oman ✆ 0845 061 6255, 0845 880 0245; www.dreamoman.com. Packages to Oman with various airlines.
Hayes and Jarvis ✆ 0870 333 3784; www.hayesandjarvis.co.uk. Tailor-made trips in conjunction with Emirates Airlines. Possibility of twin-centre holiday with Dubai in the UAE.
Key2Oman ✆ 020 7749 3627; e contact@ key2holidays.com; www.key2oman-holidays.co.uk. Tailor-made package holidays to Oman using Gulf Air as carrier; a little cheaper than most operators in this list.
Kudu Travel ✆ 01722 716167; e kuduinfo@ kudutravel.com; www.kudutravel.com. Offers 2-week tours to Oman taking in Muscat, the Jebel Akhdar range and Ubar.
Kuoni ✆ 01306 743000, 020 7374 6601; e help@kuoni.co.uk; www.kuoni.co.uk. Tailors luxury holidays.
Letsgo2 ✆ 020 8329 2647; e sales@letsgo2.com; www.oman.letsgo2.com. Holiday packages via various airlines.
Rainbow Tours ✆ 020 7226 1004; e info@ rainbowtours.co.uk; www.rainbowtours.co.uk. Offers tailor-made trips to Africa and the Indian Ocean

region, inc self-drive itineraries, escorted tours, honeymoons and family holidays. Tour guides are highly praised.
Safari Drive ✆ 01488 71140; e info@ safaridrive.com; www.safaridrive.com. Specialises in private, tailor-made safaris and offers trips to the Wahiba Sands with a Bedouin guide.
Shaw Travel ✆ 01635 47055; e info@ shawtravel.co.uk; www.shawtravel.co.uk. Shaw Travel specialises in luxury holidays to Oman using Gulf Air, and tailors your itinerary to suit.
Travel Oman ✆ 0870 748 7474; e sales@ airtravelcorp.co.uk; www.traveloman.co.uk. Arranges hotels, local tours, car rental. Also offers business-class packages to Oman.
Undiscovered Destinations ✆ 0191 206 4038; e info@undiscovered-destinations.com; www.undiscovered-destinations.com. Offers 2 tours in Oman: a 9-day trip from Muscat to Wahiba and Ras al Hadd, and a 16-day trip taking in Muscat, Nizwa, the Rub Al Khali desert, Salalah and the Wahiba Sands.
World Odyssey Ltd ✆ 01905 731373; e info@world-odyssey.com; www.world-odyssey.com. Specialises in tailor-made trips for individuals or small groups, using environmentally friendly partners.

US

SITA World Tours ☏ 818 990 9530; e sitatours@
sitatours.com; www.sitatours.com. Named one of
National Geographic's top 5 tour operators in
2004, SITA offers an 8-day tour in Oman and
Dubai including wadi-bashing and a desert safari.

Travcoa ☏ 866 591 0070; e requests@
travcoa.com; www.travcoa.com. Luxury tailored
holidays in small groups to Oman, with local guides
and lecturers.

RED TAPE

VISAS All visitors require visas and these can be easily purchased on arrival at Seeb
International Airport or at any of the border posts (after filling in a form), for
visitors from 63 countries; visas are valid for one month. For visitors from the
GCC states the visa costs RO3; all other visitors pay RO6. For all nationalities,
under 18s are free. Any further details can be obtained from the Royal Oman
Police (e *ropnet@omantel.net.om; www.rop.gov.om*) or try the very informative
website www.destinationoman.com.

CUSTOMS REGULATIONS Firearms, narcotics and pornographic material are banned.
Magazines, videos and books are sometimes confiscated and examined for
subversive or overtly sexual material. One bottle of alcohol may be brought into
the country by non-Muslims on entry at Seeb International Airport. Alcohol is
forbidden in private vehicles at land border crossings and vehicles are searched
quite thoroughly to find it among parties of expatriates travelling over from Dubai
for weekends or holidays. If found it is confiscated and you are fined. There are no
restrictions for camera equipment, computers or music players.

As for taking goods out of the country, be aware that some handles of the more
expensive *khanjars* (curved tribal sheathed daggers) are made from rhino horn or
ivory. It is illegal to take these out of the country, and indeed import them to your
own. Although these materials are no longer allowed to be used in the making of
khanjars, the authorities still permit the old stocks to be used up. Cheaper varieties
of *khanjar* are widely available as souvenirs (see box on page 20).

DEPARTURE TAX On leaving Oman, there is no departure tax.

Ⓔ OMAN EMBASSIES AND CONSULATES OVERSEAS

Austria Waehringer Strasse 2-4/24/25, 1090 Vienna
9th Quarter; ☏ +43 1 310 8643, 310 8644, 310
8684; f +43 1 310 7268

Bahrain Bldg 37, Rd 1901, Diplomatic Area, Manama
319, PO Box 26414; ☏ +973 293 663; f +973
293 540

Cyprus (consulate) 113 Prodromou Str 2064
Strovolos, PO Box 4670; ☏ +357 2 663 300;
f +357 2 663 321

Denmark (consulate) Strandvaenget SB, Dk 8240
Risskov; ☏ +45 8617 5072; f +45 8617 5058

Egypt 52 Al Higaz Str Al Muhandesin, Cairo; ☏ +20
2 303 6011, 303 5942, 303 5673; f +20 2 303
6464

France 50 Av D'lena – 75116 Paris; ☏ +33 1 47
23 01 63; f +33 1 47 23 77 10, 47 23 02 25

Germany Lindenallee 11, 53173 Bonn; ☏ +49 30

810050; f +49 30 810051

Ireland (consulate) 10A Lower Camden St, Dublin 2;
☏ +353 1 478 2504; f +353 1 478 3987

Italy Via Della Camilluccia 625, Postal Code 135,
Rome; ☏ +39 06 3630 0517, 3630 0545; f +39
06 3620 6802

Jordan Jebel Amman, between 4th and 5th Circle, PO
Box 20192, Amman 11110; ☏ +962 6 568 6155,
568 6156, 568 6157; f +962 6 568 9404

Kuwait Al Odeilia Plot 3, 3rd Str, Villa 25; ☏ +965
2561 956, 2561 957; f + 965 2561 963

Lebanon Al Remla, Al Bida Venezuele Str, Al Tyser
Bldg, PO Box 135900 Beirut Shouran; ☏ +961 1
856 555; f + 961 1 855 454

Netherlands Konginnegracht 27-2514 AB, The Hague;
☏ +31 70 361 5800, 363 3969; f +31 70 360
5364

Qatar Ibn Aiqassim Str No 41, Villa No7, Alhilal Area, Doha; ☏ +974 670 7 44, 670 745, 670 746; f +974 670 747

Russia 109180 Moscow, Staromonetny per, 14 Bldg 1; ☏ +7 095 230 1255, 230 1587, 230 2052; f +7 095 230 1544

Saudi Arabia Al Raed Quarter, opposite King Saud University, PO Box 94381 Al Riyadh 11693; ☏ +966 1 4823 120, 4823 067; f +966 1 4823 738/694. Hajj and Endowment Affairs Attaché, Al Ribat Hse, Makkah Al Mokarama; ☏ +966 1 5432 314; f +966 1 5743 263

South Africa (consulate) 3rd Fl, Export Hse, Corner of Maude and West St, Sandown, Sandton, PO Box 2142, Fourways, 2055; ☏ +27 11 884 0999; f +27 11 884 0835

Syria Mezzeh Westvillas, Al Ghazzaui Str PO Box 9635; ☏ +963 11 6110 408, 6622 506, 6130 003, 6622 194; f +963 11 6110 994

Tanzania (consulate) Hse No 2277, Vuga, Zanzibar PO 2100; ☏ +255 54 30 700, 30 066; f +255 54 31 070

Turkey Mahatma Gandhi Cad 63, Gazi Osman Basha; ☏ +90 312 4470 630, 4470 631; f +90 312 4470 632; e oman@marketweb.net.tr

UAE Al Mushraf Area next to Emigration Dept, Saeed bin Tahnon Str; ☏ +971 2 463 333; f +971 2 464 633

UK 167 Queens Gate, London SW7 5HE; ☏ +44 020 7225 0001, 7225 1622 (consular section); f +44 020 7589 2505; e omanembassy@btconnect.com

US 2535 Belmont Rd NW, Washington DC 20008; ☏ +1 202 387 1980; f +1 202 745 4933; e emboman@erols.com

Yemen Al Hoboob Corp St, Sub Baghdad St, PO Box 105, Sana'a R Y; ☏ +967 1 208 874, 208 875; f +967 1 204 586

GETTING THERE AND AWAY

✈ **BY AIR** Seeb International Airport, located 40km west of the old town of Muscat (about a 30-minute drive), is the country's main international airport, receiving flights from most of the world's airlines, as well as operating domestic flights. Salalah Airport, in the south of the country, is the only other international airport, receiving flights from other GCC countries only, as well as domestic flights from Muscat (*for flight information;* ☏ *24 519223*).

Flight prices are always subject to change, and a great site to search is www.ebookers.com. Currently, in low season, the cheapest flights from London to Muscat are offered by Qatar Airlines, costing just over £300 for an economy return flight from Gatwick with a short stop at Doha. Emirates fly from Gatwick via Dubai, taking 10½ hours, costing £330. Gulf Air fly non-stop from Heathrow, taking 7½ hours, costing £438. British Midland fly non-stop from Heathrow to Muscat, taking 7½ hours, costing £403. Etihad fly from Gatwick via Abu Dhabi, taking 8½ hours, costing £434. British Airways fly from Heathrow via Abu Dhabi, taking 8 hours 50mins, costing £441. London flights, if not direct, have a short stop in, or connecting flight from, the UAE, which then can add an extra hour or two to your journey.

For other European routes, the economy fare starts around the £400 mark for a return flight. Flights from CDG International Airport in Paris have a connecting flight from the UAE. These flight times are roughly 6 hours 50 minutes to Dubai, with an onward flight to Muscat taking an hour.

From the US there are no direct flights to Oman.

National carriers
Gulf Air (☏ +44 0870 777 1700; *Muscat* ☏ 24 703222, 24 703332; *www.gulfairco.com*). Oman is one of three owner states of Gulf Air, which has the most frequent flights into Muscat of any of the international airlines, servicing not only Europe but also the US, Asia, Africa and Australia. It operates direct daily flights from London Heathrow.

Oman Air Oman Air is the national carrier and has flights from Muscat to destinations that include Abu Dhabi, Al Ain, Bahrain, Beirut, Cairo, Chennai (Madras), Cochin, Dammam, Dar es Salaam, Delhi, Doha, Dubai, Hyderabad,

Jeddah, Kochi, Kuwait, Mumbai (Bombay), New Delhi and Trivandrum, as well as domestic flights to Salalah (in Dhofar) and Khasab (in Musandam).

Oman Air Sales Office Ruwi ✆ 24 707222, 24 750812; f 24 795546; e wytckres@omantel.net.om; www.oman-air.com
Oman Air Holidays ✆ 24 765129; f 24 765156; e wyholidays@oas.com.om
Oman Air Khasab ✆ 26 831591; f 24 831591, 99 027988

Oman Air Salalah Airport ✆ 23 296766, 23 298733, 23 294237; f 23 293242; e sllmmwy@omantel.net.om
Oman Air Seeb International Airport ✆ 24 519347, 24 519591; f 24 510550; e wymctstn@oas.com.om

Other airlines

Aeroflot ✆ 24 704455; www.aeroflot.co.uk
Air Canada ✆ 24 566046; www.aircanada.com
Air France ✆ 24 704318, 24 605761, 24 605148; www.airfrance.com
Air New Zealand ✆ 24 700326; www.airnewzealand.co.uk
American Airlines ✆ 24 604538
British Airways ✆ 24 568777, 24 565123; www.britishairways.com
Cathay Pacific ✆ 24 789818; www.cathaypacific.com
Emirates Air ✆ 24 786700, 24 792222, 24 783030;

www.emirates.com
Japan Airlines ✆ 24 704455; www.jal.com
KLM Royal Dutch Airlines ✆ 24 566737; www.klm.com
Lot Polish Airlines ✆ 24 796387; www.lot.com
Lufthansa German Airlines ✆ 24 796692; www.lufthansa.co.uk
Olympic ✆ 24 796387; www.olympicairlines.com
Qantas ✆ 24 604258; www.qantas.co.uk
Swiss International Airlines ✆ 24 787416, 24 791710; www.swissair.com.om

BY ROAD Although Oman borders three countries, it is only accessible by road through the United Arab Emirates. It is not possible to access Oman from either Saudi Arabia or Yemen.

Border crossings with the UAE From the United Arab Emirates there are six entry points: Hatta border (at Wadi Hatta and Al Wajajah); two Buraimi borders – one at Wadi Jizzi (coming from Sohar to Buraimi) and one at Jebel Hafeet (leading to Ibri/Nizwa); and Khatmat Milahah border (from Fujairah). The final two entry points are into Musandam in the north (from Ras al Khaimah emirate into Bukha, and from Fujairah emirate into Dibba). The journey from Dubai to Seeb Airport in Muscat takes approximately four hours and is a straight, uneventful drive through desert plain.

Tourists coming from the UAE by road will have their UAE visa cancelled on exit at the border posts, and Omani visas issued on entering the sultanate. All European and US nationals are eligible to get visas upon arrival at the borders, after filling in a form and paying the RO6 visa fee. For all other nationalities, and any other border post concerns, check with the Royal Oman Police via its website (*www.rop.gov.om*) It is then necessary to pass through immigration and customs formalities.

Visits to Musandam and Buraimi in Oman are a little more complex, as they each require a crossover into UAE territory. Although Buraimi is in Oman, it is frustratingly necessary to cancel your Oman tourist visa, as it is tightly juxtaposed with Al Ain (UAE) and the border posts lie quite a way out of Buraimi/Al Ain Town. Fortunately, the UAE offers a free-of-charge visit visa (*for further information visit http://www.uaeinteract.com/travel/visas.asp*), but it is nevertheless frustrating to endure the rigmarole of the paperwork and having to pay for the issuing of another Omani visa (which will last for one month from the new date) in order to continue your journey in Oman. There are no restrictions for women travelling alone, although lone female travellers are seemingly questioned more thoroughly at the border.

If you have rented a car in Oman and are taking it into the UAE (even simply in transit to Musandam or to Buraimi) then it is necessary to gain permission from your car-hire company and to confirm that the car is fully insured in both countries.

BY SEA No passenger ships terminate at Muscat, only cargo vessels, and these use Muttrah and Salalah ports. Cruise ships do day-long stops at Khasab (Musandam), Muttrah and Salalah (Dhofar).

✚ HEALTH with Dr Felicity Nicholson and Dr Jane Wilson-Howarth

PREPARATIONS From a health perspective, Oman is a relatively safe country to visit. Vaccinations are usually required only for longer-term visitors or those staying in rural areas.

There are pharmacies and clinics and good private medical-care facilities throughout the country. The heat of the country does mean that it is important to drink plenty of water.

Vaccinations
There are no compulsory vaccinations for visitors but it would be wise to be up to date with tetanus, diphtheria and polio. Long-term visitors and expatriate residents are usually advised to have typhoid vaccine and hepatitis A and B injections. A course of pre-exposure rabies vaccine is also advised for long-term visitors who will be in rural areas. It is best to check with your local clinic several weeks before departure. Yellow fever is required only for those travelling from infected areas. A valid certificate is then required, which is active ten days after vaccination and lasts for ten years. If the vaccine is contraindicated then ask your doctor or travel clinic (see below) for an exemption certificate and wherever possible obtain a letter from the Oman embassy in your starting country to accept this.

Malaria
Malaria is a limited risk in remote areas of Musandam and north Batinah, where there is high humidity and dense vegetation in the summer (April to September). For these rural areas, chloroquine and proguanil are recommended, which if it suits you needs to be started one week before entering the malarial area, continued during your stay and for four weeks afterwards. It may not be suitable for those with severe psoriasis, epilepsy and for people taking Zyban (an anti-smoking drug) or certain heart medications. If you are likely to visit rural areas, you should check with your doctor or a specialist travel clinic before departure. There is no risk of malaria in Muscat.

Extra protection
It is important to protect yourself from mosquito bites, so keep your repellent to hand at all times. Be aware that no prophylactic is 100% protective but those on prophylactics who are unlucky enough to catch malaria are less likely to get rapidly into serious trouble.

You also need either a permethrin-impregnated bednet or a permethrin spray so that you can 'treat' bednets in hotels. Permethrin treatment makes even very tatty nets protective and prevents mosquitoes from biting through the impregnated net when you roll against it; it also deters other biters. Putting on long clothes at dusk means you can reduce the amount of repellent you need to put on your skin, but be aware that malaria mosquitoes hunt at ankle level and will bite through socks, so apply repellent under socks too. Travel clinics usually sell a good range of nets, treatment kits and repellents.

Rabies
Rabies is carried by all mammals (beware the village dogs) and is passed on to humans through a bite, scratch or a lick of an open wound. You must always assume any animal is rabid (unless personally known to you) and seek medical help

as soon as possible. In the interim, scrub the wound with soap and bottled/boiled water, then pour on a strong iodine or alcohol solution. This helps stop the rabies virus entering the body and will guard against wound infections, including tetanus.

If you intend to have contact with animals and/or are likely to be more than 24 hours away from medical help, then pre-exposure vaccination is advised. Ideally three doses should be taken over a minimum of three weeks. Contrary to popular belief these vaccinations are relatively painless.

If you are exposed as described, treatment should be given as soon as possible, but it is never too late to seek help as the incubation period for rabies can be very long. Those who have not been immunised will need a full course of injections together with rabies immunoglobulin (RIG), but this product is expensive (around US$800) and may be hard to come by: another reason why pre-exposure vaccination should be encouraged in travellers who are planning to visit more remote areas.

Tell the doctor if you have had pre-exposure vaccine, as this will change the treatment you receive. And remember that, if you do contract rabies, mortality is 100% and death from rabies is probably one of the worst ways to go.

TRAVEL CLINICS AND HEALTH INFORMATION A full list of current travel clinic websites worldwide is available from the International Society of Travel Medicine on www.istm.org. For other journey preparation information, consult www.tripprep.com. Information about various medications may be found on www.emedicine.com. For information on malaria prevention, see www.preventingmalaria.info.

UK

Berkeley Travel Clinic 32 Berkeley St, London W1J 8EL (near Green Park tube station); ℡ 070 7629 6233
Cambridge Travel Clinic 48a Mill Rd, Cambridge CB1 2AS; ℡ 01223 367362; e enquiries@cambridgetravelclinic.co.uk; www.cambridgetravelclinic.co.uk. Open Tue–Fri 12.00–19.00, Sat 10.00–16.00.
Edinburgh Travel Clinic Regional Infectious Diseases Unit, Ward 41 OPD, Western General Hospital, Crewe Rd South, Edinburgh EH4 2UX; ℡ 0131 537 2822; www.link.med.ed.ac.uk/ridu. Travel helpline (0906 589 0380) open weekdays 09.00–12.00. Provides inoculations and antimalarial prophylaxis and advises on travel-related health risks.
Fleet Street Travel Clinic 29 Fleet St, London EC4Y 1AA; ℡ 020 7353 5678; www.fleetstreetclinic.com. Vaccinations, travel products and latest advice.
Hospital for Tropical Diseases Travel Clinic Mortimer Market Bldg, Capper St (off Tottenham Ct Rd), London WC1E 6AU; ℡ 020 7388 9600; www.thehtd.org. Offers consultations and advice, and is able to provide all necessary drugs and vaccines for travellers. Runs a healthline (0906 133 7733) for country-specific information and health hazards. Also stocks nets, water-purification equipment and personal protection measures.
Interhealth Worldwide Partnership Hse, 157 Waterloo Rd, London SE1 8US; ℡ 020 7902 9000; www.interhealth.org.uk. Competitively priced, one-stop travel health service. All profits go to their affiliated company, InterHealth, which provides health care for overseas workers on Christian projects.
MASTA (Medical Advisory Service for Travellers Abroad) Moorfield Rd, Yeadon LS19 7BN; ℡ 0870 606 2782; www.masta-travel-health.com. Provides travel health advice, anti-malarials and vaccinations. There are over 25 MASTA pre-travel clinics in Britain; call or check online for the nearest. Clinics also sell mosquito nets, medical kits, insect protection and travel hygiene products.
NHS travel website www.fitfortravel.scot.nhs.uk. Provides country-by-country advice on immunisation and malaria, plus details of recent developments, and a list of relevant health organisations.
Nomad Travel Store/Clinic 3–4 Wellington Terrace, Turnpike Lane, London N8 0PX; ℡ 020 8889 7014; travel-health line (office hours only) 0906 863 3414; e sales@nomadtravel.co.uk; www.nomadtravel.co.uk. Also at 40 Bernard St, London WC1N 1LJ; ℡ 020 7833 4114; 52 Grosvenor Gardens, London SW1W 0AG; ℡ 020 7823 5823 and 43 Queens Rd, Bristol BS8 1QH; ℡ 0117 922 6567. For health advice, equipment such as mosquito nets and other anti-bug devices, and an excellent range of adventure travel gear.

Trailfinders Travel Clinic 194 Kensington High St, London W8 7RG; ☎ 020 7938 3999; www.trailfinders.com/clinic.htm

Travelpharm The Travelpharm website www.travelpharm.com offers up-to-date guidance on travel-related health and has a range of medications available through their online mini-pharmacy.

Irish Republic

Tropical Medical Bureau Grafton St Medical Centre, Grafton Bldgs, 34 Grafton St, Dublin 2; ☎ 1 671 9200; www.tmb.ie. A useful website specific to tropical destinations. Also check website for other bureaux locations throughout Ireland.

US

Centers for Disease Control 1600 Clifton Rd, Atlanta, GA 30333; ☎ 800 311 3435; travellers' health hotline 888 232 3299; www.cdc.gov/travel. The central source of travel information in the US. The invaluable *Health Information for International Travel*, published annually, is available from the Division of Quarantine at this address.

Connaught Laboratories PO Box 187, Swiftwater, PA 18370; ☎ 800 822 2463. They will send a free list of specialist tropical-medicine physicians in your state.

IAMAT (International Association for Medical Assistance to Travelers) 1623 Military Rd, 279, Niagara Falls, NY 14304-1745; ☎ 716 754 4883; e info@iamat.org; www.iamat.org. A non-profit organisation that provides lists of English-speaking doctors abroad.

International Medicine Center 920 Frostwood Drive, Suite 670, Houston, TX 77024; ☎ 713 550 2000; www.traveldoc.com

Canada

IAMAT Suite 1, 1287 St Clair Av W, Toronto, Ontario M6E 1B8; ☎ 416 652 0137; www.iamat.org

TMVC Suite 314, 1030 W Georgia St, Vancouver BC V6E 2Y3; ☎ 1 888 288 8682; www.tmvc.com

Australia, New Zealand, Singapore

TMVC ☎ 1300 65 88 44; www.tmvc.com.au. 31 clinics in Australia, New Zealand and Singapore, including: *Auckland* Canterbury Arcade, 170 Queen St, Auckland; ☎ 9 373 3531

Brisbane 6th Fl, 247 Adelaide St, Brisbane, QLD 4000; ☎ 7 3221 9066

LONG-HAUL FLIGHTS, CLOTS AND DVT

Dr Jane Wilson-Howarth

Long-haul air travel increases the risk of deep vein thrombosis. Although recent research has suggested that many of us develop clots when immobilised, most resolve without us ever having been aware of them. In certain susceptible individuals, though, large clots form and these can break away and lodge in the lungs. This is dangerous but happens in a tiny minority of passengers.

Studies have shown that flights of over 5½hrs are significant, and that people who take lots of shorter flights over a short space of time form clots. People at highest risk are:

- Those who have had a clot before – unless they are now taking warfarin
- People over 80 years of age
- Anyone who has recently undergone a major operation or surgery for varicose veins
- Someone who has had a hip or knee replacement in the last three months
- Cancer sufferers
- Those who have ever had a stroke
- People with heart disease
- Those with a close blood relative who has had a clot

Those with a slightly increased risk:

- People over 40
- Women who are pregnant or have had a baby in the last couple of weeks
- People taking female hormones or other oestrogen therapy
- Heavy smokers
- Those who have very severe varicose veins
- The very obese
- People who are very tall (over 6ft/1.8m) or short (under 5ft/1.5m)

Melbourne 393 Little Bourke St, 2nd Fl, Melbourne, VIC 3000; ☏ 3 9602 5788
Sydney Dymocks Bldg, 7th Fl, 428 George St, Sydney, NSW 2000; ☏ 2 9221 7133
IAMAT PO Box 5049, Christchurch 5, New Zealand; www.iamat.org

SAA-Netcare Travel Clinics P Bag X34, Benmore 2010;

www.travelclinic.co.za. Clinics throughout South Africa.
TMVC 113 D F Malan Drive, Roosevelt Park, Johannesburg; ☏ 011 888 7488; www.tmvc.com.au. Consult website for details of other clinics in South Africa and Namibia.

IAMAT 57 Chemin des Voirets, 1212 Grand Lancy, Geneva; www.iamat.org

PERSONAL FIRST-AID KIT Pharmacies are so plentiful throughout Oman that it is not the end of the world if you don't take your own personal first-aid kit. However, If you prefer to go prepared, then the following may be helpful.

- A few small plasters or dressings
- Suncream
- Painkillers
- Antiseptic cream
- Insect repellent (only needed if camping, and then only in some remote areas)

IN OMAN
Medical facilities In the late 1960s there were only three hospitals in the country and eight out of ten babies died within ten months of conception. Old and young alike were riddled with trachoma (a contagious disease of the eye). Tuberculosis was

A deep vein thrombosis (DVT) is a blood clot that forms in the deep leg veins. This is very different from irritating but harmless superficial phlebitis. DVT causes swelling and redness of one leg, usually with heat and pain in one calf and sometimes the thigh. A DVT is only dangerous if a clot breaks away and travels to the lungs (pulmonary embolus). Symptoms of a pulmonary embolus (PE) include chest pain that is worse on breathing in deeply, shortness of breath, and sometimes coughing up small amounts of blood. The symptoms commonly start three to ten days after a long flight. Anyone who thinks that they might have a DVT needs to see a doctor immediately who will arrange a scan. Warfarin tablets (to thin the blood) are then taken for at least six months.

PREVENTION OF DVT Several conditions make the problem more likely. Immobility is the key, and factors like reduced oxygen in cabin air and dehydration may also contribute. To reduce the risk of thrombosis on a long journey:

- Exercise before and after the flight
- Keep mobile before and during the flight; move around every couple of hours
- During the flight drink plenty of water or juices
- Avoid taking sleeping pills and excessive tea, coffee and alcohol
- Perform exercises that mimic walking and tense the calf muscles
- Consider wearing flight socks or support stockings (see *www.legshealth.com*)
- Take a meal of oily fish (mackerel, trout, salmon, sardines etc) in the 24 hours before departure to reduce blood clotability and thus DVT risk

If you think you are at increased risk of a clot, ask your doctor if it is safe to travel.

Practical Information **HEALTH**

2

If someone was seriously ill with much pain, the old Arab practice was to apply the *wussum* burn. A girl who had been bitten by a poisonous snake on one leg, thus had a series of deep burns inflicted on her other leg which were then brushed with fresh camel dung. The effect was to outweigh the original pain, and sometimes to cause gangrene and death. The old customs ran deep and even in the late 1960s, a trained Omani doctor commented: 'Our people will burn and bleed a patient through trying to cure him before they would even think of taking him to the American Hospital in Muttrah, That is done only as a final resort when all else has failed.'

Freya Stark in her travels in southern Arabia commented on the same tendency. As a consequence of having two windows in every wall there were often strong draughts in Arab houses. Many caught measles, shivering, then bronchitis and pneumonia, as she herself did. But as she noticed: 'Few came to the chemist. They preferred to run hot irons down their backs.' She also noted that the people of the Hadramaut had a horror of soap or scent, convinced it weakened or even killed you if you were already poorly. After measles no-one would use it for 41 days.

common, as were malaria and chronic anaemia. Leprosy was endemic with no enforced segregation. Flies were everywhere, transferring disease from the faeces of villagers to their food with regularity and crawling over the faces of oblivious children.

Today, the situation in Oman is remarkably different. There is an extensive public health service which is free to Omanis (for foreigners, doctors and hospitals often expect cash, and costs can be high). Private medical services are excellent. Cosmetic surgery is widely available, as is laser eye surgery (tried and tested to full satisfaction by the author in Al Shatti Hospital in Muscat). Travel insurance is advised as medical treatment can be costly for foreigners. Those with specific medical conditions should wear medical alert tags and carry a list of medications related to their condition.

Hospitals For hospital telephone numbers, see the end of each regional chapter.

Pharmacies Muscat Pharmacy has branches throughout the country at Ruwi, Al Saruj, Al Khuwair, Al Ghubra north, Al Mawaleh, Sohar, Al Hail, Hamriya and Salalah. A few are open 24 hours in the capital, the details of which appear in any of the English-language newspapers.

Emergency An ambulance service was introduced in certain urban locations in 2004, using US equipment and US-trained staff. Otherwise, the availability of roadside or ambulance assistance is poor. The Royal Oman Police will assist in an emergency.

Emergency services ☏ 999   **Royal Oman Police** ☏ 24 560099

Drinking water Outside of the capital area, water should be regarded as being potentially contaminated. Bottled water, or water that has been boiled, is advised for drinking, brushing teeth and making ice. Several brands of bottled water are from Oman's own mountain sources.

Protection from the sun The summer months (April–September) can be extremely hot. Be careful to keep your skin covered and wear loose-fitting clothes for comfort. Sunglasses and hats will provide welcome relief and are recommended. Do use a sunscreen or at least a high-factor protection cream, and reapply after swimming. Try to keep out of the sun between 11.00 and 15.00 when the sun is strongest.

SAFETY

The crime rate in Oman is low and the streets of the capital are safe even for lone travellers after dark.

WOMEN TRAVELLERS Oman is one of the easiest Arab countries for foreign women to travel in without hassle, if their dress and demeanour are appropriate. There is no risk for women in using taxis, buses or hiring a car.

In the city, despite the fact that the hotel bars and private clubs are a male domain (in Omani culture), you will find that, broadly, Omanis are chatty, relaxed and helpful. Their temperaments generally are very easy-going and good-humoured. For a lone female traveller, Omani men (for men are likely all you will meet and converse with in public) make excellent, respectful and supportive company.

WHAT TO TAKE

CLOTHES For comfort, loose cotton clothing is best and a pullover will often be required in the evenings in the winter months (October through to March). In the top-class hotels dressing for dinner is normal, while in the smaller hotels, especially inland, the style is much more informal. For more details, see *Dress code*, page 57.

FOOTWEAR A lot of the exploration involves walking on uneven surfaces so ensure your footwear can cope.

OTHER USEFUL ITEMS There are pharmacies and foodstuffs stores throughout the country and so medicines, plasters, batteries etc will all be readily available. In Muscat there are several large supermarkets and one hypermarket which have excellent stocks of virtually everything you can get at home. For female travellers, it may be an idea to take a tampon supply – only a few of the supermarkets stock Tampax, and most places sell only the non-applicator variety. You will find that some pharmacies keep these under the counter too. Sanitary towels are widely available.

CAMPING EQUIPMENT Camping equipment can be hired from tour operators (see *Chapter 3*, page 117, for cost). In addition there are local shops in every village selling pots, pans and odd bits and pieces that are cheap enough and will equip you for your trip.

$ MONEY AND BUDGETING

CURRENCY The currency is the Omani rial (RO). One rial is made up of 1,000 baizas (bzs).

The Omani rial is pegged to the US dollar at RO1 = US$2.60 and the exchange rate has therefore been very stable for a number of years.

The rates of exchange in September 2006 were as follows: £1 = RO0.73, US$1 = RO0.38, €1 = RO0.50.

CASH It is best to change money once in Oman as the rates are better than can be obtained overseas. ATMs are plentiful throughout the country. There are several HSBC points in Muscat and Salalah and in other large towns. Up to RO300 in

Gordon Rattray (www.able-travel.com)

Having wheelchair access is not yet obligatory for Oman's tourist facilities, and the further you venture from Muscat, the more challenging life becomes for travellers with mobility problems. However, the tourist industry is growing rapidly and this is having a positive influence on what is available for the disabled traveller. On top of this, Omani culture is one of exceptional hospitality and friendliness, and therefore local people will always offer support and help.

ACCOMMODATION Since most hotels have been built post-1980, access is fairly good. The government has been putting pressure on hotels to provide special facilities and many have responded well (especially in Muscat and in Salalah). This does not mean these hotels will all have roll-in showers and grab handles, but some have a small number of dedicated bedrooms, and lifts and access ramps make movement within the public areas of the hotel easier. Generally, access to the pool areas in these larger hotels is quite good, but many still only have ladder entry. One exception (albeit expensive) is the Chedi (page 70), where pools have gradual steps. Access to beaches is never easy, but as always, staff are willing to help.

GETTING AROUND

In general As with tourist accommodation, most public buildings have been built in the last 30 years, meaning that they are fairly accessible. In the cities, the situation is constantly improving and several modern shopping malls and pedestrian areas even have disabled toilets and access ramps. The main mosques and museums don't cater especially for wheelchairs, but most are fairly flat with wide doors and level access. If you are intending to visit forts and castles, you can expect to find them as inaccessible as they were designed to be!

By road I am unaware of any accessible taxi companies in Oman, so you may need help when transferring in and out of the vehicle. This will be even more likely if you are planning to venture off the beaten track as 4x4s are higher than normal cars. Drivers/guides are normally happy to assist, but are not trained in this skill, so you must thoroughly explain your needs and always stay in control of the situation.

Distances can be great but thankfully the condition of the roads throughout the country is excellent. However, if you plan to go off-road in any way, for example, a wadi trip, or a desert or mountain safari, then it will be bumpy. Anyone prone to skin damage should take extra care. Place your own pressure-relieving cushion on top of (or instead of) the original car seat and if necessary, pad around knees and elbows.

Anyone planning to use Oman's coach network should be aware that it does not cater for disabled travellers. Therefore, depending on your ability, you may need assistance to get on and off buses.

By air 'Aisle chairs' are used for international arrivals in Muscat, making entering and exiting the aircraft easier for non-ambulant people, and Seeb International Airport has

cash can be withdrawn per day. On arrival in Muscat, you are able to pay for your one-month tourist visa by credit card or in currency from your country of origin, so don't worry if you haven't got Omani rials to hand.

TRAVELLERS' CHEQUES If you prefer to use travellers' cheques, these, as well as major currencies, can be exchanged for Omani rials at banks, bureaux de change, the airport and at larger hotels. Travellers are advised to purchase travellers' cheques in US dollars to avoid additional exchange rate charges. The exchange rate disabled toilets. The local carrier – Oman Air – is also reported to be of a high standard, though that is not to say that an aisle chair and full facilities are to be expected at every domestic terminal.

ACTIVITIES Local operators have assured me that the dolphin-watching and desert and wadi visits should all be possible. More challenging activities like trekking or via ferrata (mountain routes traversable by fixed cables, ladders and bridges) would obviously require more planning, but again, depending on your ability and motivation, they are not out of the question.

HEALTH General healthcare in Oman is excellent. However, as with anywhere, you must understand and be able to explain your own particular medical requirements. Comprehensive insurance is essential, and be sure the insurance company is aware of any existing medical conditions.

Pharmacies are well stocked, but it is always advisable to take all necessary medication and equipment with you, and to pack this in your hand luggage during flights in case your main luggage gets lost.

Oman is hot all year round, but every hotel is equipped with air-conditioning units for your comfort. Aerosol water sprays are widely available at chemists, and provide welcome relief as an instant cooling aid, although a cheaper and more environmentally friendly device is a plant-spray bottle filled with water.

SECURITY Oman is a relatively safe travel destination and the crime rate is low. However, it is worthwhile remembering that, as a disabled person, you are more vulnerable. Stay aware of who is around you and where your bags are, especially during car transfers and similar. These activities often draw a crowd, and the confusion creates easy pickings for an opportunist thief.

SPECIALIST OPERATORS There are, as yet, no operators who specialise in disability travel to Oman. Having said that, most travel companies will listen to your needs and try to create an itinerary suitable for you. For the independent traveller, it is possible to limit potential surprises by contacting local operators and establishments by email in advance.

FURTHER INFORMATION The most accurate and up-to-date information is available from tour operators. I found the following people most helpful:

Peter and Margaret at Omantravel Ltd ✆ +44 (0)1235 200444; e margaret@omantravel.uk.com; www.omantravel.uk.com

Sasha at Muscat Diving & Adventure Centre ✆ +968 24485663; f 00 968 24485774; e sasha@holiday-in-oman.com; www.holiday-in-oman.com

at hotels is usually worse than at a bank or money changer (sometimes up to 17% lower), but has the advantage of convenience, and where the amounts concerned are small the effort entailed in finding a bank and queuing during its opening hours scarcely warrants the saving. Banks outside Muscat will change only American Express travellers' cheques.

CREDIT CARDS Credit cards are widely accepted in hotels, restaurants, shopping complexes, petrol stations and businesses throughout Oman. It is recommended that you advise your credit card provider that you intend to use the card in Oman, and in that way you can be assured that you will encounter no hiccups and gain full approval. In smaller hotels, shops, souks and restaurants it is likely that you will need cash, especially in the interior. In the traditional souks, cash is mainly used, as it also allows for easy bargaining, which is expected in this setting as a matter of course.

BUDGETING Oman is not a cheap destination for the visitor, but it is possible to tour the country on a budget if you are prepared to forgo some comforts and luxuries. You can also eat very cheaply at the unlicensed Indian and Omani restaurants and coffee shops. A meal for two with drinks is likely to be under RO5. You can buy fresh breads of all varieties, hot chicken, delicatessen foods, pre-prepared salads, fruits and cold drinks away from any of the supermarkets for great beach or mountain picnics. A litre bottle of water costs around 250bzs, and canned drinks cost around the same. A whole chicken straight off the rotisserie costs only RO1.

Car-hire companies operate within residential areas, and these are a little cheaper than those in the airport. If a 4x4 is not necessary, go for a saloon, which is significantly cheaper. The cheapest option for getting around is to use the minibus service operating in the capital.

If you're lucky enough to have Omani friends or acquaintances, or know expats with Omani residence, then it is likely at some point that you will be invited along to one of the many private clubs in the cities. Here you will save a fortune on food and drink, as these are expensive in hotels. Postcards cost just baizas, to buy and to send home (using the post offices). T-shirts can be bought cheaply in the small shops in Ruwi Souk Street for around RO5. Camera film is inexpensive and petrol is very cheap (under RO10 to fill a 4x4 tank).

It is possible to stay in Oman for a cost of RO35 per day, staying in a budget hotel, renting a saloon car and eating in the local coffee shops and budget restaurants. This figure can be reduced further if you forego the hire car, or intend to camp in the country (although if you're camping, you will need the car for all the necessary equipment). In this case, you can get by here on a rock-bottom budget of RO20 per day.

TIPPING In hotels and restaurants a 15% service charge is added to the bill, so tipping over and above this is a matter of personal choice. It will, however, be appreciated. Any other tipping, for example for hotel porterage, airport assistance, room service or taxi service, is appreciated, but not expected.

GETTING AROUND

✈ **BY AIR** Within Oman there are domestic flights to Khasab in Musandam and Salalah in Dhofar only, operated exclusively by Oman Air (see page 36).

🚗 **BY ROAD** The road network in Oman is excellent, and so a saloon car is largely all you need to get about. The three-lane motorway (or highway) in Muscat is good (although the roads around the capital can be confusing; see page 64 for further details), and so too are the dual carriageways both in the capital and along the Batinah coast. There are good single carriageways inland to Nizwa, Sur, Ibri and down to Salalah and traffic is generally light. Roads are also excellent to Dubai. Directions are clearly signposted in phonetic English, so getting around is easy.

There are, however, a few off-road trips where a 4x4 is necessary, and these can easily be hired. Alternatively, if you arrange these trips through a tour operator, rather than going independently, the vehicle and driver/guide will be provided and included in the price. The Wahiba Sands, the Empty Quarter and the wadi trips each require a 4x4, and so does the coastal road trip to Sur (for a short part of the way). As such it may be an idea to hire a saloon, then pay a tour operator for a trip into the Wahiba or your first wadi-bashing experience. They can either drive you from the capital to your destination, or collect you from your hotel in the region.

Driving is on the right-hand side of the road, so all vehicles are left-hand drive. Be sure to carry your driving licence and hire-car agreement with you in case you are asked to produce them at any time. In the event of an accident, however slight, the police must be called and the vehicles involved not moved. Driving under the influence of alcohol is an offence. Wearing a seatbelt is mandatory and the fine for non-compliance is RO10.

Shell, Al Maha and Oman Oil fuel stations abound throughout the country. The BP stations have now been replaced with Oman Oil garages. Fuel is cheap – it costs approximately RO9 (£13, US$23, €18) to fill a 4x4 tank. Most fuel stations have toilets (albeit in various states of cleanliness), and some have shops selling foodstuffs and drinks, very cheaply.

Be aware that there may be camels, goats or donkeys crossing the road at any time. Oncoming cars may flash their headlights at you to warn you to slow down for a possible hazard up ahead.

The speed limit on the highways is 120km/h (75 mph).

Vehicle assistance The AAA (Arabian Automobile Alliance), provides 24-hour roadside assistance (✆ *24 697800*).

Car hire There is no difficulty in getting a hire car in Oman. Plenty of car-hire firms have desks immediately in Seeb International Airport arrivals area and the upper-range hotels have car-hire desks/offices within, if you prefer to wait until you are rested before arranging things. The budget and mid-range hotels will also certainly arrange a car for you on request. So, don't worry if you haven't pre-booked; you are bound to find something. Most companies will drop a car off at your hotel.

As with most places they will ask for a copy of your passport, your driving licence (either from your country of origin or an international driving licence), and a credit card or cash for a returnable deposit. Drivers have to be 21 or over. Rates for small cars range from RO10–14 per day or RO70–100 for a week, including insurance. A 4x4 jumps up to approximately RO35 per day. The costs usually include 200km mileage, collision damage waiver, theft waiver, third party insurance and local taxes. Personal accident insurance is optional, and costs around RO1 per day, and mileage above 200km is charged at approximately RO0.08 per km.

If you intend to cross any of the border posts into the UAE (even if simply in transit to Musandam or Buraimi) it is necessary to obtain permission from your car-hire company and to confirm that the vehicle is insured in both countries. For more details about crossing borders, see page 37.

Note that if returning your hire car to the airport, you need to go back to the arrivals desk (even though you are departing) as there are no car-rental desks in departures. So remember to park the vehicle closer to this end of the airport entrance.

Always keep documentation with you in case of an accident or a police stop. The majority of the car rental companies listed below are in Muscat. Where they have branches in Salalah, this has been indicated.

Advantage Car Rentals CCC, Qurum; ✆/f 24 561910; e touroman@shanfari.com; www.shanfari.com

Arabian Tours Company Salalah and Muscat; ✆ 23 290088

Avis Rent-a-Car, Ruwi; ✆ 24 692940; f 24 692239; Avis Seeb Airport; ✆ 24 519176, 24 510342; Avis Intercontinental; ✆ 24 607235, 24 601224; f 24 694885; Avis Al Bustan Palace Hotel; ✆ 24 703242; Avis Sheraton Oman; ✆ 24 799899; Avis Grand Hyatt; ✆ 24 696596; Avis Crowne Plaza; ✆ 24 566526; Avis, Salalah (Al Nahda St); ✆ 23 2022582; 23 235 582; e avisoman@omantel.net.om; www.avis.com

Budget Rent-a-Car Seeb Airport; ✆ 24 510816, 24 510817; f 24 704248; Salalah Crowne Plaza; ✆ 23 235160; f 23 235966; Salalah Airport; ✆ 23 290097; Salalah Crowne Plaza; ✆ 23 235160; f 23 235966; Al Falaj Hotel; ✆ 24 794721, 24 702311; f 24 798144; Sur Plaza Hotel; ✆ 25 443777; Ruwi Hotel; ✆ 24 561910; e budgetom@omantel.net.om. Daily rate RO14, weekly RO88 with 250km free daily, 4x4 RO36 daily, RO216 weekly with 150km free daily.

Europcar ✆ 24 700190, 24 700191; f 24 794061; Muscat Holiday Inn; ✆ 24 684093; Seeb Airport: ✆ 24 521369, 24 519014; f 24 521369; Salalah Airport: ✆ 99 341814; Salalah Hilton; ✆ 23 212460, f 23 212461; Sohar; ✆ 26 840753; Sur Beach Hotel; ✆ 25 540735; e euro@omantel.net.om; www.europcar.com

Global Car Rental Shatti al Qurum; ✆ 24 697140; f 24 696393; Sur; ✆ 25 541007; f 25 540454; e glowbal@omantel.net.om

Al Hadaf Car Rent ✆ 24 497684, 99 357953; f 24 497668. This is a local car-hire company with an office in Ghubra. It might save a few pounds, although the organisation may take a little bit more effort.

Hertz National Travel and Tourism Wattayah; ✆ 24 566208; f 24 566125; Seeb Airport; ✆ 24 521187; e nttoman@omantel.net.om; www.nttoman.com. Quotes for a Ford Focus were RO14/90 per day/week; Ford Mondeo RO17/110 per day/week.

Al Ibtisama Rent-a-Car Rex Rd, Muscat; ✆ 24 751177; f 24 796874

Mark Rent-a-Car Hatat Hse, Muscat; ✆ 24 562444, 24 565567, 24 560975; f 24 565434; Seeb Airport; ✆ 24 510033; www.marktoursoman.com/rentacar

Al Maskry Car Rentals Ghubra, Muscat; ✆ 24 505923, 24 595241; f 24 591538; e almaskrey@omantel.net.om; www.almaskryrentacar.com

Al Miyasa Rent-a-Car Salalah (Al Salam St, next to Redan Hotel); ✆ 23 296521; f 23 296521

Payless Car Rental Muttrah, Muscat; ✆ 24 567261, 24 561482; f 24 560168

Qurum Beach Hotel Car Hire Qurum Beach Hotel, Muscat; ✆ 24 564070

Shuram Shatti al Qurum, Muscat; ✆ 24 696299; f 24 600917

Sixt Seeb Airport; ✆ 24 520224, 24 510224; f 24 510933; Al Khuwair; ✆ 24 600793, 24 600835, 24 600896; f 24 601056; Crowne Plaza Hotel; ✆ 24 561427; Sheraton Oman ✆ 24 704455, 24 704458; Salalah; ✆ 23 290908, 23 294665; f 23 294213

Thrifty Car Rental Al Khuwair; ✆ 24 489248, 24 489648; f 24 602512; Seeb Airport; ✆ 24 521189; Salalah Airport; ✆ 23 290082, 99 323619; Salalah City Centre; ✆ 23 211493; Qurum; ✆ 24 567785; f 24 567784; Muttrah Business District; ✆ 24 784275; f 24 750436; e haditha@omantel.net.om; www.thriftyoman.com The Thrifty desk at Seeb Airport is very helpful. Rates only RO14 per day for a Nissan Sunny automatic.

Toyota Rent-a-Car Crowne Plaza Hotel, Muscat; ✆ 24 561427, 24 561437; f 24 565968; Seeb Airport; ✆ 24 510224, 24 510933; Salalah Airport; ✆ 23 290908, 23 294665; f 23 294213; e tracbest@omantel.net.om

Value Plus Rent a Car ✆ 24 597264; f 24 597266; Seeb Airport; ✆ 24 510292; f 24 510876; Sohar; ✆ 26 842557; Salalah; ✆ 23 298085, 23 210125; f 23 297085, 23 210145; e vic@otegroup.com; www.valueoman.com

Zubair Automotive Azaiba, Muscat; ✆ 24 592143, 24 590430; f 24 595584, 24 501376; e leasing@zaleasing.com; www.zaleasing.com

By taxi Taxis are frequent, honest and reliable and are the best means of transport in Oman. With their orange-and-white colouring they are very conspicuous. It is a good idea to agree the fare beforehand, as taxis are unmetered, although you're unlikely to be ripped off. They can be hailed on any street, and on quieter roads, if the driver sees you walking, he may toot to see if you need a taxi. Tipping is not necessary, unless you particularly want to.

Only a few taxi firms offer a pre-arranged service, and these are based in Muscat. For details, see *Chapter 3, Muscat*, page 65.

If you require something special, a chauffeur-driven limousine service is available and can be arranged through the larger hotels or at the information desk in Seeb Airport.

The maximum safe depth is to the tops of the tyres. Cross where the water is at its widest, as this tends to be where it is shallowest and with the weakest current. Keep your speed down if the water is fairly shallow so you do not splash your electrics. With deeper water, enter slowly in 4x4 low gear (first or second), then keep the revs high once the front grill is in the water to create a slight bow wave with a trough under the engine.

If your engine does get drowned do not attempt to start it as water may have entered the tops of the pistons via the exhaust or air filter which could result in a bent crank shaft or in the worst case a piston breaking through the side of the engine. Tow the vehicle out of the water, remove and dry the spark plugs, dry the ignition system, then turn on the ignition which will pump the water out of the combustion chamber. Once the water is out, you can reassemble the spark plugs and leads (taking care to get them in the right order!), then try the ignition or push start if your battery is low.

By coach For longer journeys you might like to consider taking a coach. From Muscat it is possible to get a coach from Ruwi Bus Station to Salalah (in the south), Nizwa (in the Dakhiliyah), Sohar (on the Batinah Coast), Buraimi (in the Dhahirah), Ibra and Sur (in the Sharqiya), and Dubai and Abu Dhabi (in the United Arab Emirates). Coaches make several stops along the way at allocated pick-up/drop-off points, the first being at Seeb International Airport. It is recommended that you make your booking a few days in advance, though it is possible to join any of the coach services on the spot if space allows. The air-conditioned buses take around 40–45 people. No food is provided on the coaches so you might like to take some snacks and drinks along with you. Children under 12 travel for half price. Journeys that take you into Dubai, Abu Dhabi and Buraimi cross border posts where the coaches stop for the necessary visa procedures. UAE visas are charged at RO10.

Oman National Transport Company (*Muscat office* ☎ *24 492948;* f *24 590152, 24 591791; Salalah office* ☎ *23 292773;* e *ontc01@omantel.net.om; www.ontcoman.com*). This is state owned and the only company to offer the full range of destinations: Salalah, Dubai, Buraimi, Abu Dhabi, Sur, Sohar. They have a detailed timetable on their website, some details of which are shown below.

Muscat to Salalah The Salalah Express runs four times per day, taking 13 hours from Ruwi Bus Station to Salalah Central Market. The single fare is RO10 and return is RO16, with children under 12 half fare. You can pick up the bus at any designated ONTC stop, including the one at Seeb International Airport. Seats need to be booked a few days in advance, though there is occasionally spare room available for on-the-spot passengers. The air-conditioned bus takes 40–45 people and rest stops are made at Ghaba Resthouse and Al Ghaftain Resthouse. All departure times below are from Ruwi Bus Station (the coach terminal).

Dep: 06.00/13.00/17.00/19.00; arr: 19.00/02.00/05.40/07.40.
RO10/16 one way/return; children under 12, half fare.

Muscat to Buraimi (route 41)
Dep: 13.00 (daily)/15.00 (Tue & Fri); arr: 17.40/21.00 (stopping at Sohar 15.45/18.55)

2

Muscat to Ibri (route 54)
Dep: 08.00; arr: 12.15, daily (stopping at Nizwa, 10.20)

Muscat to Sur (route 55)
Dep: 07.30/14.30; arr: 11.45/18.45, daily (stopping at Ibra and Al Mintrib 10.25/17.25)

Muscat to Abu Dhabi (route 202)
Dep: 06.30; arr: 13.00, daily

Muscat to Dubai (route 201)
Dep: 06.00/07.00/16.30; arr: 11.30/12.30/22.25, daily

Muscat to Salalah (route 100)
Dep: 06.00/13.00/17.00/19.00; arr:19.00/02.00/05.40/07.40

Salalah to Dubai (route 102)
Dep: 15.00; arr: 07.00

Comfort Line (*Muscat office* ❧ *24 702191, 24 597644;* f *24 708370; Dubai office* ❧ *00 9714 295 6733;* e *comfort@omantel.net.om; www.comexextress.com*). This company runs two services daily from Muscat to Dubai and two from Dubai to Muscat, crossing the Hatta border, where the United Arab Emirates visas will be issued.

Muscat to Dubai
Dep: 06.30/16.00; arr:12.00/21.30

Dubai to Muscat
Dep: 07.00/16.30; arr: 12.30/22.00
RO5/9 one way/return, under 12s half fare

Gulf Transport Company (❧ *24 790823, Salalah office* ❧ *23 293303;* f *23 297103*). This company operates daily coach services from Muscat to Salalah and from Salalah to Dubai.

Muscat to Salalah
Sat–Thu dep: 07.00/12.00/17.00/18.00; arr: 19.00/24.00/05.00/06.00
Fri dep: 07.00/16.00/17.00.

Salalah to Muscat
Sat–Thu dep: 07.00/12.00/17.00/18.00; arr: 19.00/24.00/05.00/06.00
Fri dep: 07.00/17.00/18.00
RO6/11 one way/return

Salalah to Dubai
Every day dep: 12.00/15.00; arr: 08.00/11.00 the following day

Dubai to Salalah
Every day dep: 12.00/15.00; arr: 08.00/11.00 the following day
RO10/18 one way/return.

Salalah Line Transport (*Muscat office* ❧ *24 709709,* f *24 708708; Salalah Office* ❧ *23 293323;* f *23 299889;* e *sltsalalah@yahoo.com*). This company offers coach services to and from Salalah only. They run three daily services from Ruwi Bus Station in Muscat and three from Salalah.

Muscat to Salalah
Dep: 06.00/14.30/18.00.; arr: 18.00/02.30/06.00 (12hr trip)

Salalah to Muscat
Dep: 08.00/14.30/18.00; arr: 20.00/02.30/06.00.
RO6/11 one way/return.

By minibus Minibuses (sometimes called baiza buses) can also take the form of small van-type vehicles, which can be flagged down at the many stops along the highway. They are certainly the cheapest way of getting around and are used largely by the Asian workforce.

MAPS Getting good, detailed maps of Oman is a problem, and, believe us, we tried. The best map we were able to find was a boxed set issued by the Geographic Information Systems Department of Muscat Municipality, which we managed to obtain through an Omani friend and is not readily available off the shelf. The tourist maps on sale in hotels and bookshops around the city are vague. They're fine for the larger picture of getting from district to district, but not for the detail of getting from door to door. The Intercontinental and Hyatt hotels floating in the sea, at the end of some road or another, in that kind of vicinity, aren't particularly helpful for the first-time visitor who has hired a car to get around and needs to rely on it. We have tried to make things clearer with the maps in this guide.

ACCOMMODATION

Muscat is home to some excellent four- and five-star hotels such as Al Bustan Palace, the Grand Hyatt, the Radisson SAS, the Chedi and the recently opened Shangri-La Barr al Jissah Resort of two five-star hotels and one six-star. There are more to come, as the government directs its energies towards its tourism sector. There are many mid- and budget-range hotels too, which offer good, clean accommodation, and so it is a misconception that the country can be visited only by the more affluent traveller.

EATING AND DRINKING

Travelling around the country you will find plenty of local coffee shop-type restaurants. Although these are very basic, it is a good, cheap way to eat when you are on the road. Chicken, mutton and fish are frequently on the menu. Each of the resthouses has a restaurant, and although these are basic and unlicensed, the curries tend to be very good. Snacks can be bought at the foodstuffs stores found beside most petrol stations, and within the shops of the petrol stations themselves. Higher-end restaurants can be found in any hotel in any town and these generally are licensed. The star rating of the hotel is indicative of the price range of the restaurant. The Bin Ateeq small chain is excellent for Omani cuisine, served in the traditional way at ground level (unlicensed); you will find these at Muscat, Nizwa and Salalah. The capital has many excellent high- to mid-end restaurants both inside and out of hotels.

ALCOHOL Alcohol is widely available at hotels, restaurants (both inside and out of hotels) and private clubs throughout the country. There are no stand-alone bars on the streets and the cheap local restaurants in every town or village throughout the

2

country are unlicensed. Expatriates are permitted to apply for a liquor licence, entitling them to buy alcohol from the discreet 'retail' shops distributed about the capital, and to drink in their homes.

PUBLIC HOLIDAYS

RELIGIOUS Each year, the religious holidays move forward by approximately 11 days in accordance with the lunar calendar.

Prophet's Birthday (*Mawlid al Nabi*)	31 March 2007; 20 March 2008; 9 March 2009
Ramadan	13 September 2007; 2 September 2008; 22 August 2009
Eid al Fitr (end of Ramadan)	13 October 2007; 2 October 2008; 21 September 2009
Eid al Adha (conclusion of the pilgrimage)	31 December 2006; 20 December 2007; 9 December 2008; 28 November 2009
Islamic New Year (*Muharram*)	20 January 2007; 10 January 2008; 29 December 2009

NON-RELIGIOUS

New Year's Day	1 January
Renaissance Day	23 July
National Day	18 November
Sultan's Birthday	19 November

WORKING HOURS

Government sector/ ministries	Sat–Wed 07.30–14.30; Thu–Fri closed
Private sector	Sat–Wed 08.00–13.00 & 16.00–19.00, Thu 08.00–13.00
Banks	Sat–Wed 08.00–13.00; Thu 08.00–noon; closed Fri
Shopping malls	Sat–Thu 09.00–13.00 & 16.00–21.00; Fri 16.30–22.00
Souks	Sat–Thu 08.00–13.00 & 16.00–21.00; Fri 16.30–21.00

SHOPPING

The main shopping complexes are in the Qurum area. These are in the form of modern, air-conditioned **malls and plazas**, selling perfumes, gold, souvenirs, furniture made in India (to Omani style), household goods, stereos, computers, mobile phones, sports equipment, clothing and photographic equipment. Shopping is not cheap (for better deals you might like to take a trip to Dubai), but it is good to have a wander, simply to spot all the things in Arabia that are familiar to us in the West. Largely, it is home from home: Gap, BHS, Next and the Body Shop all have a presence here, and so do the ubiquitous McDonald's, KFC, Pizza Hut and Burger King. A relatively new arrival is Marks & Spencer (at Al Mawaleh) so don't panic if you have forgotten to pack your undies!

A traditional shopping trip is a must, and the **souk** (or traditional market) at Muttrah is the place to go for this Arabian experience, selling souvenirs, crafts, jewellery, perfumes and oils, wooden chests, fabrics, *dishdashas* etc, not forgetting frankincense (see *Chapter 3*, page 90, for further details). Souks have been part of Omani culture for centuries, and every town or village in the country has one. It is a traditional marketplace, which doubles up as a meeting place. Those selling fruits and vegetables are well worth a visit, displaying a fantastic array of bright colours.

SOUVENIRS Omani silver *khanjars* (daggers), traditional Omani silver jewellery, coffee pots and small silver boxes all make excellent souvenirs. Omani rose-water, perfumes, frankincense and myrrh are cheaper, smaller, yet still distinctive souvenirs. Frankincense, or bakhoor (a mixture of fragrances; see *Frankincense* box on pages 254–5 for further details), and a frankincense burner make the perfect gift – Oman being famed for its frankincense production and trade throughout history. Slightly more intriguing, and certainly a topic of conversation when you get back home, would be the *hookah* pipe. Larger items are the Omani and Indian chests, and the Omani coffee tables (which use the concept of the traditional Omani door as the table top), which can be shipped or air freighted to you in your home country. The *mandoos* (Omani chests) come in all sizes, and so the smallest (which is jewellery-box size) may be a more practical purchase, in terms of transporting it home. See *Chapter 3*, page 82, for artisan/furniture shops. The *dishdasha* makes a souvenir gift to be worn, and is great to wear about the house back home. For the consumable small gift for friends and family, Omani dates are a must and you can always combine this with a packet of Omani coffee (which is mixed with cardamom), which will undoubtedly evoke memories of your Oman experience. Visit the souk at Muttrah for your souvenirs.

ACTIVITIES

The terrain of Oman, along with its climate, makes it perfect for the adventure tourist with a love of the outdoors. As mountain and desert constitute approximately 82% of Oman's geography, then mountain trekking, rock climbing, caving and wadi driving are all widely available. The treks, climbs and caves are graded in terms of difficulty. There are spectacular gorges and old mountain villages to see and camping is very popular. If you prefer water-based activities, then scuba diving, sailing, snorkelling, canoeing, dolphin and whale watching, dhow cruising and game fishing are all available. Nature and wildlife lovers can birdwatch, turtle-watch, camp or picnic in the mountains or quiet coastal bays. If local history or architecture is of interest, there are museums, mosques, forts and castles to explore (and these proliferate throughout the country). For those keen on physical fitness, there is a good selection of gyms and health clubs within the hotels, with swimming pools and tennis and squash courts attached. The beaches or beach roads are perfect for jogging. Visiting the souks (marketplaces) provides a fascinating glimpse into traditional Oman, while air-conditioned, modern shopping complexes give it its familiar Westernised feel. If you want to do nothing, there are some excellent, luxury hotels, some with private beaches, where you can simply relax.

For details of excursions beyond Muscat, including more details of the options available, see page 115.

ENTRY FEES AND PERMITS Oman's focus on the promotion of its tourism industry means that its forts and other historical buildings of significance are scheduled to undergo restoration programmes. The intention is a move towards preserving the country's heritage while simultaneously displaying and presenting it to the new influx of visitors.

It costs roughly 500bzs to visit most forts (payable at the door); others have no-one at the door and you can wander around freely with no charge; and some appear to be locked up at odd times during the day. So do interpret the opening times shown in this guide generously!

It is no longer necessary to obtain permits from the Ministry of Culture and National Heritage (opposite the Zawawi Mosque in the ministries area of Muscat) to visit forts and archaeological sites. For turtle-watching sites you can easily get a permit from the Ras Al Hadd Hotel, or your tour operator, or at the entrance of the Ras Al Jinz site itself. To dive the Daminayat Islands, the permit is easily arranged for you by any dive centre arranging the dive trip. The bureaucracy has been relaxed as part of the country's initiative to facilitate tourism.

The **Historical Association of Oman** (↖ *24 563074;* e *patricia@cfbtoman.com; www.hao.org.om*) organises regular talks (usually at the PDO oil exhibition club in Qurum) and field trips in appreciation of Oman's past.

PHOTOGRAPHY

The scenery of the country is superb for photography. The only places where it is not permitted are government and military buildings. Photographing Omani women can be offensive to them – it is safest to ask permission (and permission should generally be asked of men as well). '*Mumkin sura, minfadluk?*' is Arabic for 'May I take your picture, please?' If it's a woman, it is likely that you will be refused. By contrast, Omani men, in my experience, have always been happy to be photographed.

ℓ MEDIA AND COMMUNICATIONS

NEWSPAPERS The English-language newspapers in Oman are the *Times of Oman* (e *times@omantel.net.om; www.timesofoman.com*); the *Oman Observer* (*www.omanobserver.com*); the *Oman Tribune* and *The Week*. Foreign newspapers can be bought in the larger hotels, supermarkets and in some bookshops, but they are not cheap.

MAGAZINES *Oman 2day* (*www.apexstuff.com*) is an excellent publication in handy small size, with up-to-date information and good photo-articles on adventure days out around the capital. It also has reviews of cars and restaurants. A good adventure-based magazine is *Adventure Oman*. Foreign magazines are readily available, but are expensive.

TELEVISION AND RADIO There is one terrestrial television broadcaster in Oman which is the state-owned Oman TV. This is run by the Ministry of Information. It broadcasts two channels, one in Arabic with the other in English.

The Sultanate of Oman FM Service is the local English-language radio station, broadcasting daily. Radio Oman is the official state broadcaster, operated by the Ministry of Information and running two channels in Arabic and English. The BBC World Service is also available.

TELEPHONE The country code for Oman if dialling from abroad is 968 followed by the local number. International calls made from Oman are cheapest from 21.00 until 07.00. Local calls are around 25bzs for three minutes.

Public telephones accept phonecards, which can be bought at petrol stations, supermarkets and some small shops.

Landline numbers are six digits and are prefixed with a two-digit area code (eg: 24 for Muscat, 23 for Dhofar, 26 for Musandam and the Batinah, and 25 for the interior and Sharqiya).

Mobile phones Your first option is to check with your mobile phone provider in your country of residence as to whether there is network coverage in Oman, and establish with them the cost of calls. If there isn't coverage, and if you intend to visit Oman regularly, an option worth considering is to purchase a pay-as-you-go mobile phone in Muscat. To top up your balance scratch cards are used, and these are readily available at petrol stations, supermarkets and in some small shops, in amounts of RO1.50, RO3 and RO5. They last an age. **Hayak** top-up cards are used for Oman Mobile phones (*www.omanmobile.om*), and **Nawras** are used for Oman Telecommunications (*www.omantel.net.om*).

Mobile numbers are usually prefixed with '99' or '95'.

Useful telephone numbers

AAA (car breakdown services) ☎ 24 605555

Directory enquiries ☎ 198 (from abroad ☎ +968 24 600100)

International directory ☎ 143

International operator ☎ 195

Fire ☎ 999

Royal Oman Police Muscat; ☎ 24 560099, Salalah; ☎ 23 290099

Recorded news in English ☎ 1105 (including chemists on duty)

Flight information ☎ 1101, 24 519223

Foreign exchange rates ☎ 1106

Talking pages ☎ 24 600100

INTERNET Oman's internet service provider is Omantel. Internet cafés (or cyber cafés) can generally be found within the shopping complexes at Qurum and Al Khuwair, and some exist within the rows of shops found down side streets in any residential area throughout the country. They charge far less than the hotels and are well worth a visit. There is something quite intriguing, after retrieving communication from London, in passing groups of laid-back Omanis in *dishdashas* and sandals gathering to smoke *shisha* al fresco next door. The old and the new sit side by side like respectful neighbours. So aside from the financial saving made by visiting an internet café on the street, there is also the experience to be had; instead of being obscured from local culture inside the hotels, you are amid it.

POST OFFICES Post offices are open Saturday–Wednesday 07.30–14.00. On Thursdays they close at 11.00 and on Fridays they are closed all day. The offices aren't always easy to find, but there is one in every district in Muscat, usually with the Omani flag flying above the building. This is the cheapest way of sending postcards or parcels home; a postcard to any country outside the GCC region costing only 200bzs. More expensive, but more convenient is to ask your hotel to do it for you.

CULTURAL ETIQUETTE

On greeting, Omani men will shake hands. For friends and family the handshake is accompanied with kissing, which is a gentle touch to both cheeks, and sometimes repeated for close friends. Kissing between men in this way is common. Some will lightly touch noses. It is not customary to shake an Omani woman's hand unless she offers it first. It is quite common for Omani men to shake hands with foreign women as Omanis are highly aware of this cultural difference.

If you are invited to an Omani's home, it is customary to remove your shoes at the door before entering the house. *Kahwa* (a strong, bitter coffee, flavoured with cardamom) and dates are offered and it is considered impolite to refuse. Once the first cup of coffee (served in a tiny bowl-like container) is consumed, it is then fine to refuse further top-ups. To indicate that you have finished, the cup is gently shaken (or tilted) from side to side. The right hand is used for traditional Omani eating from a communal plate, and the same is used for drinking. This is usually performed at ground level. It is quite normal for gatherings to be single-sex groups.

Ariadne Van Zandbergen

EQUIPMENT Although with some thought and an eye for composition you can take reasonable photos with a 'point-and-shoot' camera, you need an SLR camera if you are at all serious about photography. Modern SLRs tend to be very clever, with automatic programmes for almost every possible situation, but remember that these programmes are limited in the sense that the camera cannot think, but only make calculations. Every starting amateur photographer should read a photographic manual for beginners and get to grips with such basics as the relationship between aperture and shutter speed.

Always buy the best lens you can afford. The lens determines the quality of your photo more than the camera body. Fixed fast lenses are ideal, but very costly. A zoom lens makes it easier to change composition without changing lenses the whole time. If you carry only one lens, a 28–70mm (digital 17–55mm) or similar zoom should be ideal. For a second lens, a lightweight 80–200mm or 70–300mm (digital 55–200mm) or similar will be excellent for candid shots and varying your composition. Wildlife photography will be very frustrating if you don't have at least a 300mm lens. For a small loss of quality, tele-converters are a cheap and compact way to increase magnification: a 300 lens with a 1.4x converter becomes 420mm, and with a 2x it becomes 600mm. Note, however, that 1.4x and 2x tele-converters reduce the speed of your lens by 1.4 and 2 stops respectively.

For photography from a vehicle, a solid beanbag, which you can make yourself very cheaply, will be necessary to avoid blurred images, and is more useful than a tripod. A clamp with a tripod head screwed on to it can be attached to the vehicle as well. Modern dedicated flash units are easy to use; aside from the obvious need to flash when you photograph at night, you can improve a lot of photos in difficult 'high contrast' or very dull light with some fill-in flash. It pays to have a proper flash unit as opposed to a built-in camera flash.

DIGITAL/FILM Digital photography is now the preference of most amateur and professional photographers, with the resolution of digital cameras improving the whole time. For ordinary prints a 6 megapixel camera is fine. For better results and the possibility to enlarge images and for professional reproduction, higher resolution is available up to 16 megapixels.

Memory space is important. The number of pictures you can fit on a memory card depends on the quality you choose. Calculate in advance how many pictures you can fit on a card and either take enough cards to last for your trip, or take a storage drive onto which you can download the content. A laptop gives the advantage that you can see your pictures properly at the end of each day and edit and delete rejects, but a storage device is lighter and less bulky. These drives come in different capacities up to 80GB.

BUSINESS ETIQUETTE In business, it is advisable to wait for the Omani party to initiate the greeting. As in social etiquette, men will shake hands with other men, and some (probably most) will shake hands with foreign women. It is better for a businesswoman to wait for an Omani man to offer his hand. A customary greeting is *salaam alaykum*, meaning 'peace be with you'. This is followed by *kaif halek*, meaning 'how are you?' When offered coffee, it is considered impolite to refuse. It is acceptable, however, to refuse refills. The left hand is considered unclean. Always eat with the right hand. Showing the bottom of your shoe or foot is offensive, and so too is the 'thumbs up' gesture. Gifts are not necessary. If you do offer one, it will be opened in private. When offered a gift, it is impolite to refuse. Do not discuss the subject of women, even if to enquire about an

Bear in mind that digital camera batteries, computers and other storage devices need charging, so make sure you have all the chargers, cables and converters with you. Most hotels have charging points, but do enquire about this in advance. When camping you might have to rely on charging from the car battery; a spare battery is invaluable.

If you are shooting film, 100 to 200 ISO print film and 50 to 100 ISO slide film are ideal. Low ISO film is slow but fine grained and gives the best colour saturation, but will need more light, so support in the form of a tripod or monopod is important. You can also bring a few 'fast' 400 ISO films for low-light situations where a tripod or flash is no option.

DUST AND HEAT Dust and heat are often a problem. Keep your equipment in a sealed bag, stow films in an airtight container (eg: a small cooler bag) and avoid exposing equipment and film to the sun. Digital cameras are prone to collecting dust particles on the sensor which results in spots on the image. The dirt mostly enters the camera when changing lenses, so be careful when doing this. To some extent photos can be 'cleaned' up afterwards in Photoshop, but this is time consuming. You can have your camera sensor professionally cleaned, or you can do this yourself with special brushes and swabs made for the purpose, but note that touching the sensor might cause damage and should only be done with the greatest care.

LIGHT The most striking outdoor photographs are often taken during the hour or two of 'golden light' after dawn and before sunset. Shooting in low light may enforce the use of very low shutter speeds, in which case a tripod will be required to avoid camera shake.

With careful handling, side lighting and back lighting can produce stunning effects, especially in soft light and at sunrise or sunset. Generally, however, it is best to shoot with the sun behind you. When photographing animals or people in the harsh midday sun, images taken in light but even shade are likely to be more effective than those taken in direct sunlight or patchy shade, since the latter conditions create too much contrast.

PROTOCOL In some countries, it is unacceptable to photograph local people without permission, and many people will refuse to pose or will ask for a donation. In such circumstances, don't try to sneak photographs as you might get yourself into trouble. Even the most willing subject will often pose stiffly when a camera is pointed at them; relax them by making a joke, and take a few shots in quick succession to improve the odds of capturing a natural pose.

Ariadne Van Zandbergen (e ariadne@hixnet.co.za; www.africaimagelibrary.co.za) is a professional travel and wildlife photographer.

Omani man's wife or family. Avoid admiring an item to excess, as your host may feel obliged to give it to you. Expect communication to be slow. Do not feel obliged to speak in periods of silence. Meetings can often be interrupted by phone calls and visits from friends and family. Bear in mind that the Omani doing all the talking is often not the decision-maker. The decision-maker will often be the silent observer.

DRESS CODE Considering Oman is a Muslim country, the dress code is relatively relaxed. As a gesture of respect it is advisable for both men and women to wear loose clothes that cover the shoulders and knees and are therefore not too revealing. Shorts, T-shirts and sleeveless tops are fine for the beach, but best avoided in the shopping complexes, souks, or for touring the villages and sites of the interior (where the dress code is more conservative). Lightweight and loose-fitting cotton blouses, trousers, and skirts are perfect all year round, and for your comfort in the winter, lightweight jackets, jumpers or shawls may be needed. Swimwear, including bikinis, is fine for private beaches and pools.

During the holy month of Ramadan it is respectful to observe the dress code strictly.

Business dress code For foreign businessmen, a jacket and tie are usually required for business meetings. Long trousers and preferably a long-sleeved shirt (fully buttoned to the collar) should be worn. Men should avoid wearing visible jewellery.

For foreign businesswomen, high necklines are a must, and sleeves at least to the elbows are expected. Skirts should cover the knees well, and preferably be ankle-length. As with the general social dress code, clothes should not be figure-hugging; aim for a baggy, loose-fitting look.

GIVING SOMETHING BACK

When travelling through Oman there are many small things you can do to give something back to the place you have the privilege of exploring. Every action, no matter how small, counts.

Respect the locals and their right to privacy. Bear in mind that it is their home territory. Ask permission before taking any photographs, and be aware that Omani women and girls will often refuse. Omani men and boys will often enthusiastically oblige. If you have a digital camera, showing Omani children their picture on the screen invariably delights them.

Look after your immediate environment. Limit your water usage. Do not leave water running. Take a shower, if you can, rather than use the bath. Turn lights off in hotel rooms when they are not absolutely necessary. Reuse towels (hang them back on the rail, so they will not be considered laundry). Limit your use of air conditioning, if possible. Always dispose of your own rubbish after camping or picnicking.

Purchase any locally made artefacts. Buy a pot from the Aldawi pottery factory in Bahla, or buy a rug from the locals selling their weavings in Jebel Shams and Jebel Akhdar. Don't forget the essential purchase of frankincense and a burner – you will have become part of an ancient trading history in this commodity. Every small amount you give, helps to sustain the heritage and keep alive long-standing Omani traditions.

Eat at local restaurants and coffee shops – your valued rials will help in keeping these small businesses running. Buy some fruit at a souk or roadside stall. Stay at any of the static camps in the country, for example those in the Wahhabi Sands; these make trips out to Bedouin camps where you will share lunch in a traditional home. Simply by demonstrating their way of life to you, the Bedu are able to benefit financially, and so, by using the camps, you are making a contribution to their living.

Respect the rules when visiting nature reserves and sanctuaries. Take care not to disturb the wildlife in any way. This is their habitat. Adhere to the list of dos and don'ts when it comes to viewing the nesting turtles (see page 229). Don't touch the coral when scuba diving or snorkelling – it causes damage.

An opportunity to assist with the Arabian leopard survey in Musandam is offered through www.responsibletravel.com, who are collaborating with conservation authorities in Oman. The aim is to expand the knowledge of the leopard in this vicinity. You might like to play a part.

Make that little bit of extra effort to find out more about the local charities shown at the end of this chapter. You might be able to help. Perhaps you can volunteer your time, knowledge or assistance in bringing awareness to their cause in some way when back in your country of residence. There may be a new project under way at the time of your visit. Do give them a call.

Let's be responsible and conscious tourists in the sultanate.

CHARITIES AND ORGANISATIONS

A'Noor Association for the Blind PO Box 910, Al Khuwair, Code 133; e anoorab@omantel.net.om; (email address of the vice-president, who speaks good English): bshahbal@hotmail.com

Association for Early Intervention for Children with Special Needs ☎ 24 496960; f 24 492118; e earlyint@omantel.net.om; www.aei.org.om. Looks after children from birth to 6 years of age. Hassan Moosa (☎ 99 324882) is responsible for marketing and fund raising.

Association for the Disabled Looks after those above 16 years of age.

Association for the Welfare of Disabled Children Looks after children from 6–15 years of age.

Cancer Awareness Group Fat'hiya al Hinai and Yuthar al Ruwahy (☎ 99 383070) are the two most senior ladies.

Dar Al Atta e daralatta@yahoo.com. A newly formed charity that gives assistance to underprivileged families.

Geological Society of Oman www.gso.org.om. Established in 2001, this organization promotes geotourism in Oman (considered one of the world's best 'geo parks') and facilitates knowledge sharing in the geologic community of the country, advancing

the science and increasing awareness in the lay community of the importance and relevance of their work.

Historical Association of Oman ☎ 24 563074; e patricia@cfbtoman.com; www.hao.org.om. This group organises regular talks (usually at the PDO oil exhibition club in Qurum) and field trips in an appreciation of Oman's past. The membership secretary is Rosemary Hector.

Omani Charitable Organisation Al Khuwair St 33, bldg no 173; PO Box 1998, PC 112; ☎ 25 687998; f 25 687997; www.oco.org.om. Established in 1996, to assist needy families, orphans, senior citizens and the disabled.

Royal Geographical Society www.rgs.org. This society promotes geographical research and advances geography, nationally and internationally. Prince Michael is patron. In Oman it runs the Wahiba Sands Project.

United Nations Children's Fund (UNICEF) – Oman www.unicef.org/infobycountry/oman.html. UNICEF international aid agency assists and advises Oman on all aspects of child development, malnutrition reduction, education and protection.

2

Part Two

THE GUIDE

Only one airline
flies non-stop to Oman

Enjoy Gulf Air's award winning service from London Heathrow to Muscat, on the only non-stop flights to beautiful Oman. For reservations, call 0870 777 1717 or visit www.gulfairco.com

3

Muscat مسقط

Your first encounter with Oman is likely to be with its capital city, Muscat – the hub of all international flights. On arrival at Seeb International Airport it is possible to take an immediate short domestic flight south to the province of Dhofar, or north to the Musandam peninsula; you may even choose to drive directly up the Batinah coast or into the interior. But generally, after your flight, it is likely that you'll want to rest where you land, and so Muscat will provide your first impression of the country.

Muscat proper is a small old port and harbour town, situated about a 30–40-minute drive away from the airport, and home to the Sultan's Palace, Al Alam. But since the discovery of oil in commercial quantities in 1962, and the subsequent coming to power of Sultan Qaboos Bin Said in July 1970, surrounding residential areas, which were once small villages, have expanded under the modernisation programme, spilling over and outwards. Muscat, as a governorate, in fact stretches from Seeb (the town to the west of Seeb International Airport) out to Muscat Old Town (approximately 35km away, on the eastern tip), and southwards down to Quriyat. So today, when people speak of Muscat, they tend to be speaking of Muscat in this broader sense, which encompasses the whole governorate or capital area.

Muscat is a modern, clean city. Beautified under the instruction of Sultan Qaboos, it appears just as a developer's model town made large. Date-palm trees and neat, manicured, grassed areas flank the faultless motorway that threads this narrow, elongated piece of land between the mountains and ocean and speeds you along with ease to your hotel. Once away from the initial hubbub and slight congestion of the exit road of the airport, any stress or tension soon dissolves as you observe the clean and cared-for appearance of Muscat. Under the capital's unrelenting blue sky, camel-coloured mountains trail you to your right and blue ocean trails you to your distant left; deep-green grassed verges and white low-level buildings on either side complete the picture. The boldness of nature's colours and the power of nature's heat are conspicuous. Muscat appears confident and prosperous and, like its people, self-respecting and proud.

GETTING THERE

BY AIR All international airlines serving Oman fly into Muscat's Seeb International Airport on the western edge of the capital area, close to the coast.

There is a currency exchange desk immediately in front of you as you enter the airport building from the plane, and you need to pay for your tourist visa here, after completing a form. Visas cost RO6 and may be paid for in foreign currency or by credit card. If you pay in foreign currency, you will be given your change in rials.

Once through passports, there is a small duty-free shop on the left, which also sells alcohol. You are permitted to take a bottle into the country (and if you are

3

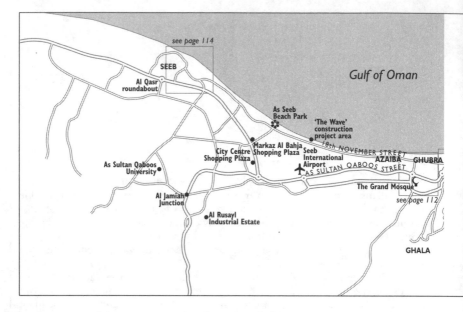

see page 114

SEEB

Al Qasr roundabout

Gulf of Oman

As Seeb Beach Park

'The Wave' construction project area

18th NOVEMBER STREET

Markaz Al Bahja Shopping Plaza

City Centre Shopping Plaza

As Sultan Qaboos University

Seeb International Airport

AZAIBA   GHUBRA

AS SULTAN QABOOS STREET

Al Jamiah Junction

The Grand Mosque

see page 112

Al Rusayl Industrial Estate

GHALA

staying at one of the upper-range hotels, you might like to consider doing so, if you want to save a small fortune on the cost of the same in the minibar in your room). A little further on past this small duty-free shop are the luggage carousels. Once you have taken your luggage through the security check, you reach the arrivals area where there are some cafés, a cashpoint (that accepts a multitude of cards) and plenty of car-rental desks. In the departures area there are two business-class lounges on the ground floor. If you don't have access to these, take the escalators up to the first floor, where there is a licensed bar, some cafés, a bookshop, music shop, souvenir shop and a small duty-free shopping area.

OVERLAND See page 37.

GETTING AROUND

ORIENTATION As the capital area is replete with roundabouts, if you are intending to hire a car, some familiarisation with the roundabout names prior to your drive will be time well spent. The city is not at all large, but it is stretched out, and the modern dual carriageway that threads through it is a great facility; but for the newcomer it can become confusing at Qurum and beyond where it splits into two, crossing over itself and continuing in distorted figure-of-eight shapes to circumnavigate the mountains, which have a constant looming presence throughout the capital. This can create havoc with your sense of direction. If you think of the airport roundabout as the starting point, the first roundabout you meet (going towards the old town of Muscat) is Azaiba (or Ghala), then Ghubra (or Bowshar), Al Khuwair, Qurum, Wuttayah, Wadi Adai, Hamriya, Ruwi, Al Burj, then Bait Al Falaj. Once you have mastered the position of these, then finding your way to specific locations becomes a lot easier.

Be prepared for several different spellings of the same place names on road signs, in books and on maps. This is because of varying interpretations of the transliteration of the Arabic. Many of the roundabouts in the capital are adorned with giant model sculptures, and these sculptures have significance for that

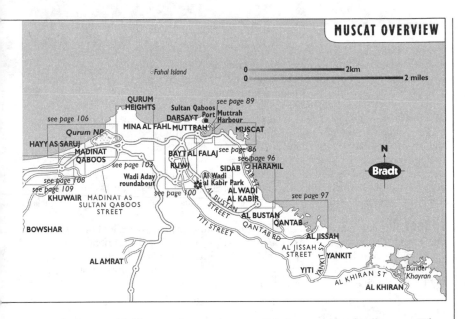

particular area. Coffee pots, incense burners, fish, boats and books all appear. When obtaining directions, the roundabouts are frequently referred to, in simple terms, by the model that sits on them. For example, the roundabout that is close to the Sultan Qaboos University displays a large model book, and so is often called 'the book' roundabout; and the one at the top end of the Muttrah corniche (coastal road), close to the group of budget hotels and fish souk, is referred to as 'the fish' roundabout.

BY TAXI Taxis are certainly the easiest option for getting around in the capital, especially if you are unfamiliar with the lie of the land. You will have no problem getting one as you step out of the airport building; the two-tone orange-and-white cars are in abundance, and drivers sometimes tout for business inside the building. Although they are unmetered, taxis operate on a standard-rate system, and so you won't be ripped off. The taxi fare from Seeb Airport to Muttrah/Muscat Old Town is roughly RO10 and it takes about 30 minutes to cover the 40km. A transfer to any of the central hotels, such as the Grand Hyatt or Intercontinental (about 20km away), will take roughly 15–20 minutes and will cost around RO7.

There are a few companies that take taxi bookings, so if you prefer to arrange things in advance, call:

🚕 **City Taxi** ✆ 24 602211, 24 603363   🚕 **Al Dar Taxi LLC** ✆ 24 700555, 24 700777
🚕 **Comfort Line** ✆ 24 702191   🚕 **Hello Taxi** ✆ 24 607011, 24 607012

BY HIRE CAR There is no difficulty in renting a car at Seeb International Airport. Plenty of well-known car-hire firms operate both here and from local hotels. There are also some cheaper local firms throughout the city. Don't worry if you haven't pre-booked; you will certainly find something (for details and car-hire firms, see *Chapter 2, Getting around* section, page 47).

BY MINIBUS By far the cheapest way to get around is by minibus – medium-sized vehicles known as baiza buses (because it costs only a few baizas for the journey), which operate in the city area. They can be hailed at any of the bus stops on the main highway, and run to all of the Muscat suburbs. Fares are charged according to your destination, and you pay on entry. This mode of transport is regularly used by Oman's large Asian labour force, but rarely by Western visitors. At busier times, be prepared to become closely acquainted with other passengers; the 'packed-in-like-dates' situation may be off-putting for some.

BY COACH Another good option in Oman is to travel by coach and there are a handful of coach operators in the capital. From Muscat it is possible to get a coach trip to Sur (in the Sharqiya) and Salalah (in the Dhofar region), making stops at strategic points in the interior (Dakhiliyah region) – Nizwa, for example. Coaches also travel to Dubai and Abu Dhabi in the United Arab Emirates, making stops at Sohar (in the Batinah region), and Buraimi (in the Dhahirah) along their respective routes. For all coach information see *Chapter 2,* page 49).

ON FOOT It is not easy to walk around Muscat as the city is so stretched out, and in the summer months it is just too hot. Nevertheless, the introduction of the occasional pedestrian walkway over the main highway makes things a lot safer; pedestrians dashing across the busy road used to be a common, if heart-stopping, sight. I would suggest saving your walks for the endless stretches of beach.

TOURIST INFORMATION

ORGANISED TOURS Many tour companies operate within the capital (listed below), each offering the usual array of tours. They are regulated by the Ministry of Tourism. If you don't want to make the arrangements yourself, explain your requirements to your hotel and they will arrange things for you; they usually work closely with one or two tour operators. Guests can be picked up from any of the city hotels (or from a private address) and this is included in the price.

TOUR OPTIONS The stock tours offered in Muscat include **sunset dhow cruises** (a dhow being a traditional wooden boat – part of Oman's seafaring history) along the coastal bays of Muscat, half-day **city tours** (which include the Sultan Qaboos Grand Mosque at Azaiba, Al Alam Palace in Muscat Old Town, the Portuguese forts of Mirani and Jalali, Muttrah souk, Bait Al Zubair Museum and Al Bustan Palace Hotel), **dolphin-watching tours, snorkelling and diving tours** and **fishing safaris**.

Off-road **4x4 safari tours** are largely to destinations beyond the capital area, and include trips up into the mountains, into the wadis and into the desert. A 4x4 is essential, and it is advisable to go through a tour operator who will provide the vehicle and an invaluable driver/guide.

For safety and comfort, these 4x4 trips offered by tour operators are based on four passengers in one vehicle with a driver/guide, and cost around RO120. Some tour companies allow you to join a tour in a convoy, if you have your own rented 4x4, and this will work out cheaper, but of course you miss the information provided by the guide en route, and you also take responsibility for the driving, which requires skill and experience. It is better to leave the driving to the guides, and more or less essential to do so for trips into the Wahiba Sands (Sharqiya) and the Empty Quarter (Dhofar). Wadis may be more manageable for the inexperienced, but only if dry. Some of the roads up into the *jebels* (mountains) can be narrow and precipitous. In this case, it is still recommended that at least two vehicles go in convoy. If in doubt, arrange your trip through a tour operator rather than drive independently.

The 4x4 tours can work out expensive if you are a lone traveller, as it costs RO120 for a 4x4 and driver/guide for the day, irrespective if you are one or four passengers. In such a situation, and if you would like to bring the cost down substantially, enquiries at any of the tour operators will establish whether it is possible for you to join another car for your chosen trip. However, you may prefer the privacy of your own car and driver/guide, irrespective of cost.

TOUR OPERATORS

Below is a list of the majority of tour operators in existence in Oman. These are all based in Muscat but arrange tours throughout the whole of the country. Some have desks within the upper- to mid-range hotels and this is generally the most convenient way to arrange a trip.

AGAS Tours PO Box 83, PC 122; ✎ 99 325441; f 24 590558; e riyadhgm@omantel.net.om. Specialising in Wahiba Sands trips but also offering canoeing, hiking, caving and trekking.
Arabian Sands Tours PO Box 35, PC 133; ✎ 24 785027; f 24 686599. Wahiba Sands camping trips, camel and 4x4 safaris.
Arabian Sea Safaris PO Box 2785, PC 111; ✎ 24 693223; f 24 693224; e arabseas@omantel.net.om; www.arabianseasafaris.com. Located in the Muscat Intercontinental Hotel at Shatti al Qurum. Offering all sorts of sea activities and tours including sailing, surfing, rowing, pedal boating, body boarding, skim boarding, fishing (beach casting), land sports, cycling, professional game fishing, traditional tuna fishing, bottom fishing, old Muscat by sea cruise, coastal cruise, sunset cruise, dolphin watching, snorkelling, birdwatching, diving safaris, land safaris, overnight beach adventures, overnight yacht safaris.
Al Azri Tours PO Box 877, PC 611, Nizwa; ✎ 25 412368; f 25 412368. This small company specialises in tours of Nizwa Old Town, walking and trekking in the Jebel Akhdar, as well as camping and camel safaris in the Nizwa area.
Bahwan Travel Agencies LLC PO Box 282, PC 113; ✎ 24 704455, 24 706798; f 24 794189; e topclass@omantel.net.om or lakshmy@bahwantravels.com; www.bahwantravelgroup.com. This operator has several offices in the capital and is one of the biggest tour operators. Locations in the Central Business District, MQ Shopping Centre; ✎ 24 601192, Ruwi; ✎ 24 706134, Sabco Centre; ✎ 24 564678, Golden Tulip Hotel; ✎ 24 510720, Al Khuwair, ✎ 24 603898; Salalah, ✎ 23 294665, 23 290908. Established 25 years, offering a full range of tours and safaris. Lakshmy is very helpful and knowledgeable.
Braema Tours PO Box 2789, PC 111; ✎ 24 552417; f 24 555591. This company specialises in caving

tours providing all necessary equipment. It operates many other adventure safaris and trips too.
Darran Tours PO Box 2540, PC 111, Seeb; ✎ 24 607311, 24 607312; f 24 607552; e darran@omantel.net.om. Located in Dhofar House in Madinat Qaboos district. City tours, dhow cruises, camping safaris with astronomical telescope, ground handling for exhibitions and conferences.
Debeek Tours PO Box 517, PC 113; ✎ 24 698555; f 24 698263; e debbek@gto.net.om. Run by a Dutchman, specialising in camping safaris, but offering historical/cultural tours as well.
Desert Adventures ✎ 95 201107. For group tours and expeditions; also offers cruises on a 30ft boat (15 passengers). Camping and expedition equipment meets international quality and safety standards. Wahiba Sands and Coastal Adventure (2 days, 1 night) RO70 pp (min 3 people); Sea Adventure (full-day cruise) snorkelling, fishing, dolphin watching, beach barbecue RO18 pp (min 4 people); Wilderness Challenge — specialising in adventure education for the young, the Wilderness programmes focus on team building, personal development and leadership for those aged 14–18 (3 days, 2 nights) RO150 pp (minimum of 4, maximum of 8).
Desert Discovery Tours PO Box 99, Madinat Al Sultan Qaboos, PC 115; ✎ 24 593232, 99 328858, 99 418664; f 24 590144; e tours@omantel.net.om; www.desert-discovery.com. This company's facilities include Al Areesh Desert Camp in Wahiba Sands, Al Naseem Turtle Beach Camp at Ras al Junaiz (close to the turtle reserve), Al Qabil Resthouse (approximately halfway between Muscat and Sur, and a good stop-off point), as well as mobile camping units. It offers professionally guided tours from one person to a large group, including cultural, historical and adventure tours.
Eihab Travels PO Box 889, PC 113; ✎ 24 796387, 24 796282; f 24 796282, 24 793849;

e eihabtra@omantel.net.om. Located in Muttrah high street, and established 20 years. Offers city tours, day trips, car hire and domestic flights.

Empty Quarter Tours PO Box 9, PC 115, Madinat Qaboos; ℑ 99 387654; f 24 698292; e emptyqtr@omantel.net.om; www.emptyquartertours.com. Operates the Nahar Tourism Camp in the Sharqiya near Ibra, and specialises in tailor-made tours with Omani guides, focusing on Omani history, culture and wildlife (for details see *Chapter 8, The Sharqiya*, page 205).

Al Ghadeer Tours ℑ 99 323399, 99 325441; f 24 590558; e riyadhgm@omantel.net.om. Offers tours to Ghubra, Wahiba trips, city tours, day trips, dhow cruises, 4x4 safaris, trekking and hiking.

Global Tours ℑ 24 484156, 24 695959, 24 695994; f 24 695969; e globtour@omantel.net.om or global@omantel.net.om. Located at Al Khuwair. For wadi and dune bashing, camping and caving, and all the usual tours.

Golden Oryz Tours ℑ 24 489853, 99 810889; e info@golden oryz.com; www.goldenoryx.com. This company offers the Muscat city tour, the Nizwa and The Grand Canyon tour, dolphin-watch tour, Wadi Shab trail, Rustaq, desert adventure and oasis trail, and the giant green turtles of Ras al Hadd tour.

Gulf Ventures PO Box 985, PC 112, Ruwi; ℑ 24 700326; f 24 795237; www.sunilp@inchcape.com. Long-established company with the full range of tours, day trips and safaris. Specialises in trekking.

Al Haditha LLC PO Box 198, PC 114; ℑ 24 479065, 24 489248, 24 489648, 24 603587; f 24 482512, 24 692681; e haditha@omantel.net.om or alhadtrs@omantel.net.om; www.alhadithaoman.com. This is a large established company, located in Al Khuwair and the Central Business District offering the full range of tours and trips. Al Haditha works in association with Thrifty Car Rental.

Mark Tours PO Box 3310, PC 112, Ruwi; ℑ 24 562444, 24 565567, 24 560975, 24 561466; f 24 565434, 24 565869; e marktour@omantel.net.om or admin@marktoursoman.com; www.mark-oman.com. Its main office is in Hatat Hse at Wadi Adai roundabout, but they have a desk at Seeb Airport and in the Radisson SAS Hotel, also a franchise in Salalah. Mark Tours will send you a list of tours on request.

Mezoon Travel LLC PO Box 629, PC 113; ℑ 24 796680; f 24 796690; e manoj.dass@mezoontravel.co.om, tours@mezoontravel.co.om or meztours@omzest.com; www.mezoontravel.com. Located in Al Burj St, Ruwi. Established 25 years with branches in Salalah; ℑ 23 297846 and Mina Al Fahal; ℑ 24 568220, although all tours are

arranged through the Muscat office. They offer an impressive, well-structured range of tours, trips and safaris through mountain, wadi and desert, including rock climbing and trekking, and can organise overnight camping tours, which are priced on any tailor-made route intended. Mezoon Travel will send you a detailed list on request.

Midland Tourism PO Box 426, PC 113; ℑ 24 566524; f 24 566524; e alwosta@omantel.net.om. Located in Qurum, and offering the full range of tours, including diving and hang gliding.

Multaqa Al Ebda'a Tourism PO Box 746, PC 112, Ruwi; ℑ 99 274755, 99 349399; e khaled_wahaibi@hotmail.com. Offers dolphin-watching trips, snorkelling trips, game-fishing trips, Muscat trip and bay trips, sunset cruises on a 28ft boat.

Muscat Diving and Adventure Centre ℑ 24 485663; e sasha@holiday-in-oman.com; www.holiday-in-oman.com. This company offers excellent adventure tours, from trekking to caving, with knowledgeable, qualified guides and equipment. The birdwatching tour guides are Hanna and Jens Eriksen, the authors of several books on birdwatching in Oman. Rock climbing, trekking, surfing, kayaking, game fishing, diving. Visit their website for a full explanation of their tours and prices.

Al Nahda Tourism LLC ℑ 24 799928, 24 795206; f 24 799928; e hbt123@omantel.net.om. Located in Al Falaj Hotel, Ruwi. In addition to the usual tours, Al Nahda Tourism offers specialist motorcycle tours and self-drive tours.

National Travel and Tourism PO Box 962, PC 113; ℑ 24 566046; f 24 566125; e nttoman@omantel.net.om. Also located at Wattayah, Qurum; ℑ 24 564783, Salalah; ℑ 23 295016, Buraimi; ℑ 25 650716. Long-established large company with 45 4x4 vehicles and 2 buses, offering city tours, day trips, dhow cruises, camel and 4x4 safaris, and scuba diving.

Al Nimer Tourism ℑ 24 603555, ext 456; f 24 694500, 92 549494, 92 529595; e alnimer_tourism@hotmail.com. Located in the Ramada Hotel at Qurum Beach offering all the stock tours as well as parasailing, sea tours, water rides for families and children on the Matrix, Viper or Jumbo Dog (inflatables, towed by a speedboat), and camping trips.

Nomadic Adventures and Tours ℑ 99 316507, 99 336273; f 24 485507; e nomadic@omantel.net.om or mail@nomadic-adventures.com. Specialises in tailoring desert adventures. Camel riding, horseriding, mountain trekking, 4x4 safaris.

Oman Discovery PO Box 3932, PC 112, Ruwi; ℑ 24 706424; f 24 706463; e omandisc@

omantel.net.om. A division of Khasab Travel & Tours offering a similar range of tours, trips and safaris but in the Omani heartland instead of Musandam.

Oman Geo Tours PO Box 122, PC 116, Mina Al Fahal; ↘ 24 536629, 24 600914; f 24 536460. Located in Qurum. Specialises in geological and scientific tours, but offers other tours as well.

Oman Orient Tours PO Box 409, PC 113; ↘ 24 685066, 24 790700, 24 790567; f 24 683491, 24 790500. Established 15 years with branches throughout the Gulf, offering city tours, day trips, dhow cruises, camel and 4x4 safaris. Also in Salalah; ↘ 23 236038; f 23 236038.

OmanHoliday.co.uk ↘ +968 95 116638; www.omanholiday.co.uk. Based in Hamriya in Muscat, this company has been operating for 20 years and will arrange bespoke trips for everyone from single visitors to large groups and business visitors.

Omani Travel and Tourism Bureau (OTTB) PO Box 532, PC 117; ↘ 24 789845, 24 789846, 24 789847; f 24 789843. Also in Seeb; ↘ 24 421469; f 24 425924, Buraimi; ↘ 25 655890; f 25 655889; e otboman@omantel.net.om or niche@omantel.net.om. Located in the Central Business District. Full range of tours from 2-hour city tours to 20-day safaris, also fishing tours. Car hire, travel insurance, hotel reservations, domestic flights and meet and greet.

Orient Holidays PO Box 198, PC 114, Muttrah; ↘ 24 478902, 24 604902; f 99 337159, 24 602512; e haditha@omantel.net.om or alhadtrs@omantel.net.om; www.visitingoman.com. Located in Al Khuwair, Muttrah Business District, Qurum and Seeb Airport. Offers all the tours, in association with Thrifty Car Rental: The Batinah Bounty, Mystical Muscat, Dune Dinner, Grand Canyon of Oman.

Sea Tourism Co PO Box 203, PC 115, Medinat Qaboos; ↘ 24 691211, 24 602949; f 24 796700; e seatour@gto.net.om or rb1968@omantel.net.om. Top-of-the-range luxury yacht trips a speciality; also adventure trips and camping safaris.

Shanfari Travel & Tours PO Box 783, PC 113; ↘ 24 700268, 25 4787271; f 24 785371; e touroman@shanfari.com; www.shanfari.com. City tours, dhow cruises, adventure trips, camel and 4x4 safaris, turtle watching.

Al Tamayim Tourism PO Box 244, PC 119; ↘ 24 571461, 24 601061; f 24 571462, 24 601082. Located in Al Harthy Complex. A medium-sized company offering city and day trips by bus, dhow cruises, 4x4 safaris, airport transfers, meet and greet.

Tour Oman PO Box 1694, PC 114, Muttrah; ↘ 24 799966; f 24 796716. Established 12 years, offering

the full range of tours and trips including scuba diving.

Tours by Heide Beal PO Box 2031, PC 112, Ruwi; ↘ 24 795206; f 24 799928. Based at Hotel Mercure Al Falaj, Heide Beal was the first person to run adventure safaris in Oman back in 1987. She offers tailor-made holidays from 1-day to 2-week study tours, including mountain trekking.

Treasure Tours PO Box 1107, PC 133, Al Khuwair; ↘ 24 789505 (Falaj Hotel desk – same number for fax), 24 488925; f 24 488924; e treasure@omantel.net.om or treasure@omantel.co.uk; www.treasureoman.com. Fully accredited and licensed, with an impressive repertoire of tours and helpful staff. They run 10 land tours, including the Wahiba Sands (full day or overnight), Wadi bani Khalid, Wadi Shab, Wadi Tiwi, Wadi Dayqah and Wadi Abyadh, Jebel Akdhar, Grand Canyon (Jebel Shams and Wadi Ghul), Wadi bani Awf, turtle tours, plus all of the sea tours, including fishing safaris (RO130 for a half day, RO200 for full day) in a 31ft luxury sports cruiser, dolphin watching (RO16), sunset cruise (RO15). They can also tailor-make any tours of 2, 3, 4, 5 and 6 days, and the cost depends on the accommodation you select and your meal requirements. Full-day tours in a 4x4 vehicle, with a maximum of 4 passengers, with an experienced driver/guide, cost RO120. In addition to the usual tours, Treasure Tours can arrange camel-racing trips, with car and driver/guide (RO80–120 depending on location of racetrack), or bullfighting with car and driver/guide (RO70), or combined with other local sites (RO100), and horseriding throughout the year.

United Tours PO Box 599, PC 114, Muttrah; ↘ 24 787448; f 24 784226; e utours@omantel.net.om; utours@unitedoman.com. Located in the Central Business District (CBD). Also in Salalah; ↘ 23 297948; f 23 297958. Large established firm with 40 4x4 vehicles and a fleet of buses offering the full range of tours, including comprehensive 8–12-day tours of Oman, camping, safari and culture.

Zahara Tours PO Box 833, PC 112, Ruwi; ↘ 24 692940; f 24 692950. Located in the CBD. Also at the Intercontinental Hotel; ↘ 24 699862, Grand Hyatt Hotel; ↘ 24 696596, Salalah; ↘ 23 202581, 23 202582; f 23 202581; e Arvind@zaharatours.com or Harsh@zaharatours.com; www.zaharatours.com. Large established firm, IATA travel agents carrying stocks of over 21 international airlines, with Avis car hire, travel and diving insurance and the full range of day trips, city tours, camel and 4x4 safaris, scuba diving and adventure trips.

From the airport it is never too far to your hotel irrespective of where you are staying in the city. The closest is the Golden Tulip, which is virtually opposite the airport; the furthest are Al Bustan Palace and the Shangri-La's Barr al Jissah (the latest addition to the city), both about a 35–40-minute drive away on good roads. A more central choice from which to explore the city would be the Chedi (about ten minutes away from the airport), the Grand Hyatt, or the Intercontinental Hotel (both roughly 15–20 minutes away from the airport). The Radisson is also a good central base (again about 15–20 minutes from the airport), although it doesn't occupy a beach location; it does have a beach club located next to the Grand Hyatt, however.

Some hotels in the city provide a complimentary transit from the airport; this is certainly the case if you have booked a package holiday. For the independent traveller it may be a good idea to confirm with your chosen hotel whether this service is included.

Note that all room rates are subject to a 17% government tax; some of the rates quoted here already include this (and this has been specified). In the same way, some of the rates quoted here include breakfast (also specified), whereas some don't.

UPPER RANGE

⌂ **Al Bustan Palace Hotel** (250 rooms) PO Box 1998, PC 114, Muttrah; ☎ 24 799666; f 24 799600; e albustan@interconti.com or albustan@albustanpalace.com; www.albustanpalace.com. Part of the Intercontinental Hotels Group, this hotel is about a 35–40-min drive from the airport. It is set on its own private beach within 200 acres of lush parkland, complete with helicopter landing pad and stark mountainous backdrop. Its bay location means that the sea is clear and calm. The hotel is regularly voted top in the Arabian peninsula competition, and is known as one of the finest in the world. Over half of its rooms overlook the sea, with a choice of style between Islamic and continental. Its sports and leisure facilities are extensive. It offers gourmet dining, including, on Sun and Wed, a traditional Omani meal in a Bedouin tent with entertainment by Omani musicians and dancers from 19.30 (Seblat Al Bustan – for reservations; ☎ 24 764111), and an award-winning buffet restaurant. For the non-guest, this place is worth a visit simply to gaze upon its atrium and admire its tranquil ambience and setting. Have a meal in the buffet restaurant or outside on the terrace, or perhaps take high tea. *From RO113/129 sgl/dbl, exc taxes and b/fast.*

⌂ **The Chedi** (161 rooms) PO Box 964, PC 133, Al Khuwair, Muscat; ☎ 24 524400, 24 524401; f 24 493485, 24 504485; e thechedi@omantel.net.om or reservation@chedimuscat.com; www.chedimuscat.com. Located in north Ghubra (also known as Bowshar beachfront), this is one of the latest additions to Muscat's luxury collection of 5-star hotels and only about a 10-min drive from the airport (7km). It is well signposted. It is a single and 2-storey hotel and spa, with 1 deluxe room and private villas, 2 swimming pools, tennis courts, treatment rooms and a boutique (which is also an art gallery). There are sports facilities, 3 bars and 2 poolside *cabanas*. One of the bars is sunken and has a beautiful outlook past the glass-like stillness of the infinity pool and directly onto the postcard-like blue ocean. At The Chedi the intention is a Zen experience of peace and tranquillity, with beauty and bathing rituals on offer, and body elixirs, in the form of massages, scrubs and wraps, for which there is a menu in your room. The award-winning restaurant (called 'The Restaurant'!) is regarded as one of the best in the city (☎ 24 524343; e restaurant@chedimuscat.com). There is a choice of Arabic, Asian, Indian and Mediterranean cuisine cooked in the 4 open-display kitchens, in addition to an extensive cellar, which houses over 300 imported wines on full display in the floor-to-ceiling glass library in the bar (called 'The Bar'!). Alternatively, there is 'The Chedi Pool Side Cabana' for evening dining, which serves a Mediterranean menu, and has a resident pianist entertaining you (on Sat and Sun). There are 3 semi-private dining rooms, all with sea views, named The Datai, The Setai and The Legian. Despite the promotion of peace and harmony, service is not always as good as it should be, with a lack of attention and slight aggression that is disappointing, especially after keenly anticipating The Chedi experience. This aside, the suites are impressive with their high ceilings and minimalist designs, although it was a shame there was no bath. Outside, a maze of paved pathways leads to the pools and private beach. There seemed a curious disparity between the romantic, glamour image of this hotel and the reality. *From RO115–300, exc taxes, inc b/fast.*

🏠 **Crowne Plaza Hotel Muscat** (207 rooms) PO Box 1455, PC 112, Ruwi; ✆ 24 560100, 24 660660; f 24 560650, 24 574462; e mcthc@interconti.com; www.cpmuscat.com. Another member of the Intercontinental Hotels Group, the Crowne Plaza has a superb location perched on a cliff in Qurum Heights, overlooking Qurum Beach. This is one of Muscat's oldest-established hotels and used to be the Gulf Forum Hotel. There is a Lebanese restaurant (Shiraz), an international buffet restaurant (Tropicana), Arabic food (Palm Café), casual dining (The Edge) and an English pub (Duke's Bar). It is recommended that you reserve a table in advance for any of these restaurants. There are good sports and recreational facilities and dive trips are arranged through Oman Dive Centre. *RO80/90 sgl/dbl, exc taxes and b/fast. Low season discounts (Apr–Sep); airport pick-up RO8.*

🏠 **Golden Tulip (Seeb)** (177 rooms) PO Box 69, Seeb International Airport, PC 111; ✆ 24 510300; f 24 510055; e admin@goldentulipseeb.com; www.goldentulipseeb.com. This is the closest hotel to Seeb International Airport, and is situated next to the Oman International Exhibition Centre. The hotel guests can use the facilities of the Oman Aviation Beach Club and the Oman Automobile Club (which has go-karting and an 18-hole brown (sand) golf course, located a few minutes from the hotel) and offers free transfer to these on request. There is an international restaurant (Le Jardin), with themed buffet nights, and nightclub. PADI dive course packages are also available. *RO60/70 sgl/dbl, exc taxes and b/fast. B/fast RO5, free airport transfer.*

🏠 **Grand Hyatt Muscat** (280 rooms) PO Box 951, Shatti Al Qurum, PC 133, Muscat ✆ 24 641234; f 24 605282; e hyattmct@omantel.net.om; www.muscat.grand.hyatt.com. About 20km from Seeb Airport, this 5-star hotel is set in 10 acres of gardens, in a good central location on Qurum Beach. It has a stylish design in traditional Arabian architecture, including a huge stained-glass window (14m high) through which you have views out towards the swimming pool and gardens. It has 4 restaurants and 2 bars. For those who would

prefer to self-cater there are Crowne Suites with 2 or 3 beds adjacent to the hotel, with private kitchens and living rooms. The Sirj tea lounge, with its bold décor and sumptuous sofas, is opulent, and, coupled with the soft piano music being played for you on the grand piano, creates an atmosphere of sheer tranquillity. Perhaps take high tea here, with cakes and pastries, or have your business meeting. There is a superb Italian restaurant (The Tuscany), decorated as a Tuscan villa, complete with iron gate and courtyard; the Mokha Café is down the stairs, and serves buffet breakfasts and Middle Eastern lunches and dinners; there is also a poolside Asian restaurant and bar (the marjan). The John Barry Bar, with its sea theme, was named after the wreck of the SS *John Barry* which sank off the coast of Oman in 1944. It has a peaceful ambience and good entertainment later on by the resident pianist. The Copacabana is the hotel's nightclub, which is underneath the hotel and at the front. Club Safari is a 2-min walk down the sloped entrance to the hotel. It is a great African-themed bar on 3 levels, with a snooker/pool area and a cigar lounge on the ground floor (Habana Café), a good, fun bar on the middle floor (Safari Pub) and a grill restaurant on the roof terrace (Grill House). Many excellent house bands play nightly in the Safari Pub and it can get full and lively after 22.00. There are all the usual 5-star facilities and services in the hotel, and watersports are available at the Hyatt Boat House (✆ 24 485663) situated on the beach. *RO108–118, exc taxes and b/fast. B/fast RO7.50 pp.*

🏠 **Intercontinental Muscat** (261 rooms) PO Box 398, PC 114, Muttrah; ✆ 24 680000, 24 600500; f 24 600012; e muscat@icmuscathotel.com or muscat@interconti.com; www.intercontinental.com. This hotel is set on Qurum Beach about a 15-min drive from the airport (21km), close to Qurum Natural Park and the museums. Set within 35 acres of private well-maintained gardens, its brown-brick structure doesn't make it the most attractive building. It is a little dated, but there is an efficient, friendly staff, and has good leisure and sports facilities. There is an American-style steak house (OK Corral), a Mexican restaurant (Señor Pico's), international snacks round the pool (Pool Deck), and Far Eastern food (Coconut Grove). The bar (Al Ghazal Pub) serves food and is popular with expats. It has a live band playing most evenings, and offers quiz nights, sport on the large screen TV and a pool/snooker area. There is a good cocktail bar and restaurant (Trader Vic's — ✆ 24 698028; f 24

605839), situated just outside the front of the hotel and on the left (as you face it), serving Caribbean and Pacific food. *RO62/67 sgl/dbl, exc b/fast.*

🏠 **Radisson SAS Hotel** (156 rooms) PO Box 939, PC 133, Al Khuleiah St, Muscat; ✆ 24 487777; f 24 487778; e reservations.muscat@radissonsas.com or muscat.info@radissonsas.com; www.muscatradissonsas.com. Located in Al Khuwair, in a good elevated and central setting in the capital (on the mountain-side rather than the sea-side of the highway), this hotel is about a 10–15-min drive from the airport (signposted from the highway, and situated just off Al Khuleiah St, at the one-way section). It has an excellent standard of modern décor and there is a great steak restaurant here (Al Tajin Grill), set opposite a romantic, dimly lit piano bar (The Coral), for pre- or post-dinner drinks. There is a nightclub (The Cellar – accessed around the back of the hotel and down the stairs), an all-day dining restaurant (Olivios Coffee Shop), serving buffet and à la carte meals, and the Fontana Heath Club. The beach club for the Radisson is located next to the Grand Hyatt – they will transport you. The staff give an excellent smiling welcome, and a swift, efficient check-in and delivery of bags to your room – no messing. Reception offers a full explanation of what the cost of an overnight stay includes without being prompted. I couldn't fault the experience of this hotel; ten out of ten. *RO60/65/80/85 standard/dbl/business/suite, exc taxes and b/fast. B/fast is RO5 pp.*

🏠 **Shangri-La's Barr al Jissah Resort and Spa** (680 rooms) PO Box 644, PC 113, Muscat; ✆ 24 776666; f 24 776677; e slmu@shangri-la.com; www.shangri-la.com. This is the newest addition to Oman's growing 5-star hotel assortment with the added tag of 'deluxe'. It is a resort of 3 top international-class hotels, set in 124 acres of landscaped gardens with a remarkable mountainous backdrop. Although this is the furthest hotel in the city from the airport it is still only a 40-min drive on roads of excellent condition. This resort is sheer relaxation and escape, just as that offered by Al Bustan a few bays earlier. The 3 hotels are geared towards different target markets: Al Husn (which translates as 'The Castle') is a 6-star luxury hotel, while Al Bandar ('The Town') is aimed at the business guest. Al Waha ('The Oasis') is aimed at families, providing a kids' club named 'Little Turtles', two kiddie pools and an internet café. An Omani heritage village and a retail souk will eventually appear here, but in February 2006 these were still under construction. So too was the

planned 1,000-seat outdoor amphitheatre. The Chi Spa, adjacent to the gym, has treatment rooms in 12 private villas, and offers traditional Himalayan and Chinese treatments. There is a protected 'turtle cove' area where turtles come to nest, and a ranger informs and educates guests on how to respect the species and their natural environment. Guests of Al Bandar and Al Waha can use each other's facilities, and a lazy river can be swum or followed, adjoining the two. There is a central bar amid the pools and surrounding flower gardens. In total 19 food and beverage outlets are planned and, in February 2006, 11 of these were open. There is a dive school planned (Euro Divers Dive Centre), and watersports facilities, with a lifeguard present. Al Husn remains exclusive, and with a huge chandelier from the Czech Republic, wall light shades from Morocco and carpets from Iran, the décor is opulent. When combined with 3 crystal-ceiling ballrooms with retracting walls (which allow it to convert into one impressive 700-seater), this place is severely luxurious. And to reflect this, transfers from Seeb Airport can be arranged for an exorbitant RO35. *Al Waha RO90–160; Al Bandar RO105–180; Al Husn RO170–1,500, exc taxes and based on dbl occupancy; inc b/fast and buffet dinner, laundry service, non-motorised watersports, local calls, internet access and 15.00 extended check-out.*

🏠 **Sheraton Oman Hotel** (217 rooms, 24 deluxe suites) PO Box 3260, PC 112, Ruwi; ✆ 24 772772; f 24 795791, 24 772542; e sheraton@omantel.net.om; www.sheraton.com/oman. Roughly a half-hour drive from Seeb (40km), set in the Central Business District at Ruwi, this is a high-rise hotel, rated 5-star by the Ministry of Tourism. To get here keep straight on the main highway until you reach the Ruwi roundabout. Turn right here and follow the road all the way up to the T-junction, to the traffic lights at the very end. The hotel lies opposite these lights. In addition to its full sports facilities it has a 6-lane bowling alley. A beach resort has recently been added with a shuttle-bus service to Qurum (see below). There is an international restaurant (Green Mountain Restaurant) with various theme nights, including barbecue night, fish night and Thai night, an Italian restaurant (La Mamma), a French restaurant (La Brasserie), Le Croissant Coffee Shop, the Piazza Bar and Saba Disco. All outlets are licensed. There is no complimentary airport transfer service. A taxi from the airport costs RO8. *RO66/76 sgl/dbl, exc taxes and b/fast.*

🏠 **Sheraton Qurum Beach Resort** (7 rooms) PO Box 3260, PC 112, Ruwi; ✆ 24 605945; e sheraton@ omantel.net.om; www.sheraton.com. This is the beach resort of the Sheraton Oman Hotel in Ruwi and guests from Ruwi can use the facilities here for free. There is a complimentary shuttle service from Sheraton Ruwi, leaving at 10.00/11.00/12.00 and returning in the afternoon at 15.00/16.00/17.00. It is located at Shatti al Qurum. All rooms have sea views, a gym and a swimming pool. The small resort is good for beach-sports lovers. The licensed restaurant used to be the Far Eastern Restaurant, but is now the Jade Garden Restaurant, and open in the evenings only. There is an Arabic/Moroccan nightclub (Cleopatra Night Club) and Feeney's Irish Bar. Non-guests can access the facilities for RO3 Sat–Wed, and RO5 on Thu–Fri. Accepts credit cards. *RO66/76 sgl/dbl, exc taxes and b/fast.*

MID RANGE

🏠 **Bowshar Hotel** (38 rooms) PO Box 1842, PC 112, Ruwi; ✆ 24 501105, 24 491105; f 24 501124; e bwshrhtl@omantel.net.com; www.bowsharhotel.com. To get here, come off the highway at the Ghubra roundabout. It is on the seaside of the highway, rather than the mountain-side, 15mins from the airport, and is signposted. The hotel is rated 3-star by the Ministry of Tourism. Al Mas Brasserie is the hotel's licensed restaurant. Accepts credit cards. *RO25/32.25 sgl/dbl, inc taxes and b/fast. RO21/29.25 exc b/fast.*

🏠 **Coral Hotel Muscat** (32 rooms) PO Box 3951, PC 112, Ruwi; ✆ 24 692121; f 24 694404; e bwmuscat@omantel.net.com; www.bestwesternmuscat.com. This hotel used to be the Best Western Muscat Hotel, and before that, the Laith Howard Johnson Hotel. Rated 3-star, it is located close to the Grand Hyatt and used to house Feeney's Bar, which has now moved to the Sheraton Beach Resort in Shatti al Qurum (see above). There is Al Radha Bistro, which is an Arabic-themed coffee shop with internet facilities open from 07.00–23.00, and one restaurant. Both are unlicensed. In early 2006 this hotel was undergoing major refurbishment, and so Al Nafoorah (a traditional Lebanese restaurant with terrace) and Rumours Café (serving international snacks), should be available to visitors from early September 2006. So too, will the internet service to each room. *RO30/37 sgl/dbl (rates different in summer) up to RO150 for the suites, depending on season, exc taxes, inc b/fast.*

🏠 **Dream Resort** (30 rooms) PO Box 609, PC 121, Al Seeb; ✆ 24 453399; f 24 453999; e drmuscat@omantel.net.om or dreamr@omantel.net.om; no website. This is a modern hotel (about 4 years old) of international standard and is certainly the best if you are planning on staying in Seeb Town. It is within easy walking distance of the beach. Rooms surround the 2 pools and lead straight out to them if you request one on the ground floor. The hotel is rather in the middle of nowhere, so unless you're coming for a complete rest, and like to beach-walk, there is not a lot to see and do. There is the Café Lounge, an international restaurant, and the Black Out nightclub. They also have a large screen for sporting events. *RO50/80 standard/suite, inc taxes.*

🏠 **Al Falaj Hotel** (143 rooms) PO Box 2031, PC 112, Ruwi; ✆ 24 702311; f 24 795853; e sales@ omanhotels.com or reservationruwi@omanhotels.com; www.omanhotels.com. One of Muscat's oldest hotels, this is set in the Central Business District of Ruwi, off Al Burj St, and rated 4-star. Private beach facilities are available on request. On the 8th floor there is a Japanese restaurant (Tokyo Taro) and a pub (Le Pub) with live band and bar-food menu, and each has scenic views over the city. Al Falaj also has a Lebanese restaurant, an Indian restaurant and a coffee shop. The sports facilities include glass-sided squash courts. *RO40/50 sgl/dbl, exc taxes and b/fast.*

🏠 **Haffa House Hotel** (120 rooms) PO Box 1498, PC 114, Jibroo; ✆ 24 707207; f 24 707208; e reservations@haffahouse.com; www.haffahouse.com. This 4-star hotel is situated in the Muttrah Business District and is affiliated to the Shanfari group of hotels (they have Haffa House and Samharam tourist village both in Salalah). It has a swimming pool and an unlicensed restaurant (Four Seasons). *RO35/48 sgl/dbl, incl taxes and b/fast.*

🏠 **Holiday Inn Muscat** (129 rooms) PO Box 1185, PC 111, Seeb; ✆ 24 487123; f 24 480986; e mcthinn@omantel.net.om. There are two Holiday Inn hotels in Muscat, but the one in Al Khuwair has the more central and pleasant location. It is on the right-hand side of the highway (coming away from the airport and towards Al Khuwair roundabout). To get here, slow down after the Ghubra roundabout on the highway, and exit at the Shell petrol station, where there is now also a McDonald's. This enables you to access Al Khuwair St (a 2-way slip road running parallel to the main road). Once on this road take the first right. The Holiday Inn sits a little way up on your left. Live music features in the restaurants and bars, and on the first floor there is a pub (Churchill's), which provides a pub-food menu. If you're missing a plate of sausage, beans and mash and a pint in dimly lit surroundings, this is the place to go, served by the ever-smiling Sri Lankan, Kumi. There is an African restaurant (Hakuna Matata). *RO45/55 sgl/dbl, exc taxes, inc b/fast.*

🏠 **Al Madina Holiday Inn (Ghala)** (81 rooms) PO Box 692, PC 130, Al Azaiba, Muscat; ✆ 24 596400; f 24 502191; e amhi33@omantel.net.om. This Holiday Inn, located in Ghala, has a coffee shop and licensed bars with live entertainment. *RO43/48 sgl/dbl, exc taxes, inc b/fast; airport transfer RO4.*

🏠 **Majan Hotel** (114 rooms) PO Box 311, PC 115, Madinat Qaboos; ✆ 24 592900; f 24 592979; e info@majanhotel.com or sales@majanhotel.com; www.majanhotel.com. For the Majan Hotel, exit the highway at Al Udaybah (Azaiba) roundabout and take the road leading towards the mountains (the hotel is clearly signposted). You will meet another smaller roundabout at which you will see the entrance to the grand mosque on your left. Go straight over this roundabout and you will meet another, at which you take a left. The hotel lies on your left, past the Royal Hospital, about halfway up the road. It is located close to the Sultan Qaboos sports stadium at Bowshar. The hotel, rated 4-star, has a 24hr licensed coffee shop (Khaboura Café) and 5 bars with live bands performing daily (Barrio Fiesta, The Oasis, Chambers Lounge, Al Khaima and Ghungroo). They can arrange diving packages to the Daymaniyat Islands, car hire and tours. Accepts credit cards. *RO25/35/50/45 sgl/dbl/executive suite/1-bed apt, exc taxes and b/fast; complimentary airport transfer.*

🏠 **Oman Beach Hotel** (20 rooms, 20 suites) PO Box 678, PC 116, Mina al Fahal, Muscat; ✆ 24 696601; f 24 697686; e info@omaninfobeachhotel.com; www.omanbeachhotel.com. This lovely small hotel is set close to the beach and the Intercontinental Hotel. It is under friendly new Omani management and has a quaint design with rooms surrounding a small swimming pool. Its international restaurant is unlicensed. *Summer RO32/40/50 sgl/1-bed suite/2-bed suite; winter RO48/60/80, inc taxes and b/fast.*

🏠 **Oman Dive Centre Beach Huts** ✆ 24 824241, 24 824240, 99 379031; f 24 799600. Located in Bander Jissah, in its own tranquil bay, this offers an alternative-type stay in Muscat. When nearing Al Bustan you descend a hill. Partway down you take the right-hand exit directing you to Qantab and the Shangri-La Resort. This road winds up and over the mountains and when you come to a roundabout take a left. This will take you down into the private bay of the dive centre. You can no longer camp on the beach here, but equipped, traditional Omani *barasti* (made with palm fronds) huts with AC are available for rent. There is a licensed restaurant (The Odyssey) open 07.00–16.30 and 18.00–22.00. This is a peaceful location where you can get on with the business of taking or completing your PADI course or doing a dive without distractions. *RO30/38/42 low/mid/high-season, includes b/fast and dinner, under 12s half price.*

🏠 **Ramada Qurum Beach** (92 rooms) PO Box 2994, PC 112, Ruwi; ✆ 24 603555; f 24 694500; e ramadaom@omantel.net.om; www.ramadamuscat.com. This hotel has a good location very close to the beach and the Intercontinental Hotel, about 10–15min from the airport. Rated 4-star deluxe by the Ministry of Tourism, it is an Arabic-style construction and the room décor is of a good standard. Inside the hotel is Nauras Al Shatti Restaurant and the Petit Café. *RO45/55 sgl/dbl, exclusive of taxes and b/fast; airport transfer available for RO7.*

🏠 **Ruwi Hotel** (116 rooms) PO Box 2195, PC 112, Ruwi; ✆ 24 704244; f 24 704248; e reservationruwi@omanhotels.com or sales@omanhotels.com; www.omanhotels.com. This is one of a chain of 4 hotels, the others being Al Falaj (also in Ruwi), Sur Plaza (Sur) and Al Wadi (Sohar). Set in the Central Business District at the 7th roundabout from the airport (Ruwi roundabout), this hotel has a 3-star Ministry of Tourism rating and has been operational for over 20 years. It has 2 licensed restaurants: the Coffee Shop offers all-day dining and Al Fakhr Restaurant has live entertainment from an Arabic band. There is also the Club Bar and the Mehfil Bar, each with live entertainment. Aside from the usual hotel services, there are 2 glass-backed squash courts. Accepts credit cards. *RO35/40 sgl/dbl, exc taxes and b/fast. B/fast RO3.50 plus taxes.*

BUDGET

🏠 **Al Bahjah Hotel** (52 rooms) PO Box 979, PC 121, Seeb; ✆ 24 424400; f 24 424620; e bahjahtl@omantel.net.om; www.ramee-group.com. This hotel is located in Seeb on the one-way system in the town, about 15km from the airport. Its rooms have full facilities, including swimming pool. On-site restaurants and bars include Al Saadah Café, Keranadu Restaurant, Al Massarrat Sports Bar, Al

Rafahia Arabic Restaurant and Al Marrah Indian Restaurant. If you are not staying here, it still makes a good stop for a cup of tea (400bzs) or something to eat, while visiting Seeb Town. Accepts credit cards. *RO20/24 sgl/dbl.*

🏠 **Corniche Hotel** (53 rooms) PO Box 1800, PC 114, Jibroo; ☎ 24 714707, 24 714636; f 24 714770; e corniche_hotel@mjsoman.com. This hotel is in an excellent spot on the Muttrah corniche with superb views, an international restaurant and friendly staff. The single rooms have a shower only. Although the hotel is worn and tired-looking it offers a welcome bed for the night in a beautiful historic location. It is unlicensed and parking can be limited at times, but the problem seems to have improved since the renovations to the area were completed (for the 35th anniversary of Sultan Qaboos's reign). There are a few chained parking spaces directly in front of the hotel, which they may reserve and unchain for you on request, or you can park directly opposite in front of the fish souk. Accepts credit cards. *RO13/20 sgl/dbl, inc taxes and b/fast; airport transfer RO8.*

🏠 **Al Fanar Hotel** (48 rooms) PO Box 3738, PC 112, Ruwi; ☎ 24 712385, 24 713142; f 24 714994; e alfanar@omantel.net.om. This 1-star hotel is located in the group that sits at the end of the Muttrah corniche. It has an unlicensed restaurant. *RO8.70/12.80 sgl/dbl.*

🏠 **Hotel Golden Oasis** (62 rooms) PO Box 353, PC 117, Al Wadi Al Kabir; ☎ 24 811655, 24 814062; f 24 814065; e hotgoldn@omantel.net.om; www.hotelgoasis.com. This hotel is rated 2-star and is located on the road to Al Bustan. To get here, exit the highway at Al Wadi Al Kabir roundabout (about 25 min from the airport) and follow Al Wadi Al Kabir St, which is the road running parallel to Al Bustan St. It is on your left-hand side. The hotel has a licensed bar and 3 licensed restaurants with live entertainment: Mer-Maid Bar, Captain's Café, Ubar Restaurant and Cleopatra Restaurant. This makes a good base for divers using the Oman Dive Centre, a 5-min drive away. The hotel provides a shuttle service for RO3 and can organise courses and dive trips. Accepts credit cards. *RO18/24 sgl/dbl (10% less in the summer), exc taxes and b/fast; airport transfer RO10.*

🏠 **Holiday Villa Hotel** (102 rooms) PO Box 191, PC 113, Muscat; ☎ 24 564443; f 24 562464; e hvllamct@omantel.net.om. This hotel has traditional Omani-style architecture and is in a good location close to Qurum Beach. It has an international licensed restaurant (Yamamah). Sea View Grill restaurant at rooftop. Accepts credit cards. *RO30/40 sgl/dbl.*

🏠 **Marina Hotel** (20 rooms) PO Box 500, PC 114, Muttrah; ☎ 24 713100, 24 714343, 24 711711; f 24 714666; e marina2@omantel.net.om or marina@omantel.net.om; www.chamberoman.com/member/marina. The 3-star Marina has Al Boom international restaurant, Dolphins Bar and Shark Night Club, all licensed. If you don't stay here, do take a trip up to the terrace floor 'P', where the restaurant and bar are located. There is a fantastic view over the port, the corniche and the minarets of the mosques. Have a drink and absorb the spirit of the place as you look out over Muttrah. If you're here at the time of the sundown call to prayer, the aura of an Arabia of old is remarkable. Watch the changing colours of the sky over the jebels as the sun goes down. It's magical. Accepts credit cards. *RO15/25 sgl/dbl.*

🏠 **Al Mina Hotel** (28 rooms) PO Box 504, PC 112, Ruwi; ☎ 24 711828; f 24 714981; e minahotl@omantel.net.om. Set on Muttrah corniche and offering scenic views, this hotel is rated 1-star by the Ministry of Tourism. Al Bahar and Al Safina are its licensed restaurants, serving Indian and continental cuisine. Accepts credit cards. *RO12/15 sgl/dbl.*

🏠 **Muttrah Hotel** (32 rooms) PO Box 1131, PC 114, Jibroo; ☎ 24 798401; f 24 790953. Set close to a rear entrance to Muttrah souk, this licensed hotel has a restaurant that serves French and continental food. There are 2 bars, a gym and a games room. Accepts credit cards. *RO18/25 sgl/dbl.*

🏠 **Al Nahdha Hotel** (40 rooms) PO Box 1561, PC 114, Jibroo; ☎ 24 714196; f 24 714994; e alnahdaha@muscatcityhotels.com. Set on the Muttrah corniche with sea views and about 30km from Seeb Airport. There is a restaurant serving oriental and Arabic food, and a snack bar. Rendezvous is the rooftop garden, which has splendid views of the harbour (for private parties). *RO8.50/14 sgl/dbl.*

🏠 **Naseem Hotel** (29 rooms) PO Box 360, PC 114, Jibroo; ☎ 24 712418; f 24 711728. Located on the Muttrah corniche, close to the souk, all the rooms have baths. There is no restaurant but they do provide room service with food from nearby eateries. Ask for a sea-facing room. *RO11/17 sgl/dbl.*

🏠 **Qurum Beach Hotel** (64 rooms) PO Box 2148, PC 112, Ruwi; ☎ 24 564070; f 24 560761; e qurumbeachhotel@hotmail.com. Located at Qurum Heights, this hotel provides good cheap accommodation and is in a great location with plentiful parking. Driving up the road to the entrance, it is almost African in feel, on account of all the greenery around. It also has 2- or 3-bedroom apts, an international restaurant (Maymoon) and two licensed nightclubs either side, which can be a bit noisy into the early hours. Still, there's a real sense of the holiday feel about the place. The hotel will store your excess baggage if you are taking short trips up or down the country. Members of staff were friendly, professional and accommodating when I visited. You are a short walk away from the fantastic stretch of beach that runs from the Crowne Plaza Hotel all the way up past the Grand Hyatt and Intercontinental hotels. Fantastic value for money. Accepts credit cards. *RO12/22 sgl/dbl.*

HOTEL APARTMENTS If you prefer a self-catering arrangement, for a stay of a longer duration perhaps, hotel apartments are widely available around Muscat. Again these vary in quality, but all are basically clean and comfortable. You will often get a discount for a longer period of stay.

🏠 **Arabian Palms Apartments** (34 apts) PO Box 2087, PC 111, CPO; ☎ 24 488562, 24 488563; f 24 488561; e apallc@omantel.net.om or arabianpalms@yahoo.com; www.arabianpalmsapartments.com. These are situated behind the Holiday Inn in Al Khuwair, and opposite the relatively new City Bowling Centre. The apts include sgl rooms, 1- and 3-bed suites. All the suites have their own kitchen. Tea and coffee are provided in the rooms. Restaurants in Muscat deliver food to the apts. *Standard room with no kitchen RO15 per night, inc taxes; 1-bed suite/2-bed suite/3-bed suite RO20/30/40.*

🏠 **ASAS Oman Hotel Apartments** (35 apts) PO Box 191, PC 113; ☎ 24 568515; f 24 560018; e asasoman@omantel.net.om. Located at Qurum, near Qurum Natural Park, this complex comprises 35 fully furnished en-suite apts, all with AC, equipped kitchens, washing machines, satellite TV, 24hr reception, daily housekeeping service, telephone, business centre, temperature-controlled swimming pool and car park. There is disabled access and pets are allowed. There is also an unlicensed restaurant. Accepts credit cards. *RO40/50 2-bed apts/3-bed apts (winter rates: RO60/RO70), inc taxes. B/fast at RO2.50, lunch/dinner at RO3.50.*

🏠 **Al Khuwair Hotel Apartments** (9 apts) PO Box 121, PC 115, Madinat Sultan Qaboos; ☎ 24 478171; f 24 489060. This is one of 4 properties owned by the Safeer Hotels and Tourism Company (the others are Safeer Hotel Suites, Nuzha Hotel Apartments and Ghaba Resthouse). *RO18/25 1-bed apt/2-bed apt.*

🏠 **Noos Hotel Apartments** (16 apts) PO Box 137, PC 112, Ruwi; ☎ 24 483314, 24 478852; f 24 478852; e nooshotl@omantel.net.om; www.omantourist.com/nooshotelapartment. Located close to the Radisson SAS Hotel, this offers 2- and 3-bedroom apts fully furnished and equipped. There is daily housekeeping and security, and a health club, swimming pool and babysitting services. There is no restaurant or airport transfer. Accepts credit cards. *RO15/16 sgl/dbl, incl taxes, exc b/fast.*

🏠 **Al Noorah Garden** (20 villas) PO Box 387, PC 133, Madinat al Sultan Qaboos; ☎ 24 697203; f 24 698631; e noorah@omantel.net.om; www.noorahgarden.com. Located close to the British consulate at Madinat Qaboos, these fully furnished 2- and 3-bed villas are rented on a monthly basis only. They have a swimming pool, daily housekeeping, a children's garden and car parking. *RO650/750 (per month) 2-bed/3-bed, or RO600/700 if rented for a longer duration.*

🏠 **Safeer Hotel Suites** (66 suites) PO Box 121, PC 115, Madinat al Sultan Qaboos; ☎ 24 691200; f 24 692227; e safeer@omantel.net.om; www.safeerhotel.net. Part of the Safeer Group, Safeer Hotel Suites is centrally situated, and each suite has fully equipped kitchens, satellite TV, telephone, fax services, laundry and dry cleaning service, porter and housekeeping. There is a restaurant. *RO35 for a standard room (2 single beds) to RO90 for a 3-bed suite for 6 persons.*

✖ WHERE TO EAT

Dispersed around the city are plenty of restaurants offering cuisines from around the globe. In addition to the ubiquitous Arabic and Indian cuisine, American, African, Chinese, French, Greek, Italian, Japanese, Mexican, Middle Eastern, Mongolian and Thai can all be found.

Most of the upmarket restaurants are situated within the five-star hotels, but other excellent places, like the Pavo Real (Mexican), the Mumtaz Mahal (Indian), or the Golden Oryx (Chinese/Thai), for example, are independent. While most of the hotel restaurants are licensed to serve alcohol, not all of the independents are, so you might like to check this before making your choice. See *Where to stay* above for brief information on hotel restaurants – the star rating of the hotel generally reflects the price range of the restaurant.

The restaurants below are the ones outside of hotels and are in price-range order. For a list of licensed restaurants organised by cuisine, see box, *Restaurants by cuisine*, pages 78–9.

INDEPENDENT RESTAURANTS
Mid range (RO20+ for a meal for two)

✕ **Bellapais Restaurant** ↘ 24 521100. Located in the Rusail commercial complex, this pleasant licensed restaurant serves Greek cuisine, and offers take-aways and home delivery. Your steak is cooked at your table for you. *Open Sat–Thu 12.00–15.00 and 18.00–23.00; Fri 18.00–23.00.*

✕ **Blue Marlin** ↘ 24 737288, 24 737291; e marina@omantel.net.om; www.marinaoman.com. Set within the marina complex at Marina Bander Al Rowdha, this international restaurant is licensed, and you don't have to be a member to access it. *Open Sat 12.00–23.00, Sun–Wed 10.00–23.00, Thu–Fri 08.30–23.00.*

✕ **Golden Dragon** ↘ 24 697374. A licensed Chinese and Thai restaurant in Madinat as Sultan Qaboos (MQ) behind the shopping complex, offering a nice ambience and décor. Also does take-aways. *Open Sat–Thu 12.00–15.00 and 19.00–23.30, Fri 13.00–15.00 and 19.00–23.30.*

✕ **The Golden Oryx** ↘ 24 702266, 24 706128; f 24 705669; e goryx@omantel.net.om. Located on Al Burj St. Ruwi, this licensed restaurant has an extensive menu including Cantonese, Schezwan, Beijing, Mongolian and Thai. It is also good for vegetarians. It is dimly lit and has a peaceful, pleasant atmosphere with instrumental versions of familiar songs playing softly in the background. The food is good, and the waiters are consistently efficient and friendly. The Thai Pavilion at the back provides a nice, private spot for dining. The Calypso coffee is a dream – snap the caramelised sugar from the top of the glass and crunch on it while enjoying the coffee. This restaurant is faultless and highly recommended. *Open Sat–Thu 12.00–15.00 and 19.30–midnight, closed Fri.*

✕ **Mumtaz Mahal** ↘ 24 605907, 24 607103; f 24 692100. Partly because of its hilltop location, which provides an elevated view over Qurum Natural Park and the city, and partly because of its good food, its ambience, its faultless waiter service, its dim lighting, and its very reasonable prices, this award-winning Indian restaurant is one of the best in Muscat. The chefs here certainly know their stuff. The Raan E Mumtaz dish, which is a delicious whole leg of tender mutton slowly cooked in spices is highly recommended. There is a good wine list, but if you are keeping an eye on costs, the carafe of house wine is cheap and easy to drink. From around 21.00, Indian musicians play softly on the low-level stage which fronts a calming waterfall feature. Another of Muscat's faultless restaurants. Do eat here. *Open Sat–Thu 12.00–14.30 and 19.00–23.30, Fri 13.00–15.00 and 19.00–midnight.*

✕ **Nuovo La Terrazza** ↘ 24 571126. A good Italian located behind Hatat House, close to the Passage to India. *Open 19.30–midnight.*

✕ **Odyssey** ↘ 99 379031. Located at the Oman Dive Centre, Bander Jissa, serving an international menu. *Open daily 07.00–16.30 and 18.00–22.00.*

✕ **O Sole Mio** ↘ 24 601343; f 24 601720. This is an excellent Italian restaurant with an extensive wine list and a live Filipino 2-piece band. On Shatti Al Qurum. *Open Sat–Thu 12.00–16.45, 19.00–23.00, Fri 18.45–23.00.*

✕ **Passage to India** ↘ 24 568400, 24 563452; www.restaurantpassageoindia.com. This licensed restaurant is located behind the Hatat House compound, near Wadi Adai roundabout. Both the food and service are excellent here, and there is an open kitchen where you can watch your fresh bread and superb tender meats being cooked. *Open Sat–Thu 12.00–15.00 and 19.00–23.30, Fri evenings only.*

✕ **Pavo Real** ↘ 24 602603. A fun, licensed Mexican restaurant at Madinat Qaboos with live music, where friendly, attentive and smartly dressed waiters serve you great food. Do go here for a good fun night out. Try the cocktails! *Open Sat–Thu 12.00–15.00 and 18.00–midnight, Fri evenings only.*

✕ **Purple Onion/Al Inshira** ↘ 24 715482, 24 713061. This restaurant sits opposite Riyam Park on Al Bahri Rd (the sea road) and used to be named Al Inshirah. Coming from the Muttrah corniche end you need to drive past this restaurant

For ease of reference, we have listed the main licensed restaurants of the capital in cuisine order, including those that are within the hotels.

AFRICAN
✖ **The Chambers** Majan Hotel; ☎ 24 592900
✖ **Hakuna Matata** Holiday Inn; ☎ 24 487123

FAR EASTERN
✖ **China Mood** Al Bustan Palace Hotel; ☎ 24 799666
✖ **Far Eastern Restaurant** Sheraton Qurum Beach Resort; ☎ 24 605945
✖ **Golden Dragon** Madinat Qaboos (MQ) behind Al Fair; ☎ 24 697374
✖ **Golden Oryx** Rex Rd, Ruwi; ☎ 24 702266
✖ **Marjan** By the pool at the Grand Hyatt Hotel; ☎ 24 641234
✖ **Mandarin** At the Happy Village, Qurum (behind Pizza Hut); ☎ 99 677267
✖ **Tokyo Taro** Al Falaj Hotel; ☎ 24 702311

FRENCH
✖ **Al Marjan** Al Bustan Palace Hotel; ☎ 24 799666

INDIAN
✖ **Copper Chimney** Fair Trade Hse; ☎ 24 780207
✖ **Khyber** Central Business District (CBD) next to the National Bank of Oman; ☎ 24 781901
✖ **Moghul** Wattayah, near the Toyota showroom; ☎ 24 562338
✖ **Mumtaz Mahal** Close to Qurum Natural Park; ☎ 24 605907
✖ **Passage to India** Behind Hatat Hse; ☎ 24 568480
✖ **Purple Onion** (also international food) Muttrah corniche; ☎ 24 715482
✖ **Woodlands** CBD, Europcar Bldg; ☎ 24 700192

INTERNATIONAL
✖ **Beach Pavilion** Al Bustan Palace Hotel; ☎ 24 799666
✖ **Bellapais** Rusail Complex; ☎ 24 521100
✖ **Blue Marlin** Marina Bander al Rowdha; ☎ 24 737940
✖ **Cote Jardin** Golden Tulip Hotel; ☎ 24 510300

(which sits on the seafront on the left) as it is not possible to do a left-hand turn. Instead continue past it and take the left-hand turn soon afterwards signposted towards Kalbooh. Go down this turning, turn around, and come back on yourself (there are signs saying no 'U' turns), taking the road back down again to the restaurant. This place used to be renowned for its fresh fish, but now has been taken over and offers an Indian and Chinese menu. The food is good. There are also 2 club bars attached to this complex – Indian and Arabic. Also does take-away and home delivery. *Open Sat–Thu 12.00–15.00 and 19.00–midnight, Fri evenings only.*

Budget (under RO20 for a meal for two)
✖ **Alauddin/Omar al Khayyam** ☎ 24 600667. Located close to Madinat Qaboos traffic lights. Now under the management of Omar al Khayyam, these restaurants have a big Indian, Chinese and continental menu served in basic surroundings. Certainly worth a visit for a good cheap eat. Has a Ruwi branch (one of the oldest restaurants in Muscat) at the Ruwi roundabout, near Everready supermarket (☎ 24 703035), a Seeb outlet (☎ 24 421435), and a Sohar branch. *Open Sat–Thu 11.00–15.30 and 18.00–midnight, Fri 13.00–13.30 and 18.00–midnight.*

✖ **Automatic Restaurant** This award-winning Lebanese food chain restaurant serving Arabian, Mediterranean

✘ **Al Falaj Coffee Shop** Al Falaj Hotel; ✎ 24 702311
✘ **Four Foods** MBD, OIFC Bldg; ✎ 24 709548
✘ **Green Mountain** Sheraton Ruwi Hotel; ✎ 24 799899
✘ **Khaboura Café** Majan Hotel; ✎ 24 592900
✘ **Al Khiran Terrace** Al Bustan Palace Hotel; ✎ 24 799666
✘ **Mediterranean Grill** Intercontinental Hotel; ✎ 24 680000
✘ **Mokha Café** Grand Hyatt Hotel; ✎ 24 641234
✘ **Odyssey** Oman Dive Centre; ✎ 99 379031
✘ **Olivios** Radisson SAS; ✎ 24 487777
✘ **The Restaurant** The Chedi; ✎ 24 524400
✘ **Al Tajin Grill** Radisson SAS; ✎ 24 487777
✘ **Tomato** Intercontinental Hotel; ✎ 24 680000
✘ **Trader Vic's** Immediately next to the Intercontinental Hotel; ✎ 24 680000

ITALIAN
✘ **Come Prima** Crowne Plaza Hotel; ✎ 24 560100
✘ **La Mamma** Sheraton Ruwi Hotel; ✎ 24 799899
✘ **Nuovo la Terrazza** Behind Hatat Hse; ✎ 24 571126
✘ **O Sole Mio** Jawaharat A'Shatti Complex; ✎ 24 601343
✘ **Tuscany** Grand Hyatt Hotel; ✎ 24 641234

MEXICAN
✘ **Chilis** Muscat City Centre Complex; ✎ 24 545815
✘ **Pavo Real** MQ, ✎ 24 602603
✘ **Señor Pico** Intercontinental Hotel; ✎ 24 680000

MIDDLE EASTERN
✘ **Al Bashasha** Near 'the book' roundabout (near Sultan Qaboos University); ✎ 24 425314
✘ **Al Madina** Madinat Qaboos, near Al Fair; ✎ 24 696515
✘ **Fakrudin** Ruwi Hotel; ✎ 24 704244
✘ **Seblat al Bustan** Al Bustan Palace Hotel; ✎ 24 799666, 24 764111
✘ **Shiraz** Crowne Plaza Hotel; ✎ 24 560100
✘ **Al Barouk** Beach Hotel, opposite Intercontinental Hotel; ✎ 24 604799

and Lebanese food has branches in Qurum (✎ 24 561500), Al Khuwair, behind the Radisson SAS (✎ 24 487200) and Seeb (✎ 24 424343). Good servings and prices, but an uninspiring name. *Open Sat–Thu 12.00–midnight, Fri 13.00–midnight.*
✘ **Bin Ateeq** ✎ 24 603225. Traditional Omani food. Next to Shell petrol station on the Khuwair slip road. The Bin Ateeq restaurants (one in Muscat, one in Nizwa and one in Salalah) are highly recommended. They are very reasonable in price, and offer good tasty food served in the traditional Omani way at ground level. Do go along.
✘ **China Town** ✎ 24 567974. Located at the Capital Commercial Centre (CCC) in Qurum, serving good Chinese food. *Open Sat–Thu 11.00–15.00, 18.00–midnight, Fri 13.00–15.00, 18.00–midnight.*

✘ **Copper Chimney** ✎ 24 706420, 24 780207. Located inside Fair Trade House in the Central Business District (opposite British Bank), serving good Indian food, licensed. *Open Sat–Thu 12.00–15.00, 19.00–midnight, Fri 13.00–15.00, 19.00–midnight.*
Al Deyar Restaurant and Cafe ✎ 24 696247. This local budget restaurant occupies a good location close to the sea (opposite Al Shatti Plaza). *Open Sat–Thu.*
✘ **Fuddruckers** ✎ 24 568618. Opposite the CCC in Qurum, serving American cuisine.
✘ **Golden Spoon** ✎ 24 482263, 24 478215. Located on the Khuwair slip road, between the ice skating rink and the Shell petrol station, near McDonald's, serving good Chinese and Indian food. Also at Seeb souk (✎ 24 424204). *Open Sat–Thu 11.30–15.30, 18.00–midnight, Fri 13.00–15.30, 18.00–midnight.*

✖ **Jean's Grill** ☎ 24 567666. Located inside the Sultan Centre (and upstairs) at Qurum, this restaurant/café serves good buffet breakfasts. *Open daily 07.00–23.30.*

✖ **Kamat** ☎ 24 479243, 24 793355, 24 783300. Located in Khuwair/RexRd/Ruwi. An award-winning Indian restaurant. *Open daily 10.00–13.00 and 17.30–23.00.*

✖ **Kargeen Caffe** ☎ 24 692269; f 24 560863; e kargeen@hotmail.com or info@kargeencaffe.com; www.kargeencaffe.com. There are 3 of these in town, but the gem is located in the Madinat Qaboos Shopping Centre area, within one of the courtyards. This unlicensed café is segregated into separate outdoor eating areas, some al fresco, some tented, screened (to enable AC units to function), benched and cushioned, some for traditional eating at ground level, some for families, and some for smoking *shisha*. Overall it imparts a real sense of being in traditional Arabia. An attractive labyrinth and a true oasis, where the bread and food on the international menu is cooked outdoors in full view. There are two other Kargeen outlets: in City Plaza (at Al Khuwair) and Al Harthy complex (in Qurum), but these are indoor and not half as interesting. Kargeen at Madinat Qaboos (MQ) is the one to visit — it is quite unique. *Open 09.30–15.00 and 17.00–01.00.*

✖ **Khana Khazana** ☎ 24 813466. Indian, Chinese and Tandoori restaurant behind Pizza Hut in Ruwi Souk St. *Open 12.15–15.15 and 19.00–23.30.*

✖ **Khyber** ☎ 24 781901. Indian cuisine in the Central Business District (CBD), next to National Bank of Oman, licensed. *Open 12.00–15.00 and 19.00–midnight.*

✖ **Mandarin** ☎ 24 564995. Located at Happy Village, behind Pizza Hut at Qurum, serving good Chinese food, licensed. *Open 12.00–16.00 and 18.30–00.30.*

✖ **Morning Rose** ☎ 24 785960. Behind Air India in the CBD in Ruwi, serving Indian, Arabic and Chinese cuisine.

✖ **The Red Lobster** ☎ 24 591993. Located close to the Ministry of Tourism between Azaiba and Ghubra this is a good cheap licensed restaurant with a large menu and live entertainment from 21.00. Although frequented by locals, and the décor isn't brilliant, you can get some tasty food and a carafe of wine for a good price.

✖ **Silk Route** ☎ 24 561741. Chinese cuisine with Chinese chefs, next to the Automatic Restaurant in Qurum. *Open daily 12.00–15.00 and 18.30–23.30.*

✖ **Woodlands Restaurant** ☎ 24 700192. Located in the CBD in the Europcar Bldg, serving Indian cuisine, licensed. *Open 12.00–15.00 and 18.30–23.30.*

FAST FOOD

✖ **Burger King** Located on Al Khuwair slip road, Al Araimi complex in Qurum.

✖ **Happy Days** Near the Radisson SAS, serving burgers and *shisha*.

✖ **Hardees** At Qurum, Al Khuwair slip road, near airport roundabout, Ruwi, Seeb and Muscat City Centre food court. Chicken fillet served in a variety of ways.

✖ **Kentucky Fried Chicken** At Qurum, Al Khuwair slip road, Muscat City Centre food court, Ruwi High St, Seeb, near airport roundabout, Azaiba roundabout, Lulu Centre in Ghubra and Madina Plaza.

✖ **McDonald's** Behind the CCC at Qurum, Al Khuwair, Muscat City Centre food court, Ghala, Seeb and Saruj Complex. Selling the usual global array of burgers, with the addition of the McArabia grilled kofta.

✖ **Magic Wok** Good Chinese fast food at Muscat City Centre food court.

✖ **Papa John's Pizza** Serving pizza, located in the Lulu Centre in Ghubra.

✖ **Penguin** Located at Ghubra and Seeb. An Omani fast-food brand, selling *halal* products, including chicken, pizzas, kebabs, burgers and fish and chips.

✖ **Pizza Hut** Total of 14 branches in Oman. Eat-in, take-away, or home delivery.

✖ **Pizza Muscat** Located at Al Khuwair and Al Harty Complex in Qurum, serving pizza made with *halal* meat, salads and lasagne.

✖ **Santino's Bistro Italiano** Located in Jawaharat a'Shatti and in Muscat City Centre food court. Serving *antipasti*, pizza, pasta, *calzone*, *risotti* and *insalata zuppa*,

✖ **Shamiana** Located at Muscat City Centre food court. Serving fast Indian food.

✖ **Taza** Located at Al Khuwair. Serving a burger with a difference in toasted *ciabatta*.

PUB FOOD There are many pub-like bars inside the hotels and generally these all serve bar food. Again, the star rating of the hotel usually reflects the price bracket.

Churchill's in the Muscat Holiday Inn, **Duke's Bar** in the Crowne Plaza, **Al Ghazal** in the Intercontinental, **Club Safari** in the Grand Hyatt and **Feeney's** in the Sheraton Qurum Beach Resort are some of the bars popular with expats and locals alike. The **Up Town** restaurant is like an English pub and located on Rex Road, Ruwi (✆ *24 706020*).

COFFEE SHOPS Both **Costa Coffee** and **Starbucks** have a large presence in Muscat now, with outlets at Madinat Qaboos (MQ), Jawharat A'Shatti, Shatti al Qurum (beach road to the Crowne Plaza Hotel), Muscat City Centre food court, Seeb Airport, Lulu in Ghubra, Oasis by the Sea (Shatti al Qurum) and Al Asfoor Plaza in Qurum.

Starbucks and **Second Cup** are the two coffee shops with an excellent location on the beach road running from Shatti al Qurum up to the Crowne Plaza Hotel.

ENTERTAINMENT AND NIGHTLIFE

BARS AND PRIVATE CLUBS There are no independent bars as such. Instead you will find 'pubs' and bars inside hotels and private clubs. There used to be an independent nightclub in the Oasis on the Sea (opposite O Sole Mio Italian restaurant), but the outlets inside this development have now closed for refurbishment (as of February 2006).

You can access a private club only as a guest of a member. If you are lucky enough to have Omani or expat acquaintances, then you can get food and drink in these clubs for a fraction of the amount you pay in the hotels. A couple of these are **Muscat Rugby Club** (✆ *24 604890; www.muscatrugbyclub.com*) located at Al Khuwair and **Civil Aviation Recreational Club (CARC)** (✆ *24 519424*) located at Azaiba Beach.

CINEMAS Films are shown in the capital in English, Arabic, Hindi, Tamil and Malayalam. The cinemas listed below all show films in English. Admission is RO2.

Al Shatti Plaza Shatti al Qurum; ✆ 24 607360, 24 692656. *Open daily 13.30–midnight.*
Ruwi Cinema Ruwi; ✆ 24 780380, 24 7a01564. *Open 09.00–13.00 and 17.00–23.00.*

Star Cinema Central Business District, Ruwi; ✆ 24 791641. *Open daily 14.30–00.30.*
Markaz al Bahja Cinema Al Khoud; ✆ 24 540855. *Open 13.30–02.00.*

NIGHTCLUBS
☆ **Al Hamra** Al Bustan Palace Hotel; ✆ 24 799666
☆ **Saba Nightclub** Sheraton Ruwi Hotel; ✆ 24 799899

☆ **Sur Nightclub** Intercontinental Hotel; ✆ 24 600500
☆ **Copacabana** Grand Hyatt Hotel; ✆ 24 641234

SHOPPING

Evening shopping is a popular pastime with Omani families. There are several modern, air-conditioned **shopping complexes** mainly in the Qurum area, where the highway splits. Each of these complexes, malls or plazas has its own selection of cafés, food courts and play areas and amusements for children, as well as fashion shops, upmarket brand-name products (such as watches and sunglasses), computer shops, sportswear outlets, CDs and DVDs, photographic retailers, electronics, perfumes, florists, opticians, interior design shops, artisanal handmade furniture and gifts, internet cafés, cards and bookshops, footwear, beauty products (for further details see *Qurum* below, page 102). There are also small, modern souks in the Sabco Centre and Capital Commercial Centre, if you haven't the time to visit the real thing in Muttrah.

SUPERMARKETS The supermarkets (dotted about everywhere) have a fantastic selection of fresh fruit and vegetables, fresh breads and hot ready-to-go foods.

Al Fair is an excellent chain of supermarkets and they are worth a browse around, especially if you fancy taking a picnic to the beach or into the mountains. Grab a hot rotisserie chicken, Arabic bread and hummus, *taboule* salad, fruits and cold drinks and head to any close destination (there is plenty of spare beach available). Simply driving the short distance from Al Fair at A'Saruj to Al Shatti Street (the beach road leading up to the Crowne Plaza), parking the car and eating on the beach is great fun. Al Fairs are dotted about throughout the city, another one being at Madinat Qaboos shopping area.

The **Lulu** chain has recently opened two excellent hypermarkets here, one near the Ghubra roundabout (on the mountain-side of the highway) and one at Darsait.

BAKERIES Branches of both the **Muscat Bakery** and **Switz** chains are dotted around the capital and the country and are worth a peek. Try those on the Khuwair slip road, in Ghubra, or Ruwi. You're never far away from a Muscat Bakery.

TAILORS Tailors' outlets too are ubiquitous. Virtually every parade of back street shops in the city has its collection. Try Ruwi, Khuwair or Ghubra. You can take in an article of clothing and they will copy it for you very cheaply in a material of your choice, in no time at all; or, alternatively, select a design from their range of catalogues.

ART AND ARTEFACT GALLERIES AND SHOPS

Abu Qais Decoration and Trading Co Qurum, near Madinat Qaboos; ℡ 24 699956. Art exhibitions by local artists, Omani handicrafts.

Bait al Muzna Gallery Old Muscat; ℡ 24 739204; e baitmgal@omantel.net.om; www.omanart.com. Situated opposite Bait al Zubair Museum in a traditional Omani villa, this gallery showcases both contemporary and traditional art by local and international artists. *Open Sat–Wed 09.30–13.30 and 16.30–20.00, closed Fri.*

Bait Al Turath Al Omani ℡ 24 593719. Sponsored by the Omani Ministry of Heritage and Culture, this place offers traditional weaving, pottery and other crafts. In a shopping plaza by the Porsche showroom in lower Al Khuwair by the ministries. *Open Sat–Wed 07.30–14.30, closed Thu and Fri.*

The Gallery Al Harthy Complex, Qurum; ℡ 24 562269. Selling fine art, originals and prints.

Jibreen Art Gallery Al Araimi Complex; ℡ 24 796925. Selling fine art, originals and prints.

Lamsat Al Khuwair; ℡ 24 698338. Selling paintings by local artist Saleem Bin Sakhi.

Al Madina Art Gallery Rd 2, Villa 1691, Madinat Qaboos; ℡ 24 691380. Selling prints, watercolours and oils.

Majid Trading Enterprises LLC ℡ 24 563098, 24 562370. Located in Al Araimi Complex, Al Harthy Complex and inside the Grand Hyatt.

Majlis Gallery St 44, Villa 57, Azaiba; ℡ 24 501057.

Selling Arabian and colonial antiques, Omani chests, silver jewellery, coffee tables, frankincense candles.

Marina Al Araimi Complex, Qurum; ℡ 24 562221; www.marinagulf.com. Also in Muscat City Centre; ℡ 24 537055 and in Jawharat a'Shatti; ℡ 24 698884. Stocks rustic wooden furniture and other unique furnishings. They arrange international shipping.

Murtada AK Trading Al Noor market, Muttrah souk; ℡ 24 711632, 24 793248. Selling original paintings by Omani artists, gifts, handicrafts and jewellery.

National Trading Co LLC Al Inshirah St, MQ; ℡ 24 601066. Near the British Council, selling restored Arabian and Asian furniture, chests, doors, tables, Omani silver jewellery and weaponry.

Omani Heritage Gallery Jawaharat Al Shatti Shopping Complex, Shatti al Qurum; ℡ 24 696974. Selling Omani handicrafts made by Omani Artisans, a non-profit organisation.

Raj Relics Ghubra; ℡ 99 329842, 24 593131. Behind Bahar soap factory (near the Chedi Hotel), selling antique and reproduction furniture, Indian and Omani chests, antique doors, dining and coffee tables and artefacts.

Riqwa Oman Intercontinental Hotel; ℡ 24 600500. Selling fine art and limited-edition prints.

SA Halela Behind Muttrah souk; ℡ 24 712627. Selling original paintings by Indian artists.

Sabco Souk Sabco Centre, Qurum; ℡ 24 563943. Selling handicrafts and artefacts. Haggling expected.

Tamimah Gallery Muscat Old Town; ☏ 24 737683. Selling Omani antiques, chests, weaponry and silver jewellery. Telephone for an appointment.

Yitti Art Gallery Al Khamis Plaza and CBD; ☏ 24 796073, 24 785696. Selling fine art, limited-edition prints and maps of Arabia.

MEDIA AND COMMUNICATIONS

POST AND COURIER SERVICES Post offices can be found in all residential districts and this is by far the cheapest way of sending letters, postcards or gifts home, costing just baizas rather than rials. Post offices are open generally from 08.00–14.00.

Post offices

Al Harthy Complex ☏ 24 563534	**Muttrah** ☏ 24 711633
Hamriya ☏ 24 789311	**Ruwi** ☏ 24 701651
Madinat a'Sultan Qaboos ☏ 24 697083	**Al Wadi al Kabir** ☏ 24 816275
Muscat ☏ 24 738547	**Seeb** ☏ 24 519922

In addition, there are branches of the major international courier services in the city:

DHL Rumaila Bldg, 106 Sultan Qaboos St, Wattayah, PO Box 818, Al Hamriya 131, Muscat 112. *Open Sat–Thu 07.00–21.00, Fri 09.00–18.00.*
FedEx Sinaw Hse, opposite Al Nahda Hospital; ☏ 24 793311; f 24 795554. FedEx is represented in Oman by a nominated service contractor. For further information call Oman Postal Express (☏ 24 833311; f 24 835554).

INTERNET Internet cafés can generally be found within the shopping complexes at Qurum and Al Khuwair, as well as within some residential areas in the rows of smaller shops on the street. These all charge far less than the business centres of the hotels.

OTHER PRACTICALITIES

USEFUL TELEPHONE NUMBERS
Hospitals

Khoula Hospital ☏ 24 563625, 24 560455	**Royal Hospital** ☏ 24 592888, 24 599000, 24 590491
Muscat Hospital ☏ 24 738036	
Al Nahda Hospital ☏ 24 707800, 24 837800	**Al Shatti Hospital** ☏ 24 604263
Quriyat Hospital ☏ 24 645003	**Sultan Qaboos Hospital** ☏ 24 211151

EMBASSIES AND CONSULATES IN MUSCAT Many countries have embassies in Oman, and these are largely concentrated in the Shatti al Qurum diplomatic area of Muscat (close to the A'Saruj area). Opening hours generally are 08.00–14.00, with some slight variations. They are closed on Thursdays and Fridays.

Austria PO Box 2070, PC 112, Ruwi; ☏ 24 793135, 24 793145; f 24 793669; e maskat-ob@ bmaa.gv.at; www.austriantrade.org; location: Moosa Abdul Rahman Hassan Complex, Bldg No 477
Bahrain PO Box 66, PC 115, Madinat Al Sultan Qaboos; ☏ 24 605074, 24 605075, 24 605133; f 24 605072; location: Shatti Al Qurum, Way No 3017, Villa No1345
Belgium (consulate) Al Wattayah, Al Rawahy Bldg; ☏ 24 562033, 24 563011; f 24 564905

Canada (consulate) Flat 310, Bldg 477, Way 2907, Moosa Abdul Rahman Hassan Bldg, A'Noor St, Ruwi; e canada_consulate_oman@hotmail.com
Cyprus (consulate) PO Box 603, PC 113; ☏ 24 590200, 24 590285; f 24 590699; location: Al Azaiba, J & P Camp Azaiba
Denmark (consulate) PO Box 1040, PC 112, Ruwi; ☏ 24 708304; f 24 793892; location: W J Bldg, MBD
Egypt PO Box 2252, PC 112, Ruwi; ☏ 24 600411,

24 600982; f 24 603626; location: Diplomatic Area, Jami'at al Dowal al Arabiya St
Finland (consulate) PO Box 84, PC 113; ✆ 24 702133; f 24 703826; location: Getco Tower, MBD Area, Bldg No 1704, Way No 2726
France PO Box 208, PC 115, Madinat al Sultan Qaboos; ✆ 24 681800; f 24 681843; www.ambafrance-om.org; location: Al Khuwair, Diplomatic Area, Jami'at al Dowal al Arabiya St
Germany PO Box 128, PC 112, Ruwi; ✆ 24 832164, 24 832482; f 24 835690; e diplofrg@omantel.net.om
Iran PO Box 3155, PC 112, Ruwi; ✆ 24 696944, 24 696947, 24 696919; f 24 696888; location: Diplomatic Area, Jami'at al Dowal al Arabiya
Ireland (consulate) PO Box 424, PC 113, Ruwi; ✆ 24 701282, 24 797083; f 24 701278; location: OC Centre, 8th Fl, Suite 807
Italy PO Box 3727, PC 112, Ruwi; ✆ 24 560968, 24 564832, 24 564838, 24 695223; f 24 564846; e ambamasc@omantel.net.om; location: Al Qurum, Hse No 842, Way No 2411
Jordan PO Box 70, PC 130, Al Azaiba; ✆ 24 692760, 24 692761; f 24 692762; location: Diplomatic Area, Jami'at al Dowal al Arabiya St
Kuwait PO Box 1798, PC 112, Ruwi; ✆ 24 699626, 24 699627, 24 696095; f 24 600972; location: Diplomatic Area, Jami'at al Dowal al Arabiya St
Lebanon PO Box 67, PC 118; ✆ 24 695844, 24 693208; f 24 695633; location: Shatti al Qurum, Villa No 1613, Way No 3019
Netherlands PO Box 3302, PC 112, Ruwi; ✆ 24 603706, 24 603719; f 24 603778, 24 602254; location: Shatti al Qurum, Villa No 1366, Way No 3017
New Zealand (consulate) PO Box 520, PC 113, Muttrah; ✆ 24 794932, 24 795726, 24 786039; f 24 706443; location: Muttrah St, Bldg No 387, Way No 3007
Norway (consulate) PO Box 89, PC 112, Ruwi; ✆ 24 708304, 24 703289; f 24 793892; location: W J Towell Bldg
Portugal (consulate) PO Box 1812, PC 112, Ruwi; ✆ 24 561400; f 24 562377; location: Al Watteyah,

Al Asfoor Furnishing LLC
Qatar PO Box 802, Muscat; ✆ 24 691152, 24 691153, 24 691154; f 24 691156; location: Diplomatic Area, Jami'at al Dowal al Arabiya St
Russia PO Box 80, PC 112, Ruwi; ✆ 24 602894; f 24 604189; location: Shatti al Qurum, Way No 3032, Surfait Housing
Saudi Arabia PO Box 1411, PC 112, Ruwi; ✆ 24 601744, 24 601743, 24 601791; f 24 603540; location: Diplomatic Area, Jami'at al Dowal al Arabiya St
Spain (consulate) PO Box 3376, PC 112, Ruwi; ✆ 24 698381; f 24 695796; e spanishconsulatemct@hotmail.com or spaconsl@omantel.net.om; location: Shatti al Qurum, Villa No 1386, Way No 2818, Villa 1386
Sweden (consulate) PO Box 1, PC 112, Ruwi; ✆ 24 708693; f 24 794283; location: 8th Fl, Bahwan Business Centre Bldg
Switzerland (consulate) PO Box 385, PC 118, Al Harthy Complex; ✆ 24 568202; f 24 568206; location: Al Asfoor Plaza, Qurum, 1st Fl, Flat No 104
Syria PO Box 85, PC 115, Madinat al Sultan Qaboos; ✆ 24 697904, 24 695917; f 24 603895; location: Madinat al Sultan Qaboos, Al Inshirah St, Villa No 201
Turkey PO Box 47, PC 115, Madinat al Sultan Qaboos; ✆ 24 697050, 24 697051; f 24 697053; location: Shatti al Qurum, Villa No 3270, Way No 3042
United Arab Emirates PO Box 55, PC 111; ✆ 24 600302, 24 600988; f 24 602584; e uaeoman@omantel.net.om
United Kingdom PO Box 300, PC 113; ✆ 24 693077, 24 609000; f 24 693 087; www.britishembassy.gov.uk/oman; location: Diplomatic Area, Jami'at al Dowal al Arabiya St
United States PO Box 202, PC 115, Madinat al Sultan Qaboos; ✆ 24 698989, 24 699049; f 24 604316, 24 699778; www.muscat.usembassy.gov; location: Diplomatic Area, Jami'at al Dowal al Arabiya St
Yemen PO Box 105, PC 115, Madinat al Sultan Qaboos; ✆ 24 600815, 24 604172; f 24 605008; location: Shatti al Qurum, Bldg No 2981, Way No 1840

MISSIONS
UNICEF PO Box 3787, PC 112, Ruwi; ✆ 24 602624, 24 601398; f 24 698429; location: Al Khuwair National Automobiles Bldg (BMW), 1st Fl

WHO PO Box 1889, PC 112, Ruwi; ✆ 24 600989, 24 602177, 24 605860; f 24 602637; location: Ministry of Health Bldg

WHAT TO SEE AND DO

There is a variety of things to see and do in the capital area, including scuba diving, dolphin, whale, and birdwatching, dhow cruising, fishing, watersports, sailing, beach walking and jogging (for further information see *Excursions beyond Muscat*, page 115). There are museums, mosques and forts to visit, or you can shop in the souks and modern shopping complexes. You can opt for a tour with one of the many tour operators, or hire a car and travel independently. For the less active, there are endless beaches and bays within the capital that are crying out for you to relax, perhaps with a picnic. Or if you don't want to move, there is the beach or pool of your hotel.

BIRDWATCHING Birdwatching sites in the capital include Qurum Natural Park, Al Ansab Lagoons, the gardens of the Intercontinental and Grand Hyatt hotels, and any of the beaches.

In Qurum Natural Park species such as the purple sunbird, Indian silverbill, laughing dove, Indian roller, little green bee-eater, yellow-vented bulbul, graceful prinia, grey francolin, the common mynah and the house crow are likely to be spotted. On the beaches species such as western reef heron, swift tern and sooty gull will undoubtedly be seen. For further detailed information, any of the publications by Hanne and Jens Eriksen are highly recommended (for details see *Appendix 3*, page 276). Speak to any tour operator in the capital if you would like to join a set birding excursion.

DIVING

Dive sites *Al Munassir* wreck was offered by the Royal Navy of Oman for an artificial reef project and was sunk on 22 April 2003. It is a short boat trip away from Marina Bander al Rowdha. Fahal Island, 4km offshore, is also a short boat trip away.

Diving here involves finning through an L-shaped tunnel through the island. There are many corals to be seen and the area attracts numerous sharks. Other popular dive sites include Cemetery Bay, Cat Island, just off the coast of the Marine Science & Fisheries Centre at Sidab, and the Kalbou area (east of Muttrah harbour). East of Al Bustan Palace Hotel there are the three bay areas of Bander Jissah, Bander Khayran and As Sheik. Any dive centre will provide you with further information.

Dive centres

Bluzone Watersports Oman Marina Bander al Rowdha, PO Box 940, Muscat 113; ✆ 24 737293; f 24 737293; e bluzone@omantel.net.om; www.bluzonediving.com. This is a PADI Gold Palm resort and a BSAC resort diving centre, offering 2 dives in the morning with the option of a single dive in the afternoon or a night dive. Scuba courses of all levels can be taken here. It is possible to complete the basic level course in 4 days (courses available during the week, weekend or evenings) with their qualified instructors, although, if you want to combine diving with sightseeing and relaxation, it may be an idea to take all the theory aspect of the course in your home town and simply complete the practical side of things out here. Equipment can be hired here, and dive masters are on hand. Bluzone offers dolphin-watching expeditions, snorkelling lessons and trips and sunset coastal cruises, in addition to arranging dive packages with the Ruwi Hotel, Al Falaj Hotel and Golden Oasis at RO40 pp per night based on a dbl room sharing, including b/fast, 2 dives pp with tanks and weights provided, dive permits, tax, and tea/coffee/water on the boat. This is booked through Bluzone. Accepts credit cards. There is a licensed pool bar and restaurant.

Euro Divers Dive Centre ✆ 24 776666. This is to be located at the Shangri-La's Barr al Jissah Resort, but as of July 2006 there was no information available. Check with the Shangri-La for updates.

Muscat Diving & Adventure Centre The Boat House, Grand Hyatt, Muscat, Shatti al Qurum; ✆ 24 602101; f 24 602542; e diveco@omantel.net; www.holiday-in-oman.com. Operating from the beach of the Grand Hyatt and offering all of the stock dive tours around Muscat.

Oman Dive Centre/Extra Divers Muscat Barr al Jissah, ✆ 24 824241, 24 824240, 99 379031; f 24 824241; e muscat@extra-divers.li or info@omandivecenter.com, www.extra-divers.li or

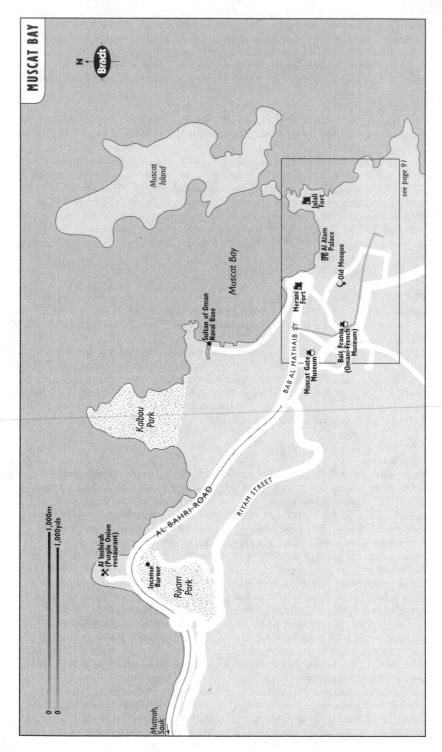

MUSCAT BAY

N

Bradt

Muscat
Island

Muscat Bay

Sultan of Oman
Naval Base

Jalali
Fort

Al Alam
Palace

Old Mosque

Merani
Fort

BAB AL MATHAIB ST

Muscat Gate
Museum

Bait Fransa
(Omani-French
Museum)

see page 91

Kalbou
Park

AL BAHRI ROAD

RIYAM STREET

Al Inshirah
(Purple Onion
restaurant)

Incense
Burner

Riyam
Park

Muttrah,
Souk

0   1,000m
0   1,000yds

www.omandivecenter.com or www.diveoman.com.om. Located in its own peaceful bay, the Oman Dive Centre is a PADI Gold Palm 5-star resort and is managed by Extra Divers Worldwide. They have 4 custom-made boats and offer: 1 dive RO12; 2 tank dives RO22; night dive RO15 (mininum 4 people); snorkelling RO10/6 am/pm. Courses include Discover Scuba (full day) RO32; Open Water diver (3–4 days) RO140; Advanced Open Water (5 dives) RO100. Dolphin watching RO15; coastal cruise RO15. For dives, proof of dive certification and logbook is required. It has AC, equipped, traditional Omani *barasti* beach huts in which you can stay (RO30/38/42 low/mid/high season, includes b/fast and dinner, under 12s half price). There is a licensed restaurant called The Odyssey (*open 07.00–16.30 and 18.00–22.00*). To get there follow the road towards Al Bustan Palace. As you descend the hill take the right-hand exit directing you to Qantab. This road winds up and over the mountains, towards the new Shangri-La resort. When you come to the first roundabout take a left. This leads down to the dive centre. Camping is no longer permitted here.

HEALTH CLUBS Health and fitness clubs and gyms can be found in most of the hotels in Oman and, as expected, the standards vary according to the star rating of the venue. If you are resident in the country you can arrange annual membership at most of the clubs. If you are a guest, then usage is included in your room rate. Non-guests can use the gym and pool facilities of most hotels for the day, for a charge of approx RO2 per person plus taxes – check with the specific venue.

SPORTS

Bowling There is City Bowling opposite the Holiday Inn Hotel in Al Khuwair (↘ 24 541277), and one in Al Hail in the Markaz al Bahja. The Sheraton Hotel at Ruwi have a bowling alley (↘ 24 772772) and a further bowling centre is being constructed opposite the Saruj Centre in Shatti al Qurum.

Golf 'Brown' golf courses (sand) exist in Muscat. Call Jeff Hutchenson (↘ 23 467192); Ghala Wentworth (↘ 24 591248) or Al Maha Golf Club (↘ 24 522177). There are currently no 18-hole green golf courses on offer to the tourist in the capital area. However, there is the Muscat Golf Course Project (*MGCP;* ↘ 24 510065; *www.muscatgolf.com*) scheduled for completion at the end of 2006, which will be the Muscat Golf and Country Club. This is to be an internationally recognised 18-hole PGA championship-standard golf course, with world-class tournaments envisaged for 2007, and is the first green golf course in Oman (there is a 9-hole green golf course at the Crowne Plaza, Salalah). There will be a clubhouse, a restaurant, swimming pools, tennis and squash courts, as well as a driving range and a 9-hole practice course.

Horseriding

The Royal Stables at Seeb (↘ 24 420444) are considered one of the top riding arenas for watching equestrian events, although the best breeders and trainers are located in Al Kamil and Al Wafi regions in the Sharqiya. The Royal Stables offers horse riding lessons and trails. Riding groups are kept small in the interests of safety, and are accompanied by an experienced guide.

Other riding schools are based within easy reach of Muscat, at Qurum Natural Park and by the sea:

Qurum Equestrian School ↘ 99 832199; f 24 703006. Located in Qurum Natural Park and is signposted once inside the park. For an hour's ride it is RO8, but if there is a group of you, this reduces to RO6 pp, with a maximum of 6 people in the group.

Al Sawahil Horse Riding ↘ 95 177557; e ahmad-565@hotmail.com; open 16.00–19.00. Located at the seaside, behind the park, at Al Bahja, Al Hail. RO7 per hour for lessons; beach RO10 per hour for a ride along the beach. Beginners welcome.

Shah Mohammed al Khalili \ 99 386978; f 24 692300. Located in Qurum Natural Park. Shah Mohammed will meet you and your group at the main gate of the park. Beginners are welcome and can take a ride through the park and along the beach for RO10. For the more experienced, the ride can be tailored to you. An experienced guide accompanies all rides. Lessons are also available at RO10, however, if you have a group of 4 people (which is the maximum number for a group ride), this reduces to RO7.

Seeb Horse Riding Centre \ 24 603501, 24 694303. Horseriding trails.

Ice skating

Al Khuwair Centre Ice Rink \ 24 489492. Regular sessions Sat–Thu 09.00–20.00, Fri 11.30–20.00. Sessions cost RO2.50 inc skates, RO2 exc skates.

Motorsports

Oman Automobile Association \ 24 510239, 24 510630, 24 522177. Offers go karts, motorbikes, motorcross/dirt bikes, rallies, golf, softball, football, basketball, tennis, table tennis, BMX bicycles, children's playground, remote-controlled cars, roller skates, skateboards and cricket. There is also a campsite and party hall.

ACTIVITIES AND SPORTS CLUBS FOR THE LONG-STAY VISITOR For those planning a longer stay in Oman, or, more specifically, in Muscat, there are excellent health clubs attached to the larger hotels which you can join. There are also several sports clubs:

Team sports

Basketball Oman Basketball Association \ 24 793802

Cricket Oman Cricket Association \ 24 703142; British Cricket Club \ 24 673910; Oman Cricket Club \ 24 791270

Football Muscat United Football Club \ 24 542920

Hockey RAH Hockey Club Muscateers \ 24 675355

Netball PDO \ 24 675334; Red Devils Costains \ 24 595011

Rugby Muscat Rugby Club \ 24 604890; Women's Rugby Team \ 24 544806; Dhofar Nomads Rugby Club \ 99 291548

Softball Muscat Softball League \ 24 680453, 99 336015, 99 235291

Volleyball Oman Volleyball Association \ 24 705567

Cycling and running

Cycling Muscat Cycling Club \ 99 324594

Running Muscat Hash House Harriers \ 24 316127; Jebel Hash House Harriers \ 24 494226; Oman Athletic Association \ 24 797233; Muscat Road Runners \ 24 692903

Watersports

Sailing and boating Beach Catamaran Owners Club \ 24 604307; Capital Area Yacht Club CAYC \ 24 737712; Castaways Sailing Club \ 24 494751; Civil Aviation Yacht and Beach Club \ 24 519424; Marina Bandar Al Rowdha \ 24 737288

Racquet games

Squash Muscat Squash League \ 24 677414

Tennis Oman Tennis Association \ 24 751402; Muscat Tennis League \ 24 675210

Motorsports

Bikers Oman claims to be 'the most happening bikers' fraternity in Oman today', participating in motorbikers' events and 'members only' events with discounts on accessories among other benefits www.bikersoman.com. There is also the Harley-Davidson Owners' Group \ 99 310853, otherwise known as the HOG. There is an annual HOG Middle Eastern Rally held in Muscat or Dubai. In 2006, this will be from 6–9 December in Muscat. There is a Harley-Davidson dealership at Khuwair Muscat Bikers; \ 24 561749

Other

Bridge Muscat Ladies \ 24 590167; Muscat Open \ 24 797597

Darts Oman Darts Club \ 24 618426

Game fishing Muscat Game Fishing Club \ 99 322779

Muttrah is superficially similar to its close neighbour (Muscat Old Town) with its bowl-shaped harbour and seafront crescent of impressive merchant houses. Its solitary fort is smaller than the Merani or Jalali forts in Muscat's bay, perched up on a rocky crag guarding the harbour. It too is out of bounds to visitors, as it is still in use by the military police.

Muttrah has less political significance than Muscat, yet it has always been larger than Muscat with a bigger souk and at least three times the population. The port here was the traditional starting point for commercial caravans to the interior. The city gate was ceremonially shut and guarded at night until the 1970s.

The modern Mina Qaboos Port (completed in 1974) has replaced the ancient trading port and now fills most of the bay. The traditional industries of the area include perfumery, the crafting of silver and gold, weaving, textiles and fishing.

Close to the fish roundabout (As Samakah roundabout), at the beginning of the corniche, there is a group of budget hotels: The Corniche, Marina Hotel, Al Nahdah Hotel, Marina Hotel and Al Fanar Hotel are grouped together at the very end, and Al Mina Hotel is a little further along the corniche towards the souk (see *Where to stay*, page 75). It is good to stay in one of these, if only for one night, to get a real sense of being in the Oman of old. Request a room at the front of the hotel for the views up the corniche. Or take the lift up to the bar of the Marina Hotel and sit on the terrace, with a glass of something nice, and watch the sun go down in this evocative and historical setting – the night lights of both the port and the minarets come on, and the call to prayer starts up.

If you need to pick up your emails, there is an internet café just past the Muttrah

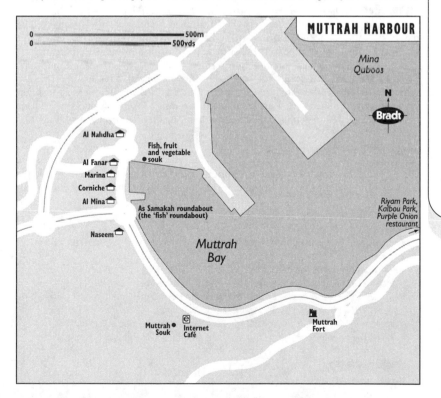

souk entrance (400bzs per hour's usage). If you don't want to walk the corniche, taxis are plentiful.

WHAT TO SEE

Muttrah souk (*Open Sat–Thu 09.00–13.00 and 16.30–23.00, Fri 16.30–23.00*). Muttrah souk (or *Souk al Dhalam* – Market of Shades) is the oldest in Oman and the most popular with visitors. This is probably due, in part, to its accessibility and proximity to the airport (it can easily be visited by short-stay visitors), as well as the fact that it occupies such a scenic location on Muttrah harbour. Since completion of the modernisation project for the corniche for the 35th National Day (in 2005), the souk now is adorned with a domed entrance. So, if you had problems finding the entrance before, you won't now.

The souk consists of a covered intricate labyrinth of stalls, curio shops and winding alleys, more extensive and complex than anywhere else in the country. Indian merchants are predominant. Even in the 1960s you could buy a Chinese tricycle, a Mexican gold sovereign, an old bedstead or a Penguin paperback. The basis of the economy in trading here was selling dates and limes in exchange for cloth, rice and coffee. Today you can buy coffee pots, incense burners, rose-water sprinklers, henna, Arabic coffee, oregano, dried limes, dried chilli peppers, frankincense, perfumes, pashminas, *dishdashas*, antiques, gold, silver, chests, rugs, handicrafts and even the essential Teletubby. Khanjars are popular souvenirs. The aromas from the spices, the incense and the perfume shops evoke an exotic sense of Arabia. In all of the souks, friendly haggling is expected. Try one of the fantastic milkshakes or fruit juices in the air-conditioned juice shops. The souk can get busy in the evenings.

Riyam Park (*Open Sat–Thu 15.00–midnight, Fri 08.00–midnight*). This well-maintained park overlooks the sea in the Muttrah area and is clearly landmarked by the large model incense burner that sits atop a cliff. There is a children's playground. It is a lovely, peaceful spot to wander around in the early evening.

Kalbou Park (*Open Sat–Wed 15.00–23.00, Fri 08.00–midnight*). This smaller park also overlooks the sea at Muttrah, but is located on the seaward edge, close to Al Inshirah (which is now the site of the Purple Onion Restaurant). Take a left into small village of Kalbou. Snacks and drinks can be bought here. Again, it is another lovely spot.

MUSCAT OLD TOWN

The original old town of Muscat, although only small in area, held a strategic commanding position on the entrance to the Persian Gulf, and so was chosen for

---

SHIFTING CAPITALS

Throughout its history, Oman's capital has moved locations and, although the dates are unclear, it has at various times been assigned to Qalhat, Sohar, Bahla, Nizwa and Rustaq, according to the various ruling imams and sultans. Muscat has been its capital since 1786, when the third Al Bu Said leader established residence there.

Prior to 1970, Muscat was classed as separate from Oman and the country as a whole was known as Muscat and Oman, Oman being the interior and distinctly different in character from coastal Muscat. Sultan Qaboos – the current ruler – unified the country, naming it simply Oman, and today, Muscat is the hub: the site of the main international airport, the embassies, ministries, international banks and large businesses.

its excellent harbour and natural defences. Prior to 1929, Muscat was so ringed by steep jagged rocks that it was accessible only by sea or by footpaths over the hills behind, each of which was closely guarded by watchtowers.

The first land approach by vehicle was made possible in 1929 by the hacking out of a one-lane track through the mountains by the British Royal Engineers. The name 'Muscat' means 'place of falling', thought to refer to the falling of the anchor chain (a reference to the harbour).

In the late 1830s one European said of Muscat:

> With all its barrenness and unpromising appearance, such is the advantage of position enjoyed by Muscat, commanding, as it does, the entrance to the Persian Gulf, that its harbours are filled with vessels from all ports of the East, and the busy din of commerce constantly enlivens its streets. In few parts of the world can the necessaries, nay even the luxuries, of life, be obtained in greater profusion.

With such an isolated location it is surprising that Muscat was favoured as the capital city. Muttrah, just a few bays further west, had direct access to the hinterland and was just as good a harbour as Muscat, yet was considered to be a more suitable commercial rather than political capital. Muscat also had very little fresh water within its walls, and the ring of bare hills served as a bowl which magnified the extreme heat and humidity trapped within them, preventing any cooling breezes off the sea from fanning the walled town.

The town walls which stand today were built round about the time of the Portuguese. There were only three gates: the Bab Saghir (small gate) was for pedestrians and donkeys, Bab Kabeer (big gate) was the main gate for smallish vehicles and Bab Mathaib (or Matha'eeb) was the third, used by large vehicles only permitted to drive between Muttrah and Muscat, and even then only with special dispensation granted infrequently. Curfews were imposed on the residents of Muscat; the Bab Kabeer main gate was shut three hours after sunset and could only be opened after that with special written permission from the *wali* (governor). Anyone walking within the walls at this time had to carry a *butti* (a lantern). To ensure everyone remembered, a drum was beaten from the top of Fort Merani for 20 minutes beforehand, followed by three explosions, three hours after sunset. In Muttrah there was one explosion instead of three, and even long after the gate was detached from its wall, it was still ceremonially closed each night because no one gave the order to stop doing so. Different tribes had responsibility for different

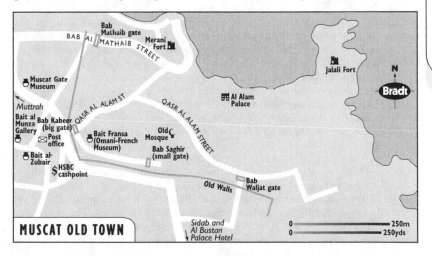

MUSCAT OLD TOWN

It was from the harbour of Muscat on 23 November 1980 that Tim Severin's ship, *The Sohar*, set sail as part of Oman's tenth National Day celebrations. It was the start of a 6,000-mile journey to China and took place amid cannon fire, bands playing and tears streaming down the face of every Omani who had been involved in building the remarkable ship. It took 165 days to build, ahead of schedule.

The project had been three years in the planning and Severin lived in the country for 12 months during the preparations and the building of the boat in Sur. He was given a mansion, rented for him by the Ministry of National Heritage and Culture, in Sur in 1980. The house was built 200 years previously by wealthy Sur merchants, had a large courtyard, and was made of crushed coral. He lived in the upper rooms where the original owners would have lived, and even in the height of summer the 3ft-thick walls and wooden shutters kept the rooms cool. When he first arrived, the place was filthy, with goats browsing in the rooms and a cow penned in the yard; it took nearly two weeks for it to be cleaned up by a veritable army of 20 workers. The house was set on slightly raised ground on the foreshore, close enough to walk to the spot where the boat would be built, but too far away to sneak back to during the day.

The boat was built in traditional fashion using timbers held together with coconut rope and painted with fish oil and sugar. Severin went to the coast of Malabar in India (1,300 miles away) to get timber for the ship. All timber for Omani ships had originally come from there, since Oman had always lacked trees large enough to provide first-class boat timber. Severin and his men made excursions into the forest to hand-pick the timber, called *aini*, which did not need to be seasoned for boat building.

Severin's boat was named *The Sohar* (which was reputedly Sindbad's birthplace) on the express wish of the sultan, who sponsored the entire project as a tribute to Oman's seafaring heritage. The journey took a total of seven months to sail to China. The first stretch from Muscat to Calcutta took one month. There was a crew of 28, eight of them Omani traditional sailors, all volunteers. All but one of these married young Muslim girls when they docked in Calcutta – a custom as old as the hills. They never had any intention of returning, but had to pay the girl a sum of money, which her family eagerly accepted. There was no stigma attached, even some pride in fact, and after three years the girls were free to marry again if the husband did not return. Indeed, Sindbad himself seemed to acquire a wife at every port. On the recreated journey, boxes of nuts, dried fruit, hundreds of eggs wrapped in sawdust, sacks of onions, dried peas, rice and spices were stowed aboard along with tinned foods, sauces, Omani dates and fresh fruit. The bilges stank of rotten eggs, giving off hydrogen sulphide gas. The navigation manual which Tim Severin took on board was written by a master of 15th-century navigation – Ibn Majid, from Sur – one of the most skilled seafarers of his time. It was however difficult to follow, not least because it was written in verse. Severin managed, however, on the strength of this manual, and after some practice, to navigate from the Pole Star using nothing more than a piece of string with a knot and cardboard. Severin's book, *The Voyage of Sindbad*, was published in 1983 (see book list on page 277). The dhow now sits on the roundabout at Al Bustan Palace Hotel in Muscat.

gates: the Hawasina provided ten guards each for the Bab Saghir and Bab Mathaib, while the Beni Umr guarded the Bab Kabeer Gate.

The Al Bu Said dynasty, of which Sultan Qaboos is the current representative, made Muscat its seat of power in the latter half of the 18th century. The old houses were built c1820–40. Though huge from the outside, they had surprisingly small living spaces, usually just the first floor being habitable with some five rooms. The ground floor tended to be lost to a spacious hall, a small guardroom by the entrance, and lots of tiny windowless storerooms. Even the inner walls were massively thick, up to 1m, to help keep the rooms cool in summer. Their design was a mix of Arab, Persian, Indian and African styles. On the flat roof there was generally a raised wooden platform, high enough to give a view over the rampart wall, offering a peaceful spot on summer evenings to catch the breeze. In the late 1800s, Muscat was said to have a faintly zoological quality with a tame lion and ostrich roaming the streets, together with an elephant that would regularly plod round to the British consulate where he was duly given sugar lumps. Descriptions of the magnificent consulate built around 1880 all speak of its splendid flagstoned veranda, overlooking the harbour and towered over by Fort Jalali (at that time the sultan's main prison), as one of the 'noblest' in the world. It was demolished in the mid 1990s to improve the view from Al Alam Palace – the sultan's palace – and to make way for more palace buildings.

Until the 1960s most of Muscat's houses were supplied with water by donkeys strapped with pairs of four-gallon tin drums or even by men trudging to and from Wadi Kabeer with goat skins. Only a handful of privileged houses were supplied by private pipelines. As there were no newspapers or radio stations, under Said bin Taimur's rule (Qaboos's father), his only means of communicating with his people was by notice board. So the gates of Muscat were utilised as message boards, announcing matters to the Omani people. Said bin Taimur's first ever public statement was made by this means in 1968 and was entitled 'the word of Sultan Said bin Taimur, Sultan of Muscat and Oman, about the history of the financial position of the sultanate in the past and the hopes for the future, after the export of oil'. Bin Taimur also had total control over all imports to the country. No car could be imported for example without his express permission, and there were no tractors in the sultanate because he refused to give permission for them to be imported. Sometimes if he forgot or failed to reply to a request, new businesses which had already invested in buildings were left waiting over six months in limbo, unable, after all, to send reminders to the sultan himself.

GETTING THERE To get here, take the Qurum Heights Road (which is the exit on the right of the highway just before the Qurum roundabout, where the highway splits) and then follow signs to Muscat and Al Madina Sultan Qaboos.

WHAT TO SEE The sultan's modest palace was built in the 1970s at its seafront location here in the old town. Its blue-and-gold colouring make it an unusual spectacle. If you take a boat trip (arranged through any tour operator) you will be able to observe the immaculate lawn which extends from the palace to the seafront.

A good half-day trip would be to combine an exploration of both Muscat Old Town and Muttrah corniche and souk.

Jalali and Merani forts The Portuguese began to build these forts in 1527, though their current versions date from 1587 and 1588 respectively. They were originally known as São João and Fort Capitan. Neither is open to the general public.

Until recently, Jalali was Oman's main jail, with many sinister tales of torture under the old sultan, Said bin Taimur. British army officers can still recall the awful conditions inside and one such officer remembers how during interrogation of a rebel of the Jebel War, he dangled the suspect rebel out of a high window by his *dishdasha* in an attempt to persuade him to talk. When the *dishdasha* began suddenly to rip, the British officer pulled him in quickly in a panic, but the Omani was so terrified by the experience that he told all he knew forthwith.

Qaboos's father, Said bin Taimur, had no links outside his country except with Britain and India, the only two countries to have consulates in Muscat before 1970. He considered membership of such bodies as the United Nations completely unnecessary and useless, especially as its first early involvement with Oman was to condemn Britain for aggression when it responded to his request for help in the 1957 imamate revolution, stating that Oman's right to self-determination was being prevented by the United Kingdom. The old sultan's relations with his Arab neighbours and brethren were also hostile, not least because several of them had imamate in Arab capitals like Baghdad, Damascus, Cairo, Riyadh and Kuwait. The imamates was the opposition led by Ghalib, Talib, Suleyman bin Himyar and Salih bin Isa, and they were seeking independence for the tribal-led interior of Oman (considered the Oman 'proper'). The sultan was therefore hostile to Omanis who left Oman to seek education in these conniving countries, and whom he would not then allow to return to Oman to take jobs. Ghalib was the imam-in-waiting; Talib – his brother, Suleyman – a political opportunist and Salih – an old man with little tribal influence. Sheikh Zayed of Abu Dhabi was the only neighbour whom the sultan trusted and had time for. He once invited Zayed to Salalah and he came, after which they had a hotline installed between them. Logically, from a geographical point of view, Oman would have done well to link up in a Trucial States Federation with the Emirates – its agricultural potential and larger population (750,000 in 1968) would have complemented perfectly Abu Dhabi's colossal oil wealth, Dubai's merchant spirit and the tiny Emirates populations. Together they would have made a viable state – but personalities made such a vision impossible. Those who were true tribal Omanis of the interior remained very cut off from the commercial activity of the coast, and therefore the big Muscat or Muttrah merchant could not easily expand through branches into the interior.

Today Jalali can be visited only by VIPs with special permits. It is still in use as a garrison for Omani troops.

Merani (also Mirani) is still the headquarters of the Muscat garrison and in the 1960s was described as a homely military barracks with iron bedsteads and socks dangling over the bed rails. Besides these forts, nothing remains of the Portuguese occupation of Muscat. Some remnants of the cathedral and the governor's residence and barracks survived as late as 1895, but were then knocked down to make way for other dignitaries' buildings.

Museums

Bait Fransa (Omani–French Museum) (*Qasr Al Alam St, Old Muscat;* ☏ *24 736613; open Sat–Thu 09.00–13.00; admission 500/200bzs adults/children 6–12*) is on the right-hand side after going through the gate (under the Gate Museum). Parking is not easy in the old town, but there is a small car park here and with persistence it is usually possible to find a space.

Bait Fransa (or French House) was the original French consulate and now is a museum chronicling Omani–French historical links from the 18th century. Although no French consul arrived to live in Muscat until 1894, there had been attempts to send one since a decree in 1795 (issued in Paris) announced the establishment of a Muscat consulate. Mr Beauchamp, the first appointee, spent four years in Egypt en route to the post and was then diverted to Constantinople by Napoleon in 1799, where he was arrested and imprisoned. The next attempt was in 1802 when Talleyrand and Napoleon appointed Cavaignac as consul. On arrival in

Muscat in 1803 Cavaignac found the imam out of town (he was further up the coast fighting Wahhabi incursions) and was told he could neither disembark his baggage nor occupy the house that had been made available until the imam returned and gave his express permission. When the imam did eventually return, he did not give permission and Cavaignac was obliged to leave. Bitterly he wrote of Oman *'Ce pays et ses inhabitants sont tout à fait misérables. Le souverain n'est qu'un clef de Bédouins'* – 'This country and its people are simply wretched. The sultan is nothing but a Bedouin pawn.' The lease of the house was returned to the Omani government in 1945, despite the fact the last French consul to live there left in 1920.

Bait Al Zubair (*Al Saidiya St, Old Muscat;* ↘ *24 736688;* f *24 740913;* e *bazubair@ omantel.net.om; open Sat–Thu 09.00–13.00 and 16.00–19.00; admission RO1/500bzs/ 250bzs expats/Omanis/children*) This museum is signposted off the Muscat to Muttrah road. Go through the gate and just past the bend and it is on the right-hand side, with its own car park. There are daily tours of this traditional Omani townhouse at 11.30 and 17.30. Opened in February 1998 as an Omani heritage museum and cultural centre, this museum is set in a renovated historic house, designed to give an insight into Omani lifestyles and traditions.

Inside there is a small lecture theatre, gift shop and coffee shop as well as a reference library and a *majlis* (meeting room) with an exhibition of old maps, seafaring information and models of traditional dhows. The museum on the ground floor displays khanjars, men's dress, swords and weapons, women's dresses, jewellery, chests and household items, all well labelled and explained. Outside there are reconstructions of traditional stone and *barasti* houses, even with a working model of a pottery kiln.

Muscat Gate Museum (*Al Bahri Rd;* ↘ *24 739005, 99 328754; open Sat–Thu 09.30–11.30 and 16.30–19.00*). This museum is operated by Royal Court Affairs (the curator is Homaid al Rajhi) and is located on Al Bahri Road (which is the continuation of Muttrah corniche on towards Old Muscat, literally 'the sea road'). It is located inside the gate which spans the road. You can park in the turning on the right-hand side just before the gate, or go through it (under the museum) and follow the immediate signs into Riyam Street. You can then walk up the steps to the museum courtyard. This museum, opened in 2001, covers the history of Oman with detail of the country's ancient wells, *falaj*, forts and harbours.

COAST EAST OF MUTTRAH

SIDAB سداب If you continue south out beyond Muscat Old Town you come next to the small village of Sidab, a bay area, with its fishing community. There is also a marina.

What to see and do
Marina Bandar Rowdha (*www.marinaoman.com*). Those interested in boating, diving, taking a dhow trip, or simply having a meal in a beautiful, peaceful location, must visit this marina. It is open to the public and not a private members' club. It has 140 wet berths, 90 dry berths, a marine control tower, a pool, a licensed restaurant (Blue Marlin) and bar, an upstairs bar (Lighthouse Bar), and offers all the sea-based tours. The *Hatteras* is a 58ft-long luxury motor cruiser with air conditioning, television/video, stereo, microwave, fridge and radar equipment and is chartered for fishing trips. A 32ft-long open boat is used for dolphin-watching trips. A traditional dhow is used for sunset trips or scenic coastal tours. The full array of tours includes diving, game fishing, snorkelling, camping, sailing, scuba,

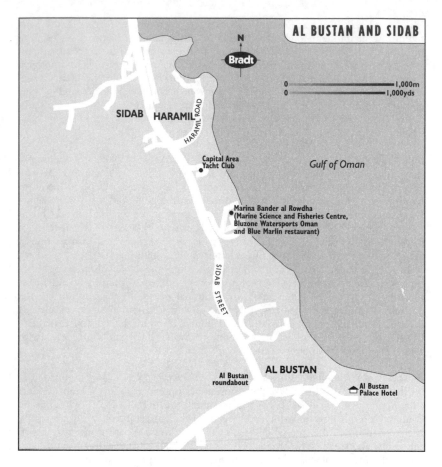

Gulf of Oman

SIDAB   HARAMIL

Capital Area
Yacht Club

Marina Bander al Rowdha
(Marine Science and Fisheries Centre,
Bluzone Watersports Oman
and Blue Marlin restaurant)

AL BUSTAN

Al Bustan
roundabout

Al Bustan
Palace Hotel

whale and dolphin watching, dhow cruising and jet skiing, or you can be asked to be taken to your own private beach and arrange to be collected. You might simply like to visit this place for a meal by the pool or inside, under the protection of the air conditioning, with full marina views.

HARAMIL A few bays after Sidab (and before Al Bustan) is the **Capital Area Yacht Club** (⟍ *24 737712*), which sits next to another private-club marina. Beside this, set right on the water's edge, is the **Marine Science and Fisheries Centre** (⟍ *24 736449; open Sat–Wed 08.00–14.30, Thu 08.00–13.00, Fri 15.00–19.00; admission free*). Opened in 1986, the centre belongs to the Ministry of Agriculture and Fisheries. Inside there is an aquarium, which has recently updated its tanks and has expanded its varieties of fish. It has a particularly fine collection of turtles and its emphasis is on conservation of ecosystems.

AL BUSTAN البستان A few bays further on you come to Al Bustan Bay, where the village of Al Bustan has long been moved to the northern corner of the bay and modernised, to make way for Al Bustan Palace Hotel, which dominates the mountain-hemmed bay.

It is common to see women and children selling small bundles of jasmine. At the roundabout leading up towards Al Bustan Palace Hotel, sits the *Sohar* dhow, which was used by Tim Severin in his 'Sindbad' journey (see box *Sindbad's voyage recreated*, page 92).

QANTAB قنتب Qantab is another fishing village and local fishermen will take you fishing if you ask.

BANDER JISSAH بندر جصة There are five dive sites in this area (also spelt Bandar Jussa), and its shallow depths are particularly suited for beginners and night dives. Turtles, spiny lobsters and cuttlefish have all been spotted here. It is a rocky coastline with small bays, one occupied by the Oman Dive Centre (see *Diving*, page 85 for more details).

BANDER KHAYRAN The small secluded bays of Bander Khayran (or Bandar Khairan) make excellent camping, picnicking, diving and snorkelling spots. There are several dive sites in this area, which you can only access by boat.

FAHAL ISLAND Otherwise known as 'Shark Island', this is reportedly excellent for diving, offering the largest variety of coral in the capital condensed into one area. There is a tugboat wreck close to North Bay. Black-tip reef sharks, rays and turtles are all to be found here.

YITI Yiti beach is a good place to take a picnic, and is close enough if you want to escape the hubbub of the city for an afternoon. For the future there is a Yiti Beach tourism project being planned.

Getting there The road to Yiti is accessed by exiting at the Hamriya roundabout in Ruwi then continuing straight on, taking the small right-hand turn at the place where the road bends round at a right angle (the start of Ruwi Souk Street). This small road will take you through a narrow street and upwards steeply, and you can look back over fantastic elevated views of the large town of Ruwi.

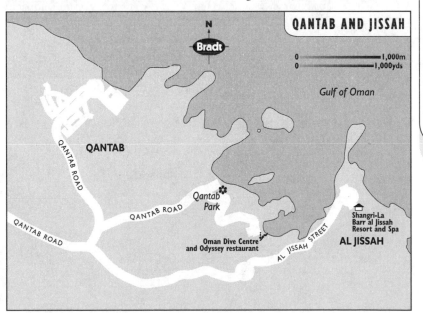

QURIYAT قريات Historically one of the main coastal towns of Oman, Quriyat refused to submit to the invading Portuguese in the early 16th century, and had its inhabitants slaughtered as a result. Set at the start of a wide plain, its salty *khor* (or creek), which centuries ago was a major port and famous harbour, has now silted up. Fishing and agriculture remain the mainstay of the local population and the fish souk is busy. It has been known for rows of sharks, including hammerheads, and stingrays to be sold here. The sharks used to be dried in the sun, and then cut into strips of dried flesh, which were used as flavouring for rice. The plain in which the town is set used to be breeding grounds for the horses for which Quriyat was famous for exporting.

Getting there To join the road to Quriyat, you need to exit the main highway at Wadi Aday roundabout. The tarmac road to Quriyat winds and climbs passing en route the Wadi Sareen Nature Reserve, created for the protection of the Arabian *tahr* (the half-goat) and not open to the public. After less than an hour's drive from Muscat you climb to a plateau, from which there is a steep descent for several hundred metres onto the plain of Quriyat (90km from Muscat). The distance from Quriyat to Sur is 120km.

What to see and do There are three fortifications here. Opposite the souk is Quriyat Castle, open to the public, restored and fully furnished to help you

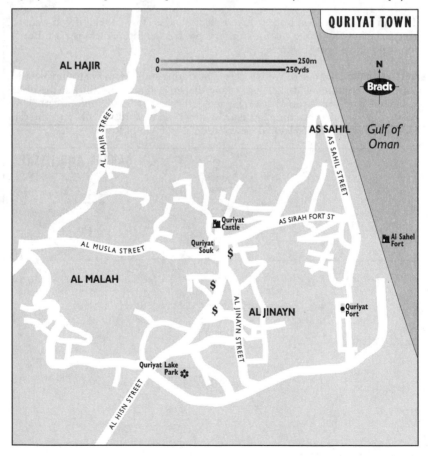

imagine readily what life was like for its inhabitants. It is open seven days a week and the watchman takes pleasure in showing visitors around. On the coast is Al Sahel Fort. The third fort of the area is Dagh Fort, which was built when the Portuguese occupied the country. Inland the dominant mountain is Jebel Aswad (the Black Mountain), peaking at 2,050m.

For the serious adventurer it is possible to trek the canyon that runs from Suwqah to Al Suwayh in the Quriyat wilayat. Known as the Quriyat Canyon, it is not for the faint-hearted and it would be advisable to take an accompanying guide with knowledge of the route, and be prepared and fully equipped. The 15km trip is about a six-hour trek, reportedly far more difficult than the 18km trek through Wadi Dayqah (see *Chapter 8, The Sharqiya*, page 205). At Quriyat roundabout, turn right in the direction of Daghmar and about 7km further along this road there is a signpost for the highlight of Wadi Dayqah. Head along this off-road trail for roughly 8km before turning right for Wadi al Arbiyeen, where this trek begins. Suwqah is the upstream end of the canyon and can be reached only from the Dima wa'Tayeen side (also in the Sharqiya region). For this upstream end, you will need to drive from Ibra, following signposts to Wadi Na'am to reach Samaiya, an oasis village in Dima wa 'Tayeen wilayat. Just 3km before Samaiya there is a trail that leads you to Suwqah, about a 27km off-road route. The canyon at this point is usually dry.

RUWI روي Map page 100

Ruwi is now a busy business district and suburb, with the greatest concentration of high-rise buildings in the whole country. The business district is sometimes referred to as the Central Business District (CBD) or the Muttrah Business District (MBD).

Until the 1960s, Ruwi was a small village serving as the market garden for Muscat and Muttrah. It had a large fish shop with an open-roofed kitchen beside the road, and donkeys would bring panniers full of fish from Muttrah souk to be cooked here. Ruwi was also the location of the customs checkpoint, comprising only a mud hut with a red flag, where taxes were levied on goods moving between Muscat and Oman. Complex rates of tax were levied: 5% for dates and 15% for tobacco for example, with everything having its own rate.

The Ruwi area may at first seem a little difficult to negotiate for the newcomer, as one roundabout can seem to resemble another. The dual carriageway also bends round sharply at Ruwi, which can play havoc with your sense of direction. The Sheraton Hotel is a good landmark from which to re-establish direction. Coming from the airport end of the motorway it is useful to remember that Qurum Heights Road (the exit on the right, just before Qurum, and where the motorway splits into two) leads up and over to the Sheraton. Alternatively, keeping straight on the motorway leads you to Ruwi Souk Street (see *Shopping*, page 101). There are various budget hotels in the Central Business District off Al Fursan Street and Al Baladiyah Street.

WHAT TO SEE
Currency Museum (*Inside Central Bank of Oman, CBD;* ☏ 24 796102; *open Sat–Wed 08.30–12.30; admission 500/200/100bzs adults/children/children under 6*). Opposite the HSBC Bank, this museum showcases a collection of coins and notes.

National Museum (*Above the Islamic Library, off A'Noor St in Ruwi;* ☏ 24 701289; *open Sat–Thu 09.30–13.30; admission 500/200/100bzs adults/children/children under 6*). Operated by the Ministry of Heritage and Culture, this museum is close to the

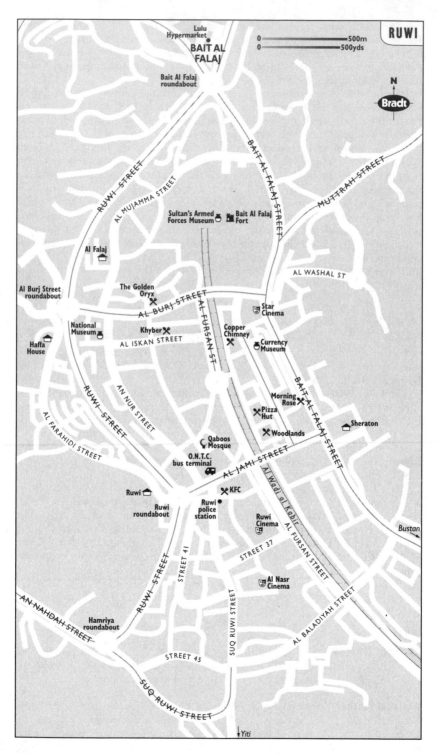

RUWI

0 — 500m
0 — 500yds

N

Bradt

Lulu Hypermarket
BAIT AL FALAJ
Bait Al Falaj roundabout

Sultan's Armed Forces Museum
Bait Al Falaj Fort

Al Falaj

Al Burj Street roundabout

The Golden Oryx

AL WASHAL ST

Star Cinema

National Museum

Khyber

Copper Chimney

Currency Museum

Haffa House

AL ISKAN STREET

AL FURSAN ST

AL BURJ STREET

RUWI STREET

AL MUJAMMA STREET

BAIT AL FALAJ STREET

MUTTRAH STREET

AN NUR STREET

RUWI STREET

AL FARAHIDI STREET

Morning Rose
Pizza Hut
Woodlands
Sheraton

BAIT AL FALAJ STREET

Qaboos Mosque

O.N.T.C. bus terminal

AL JAMI STREET

AL WADI AL KABIR

Ruwi
Ruwi roundabout

KFC

Ruwi police station

Ruwi Cinema

STREET 37

AL FURSAN STREET

Bustan

STREET 41

Al Nasr Cinema

SUQ RUWI STREET

AN NAHDAH STREET

Hamriya roundabout

RUWI STREET

STREET 45

AL BALADIYAH STREET

SUQ RUWI STREET

↓ Yiti

Abdulredha Mosque (not far from Al Falaj Hotel). It houses traditional Omani costumes and household items retrieved from Bait Nadir (a traditional home that was destroyed by fire in 1988), and has a room displaying medals and regalia, photographs, portraits and jewellery from the history of the royal families of Zanzibar and Oman. It also temporarily houses archaeological artefacts (some from the Bat tombs near Ibri) from the Oman Museum (near the Ministry of Information), which is being renovated.

Sultan's Armed Forces Museum (*Al Mujamma St, Ruwi;* ⟍ *24 312642; open Sat–Thu 08.00–13.30; admission RO1/500bzs adults/children; military personnel exempt*). Operated by the Ministry of Defence, this museum is reached by heading past Al Falaj Hotel (coming from Al Burj roundabout). You may alternatively approach it taking the first or second exit off Bait al Falaj Street (from Bait al Falaj roundabout). Opened in 1988, it is set in the immaculately groomed gardens of the Bait al Falaj Fort whose tall white tower dominates the surrounding area. It has an impressive display of Oman's military history: the land force, air force, navy and royal guard, and an informative guide leads you around. Downstairs has an account of Oman's wars against the Portuguese, while upstairs there is information about the Dhofar War against the communists in the south and about the armed forces in Oman today.

Bait al Falaj Fort (*open Sat–Thu 08.00–13.30*) was said to have been built as Sultan Said bin Sultan's weekend country house in the early 1800s, but from 1957 until 1978, served as the Sultan's Armed Forces (SAF) headquarters. Squeezed into the space beside it was the country's only civil and military airport until the 1970s, when the Seeb International Airport was built. Most visitors to Oman arrived by plane and used to watch anxiously as the hills got closer before the plane dipped in through an obscure gap to land on the small plain. The explorer Ranulph Fiennes arrived this way in 1968 and stepped out into a heat he would not have believed possible, only to be told: 'It's just beginning to get hot here, but not too bad yet. Just wait till July.'

SHOPPING
Ruwi Souk Street For Ruwi Souk Street, exit the main highway at the Hamriyah roundabout and continue along the road straight ahead (the main highway bends sharply off to the left here). This road is the start of Ruwi Souk Street, which itself

> ### INDIAN MERCHANT COMMUNITY
>
> A considerable vacuum would be left if every Indian merchant left the country. The most powerful ones are in Muttrah and Ruwi, but even in the interior most shops are run by Indians, with Omanis running only a few stalls in the older souks like Rustaq and Nizwa. Elsewhere, especially all along the Batinah, at the meat, fish and vegetable souks, you will be hard pressed to find an Omani selling instead of buying. The Omanis who are most active in business and trade tend to be the Beluch, the Baharina and the Khojas (Hyderabadis) whose families came originally from Iran, Pakistan, India or Iraq, but who now hold Omani passports and are Omani citizens. In the past these Omanis, all of whom settled on the Batinah coastal plain, were not permitted into the interior, or only with special permission. This meant that the true tribal Omanis of the interior remained very cut off from the commercial activity of the coast, and therefore the big Muscat or Muttrah merchant could not easily expand through branches into the interior.

loops around to the left (virtually parallel to the highway). Soon after joining this road you will find metered parking on the right-hand side (you will need 50 baiza coins). There are usually plenty of free spaces at this upper end of the street, so it might be best to park here and walk down, rather than get caught up in the traffic congestion that usually ensues further down.

In this street, there is a plentiful selection of shops selling gold and silver, fabric, electrical goods, souvenirs and fake designer wear, as well as the street traders that sell DVDs and clothes from mats laid out on the floor. Ruwi Souk Street can become busy in the evenings and even more so on Friday evenings, when it turns into a miniature Mumbai!

QURUM القرم

Originally just a little fishing village on the southern end of the Batinah, Qurum (which translates as 'mangrove') is now part of the modern sprawl of the capital area, where most of the beach hotels are situated along the wide sandy shore. The marshy estuary with mangrove swamps, now designated a nature reserve, is in fact the mouth of the Wadi Adai and still floods into the sea after heavy rains. It is a good birdwatching spot, more peaceful than most places within the capital area. The landscape is enhanced by the rocky headland at the far eastern end of the beach, now built up with apartment blocks and home to the Crowne Plaza (which used to be the Gulf Hotel), which benefits from the breezes and elevated views.

Qurum can appear rather complicated on first arrival, but once you have mastered the positioning of the two roundabouts (at the splitting of the highway), things become a little easier.

SHOPPING Qurum is home to most of the modern shopping plazas; to access these you will need to keep straight on the dual carriageway and come off at the main Qurum roundabout (which is the next one along from the Khuwair roundabout). Taking the left turn at the roundabout (last exit) and the subsequent first right will lead you into the main group of shopping malls. They are all generally open 09.00–13.00 and 16.00–22.00, with some slight variations.

Al Araimi Complex ✆ 24 566180; f 24 566186; e alarami@omantel.net.om. There is a Burger King here.

Al Asfoor Plaza ✆ 24 564686. Inside is a Papa John's pizza restaurant.

Capital Commercial Centre ✆ 24 563672; f 24 564938; e cccqurum@omantel.net.om. This centre combines a supermarket and a mall. Fast-food eateries here include McDonald's, Fuddruckers, Pizza Hut, Bollywood Chaat, Subway and Baskin Robbins (ice cream). There is a small souk inside here, for handicrafts and souvenirs, and a good internet café with a drinks menu. Open Sat–Thu 09.00–13.00 and 16.30–23.00, Fri 16.30–22.00.

Capital Stores ✆ 24 797236; f 24 797277; e csoman@omantel.net.om. This store is located close to Sabco Centre. There are also branches at Ruwi, Muttrah and Seeb (as well as Salalah in the south of the country).

Al Harthy Complex ✆ 24 564481; f 24 560581; information desk; ✆ 24 560454; e ahcmpx@omantel.net.om. This is located on the right-hand side of the highway (away from the main group) and stands out for its interesting dome design. For access to this complex (and the Sultan Centre, below), keep straight on the highway and once you have passed the Qurum roundabout (over the flyover) get over to the right and slow down. The entrance comes up immediately after the flyover. There are plenty of ATMs outside, and as you enter, there is an upmarket chocolate gift shop on the right, just inside the automatic doors. There is another Kargeen Café located upstairs. For the children, there is an extensive play and amusement area called Sindbad's Play City as well as a novel 'Happy Child' hairdresser's dedicated to distracting children while they have their hair cut (one TV per chair, playing cartoons continuously).

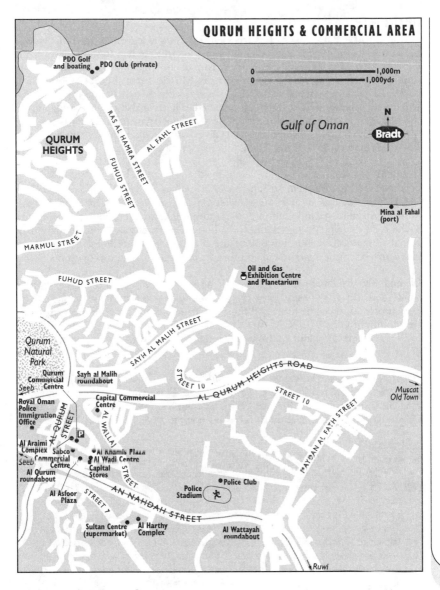

Gulf of Oman

Bradt

Mina al Fahal (port)

QURUM HEIGHTS

PDO Golf and boating — PDO Club (private)

RAS AL HAMRA STREET

AL FAHL STREET

FUHUD STREET

MARMUL STREET

FUHUD STREET

Oil and Gas Exhibition Centre and Planetarium

SAYH AL MALIH STREET

Qurum Natural Park

Qurum Commercial Centre

Seeb

Sayh al Malih roundabout

AL QURUM HEIGHTS ROAD

STREET 10

STREET 10

Muscat Old Town

Capital Commercial Centre

Royal Oman Police Immigration Office

Al Araimi Complex

Seeb

AL QURUM STREET

AL WALLAI

Sabco Commercial Centre

Al Khamis Plaza

Al Wadi Centre

Capital Stores

MAYDAN AL FATH STREET

Al Qurum roundabout

Al Asfoor Plaza

STREET 7

AN NAHDAH STREET

Police Stadium

Police Club

Sultan Centre (supermarket)

Al Harthy Complex

Al Wattayah roundabout

Ruwi

Muscat QURUM

3

Al Khamis Plaza ☎ 24 562791; f 24 563009; e alkhamis@omantel.net.om
Sabco Centre ☎ 24 563943, 24 562761, 24 566701; e sabcocen@omantel.net.om; www.sabcogroup.com. This is the longest-established complex (opened in 1985) and apart from the usual array of shops, it has the Body Shop, Nine West, Elle, Godiva, Wrangler, a pet shop, a beauty salon and a small-scale, modern, air-conditioned souk, which has 27 small individual units selling silver jewellery and handicrafts, incense burners,

dishdashas, kummahs, mussars, pottery, khanjars, leather goods, bakhour (traditional scented wood), frankincense and other artefacts. If you haven't got the time to visit the real thing at Muttrah, this miniature souk is a good place for buying gifts to take back home. Open Sat–Thu 09.00–13.00 and 16.00–22.00, Fri 16.30–22.00.
Sultan Centre This is located next door to Al Harthy Complex. It is a large, excellent supermarket, which has a restaurant upstairs called Jean's Grill (☎ 24 567666), serving good buffet b/fasts.

WHAT TO SEE

Qurum Natural Park The park is accessed from two sides: either from the gate at the base of the hill that is home to the Mumtaz Mahal Indian Restaurant, or from the road that extends from the Qurum roundabout up to the Qurum Heights peninsula. This is one of the venues for the Muscat Festival (see box opposite), held each January, when a traditional village is constructed beside the lake, and Omani rural lifestyles and crafts are depicted. There is also camel racing and an equestrian show, art exhibitions, a laser show and poetry recitals, as well as concerts with popular Arab singers held in a specially constructed temporary amphitheatre. The amusement park – Marah Land – includes rides, games and a food court.

Museums

Children's Science Museum (*A'Saruj/Shatti al Qurum;* \ *24 605368; open Sat–Thu 09.30–13.30; admission 500/100bzs adults/children under 12*). Operated by the Ministry of Heritage and Culture, this museum is located on the right-hand side of the road that approaches the Qurum Natural Park entrance and the Mumtaz Mahal Restaurant. It is inside one of the dome-shaped buildings. It focuses on interactive scientific experiments to promote interest through exploration.

Oil and Gas Exhibition Centre (*Seih Al Maleh St, Qurum;* \ *24 677834; open Sat–Wed 07.00–12.00 and 13.00–15.45, Thu 08.00–13.00; admission free*). The exhibition centre can be found on the right-hand side just before the Petroleum Development Oman (PDO) Gate No 2. It was donated to the people of Oman by PDO back in 1995 and guides you through the discovery and excavation of oil in the country.

Planetarium (\ *24 675542;* e *planetarium@pdo.co.om;* *www.pdo.co.om/planetarium; admission free*). There are shows in Arabic: Wed 17.00 and Thu 11.00; shows in English: Wed 19.00 and Thu 10.00. This was built in 2000 and is adjoined to the Oil and Gas Exhibition Centre. It is best to book in advance for the shows.

PDO

Petroleum Development Oman (PDO) is the main oil company of the country, 60% owned by the government, with Royal Dutch Shell as its operator and main private partner. In the late 1960s, Petrol Development Oman Ltd, a subsidiary of Shell, constructed the Mina al Fahal oil terminal and refinery at this hilly outcrop at Qurum. They accompanied it with its own purpose-built village called Sahil Mahla, set on a cliff above a sandy cove known as Blackpool Beach! Many PDO officials had their wives and children with them, and a car to take them shopping in Muscat or Muttrah. Each employee had his own Portakabin with air conditioning, freezer and sea view, and fresh food coming in each week from Australia in refrigerator ships. The technicians spent 11 days upcountry at the well-heads followed by four days' rest back at the village. The pay was high, with extra hardship money for the difficult climate. Bored by the long separations, some European wives began affairs with young bachelors on the compound. Omanis employed as caterers or cleaners on the compound observed everything at first hand and went back to their villages reporting on the European lifestyle, the plush bars, the well-equipped hospital kept busy with cases of mild sunburn and stomach ulcers, the piped water, the light switches and the children's schools. The contrast of lifestyle with their own was enormous: could they be blamed for wondering when, if it was the oil that was making these foreigners so rich, they would enjoy a little of the same.

Qurum Beach, or *Shatti Al Qurum* in Arabic, is a prime beach area where three excellent five-star hotels (Grand Hyatt, Intercontinental and Crowne Plaza) and two five-star hotel beach clubs (Sheraton and Radisson SAS) are located. The beach is popular with Omani families in the early evening as well as hotel guests. It is a lovely place to watch the sun go down before going for a meal in O Sole Mio or a cocktail in Trader Vic's.

SHOPPING

Jawharat A'Shatti Commercial Complex (Jewel of the Beach) *(Shatti al Qurum;*
☎ 24 692113; f *24 607412;* e *jasco@omantel.net.om).* Instead of turning right into the entrance of the Intercontinental Hotel, keep straight and this will take you to this shopping complex, which has O Sole Mio (a good Italian restaurant) on its corner. There are plenty of spaces to park, but in the evening it can get busy. Inside the complex there is a Starbucks coffee shop, a café with outdoor terrace (D'Arcy's Kitchen), the Omani Heritage Gallery (shop), a card shop, Muscat Pharmacy, and even a balloon shop. This area is popular with Omani families in the evening, as access to the beach is good. It is an excellent place to take a stroll. You might like to pop into the Sheraton Beach Hotel (which is the beach club of the Sheraton in Ruwi), located on the beach (at the opposite end to O Sole Mio), and have a drink in Feeney's Bar *(open 12.00–15.00 and 18.00–midnight).* This area is within easy walking distance of both the Intercontinental and Beach hotels.

Oasis by the Sea This complex, opposite the Jawharat A'Shatti, is now largely empty, owing to a renovation project under way here. It used to house the Samarkand Restaurant and the Med Restaurant, as well as Oman's only independent nightclub, but these are now closed while work takes place. A good cigar shop still remains, however, and a Costa Coffee sits on the corner fronted with a patio area, which overlooks the sea. This is a great place to sit in the late afternoon or early evening time, as the area is popular with evening strollers and Omani families. Check for updates on the state of play of this beautifully located complex.

Omani Heritage Gallery *(Jawharat A'Shatti Shopping Complex;* ☎ *24 696165, 24 696974).* Authentic crafts, jewellery and clothing are for sale here, close to the Intercontinental Hotel in Shatti Al Qurum. This gallery is a not-for-profit company and therefore all profits go direct to the artisans themselves.

Al Saruj Complex *(☎ 24 691311;* f *24 692300;* e *taherent@omantel.net.om).* This complex is situated close to Shatti Al Qurum, but just a little further back (and adjacent to) the highway. It is accessible from both the highway side and Al

---

MUSCAT FESTIVAL

This is a six-week-long annual cultural festival held from January until early February at various park, beach and shopping centre locations in the capital and arranged by Muscat municipality. The festival focuses on Omani heritage and culture. Entertainment includes funfairs, fireworks, entertainment and raffles. Traditional villages are constructed and Omani crafts and culture demonstrated and celebrated. Oman Air offers promotional fare deals, and discounted packages are available at the hotels, which can become full.

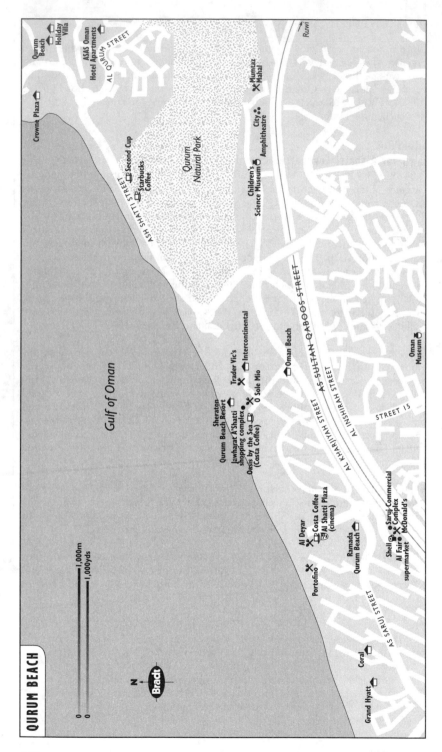

QURUM BEACH

Gulf of Oman

Qurum Natural Park

Ruwi

Crowne Plaza

Qurum Beach

Holiday Villa

ASAS Oman Hotel Apartments

AL QURUM STREET

Mumtaz Mahal

City Amphitheatre

Children's Science Museum

Second Cup

Starbucks Coffee

ASH SHATTI STREET

AS-SULTAN-QABOOS STREET

Intercontinental

Trader Vic's

Sole Mio

Oman Beach

Sheraton Qurum Beach Resort

Jawharat A'Shatti shopping complex

Oasis by the Sea (Costa Coffee)

Oman Museum

AL KHARJIYAH STREET

AL INSHIRAH STREET

STREET 15

Al Deyar

Costa Coffee

Al Shatti Plaza (cinema)

Portofino

Ramada Qurum Beach

Shell

Saruj Commercial Complex

Al Fair supermarket

McDonald's

AS SARUJ STREET

Coral

Grand Hyatt

N

Bradt

0   1,000m
0   1,000yds

Kharijiyah Street on Hayy as Saruj. It has a Shell garage, a car wash, a drive-in McDonald's, an Al Fair supermarket and an HSBC cashpoint. There is also a pharmacy and coffee shop, a Baskin Robbins, a physiotherapy clinic and a small outdoor amusement area for children. It's a good little area to get all things done. A bowling centre is being constructed almost opposite (as at February 2006).

MADINAT QABOOS مدينة قابوس *Map page 108*

This area is known locally as MQ, and you will probably see it shown as Madinat Al Sultan Qaboos, Madinat Qaboos, Madinat A'Sultan Qaboos, Medinat Qaboos etc in various maps and publications! It is a modern residential area popular with Western expats, and occupies an elevated position on the right-hand side of the highway immediately after the Khuwair roundabout. The central shopping arcade has some good restaurants as well as an Al Fair supermarket, a Family Bookshop, a Muscat Pharmacy, an HSBC cashpoint, Pizza Hut and a Starbucks coffee shop. The Pavo Real Restaurant, the Golden Dragon Restaurant and the quaint Kargeen Caffe labyrinth are all highly recommended, and make this small MQ arcade area worth a visit.

GETTING THERE One way of getting there is to exit the highway at Al Khuwair roundabout. Once at the roundabout (and therefore off the highway), take the first roundabout exit leading up to Madinat Qaboos traffic lights (which are referred to often when asking directions, and thus a useful landmark). Go straight over the lights, and a little further along the road at the bend you need to take a left. Follow this road round until you spot the Pizza Hut on your left. This is the start of the shopping complex (see map).

Alternatively, you can exit the highway taking the slip road immediately after Al Khuwair roundabout. This will lead you along parallel to the highway for a little way, before you need to take the right up Al Bashir Street and then the first left. The British Council is located on the left, close to the beginning of this road. Follow the road up the hill and you will come to the MQ complex on the right-hand side, where there is plenty of parking

WHAT TO SEE
Bait Adam Museum (*Bldg 2881, Way No 2333 [in the area opposite MQ bridge turning];* \ *99 356676;* e *baitadam@omantel.net.om; admission RO3 museum only, RO15 pp museum and lunch or dinner, 2–3hrs in duration*). This is so much more than a museum. Relatively recently opened, this private collector's home in Qurum displays art, coins, maps, books and treaties and other treasures and artefacts from Omani history, dating back to pre-Islamic times. Latif al Bulushi (whose English is excellent) and his family offer you the chance to join them in either an authentic Omani lunch or dinner in their home. Here you will experience Omani etiquette and hospitality first hand, from taking your shoes off when you enter the home, being served coffee and dates, and sitting at ground level to eat with your hands. It is a great opportunity to experience a slice of the Omani way of life Call in advance to arrange your visit, as this is a real Omani home. Highly recommended.

The Oman Museum (*Al Alam St;* \ *24 600946; open Sat–Wed 09.30–13.30, Thu 09.30–12-30; admission 500/200/100bzs adults/children/children under 6*). This museum was closed for major renovation works in February 2006, so do call before visiting to see whether it has reopened. Some artefacts from this museum have been temporarily housed at the National Museum at Ruwi (see page 99).

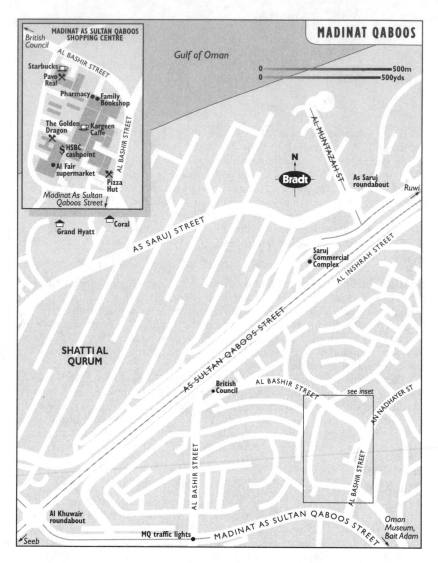

Gulf of Oman

MADINAT AS SULTAN QABOOS
SHOPPING CENTRE

British Council

AL BASHIR STREET

Starbucks
Pavo Real
Pharmacy
Family Bookshop
The Golden Dragon
Kargeen Caffe
HSBC cashpoint
Al Fair supermarket
Pizza Hut
Madinat As Sultan Qaboos Street

AL BASHIR STREET

0 ————————— 500m
0 ————————— 500yds

N

Bradt

AL MUNTAZAH ST

As Saruj roundabout

Ruwi

Grand Hyatt
Coral

AS SARUJ STREET

Saruj Commercial Complex

AL INSHRAH STREET

AS SULTAN QABOOS STREET

SHATTI AL QURUM

British Council

AL BASHIR STREET

see inset

AN NADHAYER ST

AL BASHIR STREET

AL BASHIR STREET

Al Khuwair roundabout

Seeb

MQ traffic lights

MADINAT AS SULTAN QABOOS STREET

Oman Museum, Bait Adam

Tucked behind the Ministry of Information on a hilltop overlooking Madinat Qaboos, between MQ and Qurum, this rarely visited museum, established in 1974, is a real treasure trove. Operated by the Ministry of Heritage and Culture, the carefully arranged displays take you through Oman's earliest history from the Stone Age, covering in some detail the various copper mining settlements of the 3rd and 2nd millennium BC, then moving on to explain the frankincense trade as well as the history of Oman as a seafaring nation and naval power.

To get there, exit the highway at Al Khuwair roundabout, then take the first exit of the roundabout (to the right) up to MQ traffic lights. Go straight over the lights and continue along the road until you see a sign indicating left for the Ministry of Information. Take this left and follow the steep road as it bends round and up. The museum is at the end of this road at the very top, past the Ministry of Information. There are great ocean views from this hilltop.

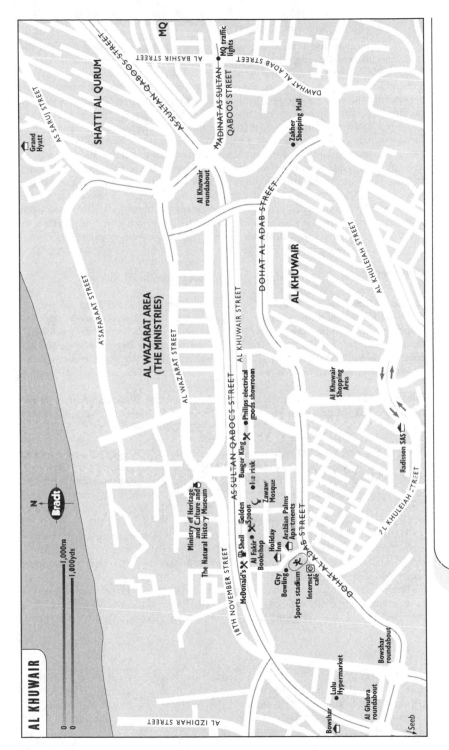

AL KHUWAIR

0 ————— 1,000m
0 ————— 1,000yds

Bradt

N

SHATTI AL QURUM

Grand Hyatt

AS SARUJ STREET

AS SULTAN-QABOOS-STREET

AL BASHIR STREET

MADINAT-AS-SULTAN QABOOS STREET

MQ

MQ traffic lights

DAWHAT AL ADAB STREET

Zakher Shopping Mall

Al Khuwair roundabout

DOHAT AL ADAB STREET

AL KHULEIAH STREET

AL KHUWAIR

A'SAFARAAT STREET

AL WAZARAT AREA (THE MINISTRIES)

AL WAZARAT STREET

AS-SULTAN-QABOOS-STREET

AL KHUWAIR STREET

Phillips electrical goods showroom

Burger King

ice rink

Zawaw Mosque

Al Khuwair Shopping Area

Radisson SAS

AL KHULEIAH STREET

Ministry of Heritage and Culture and The Natural History Museum

Golden Spoon

McDonald's Shell

Al Fakir Bookshop

Holiday Inn

Arabian Palms Apartments

City Bowling

Sports stadium

Internet café

DOHAT AL ADAB STREET

18TH NOVEMBER STREET

Lulu Hypermarket

Al Ghubra roundabout

Bowshar

Bowshar roundabout

Seeb

AL IZDIHAR STREET

Muscat MADINAT QABOOS 3

Lower Khuwair is home to all the various ministries, and lies on the left of the highway (the seaward side, when coming from the airport). This ministries' area is now clearly signposted 'Wazarat' (meaning 'ministries'), since the new flyover section here was completed in about 2004. The flyover has been brilliant at eliminating the extreme congestion that was once commonplace at the beginning of 18th November Street.

Upper Khuwair is largely residential, but there is a selection of furniture shops, fast-food establishments, bakeries, a book/stationery shop, electrical goods shops, and even an ice rink on the Khuwair slip road, running parallel to the highway on the right-hand side (coming from the airport) and accessed via the Shell petrol station. The Khuwair slip road is often referred to when obtaining directions, so it will be useful for you to keep an eye out for it. Khuwair is also home to the Radisson SAS Hotel, which lies further back from the highway and elevated from it. At the furthest end of Khuwair, just before MQ traffic lights, is the large City Plaza and Home Centre furnishings and clothing shop, and the Alauddin Restaurant (see *Where to eat*, page 78).

SHOPPING There are several shopping malls (or plazas) in Al Khuwair:

City Plaza and Home Centre Near Safeer Suites Hotel; ↘ 24 698988. Sells sportswear, clothes, makeup, toys and Western-style furniture and homeware.
Zakher Shopping Mall ↘ 24 730619; f 24 732677; e zakii@omantel.net.om. This mall is located in an area far less busy than both Qurum and Ruwi. There is a CD/DVD shop inside here, an internet café, clothes shops, sporting and diving equipment, a card shop, a Body Shop, a café area, a good Al Fair supermarket, a good Iranian restaurant (unlicensed) and a Pizza Hut.

WHAT TO SEE The ministries are largely located in Al Wazarat Street in lower Khuwair. The Ministry of Heritage and Culture houses the Natural History Museum.

Natural History Museum (*Al Wazarat St;* ↘ *24 604957, 24 641510; open Sat–Thu 09.30–13.30; admission 500/200/100bzs adults/children/children under 6*). This is a small museum, opened in 1985, next door to the Ministry of Heritage and Culture in the ministries area of lower Khuwair. The entrance is virtually opposite the large Zawawi Mosque (all the way over the other side of the highway) and close to the small roundabout. There is ample parking space.

The displays cover a small area on the ground floor, with examples of the natural environment and wildlife heritage of the country: mammals, reptiles, birdlife, insects and seashells. The Whale Hall next door has an impressive collection of skeletons.

Turtle permits used to be issued from the Ministry of Heritage and Culture here, but are now easily obtained on site in the Ras al Hadd and Ras al Jinz turtle reserves in the Sharqiya region – part of the country's drive to facilitate tourism.

BOWSHAR بوشر

Before the construction of the dual carriageway, Bowshar used to be a six-hour journey from Muscat Old Town. Now it is a swift 30 minutes. Head for the Ghubra roundabout and it is signposted from here. It lies off the main dual carriageway back inland towards the mountains. It is not yet quite a suburb. There are two separate areas of Bowshar which deserve exploration. One is the signposted

Bait al Makham. The other is behind Bowshar in Wadi al Ghail, where a path leads for a 30-minute walk over the hills to the village of Al Ghala where there are hot springs (30°C) called Bou Souman. Following the tarmac road back towards the sprawl of Muscat, watch out for the ruins of two large fortified castles, one heavily crumbling to the left of the road, the other still kept locked and very fine indeed, to the right of the road. Behind this fine ruin you can explore an extensive site, as yet unexcavated, which appears to have a huge rampart wall round it. On the hillside ridge above are ancient beehive-style graves, mainly collapsed.

WHAT TO SEE

Bait al Makham (↘ *24 641300, ext 142 (call in advance); open Sat–Wed 08.00–14.00; admission 500bzs*) is a fortified house built at the turn of the 20th century for a wealthy lady. Restored in 1992, her apartment was at the top of the house with excellent views. Local boys from the village will delight in showing you round, leaping about on the walls and towers.

Bou Souman Springs The mineral-rich waters are said to cure arthritis and rheumatism.

GHUBRA *Map page 112*

Ghubra is largely a residential area, with older buildings. There is a handy HSBC cashpoint at the first mini-roundabout you reach (coming off the highway at Ghubra and going towards the sea). In the evenings this can become quite a busy little area. There is a variety of small street shops here, namely fruit and veg, foodstuffs, building materials, a pharmacy, an optician's, a bakery, coffee shops/café-type local restaurants and an internet café. The **National Trading Company** (*Showroom at St 44, Villa 57, near Bowshar roundabout;* ↘ *24 697014*) sells Omani carved doors or shutters converted into coffee tables, Omani chests, traditional weaving and jewellery.

AZAIBA *Map page 112*

Azaiba (also Al Udhaybah or Al Athaibah) is the newest of the residential areas in the city and you will find large, detached and quite grand homes here. There is a seemingly endless stretch of beach close by, the potential of which has been fully recognised, and so will be utilised by the up-and-coming development projects of The Wave and The Journey of Light. This same stretch has been enjoyed now for many years, almost exclusively, by the Civil Aviation Recreational Club, which now is housed within a smart, sizeable building (constructed c2002), and contains the longest bar in the country (or probably in most countries come to that, much to the chagrin of its bartenders, who clock up plenty of extra mileage!). It has been a bold, optimistic step away from its small, dated Portakabin-type origins, which remain next door.

Azaiba Beach is excellent for morning or early-evening walks, and local fishermen will sell their latest catch to you. The tides can be strong at times and there have been fatal accidents in the nearby waters. So if you want to swim here, do take advice (speak to any dive centre representative), and use your common sense. Note that there are no lifeguards on duty. The calm bays of the Oman Dive Centre, Al Bustan and Shangri-La hotels, for example, offer a far safer and inviting experience.

GETTING THERE To get here, exit the highway at the Azaiba roundabout (also referred to as the Ghala roundabout). For the Grand Mosque, take the road up to the mountains (rather than down towards the sea) and you will soon reach a

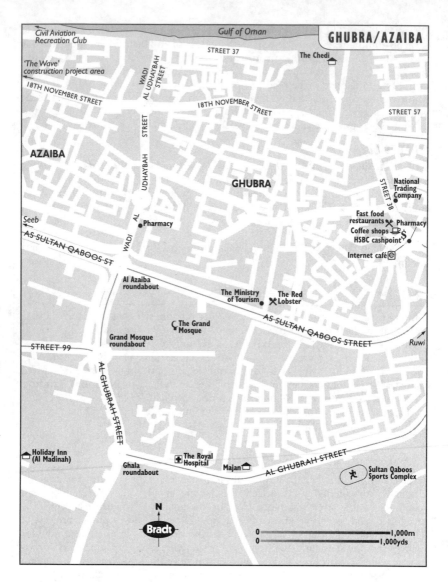

Civil Aviation
Recreation Club

Gulf of Oman

GHUBRA/AZAIBA

STREET 37

The Chedi

'The Wave'
construction project area

18TH NOVEMBER STREET

WADI
AL UDHAYBAH
STREET

18TH NOVEMBER STREET

STREET 57

AZAIBA

STREET
UDHAYBAH

GHUBRA

STREET 38

National
Trading
Company

Seeb

AL
WADI

Pharmacy

Fast food
restaurants   Pharmacy
Coffee shops
HSBC cashpoint

AS SULTAN QABOOS ST

Internet café

Al Azaiba
roundabout

The Ministry
of Tourism

The Red
Lobster

The Grand
Mosque

AS SULTAN QABOOS STREET

Ruwi

Grand Mosque
roundabout

STREET 99

AL GHUBRAH STREET

Holiday Inn
(Al Madinah)

The Royal
Hospital

Majan

AL GHUBRAH STREET

Sultan Qaboos
Sports Complex

Ghala
roundabout

N

Bradt

0   1,000m
0   1,000yds

smaller roundabout. Take the last exit on this roundabout and you will clearly see
the large entrance and road leading up to the extensive car-parking area.

WHAT TO SEE

The Grand Mosque (*Open Sat–Wed 08.00–11.00. Women need to cover their hair with a
headscarf – don't rely on the men at the entrance to lend you one – and all visitors need to follow
the conservative dress code*). This mosque is awe-inspiring and is certainly worth a
visit, if simply to appreciate its magnitude, craftsmanship and the architectural
design-and-build achievement it represents. Even the non-religious visitor can't
help but be moved in some way by a tour of its interior. Construction began in
1995 and took six years to complete. Made from marble, sandstone and wood, the
four corner minarets measure 148ft high, and along with the taller central minaret,

represent the five pillars of Islam. There are ablution areas, a library, an administrative quarter, stained-glass windows, carved wooden doors and 35 chandeliers. The Persian carpet (in the main prayer hall), is made of fine wool and cotton in 28 colours, measures 70m by 60m, includes 1,700 million knots, and weighs 21 tonnes. It was made in Khurasan in Iran and occupied 600 female weavers fully for four years. The appearance of the magnificent 50m-high central dome and the 8m-wide x 14m-high central Swarovski crystal chandelier in the main prayer hall with its 1,122 lights is breathtaking. The hall has a capacity of around 6,600 and the total capacity is estimated at 20,000 worshippers. The tranquillity and serenity of the *riwaqs* (open-air arcades), archways and courtyards is quite an experience in itself. The Grand Mosque in its entirety stands as an assertive symbol of Oman's confidence and spirituality.

SEEB السيب *Map page 114*

Seeb is like Muscat's garden suburb, with many fine weekend villas of the wealthy set among gardens and palm groves. **The Royal Stables and Equestrian Centre** and the **Royal Guard** of Oman are both here, and just off the dual carriageway is the private road leading to the sultan's Seeb palace – **Bait al Baraka** – which is not open to the public. Between the highway and Bait al Baraka is the First Royal School of Music which houses the **Royal Oman Symphony Orchestra**, formed in 1985. It may be that you will be in town to hear one of their regular performances (see local papers and publications such as *Oman Today* for details, or call ✆ 26 894021).

Seeb is a relatively large town, with a one-way system. Follow the signposts from the highway to A'Seeb. If you approach it from the coastal road (continuing from Azaiba), you will pass many gardening and plant shops on both sides of the road. Follow the road all the way along. When you reach the town you will notice the plentiful fabric shops. Continue on this road till you come to a large impressive gold-domed mosque. The right-hand turn just before the mosque leads you to a small parking area. You might like to park your car here and wander around the fruit and vegetable souk. The fish souk is over by the sea's edge.

WHAT TO SEE

Naseem Garden (*Open Mon and Wed 16.00–23.00, Tue 16.00–23.00 (women and children only), Thu and Fri 09.00–23.00, closed Sat and Sun*). Opened in 1984, this vast park, set between Seeb and Barka (on the very outskirts of the Muscat region – see Batinah coast map on pages 120–1), is about 30km away from the airport on the coast and is signposted from the dual carriageway. It has an aquarium, lake, waterfall, flower garden, Arabic and Japanese gardens, a maze and a playground. A railway transports you around, on account of the park's size. The park is popular with Omani families, and gets crowded at weekends (Thursdays and Fridays).

The Amouage Perfumery (*PO Box 307, CP 111, Seeb;* ✆ *24 540757 ext 103, 110 or 111;* f *24 540057;* e *javed@amouage.com; open Sat–Wed 09.00–16.30; admission free*). Sayed Javed is the chief operations manager here, where you are shown around by a guide for a tour of the perfumery and an explanation of how the Amouage perfume is created. Perfumery has a 2,000-year history in Oman. (See *Chapter 10, Frankincense* box, pages 254–5.)

SHOPPING

Markaz al Bahja (*Al Mawaleh roundabout;* ✆ *24 540200;* f *24 815490;* e *markaz@ ajaygroup.com; www.markazalbahja.com*). To get here you need to drive north from Seeb International Airport roundabout and exit the highway at Al Mawaleh

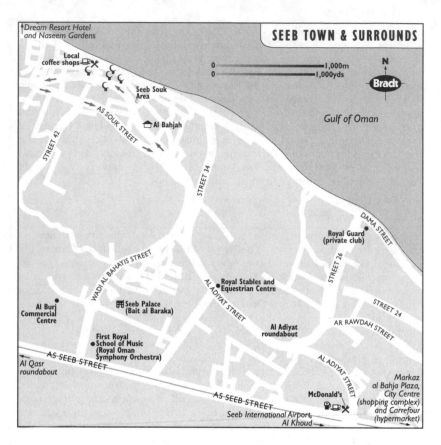

Dream Resort Hotel
and Naseem Gardens

Local
coffee shops

Seeb Souk
Area

AS SOUK STREET

STREET 42

Al Bahjah

0   1,000m
0   1,000yds

N

Bradt

Gulf of Oman

STREET 34

DAMA STREET

Royal Guard
(private club)

STREET 26

WADI AL BAHAYIS STREET

Royal Stables and
Equestrian Centre

AL ADIYAT STREET

STREET 24

AR RAWDAH STREET

Al Burj
Commercial
Centre

Seeb Palace
(Bait al Baraka)

Al Adiyat
roundabout

First Royal
School of Music
(Royal Oman
Symphony Orchestra)

AS SEEB STREET

Al Qasr
roundabout

AL ADIYAT STREET

Markaz
al Bahja Plaza,
City Centre
(shopping complex)
and Carrefour
(hypermarket)

McDonald's

AS SEEB STREET

Seeb International Airport,
Al Khoud→

roundabout (as for City Centre and Carrefour). You will see it on the right-hand side of the highway here at Al Hail. Marks & Spencer and McDonald's are also here. It is a large, new, three-level complex with two cinemas, fast-food outlets, bowling alleys, a snooker and pool centre and an internet café.

Muscat City Centre and Carrefour Hypermarket (24 558888; f 24 545320; e mccinfodesk@mafgroup.co.ae; www.citycentremuscat.com). This is the first 'super-mall' in Oman (similar to those in Dubai), with 1,500 parking spaces, and can be a little difficult to access if you are a first-time visitor. Keep on the main highway north past Seeb Airport (going away from Muscat). Don't take the Nizwa exit. Although it is very close to 'the clock' roundabout (and only 3km from the airport), you need to continue straight up the highway and exit at Al Mawaleh/Al Hail roundabout. Go all the way around this roundabout and come back on yourself on the highway. Get onto the parallel slip road as soon as you can (the bus-stopping areas can make this a little confusing). If you've missed it and find that you are driving past it again on the main highway don't worry. You can drive into the Shell petrol station (just past City Centre), and go round the back of it, and to the right, and enter City Centre via this back way.

Inside City Centre there is a Woolworths, Mango, Next, Mothercare, Adams, Starbucks, the Body Shop, among others. There is a KFC, a McDonald's and others in the large food court section at the far end, and an amusement and play area for children.

AL KHOUD

A little north of Seeb International Airport is 'the book' roundabout from where you can turn off in an inland direction to Al Khoud and the Sultan Qaboos University. It took its first students in 1986 (557) and by 1995 had a total of 3,500, one-fifth of whom were female. By 2002, the university had in excess of 10,000 students.

The university campus lies on the flat open plain but beyond it the road climbs through the foothills to drop again to the old town of Al Khoud, the place where the historic Treaty of Seeb was signed in 1920, a British-mediated truce between Muscat and the tribes of the interior. Here on a hill to the right rising above the palm plantations is the magnificent Al Khoud castle fort built in 1865, with a Zanzibari carved door and elegant windows showing east African influence. It was lived in continuously by the descendants of the original sheikh until 1979, when the 90-year-old resident finally moved into the modern buildings next door.

Also in Al Khoud dinosaur and fossilised tree remains, 65 million years old, were discovered in 1997, indicating the existence of large forests in the area at the time. They were carnivorous Therapods and giant long-necked herbivorous Sauropods.

EXCURSIONS BEYOND MUSCAT

Most of the trips in and around Muscat will provide you with a taster of the country. However, a short journey outside of the capital will allow you to see more of Oman's natural wonders and allows for the more adventurous of trips. You could go 'wadi bashing' (riding in a 4x4 through the dry riverbeds in the mountains), or picnic by peaceful hot springs (see *Chapter 4*, pages 137 and 144).

For the seriously adventurous and energetic there is rock climbing, mountain ravine trekking, and even caving (see page 116). The stock tours include visits to the Wahiba (usually including overnight camping in the desert), the wadis (Wadi Beni Khaled, Wadi Tiwi, Wadi Shab, Wadi Dayqah and Wadi Abyadh being the most popular), the jebels (Jebel Shams and Wadi Ghul, Jebel Akhdar), the turtle reserves at Ras al Hadd and Ras al Jinz, mountain village tours, fort tours, coastal towns and villages tours and desert towns tours.

Most tours to places beyond Muscat need to be arranged through one of the tour operators in the city (see page 67). If you are travelling independently around your chosen region, yet want a sand safari (which requires a 4x4, and a driver/guide) it is safest to pre-arrange this through a tour operator in Muscat who will collect you from your hotel, if you are already in the region.

Jebel Akhdar is a great full-day trip (see page 185). Nakhal Springs and the Rustaq Loop is another excellent day trip from Muscat (see page 136). Wadi bani Awf and Bilad Sayt is a popular 'wadi bashing' destination for those staying in Muscat.

For further information see *Chapter 2, Suggested itineraries*, page 31.

LAND-BASED ACTIVITIES

Birdwatching For information on birds and birdwatching see *Chapter 1, Natural history and conservation*, pages 27–8.

Camping The desert (whether rubbly – that is to say, in the vicinity of mountains – or sandy) and the beaches of Oman are perfect for outdoor adventure. You have virtually free rein of the country for camping spots.

The small secluded bays of Bandar Khayran (or Khairan) make excellent camping and diving/snorkelling spots accessible by boat only. Seifa too is excellent for camping. The Oman Dive Centre bay no longer permits camping, but they have *barasti* huts on the beach available for rent (see *Where to stay*, page 85).

Various tour operators offer equipment rental on request, tailored to your requirements. Owing to large tour groups organising camping tours, it would certainly be best to reserve your equipment in advance with a tour operator, if you are not travelling independently. They provide everything, except a sleeping bag. If you're not bringing one from home, sleeping bags can be purchased in Muscat at the hypermarkets. Try Lulu, Al Fair, Sultan Centre (up the stairs) or Carrefour. Alternatively, the sports shops may have a supply (within the plazas at Qurum, and dotted around the capital as independents). Try Ruwi or Rusayl industrial area, if you can't find what you're after in Qurum. Other camping equipment can be bought easily from the hypermarkets.

Caving and rock climbing
The more adventurous excursions of caving and rock climbing take you outside of the capital area. **Jebel Ghul**, **Jebel Misfah** and **Jebel Misht** in the Dakhiliyah region offer excellent rock climbing possibilities. Jebel Misht has the biggest rockface of all. Tour operators in the capital will advise you of the various levels each site offers, and it is necessary to join an organised group session with skilled guides.

For those interested in caving, the **Majlis al Jinn** (the meeting place of the spirits) is located in the Sharqiya region. The main cave chamber is said to be larger than the great pyramids of Egypt. The Majlis al Jinn is accessed by a free abseiling descent. Again it is imperative that you are accompanied by experienced cavers (speleologists), arranged through a tour operator, who will also provide the necessary specialist equipment.

The **Hota cave** in Dakhiliyah region, near Hamriya, is more easily accessible for the beginniner, and is being developed for tourism (see *Chapter 7*, *The Dakhiliyah*, page 177). So too is **Al Kittan Cave**, near Ibri, in the Dhahirah region (see page 169), which contains gypsum flowers and tiny fibrous hair-like crystals formed by water. The **Teyq Cave** in Salalah is one of the largest in the world.

Caves of Oman, by Dr Samir Hanna and Mohammed al Baloushi, is published by Sultan Qaboos University, and is a recommended read.

Desert safari
For desert safaris or dune bashing, as it is otherwise known, you will need to make arrangements through a tour operator, because of the potentially dangerous nature of the terrain. A 4x4 is a necessity; so too is the driver/guide that comes with it. See pages 67–9 for further details.

Horseriding
Outside of Muscat, trails are offered by Al Sawadi Beach Resort in the Batinah region.

Mountain trekking
Trekking is a fantastic way to see and experience Oman's mountainscape (see page 53). As this needs no specialist equipment, you can do this trip independently. Trekking trips can be organised through tour operators, who offer a choice of itineraries with different degrees of difficulty. With trekking, a certain level of fitness is necessary and it is always recommended that you join an organised trek, for safety reasons.

A global positioning system (GPS) is a great tool if you like to stay informed of which direction you are walking in, and your position within the globe! You can track your walks, which can be quite thrilling when you take a later trek elsewhere and discover it brings you out very close to where you had travelled previously (perhaps just the other side of the mountain). Some GSMs (mobiles) do, however, work in the mountains. Equip yourself with enough food and water for the journey. A useful guide to get hold of is *Adventure Trekking in Oman* (see *Appendix 3*, page 276).

Wadi bashing For 'wadi-bashing' trips, you will need to venture out of Muscat. See any of the regional chapters for further details of particular wadis which are worth a visit. As just one example, Wadi bani Auf in the Batinah region is a 'must-do' wadi, and can be done easily in a day trip from Muscat. Tour operators will arrange a trip for you, if you are not wishing to explore independently. It is always sensible to go in a convoy of at least two cars for your wadi initiation.

WATER-BASED ACTIVITIES
Diving and snorkelling Oman's waters have much to offer in the way of scuba diving. There are 63 registered dive sites. The Daymaniyat Islands, the waters off the eastern coastal bays of the capital, the Musandam peninsula and Dhofar region all offer excellent diving and have nearby dive centres (see the regional chapters for further details).

Special diving packages with accommodation are offered by Al Bustan Palace Hotel and Al Sawadi Forum Resort, to name but two, and there are also independent dive centres (not linked to hotels), like the Oman Dive Centre and Bluzone, offering their own packages. Hire of equipment is included in the dive trip or course costs, as are dive permits. The full range of courses from beginner to advanced diver are offered, culminating in the award of internationally recognised certificates from PADI (Professional Association of Diving Instructors) or BSAC (British Sub Aqua Club). In addition to the details in this guide, the magazine *Adventure Oman*, available in bookshops and newsagents in the country, gives a complete up-to-date listing of dive clubs throughout the country and exactly what they offer.

The spring and summer months are best for diving with clear and settled water, but diving is possible all year round, except in Salalah (in the Dhofar region) during the June to September monsoon period.

Fahal Island, which is about a 30-minute boat trip from Oman Dive Centre, is one of the most popular dive sites in the capital, along with Ras Abu Daoud, the MS *Mimoona* wreck at Quriyat, Bander Khayran (about 15–20 minutes away by boat) and Bander Jissah. The Daymaniyat Islands are a top dive site and are about a 45-minute drive from the capital (or 1½ hours by boat) Night dives, wreck dives and dive courses are widely available. Cemetery Bay is another good location for diving, and the *Munassir* wreck has been purposefully sunk. For night dives in the winter a 5mm-thickness wetsuit is recommended; night dives in the summer require a 3mm wetsuit. To arrange a dive, contact or visit any of the dive centres in Muscat (see page 85).

Snorkelling costs around RO15 per person based on a minimum of three passengers and can be arranged through most tour operators. This can be combined with dolphin watching for a cost of around RO25.

Dolphin and whale watching Dolphin-watching tours generally last for around 2½ hours and cost about RO16 per person. Fahal Island is good for whales and spinner, common and bottlenose dolphins both in the early morning and around sunset.

Game fishing It is possible to charter a private boat for a half-day fishing trip (four–five hours) with a boat captain and experienced local fisherman for a cost of RO130, up to a maximum of six people (two rods in the water). A full day's fishing costs RO200. Call Treasure Tours (↘ *24 789505*), Arabian Sea Safaris (↘ *24*

693223), Grand Hyatt Boat House (☎ 24 602888), Muscat Game Fishing Club (☎ 99 322779), Marina Bandar al Rowdha (☎ 24 737288), Muscat Diving and Adventure Centre (☎ 24 485663) and Oman Dive Centre (☎ 99 379031). Also call any of these tour operators for **surfing** or **kayaking**. A permit is no longer required for game fishing, bottom fishing and deep-sea fishing. Spear-gun and arrow fishing are not permitted, and net fishing is permitted for traditional Omani fishermen only. This can be observed along many of the extensive beaches along the sultanate's coastline.

Sailing and boat trips Sailing, boat trips and dhow trips are all available and can be tailored to suit your requirements; speak to any tour operator for full details. Generally, these cost around RO30–40 per person (for a minimum of two people) and last for about four hours. You can try your hand at fishing in the traditional Omani way with a handline, or the modern way with rods (all equipment provided). You are even invited to cook your catch.

Sunset or scenic cruises cost around RO15 per person and again can be arranged through most tour operators. The tour takes you past the two 16th-century Portuguese forts of Muscat Old Town, and the surrounding bays of Bander Jissah and Muttrah harbour.

Capital Area Yacht Club ☎ 24 737712
Castaways Sailing Club ☎ 24 494751
Grand Hyatt Boat House ☎ 24 641234

Marina Bander Al Rowdha ☎ 24 737288
Muscat Diving and Adventure Centre ☎ 24 485663

Desert rose

4

The Batinah الباطنة

THE BATINAH COAST

The Batinah coast is an extensive stretch of beach beginning at Barka and running unbroken (except by wadis running out to sea) for some 200 miles (320km) all the way up to the Khatmat border at the entrance to Fujairah in the United Arab Emirates. After the Muscat governorate it is Oman's most populated region. To use an anatomical analogy (see *Chapter 1*, page 4), the flat coastal plain, which runs for about 25km inland, is Oman's 'underbelly', and that is the literal translation of 'Batinah'; in the same vein, the western Hajar Mountains, which lie at the end of the plain, are the 'spine'.

Until the 1970s, the easiest way to visit was by boat, as the roads between the settlements were poor and intermittent. Eccentric British consuls used to wear bathing suits under their clothes, so that they could disrobe and leap ashore, then reappear in immaculate clothing to meet local dignitaries. In 1930, it took seven days by camel to reach Sohar from Muscat, and the first graded track was not built until 1930. Today, populations in the Batinah have expanded so much that the settlements virtually run into one another for the full length of the coast. A dual carriageway has now been built from Muscat to the UAE Wadi Hatta border post, running 2–3km inland, so that the sea is never visible unless you take one of the many turn-offs down to it through the towns and plantations.

The region has a history of maritime and commercial industry and activity. Centuries ago, Sohar (located roughly halfway up the full coastal stretch) was the main trading city, renowned for its copper, and archaeological evidence of the extraction of this resource dates back 5,000 years. The whole of the Batinah coast is littered with forts and fortified enclosures (*surs*), evidence of Oman's problematic history of tribal warfare – although the warring between neighbouring tribes in this region was less than in the interior. Both Sohar and Rustaq have been the capital of Oman at various times in the past, reflecting their respective strategic positions.

Today, fishing is the mainstay, and most of the settlements along the coast are fishing towns and villages first and foremost and agricultural centres second.

GETTING THERE

From the airport Seeb International Airport is situated on the southern extremities of the Batinah in the Muscat region. You will need to rent a car or take a coach or taxi from the airport to your destination (see *Chapter 3*, page 65). Taxis are around RO20 from the airport to Al Sawadi Beach Resort.

By road A good dual carriageway runs parallel with the Batinah coast, and it is an easy, pleasant drive. The road is quieter at the weekends (Thu–Fri), when the large industrial traffic lessens.

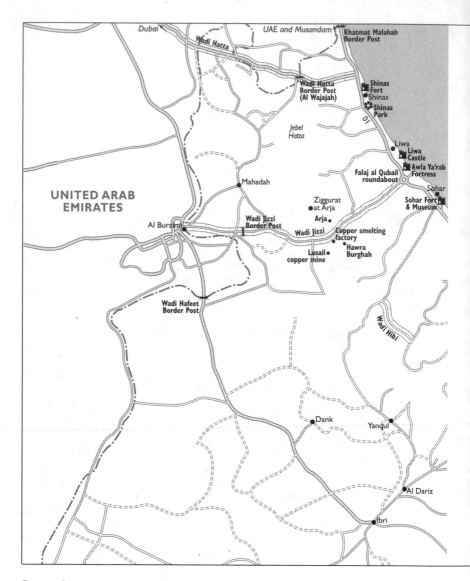

By coach All coaches from Buraimi to Muscat take the Batinah coastal route, with request stops along the route. The main Sohar stop is at the Penguin Restaurant on the highway.

WHERE TO STAY Any of the three international-standard hotels along the Batinah coast (Coral al Nahda Resort & Spa, Al Sawadi Beach Resort and Sohor Beach Hotel) make a good base from which to explore the region, and eliminate the extra driving time from Muscat. However, don't dismiss the mid- and lower-range hotels, if you are simply looking for a cheap room for a night or two.

WHERE TO EAT Good restaurants can be found within the upper- and mid-range hotels of the region. However, there are many cheap eating places outside of the

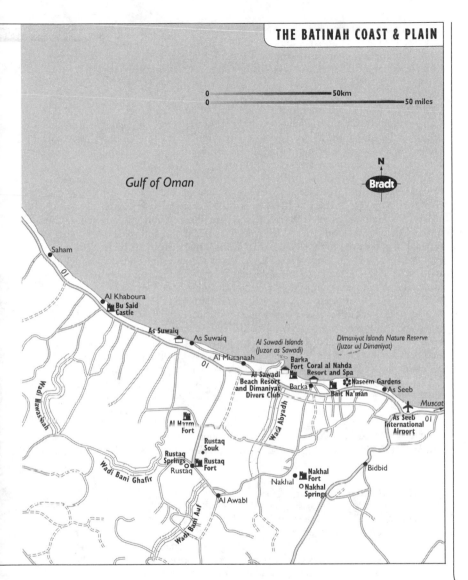

0 ———————— 50km
0 ———————— 50 miles

N

Bradt

Gulf of Oman

Saham

Al Khaboura
Bu Said Castle

As Suwaiq   As Suwaiq

Al Musanaah

Al Sawadi Islands
(Juzor as Sawadi)

Dimaniyat Islands Nature Reserve
(Juzor ud Dimaniyat)

Barka Fort
Coral al Nahda Resort and Spa

Al Sawadi Beach Resort and Dimaniyat Divers Club

Barka

Bait Na'man

Naseem Gardens
As Seeb

Muscat

Al Hazm Fort

Wadi Abyadh

As Seeb International Airport

Rustaq Souk

Rustaq Springs   Rustaq Fort

Rustaq

Wadi Bani Ghafir

Nakhal   Nakhal Fort
Nakhal Springs

Bidbid

Wadi Bani Auf

Al Awabi

Wadi Nawassiah

hotels, which are worth a try, largely in the form of Indian-run coffee shops, serving the local community. They can be found in any row of shops on the street and serve largely chicken, fish and rice dishes. Those looking for a simple Omani meal could try Alawi al Ghawi, just north of Sohar (see *Sohar*, page 131).

OTHER PRACTICALITIES
Useful telephone numbers
Batinah Police HQ ☎ 26 840096   Sohar Hospital ☎ 26 840299
Rustaq Hospital ☎ 26 875055   Sohar Post office ☎ 26 840003

WHAT TO SEE AND DO
Bullfighting Bullfighting is popular in this region and takes place on Fridays in the

winter months, rotating between Seeb, Barka, Sawadi, Sohar, Suwaiq and Saham. Any hotel along the Batinah should be able to advise you of the venue for the next event. Alternatively, you can arrange for a tour operator to transport you from Muscat, taking in other sights as well (see *Chapter 3, Treasure tours*, page 69).

Diving

Daymaniyat Divers Club (Ocean Extreme) (*Al Sawadi Beach Resort;* ⟍ *26 795545, 26 895545;* e *dive@alsawadibeach.com; www.alsawdibeach.com/dimaniyatdivers*). This dive centre is the only one in the region and is a PADI five-star Gold Palm Resort. Owing to its commitment to marine environmental conservation, it is also a *National Geographic* dive centre.

In addition to the usual half-day dive trips, two-day diving packages to the Daymaniyat Islands are offered. Boats to Al Sawadi Islands leave from here at 09.30/11.30/14.00 and return at 12.00/14.30/17.00, costing RO3/5 for children under 12/over 12. Night dives to Al Sawadi Islands can also be arranged. Snorkelling trips to the Daymaniyat Islands leave from here at 09.00 and return at 14.30, costing RO14/17 for children under 12/over 12. Hiring a mask, snorkel and fins (for either trip) costs RO5. Diving costs RO26 for a day of two dives, permit, dive equipment and snacks. PADI dive courses are available: Discover Scuba (for over 10s), taken in the safety of the swimming pool, costs RO30/36 for one/two dives at Al Sawadi Islands, RO42/50 for one/two dives at Daymaniyat Islands; PADI Open Water diver RO145, taking about four days to complete; Advanced Open Water course RO120; Open and Advanced watercourse combo RO250; Rescue Diver RO110; Emergency First Responder, CPR and Rescue Diver combo RO160; Divemaster RO250, and Bubblemaker for children 8–10 takes place in the swimming pool and costs RO20 per child per day. All-inclusive diving and weekend packages are available.

Horseriding Your best option for horseriding in this region is to enquire at Al Sawadi Beach Resort, who offer escorted horseriding trails along the beach.

Wadi trips These can be arranged either through your hotel in the region, or in advance through any tour operator in Muscat. Wadi bani Auf, Wadi Sahtan and

---

WADI BASHING

A wadi is a dried natural watercourse which has formed naturally over millennia, by rains washing down from the mountains and out to sea. Wadi bashing is the popular name for taking a 4x4 through these dried mountain riverbeds. Although the name sounds quite severe, you might be relieved to hear that the 'bashing' can be done gently or exhilaratingly, depending on your personal preference. Flash floods have been known to occur, whereby rare and short-lived storms in distant mountains can result in trails of rushing water in these mountain valleys which sweep away everything in their path. The experienced drivers provided by the tour operators in Muscat know their stuff though and there are plenty of wider wadis that have been dry for years.

Locals, tourists and expats alike enjoy this off-road adventure, which can be done as a half-day or full-day trip, or an overnighter (if you are keen on camping) taking along a picnic or barbecue and plenty of drinking water (filling up a cool box with ice and bottled drinks is recommended). In the same way, a 4x4 can be taken through the sand deserts of the country – known as dune bashing – and these can be quite breathtaking. These trips provide the opportunity to savour vast empty wilderness, which Oman has aplenty.

Wadi bani Ghafar are the three most popular wadis of the region, all of which are easily explored in day trips from Muscat.

Options for exploring the Batinah You may like to explore the whole of the coast up to the Khatmat border, before coming back on yourself and taking the two main roads inland – one being the hinterland of Sohar, the other being the Rustaq Loop. Alternatively you might like to exit the dual carriageway at the Barka roundabout to do the Rustaq Loop first, and then further up at the Sallan roundabout (after Sohar roundabout), exit the dual carriageway again in through Wadi Jizzi towards Buraimi.

It is quite possible to visit the attractions of the Batinah coast as day trips from your base in Muscat. The Rustaq Loop, for example, would make a good day trip. Or you might like to visit the Nahkal Springs as a relaxing afternoon trip. It is even possible to dive the Daymaniyat Islands as a day trip from Muscat; this can be done either as a pre-arranged boat trip from one of the dive centres in the capital, or by driving up the coast to Al Sawadi Beach Resort and arranging the trip from the dive centre there. Your choice will depend on your plans post-dive. For all of these days out, aside from the diving trip (where food may be provided on the boat), taking along a picnic is highly recommended, as there are no good restaurants hidden amid the date-palm plantations to pander to the needs of the tourist. This is the Omani countryside in its raw and natural state, thankfully. However, as an alternative you might like to pick out a hotel in the region, so that you eliminate the drive from Muscat. Al Sawadi Beach Resort, although great for sheer relaxation in its isolated spot, is not the cheapest of options as a place to stay, so do consider some of the good alternatives.

Sur Rumeis Unusual because it is built of stone rather than mud brick, Sur Rumeis is worth a brief detour off the dual carriageway (30 minutes). It also makes a good picnic stop. Take the signposted track off to Rumeis, zigzagging between walled plantations for 1–2km until you reach a small town with shops. The road is now tarmac and you can turn left parallel to the sea for a further 1km until you see its towers on the right among the trees. Follow the track round to it and you will see that it had a moat with an old drawbridge. A crumbling mosque with a *mihrab* stands beside the moat outside the walls and inside you can still climb up onto one of the towers. The internal mud-brick rooms have largely collapsed.

BARKA بركاء

Barka was one of the prosperous historic cities along this coast, and was important as an area of export to Basra (Iraq), India and east Africa. It is about a half-hour drive from Seeb Airport. The exit is clearly signposted on the dual carriageway and once you have taken the turning, the road continues for 5km towards the sea, taking you right up to the fort and fish souk. Vegetables and fresh herbs are sold from mats laid out on the ground or from the back of pick-up trucks surrounding the fish souk. And to one side, animal guts and skins are laid out in a small walled-off enclosure. A few interesting old derelict buildings remain in the open space beside it, attractively shaded by dark-green mango trees. Virtually every other shop in the village is for 'Ladies' Tailoring', except, notably, the one for the 'Sale of Ice Cubes'.

⌂ WHERE TO STAY

⌂ **Coral Al Nahda Resort & Spa** (109 chalets) ☎ 26 883710; f 26 883175; e stay@coral-alnahda.com; www.coral-alnahda.com. Located in Barka, this luxury hotel is set in 30 acres of gardens. Due to open in November 2006, it will be marketed as a 'wellness retreat', with a gym, fitness studio, spa and volleyball/tennis courts. Rates were not available at the time of publication.

WHAT TO SEE

Barka Fort (*Open daily 08.00–17.00 except when the guardian is praying or eating*) was restored in 1986 and is in fact two forts – the first Ya'arubi, the second Al Bu Said. This is the reason for the double gate, the original Ya'arubi one now being on the inside. The inner ground level is raised up to allow good drainage of rainwater or even seawater in heavy storms. There are three gun towers (look out for the bats) and two wells.

Barka Fort in its Ya'arubi form was the scene of the historical event that resulted in the ousting of the Persians from the Batinah coast and the start of the current Al Bu Said dynasty. Ahmad Al Bu Said, a merchant promoted to Wali of Sohar, signed a trick agreement with the Persians in 1748, then invited them to a grand feast in celebration at Barka Fort. After the Persians had feasted themselves witless, the Omanis slaughtered them. Ahmad's position was therefore consolidated and he founded the dynasty the following year in 1749, before setting about the reconstruction of the Omani navy.

Ostrich Breeding Farm Also in the wilayat of Barka there is an ostrich farm open to the public (⟍ 26 884869; *admission 500bzs, open Sat–Wed*), which is also an agricultural business unit. Ostrich produce, such as leather and meat, are sold on the international market. These inquisitive flightless sizeable birds come to greet you, surrounding your vehicle, before casually walking away. The breeding season is April–September and there is a souvenir shop here. Exit the highway at the Barka roundabout and travel inland for about 4km in the direction of Nakhl to reach it.

Safari Park A safari park is to be built with wild animals and amusement facilities on a 1.8million m² site (467 acres), and it is estimated that this will take at least another four–five years to come into operation.

Bait Na'man (⟍ 24 641300, ext 142; f 24 641525. *Open Sat–Wed 09.00–13.30; admission 500bzs*). An English-speaking Omani will guide you around. Signposted off the main dual carriageway just south of Sawadi (roughly half an hour's drive from Muscat), this unusual castle (fortified country house) restored in 1990 and recently renovated, is easily the most charming of its type in Oman, and made very accessible by the furnishings that bring it to life. The scale, unlike so many of the vast forts which become rather indigestible after a while, is domestic and homely, and most visitors have no trouble imagining what it would have been like living in such a house a century or two ago.

Built by Imam Saif bin Sultan (who died in 1711) in the prosperous Ya'arubi times, the house was for his exclusive use as a country retreat (a sort of Chequers); it was originally three days' journey from Muscat, but is now just half an hour away. He planted 30,000 date palms and 6,000 coconut trees around it. The gardens were irrigated by a *falaj* from Nakhl, 25km away, which is now dried up. The outside courtyard was where the soldiers would have camped, several hundred of them, to protect the imam, and there was a big raised-up cistern where rainwater collected. Inside, the high ceilings are attractively decorated and allow for coolness. The accommodation was suitable for a family of eight or nine members. On the ground floor were the toilet, bathroom, date store, kitchen and women's jail. New carpets have been laid as floor covering, too big to give an authentic feel – as original Omani rugs were and still are very small. Rush matting would have been the usual floor covering.

Halfway up the stairs was the guards' room, to stop people entering the private quarters, and the first floor had living areas only. The towers on the roof floor have cannon holes, though the cannons themselves have been taken off to Barka Fort or to the Ministry, as they were too heavy to get back *in situ* after the restoration. The walls are 1.5m thick, made from traditional Omani *sarouj* plaster which was typically soaked for 25 days, not just the one day as is the practice today. As a result the *sarouj* is less strong now than it used to be centuries ago.

AL SAWADI السوادي

There are beautiful stretches of beach at Al Sawadi, where there is a beach resort of the same name, and from where you can take boating and other adventure trips out to the Daymaniyat and Al Sawadi Islands.

WHERE TO STAY

Al Sawadi Beach Resort (100 rooms) PO Box 747, PC 320, Barka; 26 795545; f 26 795535; e sales@alsawadibeach.com; www.alsawadibeach.com. Situated on a beautiful expanse of sandy beach in a very peaceful and picturesque setting, this upper-range resort was built in 1996. Roughly 45 minutes' drive from Seeb Airport (90km from Muscat), or two hours' drive from the Wadi Hatta border, it lies approximately 15km off the main dual carriageway, and is well signposted. The disabled are catered for, and a concrete path to the sea edge facilitates easy access. Rooms are all single-storey and just big enough to squeeze in 2 extra beds for children. Each has a good-sized private sea-facing patio area where you can make your own barbecue (the hotel can provide equipment and food for RO5 pp, or alternatively you can take along your own). Its food outlets include the Periwinkles Pub, the Supper Hut

nightclub, Coral Reef Café, Sundowner's Beach Bar, Al Khanjar Omani Restaurant, Fire 'n' Spice Restaurant, Neptune's Pool snack bar, and the Waheeba Bar nightclub — all licensed. Although the beach is not private to the hotel, they have erected *barasti* (made from palm leaves) sunshades for the benefit of guests. Being driven by golf cart to your room is a nice touch. This resort is for total relaxation. The hotel supports the cleanliness and marine life preservation campaign of the government and conducts a 'beach cleaning day'. There is a Bodylines health and fitness centre and a business centre. There are good health and sports facilities and the Daymaniyat Islands are on the doorstep. Boat, dive or snorkelling trips to the Daymaniyat and Sawadi Islands are arranged from the dive centre of the hotel. Permits are easily arranged also, as a matter of course (see page 126). RO50/60 sgl/dbl (winter), exc taxes. Airport transfer RO20.

WHAT TO SEE

Al Sawadi Islands These islands lie just offshore and boat trips can be arranged through the dive centre of Al Sawadi Beach Resort. Alternatively you can negotiate with the local fishermen to take you to them. One has a sandy beach where you can picnic (Al Mugabra Island) and shelters have been erected here by the municipality. On another island (Jebel Sawadi) there is a watchtower whose stairs you can climb. These islands are also good for birdwatching. Snorkellers and novice divers are taken here

Daymaniyat Islands Nature Reserve These are a string of nine small islands situated about 16km off the Batinah coast (in both the wilayat of Seeb and the wilayat of Barka). They are about a 40-minute boat trip away from the nearest resort, which is Al Sawadi Beach Resort. The waters around the islands look remarkable from the air, when coming in to land at Seeb Airport.

The islands have been proclaimed a conservation area since 1996, and are rife in bird and marine life. You can explore the waters around the islands by diving, snorkelling or swimming, but the islands themselves are protected and inaccessible. They are nesting grounds for the endangered hawksbill turtle and the green turtle, and from April to September it is the birds' breeding season, when ospreys and red-billed tropicbirds, among others, nest here. The surrounding waters also have protected zones, the purpose of which is to preserve the coral reef. Al Sawadi Beach Resort obtains permits from the Ministry of Regional Municipalities and Environment to take guests and tourists to the waters surrounding the islands, and so all the formalities are done for you these days.

Reportedly one of the best dive sites in Oman, there are more than 20 set dive locations where coral reef, clown fish, rays, honeycomb moray eels, barracuda, tuna, green turtles, fusiliers, zebra sharks and leopard sharks have all been seen. In addition there are marine and terrestrial snake species and marine mammals such as the bottlenose dolphin, the common dolphin and the humpback whale.

The islands are broken up into western, central and eastern areas and they are named Al Kharaabah, Al Hayoot, Al Jibaal al Kibaar Island, Al Joon, Al Jebel as Sagheer, Memlehah, Al Loomiyah, Qismah and Awlad al Joon. Camping is permitted on Jibaal al Kibaar and Al Joon only, with designated areas for camp fires, and a list of strict rules and regulations.

At Al Sawadi Resort there is the Daymaniyat Divers and Watersports Club (✆ 26 795545, ext 193; f 26 795535; e dive@alsawadibeach.com; www.alsawadibeach.com/dimaniyatdivers). Boat trips, dive and snorkelling trips can easily be arranged from here (see page 121 for further information about departure times and costs).

AS SUWAIQ السويق

From the dual carriageway Suwaiq is clearly signposted off to your right taking you out towards the sea. It's quite nice to take a detour here, if simply to break the monotony of the dual carriageway. It is a quaint old village with a restored seafront fort and its share of mosques. There are four springs, the most picturesque being at Wadi Jahawar. The beach is deserted and makes a great picnic stop. The area is known for its agriculture. Bananas, citrus fruits, mangoes and herbs are grown. Bullfighting takes place here. From Suwaiq you can follow the tarmac road close to the coast for roughly 15 minutes north to Khadra Al Bu Rashid, which winds through fishing villages, past a crumbling fort and palm plantations.

Between As Suwaiq and Al Khaboura there is a cluster of three restored *surs* (walled fort enclosures) standing close to the roadside. They all have either square or round towers at their corners with gun ports. Their doors are always kept locked, but in any event they look impressive from the outside.

⌂ WHERE TO STAY

⌂ **As Suwaiq Motel** (15 rooms) PO Box 455, PC 315; ✆ 26 862241, 26 862243; f 26 862242. This simple, 1-star hotel lies about 100km from Seeb International Airport towards Sohar. Take the right-hand turn towards the sea, and the motel is about 3km down the road, about 4km away from the sea. Licensed restaurant; live Arabic and Indian entertainment. No pool. RO13/16 sgl/dbl.

Coming from the Wadi Hatta border post there is, almost immediately, a delightful area to the right, with mountain wadis flowing all year round. There are many places where cars can get close to the wadi bottom and the only downside here is the accompanying litter, especially at weekends.

The road south passes out of the mountain scenery within 15 minutes, and after that the easiest picnicking spot is not until Sohar, 45 minutes further on. Take the same signpost off towards the coast as for the Sohar Beach Hotel from the Sallan roundabout and in less than 1km you will see an extensive landscape park to the left of the road. You can enter it from either end, inland by turning left at the traffic lights, or at the shore end where you can turn left into a car park area. There are toilet blocks and water fountains, shaded pagodas and children's playgrounds with a central lake. You will find it near-deserted, except on Fridays. The Sohar Beach Hotel lies just beyond it.

If you want a wilder spot, another option is to drive further on south of Al Khaboura (1½ hours from the Wadi Hatta border). Turn off towards the coast at Qasabiyat along dirt tracks through the banana and mango plantations until you reach the tarmac road parallel to the main dual carriageway. Follow this as it winds scenically past date palms till you come to the point where the tarmac crosses a picturesque wadi flowing with a wide river. Leave the car beside the main road and then walk along either side of the riverbank to find a picnic spot among the palm trees. The birdlife here is stunning.

WHAT TO SEE

Bu Said Castle Just before (south of) Al Khaboura look out for signs to Qasr Bint Al Za'ad (towards the sea) and follow the dirt track as it leads between two shops and into the lush date-palm plantations. After about 1km you will hit tarmac again and turn left to follow the road at right angles to the coast. This is an extremely attractive road, almost devoid of traffic, and gives you a real feel of the fertility of the Batinah and the serenity it enjoyed before the days of the dual carriageway. It passes a very pretty wadi outlet to the sea, making a good picnic stop. Keep going and follow signs for Qasr Bint Al Bu Said until you reach the crumbling *sur* of that name, set right on the beach beside a small modern village, disappearing further into the sand year by year. The cannon, once wedged on one of the walls, has now vanished.

AL KHABOURA الخابورة

Al Khaboura itself is unremarkable except as a centre for traditional weaving, the products of which are sold in the Muscat heritage shops. Leather tanning and boat building are other occupations, and sugar cane, dates, wheat and cotton are grown here. Its fort is in ruins except for one tower by the beach.

WHAT TO SEE

Wadi Hawasinah At Al Khaboura a left turn at the roundabout heads you towards Ibri through the Wadi Hawasinah. The tarmac runs out fairly soon and the 130km drive is difficult, requiring a 4x4 and taking around three hours. The proposed tarmac road shown in some maps is unlikely to be built for years, as the terrain makes it a tricky and expensive engineering feat, Wadi Hawasinah being narrower than the other two inland routes of Wadi Sumail (the Sumail Gap) and Wadi Jizzi.

Saham صحم Just south of Sohar, Saham is signposted 3km off the main road. It is about 1½ hours from Seeb International Airport – or 1½ hours from the Hatta border.

Saham is an attractive old fishing town with an interesting seafront. Camel and horse racing are popular events here, along with bullfighting events, which are held on alternate Fridays to Sohar's. Keep straight on over the roundabout with the herons, following signs to As-Souk, until the road leads you onto the seafront, where it fronts the beach for 1–2km to reach the fort with its red flag flying at the far end. On the way you pass some decayed seafront houses, once the homes of rich merchants. Traces of blue and white paint remain along the decorated arches and windows that look out across the sea from the balustraded verandas. A few old *shasha* (reed) boats are usually pulled up onto the beach, still in use. The town souk is beside the fort, on the beach, and though the fort is theoretically open to the public it is in practice difficult to coincide a visit with a guard being present to open the door. Sultan Qaboos holds one of his royal camps at Seih al Taybat, which is in this wilayat.

SOHAR صحار

Muscat to Sohar is 230km and takes about 2½ hours. Sohar, once known as Majan (*ma-jan* means 'ship's skeleton' or 'chassis'), has great historical significance as a major trading port in the past and for this reason stood as the capital of Oman in past centuries.

Sohar in its heyday was described by the 10th-century Arab geographer Istakhri as 'the most populous and wealthy town in Oman. It is not possible to find on the shore of the Persian Sea nor in all the land of Islam, a City more rich in fine buildings and foreign wares than Sohar.' His contemporary, the Arab historian Al Muqaddasi described Sohar as 'the hallway to China, the storehouse of the East'. Traders disembarked from Sohar on their journeys to China, and the legend of Sindbad is said to have originated from here. The city was destroyed in the 10th century and never regained its former glory.

However, for over 1,500 years until 1749 when the Al Bu Saids moved their headquarters to Muscat, Sohar was still Oman's most prestigious and influential town. The *khor* (creek) beside the fort, which was once its splendid harbour, is now silted and almost completely vanished. The only evident reason today for the success of the town's location is its situation at the end of the Wadi Jizzi, one of the few east–west passes across the Oman mountain range, and from where copper was exported to Mesopotamian cities over many centuries.

When the Portuguese arrived in 1507 they found it a thriving town needing 1,000 people to defend the fort alone. An Augustine church was subsequently built there by the Portuguese, who retained it until they were driven out in 1650 by the native Ya'arubi sultans of Oman.

Sohar during the Al Bu Said dynasty was the stage for just two more moments of high drama: one in 1866 when a sultan was shot by his own son whilst asleep and the other in 1952 when the present sultan's father, angered by the Saudi occupation of Buraimi, ordered his army to gather at Sohar for the march up Wadi Jizzi to Buraimi; in the event the army never set off, dissuaded from action by the British.

GETTING THERE Taking the right-hand turn at Sohar roundabout you pass over several smaller roundabouts. Keep straight over these smaller landscaped roundabouts until you come close to the sea then you have the choice of turning right or left at the final mini-roundabout. The left turn takes you past a Shell garage

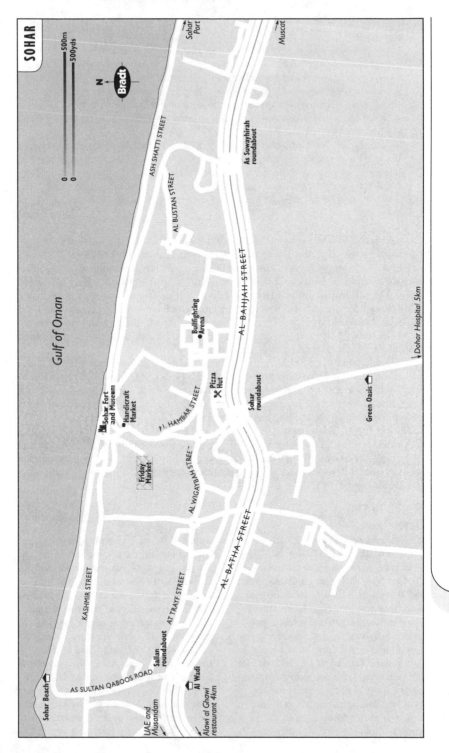

(on your left) and if you continue onwards the Sohar Beach Hotel lies on the right-hand side of the road just before the traffic lights crossroads. The hotel is set in a whitewashed stone wall enclosure, with large impressive wooden gates. This hotel is frustratingly not signposted. Back at the final mini-roundabout the right-hand turn takes you round to the coast road which, a little later, bends round and back on itself past the Sohar Fort (now on your left) which occupies an elevated position opposite the clearly signposted wali's office. For a visit to the fort you can drive up its sloped frontage to a car-parking area. The entrance door is just here, hidden behind a tree and flanked by two cannons.

Today the sprawl of Sohar remains considerable. The northern edge is at the Sallan roundabout, from where the Sohar Beach Hotel is signposted. The southern edge is the Sohar roundabout, which is identified by its vast globe statue. From here, Sohar town centre is signposted off towards the sea. The old part of town is called Harat al Hajara, and the fort and wali's office are located here.

Simple fishing boats lie on the dark sand and after 2–3km you will see the Sohar fish souk, a series of stalls set right on the beach. This is a hive of bustle in the mornings, when the freshly caught fish are laid out. You need a fairly strong stomach to stroll through it, especially as the sun gets stronger, heating the mounds of entrails.

WHERE TO STAY
Upper range

Sohar Beach Hotel (40 rooms) PO Box 122, PC 321, Al Tareef,Sohar; ☎ 26 841111; f 26 843766; e soharhtl@omantel.net.om; www.soharbeach.com. The Sohar Beach Hotel is about a 3hr drive from Seeb Airport — or a 45min drive from the Wadi Hatta border post. It is roughly halfway between Muscat and Dubai airports and provides a good stopover if you want to split the approximate 4hr drive either to or from Dubai. This is a gem of a hotel, on Sallan Beach in Sohar. It sits on the road that loops through Sohar and rejoins the highway, although not at all clearly signposted from the Sohar roundabout. Instead continue on the dual carriageway past the Sohar roundabout, and exit at the Sallan roundabout (north of Sohar) in the direction of the sea. The hotel is signposted from here, and from this end it is just past the only set of traffic lights on the loop road, and sits within its high walls on the left-hand side. The hotel is like an Omani fort in appearance, with 4 round crenellated towers. The rooms, suites and chalets are arranged on 2 storeys in a semicircle round a large pool and situated within 11 acres of landscaped gardens. Facilities include Al Sallan coffee shop, Al Zafran Arabian nightclub, serving meze, seafood and grills, Al Jizzi lounge for residents and members and Al Taraif lounge public bar. Barbecue evenings every Thu in winter, and private barbecues for 5 or more guests can be arranged. There are lots of activities for kids, like crazy golf, croquet, go-karts, beach buggies, beach volleyball, water scooters, watersports and pleasure boat rides. The room rates were cheaper than the Sawadi Beach Resort, and the décor and the welcome far superior. Accepts credit cards. *RO45/50 sgl/dbl, exc taxes and b/fast.*

🏠 **Al Wadi Hotel** (80 rooms) PO Box 459, PC 311, Sohar; ☎ 26 840058, 26 841995; f 26 841997; e gmalwadi@omanhotels.com or reservationsalwadi@omanhotels.com; www.omanhotels.com. At the Sallan roundabout (the next one up from the Sohar roundabout, 10km from Sohar), take a left. The hotel is signposted and has

a small pool. Al Sallan is the licensed restaurant offering continental, Indian and Chinese cuisine (open 06.00–23.00). There is Al Waghbah bar (open 12.00–15.00 and 18.00–01.00), and a new licensed restaurant – The Oasis (open 19.00–01.00). Al Majaz is the club bar for residents only (open 19.00–01.00). This hotel is one of four in the group which includes Al Falaj Hotel, Ruwi Hotel and Sur Plaza. They do not provide airport transfers. They use Budget and Hertz for arranging hire cars. *RO35/40 sgl/dbl, exc taxes and b/fast.*

Mid range
Green Oasis Hotel ☎ 26 846442; f 26 846441; e alwaha@omantel.net.om. There is a restaurant here. *RO22/28 (old building), RO40/45 (new rooms) sgl/dbl, incl taxes and b/fast.*

✖ **WHERE TO EAT Alawi al Ghawi** (nicknamed Cute Ali) at the roadside 9km north from Sohar roundabout and 4km north from Sallan roundabout. On the coastal side of the road, this is a simple house made of *barasti*, serving rice with fish in spicy sauce with onions, limes and lettuce, dates and water, followed by sweet herb tea. The menu is fixed and the prices low, although it is unlicensed. You eat on the floor in traditional style under ceiling fans in the room to the right. The room to the left is for prayers.

WHAT TO SEE
Sohar Fort Museum (☎ 26 844758; open Sat–Thu 09.00–13.30, admission RO1/500/250bzs non-Omanis/Omanis/children). To reach Sohar Fort from the Sallan roundabout take the road towards the coast, passing the Sohar Beach Hotel on your left and following the tarmac as it bends to run parallel to the coast. From the 'globe' roundabout follow the road for some 2–3km until you reach the white painted fort of Sohar, now converted to a museum, and set overlooking the black sandy beach.

Passing through the gateway into the Sohar Fort courtyard there are various outbuildings including a prison. Before you walk over to the tall square keep, which houses the museum proper, you will need to pop into a small central building to pay your entrance fee. A small booklet can also be bought for 200bzs. On the left of this central reception building are the visitors' toilets.

The four-storey keep/museum, opened in 1993, is laid out well with many old weapons, rifles and navigation equipment, including artefacts from the area's ancient copper trade. These are accompanied by a comprehensive historical summary of Sohar's navigational and overseas trading history, especially of the princes of Hormuz and the medieval fortress of Hawra Burghah (see page 134).

Sohar Fort dates to AD795, although it was renovated in the 14th and 15th centuries by the emirs (or princes) of Hormuz. There is said to be a 10km-long escape tunnel, leading from the fort to the beginning of the wilayat of Buraimi, which was used during sieges. The current buildings are thought to be 200–300 years old. Fully restored in 1985, it has a commanding location just in front of the beach, opposite the wali's (governor's) office. The surrounding gardens have been well landscaped.

Outside, excavations in the sand are clearly visible. Conducted in 1980–82, these revealed fine quality brick-built foundations of a 14th/15th-century fort and houses of rich merchants thought to be the princes of Hormuz, who had a strong garrison here. Many fine pieces of Chinese porcelain were discovered, confirming

Sohar's extensive trade links. The empire of the princes of Hormuz, with their headquarters on the island of Hormuz (in the strait of that name), fell to the Portuguese in 1507 after two centuries of rule here.

Just behind (inland from) the fort a new handicraft centre has been built in traditional style with domes and courtyards, selling and displaying local crafts.

Sohar Port There is now a modern fully operational industrial port at Sohar, a little further along the coast from Sohar Town (in the direction of Muscat), which received its first vessel in 2004, although fully opened in 2006. Oman's other two ports are the Raysut Port in Salalah and the Sultan Qaboos Port in Old Muscat. *Mina* is the Arabic for port.

LIWA لواء

Continuing up the main highway from Sohar, the next village you reach is Liwa, signposted 2km off the main dual carriageway. Past the village and date plantations is the castle. To reach another picturesque picnic spot or campsite, continue on, after Liwa Castle, towards the beach turning off to the right before the houses along a track that leads to a smaller ruined fort. Beyond lies a stretch of water like a lake bounded by low dunes, rich in birdlife and pleasantly wild. In the Harmul area the Awla Ya'rab Fortress, built of white clay, is located on the beach.

WHAT TO SEE

Liwa Castle The central keep has very elaborate decoration and with care you can still climb up to the upper rooms via a crumbling outer staircase to see the decorative niches and plasterwork of the top *majlis* (men's sitting room). A modern settlement just behind the fort means that young children are prone to follow you round the fort, not always in a way that is welcome.

SHINAS شناص

This town is the most northerly of the Batinah region and has a number of castles and forts, including Shinas Fort and Ras al Malah Castle, as well as a park noted for its forest of mangrove trees (or *qurum*, in Arabic). Fruits and vegetables, such as bananas, mangoes, lemons and tomatoes are grown in the vicinity.

WHAT TO SEE

Shinas Fort Shinas Fort, restored in 1997–98 and now open to the public, is signposted 2km off the main highway towards the sea. The simple classic coastal design has four crenellated walls enclosing a rectangular courtyard with a round tower at each corner, built of mud brick and faced with traditional Omani *sarouj* plaster. There is a freestanding mosque in the courtyard. The fort was built in Shinas's heyday around 1800 when the town was allied with the Persians, and quite separate to the rest of Oman. Shinas fought with the Ras al Khaimah Qasimi tribe against British shipping in the Gulf. The British and Omani mainstream retaliated and in 1810 the fort was sacked and forced to surrender.

FROM SHINAS TO THE KHATMAT MALAHAH BORDER POST From Shinas, the road to the north leads to the Khatmat Malahah border post with Fujairah, which would be the way to travel to reach Musandam, or Sharjah or Ras al Khaimah emirate.

FROM SHINAS TO THE WADI HATTA BORDER POST AND WADI KHABAB Instead of continuing straight up the coast road to the Khatmat border and on to Musandam, taking a well-signposted left at the roundabout leads you to Dubai and the Wadi Hatta border post. There is magnificent scenery along this route, which culminates in the Wadi Khabab.

The drive from Muscat to the Wadi Hatta border post, non-stop cruising at the 120km/h speed limit, takes three hours minimum – roughly one hour to Sawadi Beach, another hour to Sohar, and the third to reach the border post – though in practice, with stops for petrol and leg-stretches, most people would allow at least four hours. Coming the other way, from the UAE into Oman, the Wadi Hatta border post is the easiest and quickest of all the crossing points, mainly because there is no UAE exit post. This means that only one set of forms needs to be filled in and only one checkpoint needs to be crossed, followed by the standard vehicle search.

Wadi Khabab Immediately before the border (on the Oman side) the scenery is magnificent with jagged mountain peaks dominating the wadi gorges, many of which have year-round running water. If you want to camp in this area of the northern Batinah, but more off the beaten track, follow the sign left to Tumait for 9km, shortly before the Wadi Hatta border post. The dirt track crosses the wadi bed and climbs a steep track out of the valley. Take the first left fork after the wadi (approximately 500m from the Tumait sign) and stay on this for some 6km until you reach date plantations set above a gorge, flowing with water. This is the Wadi Khabab, known for its blue pools, created by deposits of calcite in the rock and the reflected light. It has to be full daylight for you to appreciate the colour, with the blue sky above. There is no village here and the track continues along the right of the wadi, arriving at an open space beyond the plantations, which is ideal for camping. The track is good and can be negotiated by a saloon car, as long as the water level in the first wadi by the tarmac is low. The pools themselves are not deep and are more for splashing and wallowing than swimming.

THE BATINAH PLAIN

The Batinah Plain is fertile from the mineral-rich soil washed down from the mountains into the wadis, namely Wadi Jizzi, Wadi Hibi and Wadi Ahin, and it is watered by many wells. These have been drilled to excess in recent years, which has led to seawater seepage into the soil. However, the land still produces dates and limes together with tomatoes, carrots, onions, aubergines, cauliflowers, peppers, lemons, bananas, mangoes, guavas and even tobacco. Inland, this fertile plain gives way to gravel plain that reaches back to the mountains, broken up only by a few scrubby bushes and trees.

WADI JIZZI وادي الجزي Few people are aware how much there is to see in the hinterland of Sohar, but an enjoyable few days can be spent based at the Sohar Beach Hotel exploring Wadi Jizzi with its ancient copper mining sites, the medieval stronghold of Hawra Burghah and the ziggurat (temple) at Arja. All are likely to be deserted and all are set in landscapes of wild beauty. This wadi was one of the two major inland corridors permitting access to the sea; the other was the Sumail Gap that links Muscat with Nizwa and the interior. Sohar grew up here because it was the natural port for the copper dug from the ancient mines along the Wadi Jizzi, copper that was destined eventually for Mesopotamia via Umm Al Nar (now Abu Dhabi) and Dilmun (now Bahrain).

Getting there Wadi Jizzi is reached by forking inland at Falaj Al Qubail roundabout some 20km north of Sohar, a roundabout recognisable by its landscaped artificial rocks, model goats and waterfall. It starts off very wide and becomes narrower and more mountainous as you head further inland towards Buraimi.

HAWRA BURGHAH FORTRESS This worthwhile excursion from Sohar is now easily drivable even in a saloon car since the construction of the wide graded track to the Wadi Al Jizzi Dam. The 13th-century fortress is dramatically sited on the summit of a rock outcrop that rises 200–300m above the Wadi Jizzi which it straddles.

The medieval fortress was the most important of several forts built by the Nabahina dynasty of hereditary kings in their attempts to resist the invading Hormuz princes. Its strategic location at Hawra Burghah enabled it to dominate the passageway through Wadi Jizzi to Buraimi. Beyond it to the south stands the unmistakable triangular **Sohar peak**, the highest mountain in the area at 1,600m and used by early navigators as a landmark. Its huge white limestone cone rises directly behind the town of Sohar as seen from the sea.

The name *Hawra* means 'white limestone' in Arabic and *Burghah* means 'garden' in Persian. Besides the defence walls it is the elaborate water system of dams, cisterns and plaster-lined *falaj* channels (see box, *Chapter 7, The falaj system*, page 179), which make the exploration of the hilltop interesting and which give it its name. In its heyday the various terraces and levels must have been lush with crops and vegetation, enabling the inhabitants to hold out against long-term sieges, and testament to the fact that rainfall must always have been high enough to sustain life on this magnificent hilltop.

The ascent of the steep hill takes 10–15 minutes and is best made from the north side where the track nearly touches the foot of the hill and where there is a breach in the walls through which you can enter. The upper section of the hill is quite a scramble and requires good strong footwear. Once on top it takes the best part of an hour to look around the surprisingly extensive city. Try to avoid the midday period as there is no shade on the summit.

Getting there Take the road inland towards Buraimi from the Falaj al Qubail roundabout for some 13km until you reach the blue sign marked left for Wadi al Jizzi Dam (4km). As you head inland, and once you reach the foothills, try to attune your eyes to the beehive tombs along the ridges on both sides of the road – there must be upwards of 50. Before reaching the turn-off to the Wadi al Jizzi Dam, archaeology enthusiasts who want to take a closer look at these tombs might like to turn off to a town called Willi – a sorry collection of hovels to the left of the road.

From Willi a dirt track to the left leads on through the low hills with many beehive tombs lining the ridges to either side, within easy scrambling distance of the track. Though they are mainly in a collapsed state, their sheer size and number is nevertheless impressive. Following the track out beyond these hills brings you close to an interesting group of rocks shaped like a falcon's head, an excellent perch for a picnic.

Back at the Wadi Jizzi turn-off after this detour (take the second turn after the sign to avoid the village), follow the track for 3km and continue straight at the fork that heads left towards the dam. It is a wide, dark-brown graded track that crosses the wadi stream in two places before reaching the foot of the distinctive outcrop which it skirts right round to the left. At times of heavy rain the wadi crossings can be impassable to all but 4x4s.

THE ZIGGURAT AT ARJA This archaeological ruin is remarkable not for its scale or size, but for the fact that it exists at all. The only one of its kind in the whole

Arabian peninsula, a ziggurat is a very early kind of temple, built in terraces, similar to a step pyramid. The earliest and most famous ziggurat was at Ur of the Chaldees in southern Mesopotamia. Arja itself was the main centre for copper mining in Oman up to the 12th century. A total of 32 copper smelting sites have been identified in this area, centred on Wadi Jizzi. Estimates suggest that in medieval times Arja produced 48,000–60,000 tonnes of copper. Copper was massively exploited here for nearly 4,000 years. The result was the gradual deforestation of the entire mining area to provide fuel for smelting. Omani copper has a high nickel content and the copper deposits here were formed millions of years ago at the bottom of the ocean, in the lavas now exposed in Oman ophiolite rocks.

One side of the ziggurat has a clearly recognisable processional ramp leading to the summit, which would have been used by early priests making sacrificial offerings. The exact nature of these practices is a matter of pure speculation – as is the position of this ziggurat which appears to be oriented towards a dramatic dark pyramid-shaped peak on the far side of the valley.

Archaeologist Paolo Costa and English Orientalist T G Wilkinson conducted an archaeological study in 1978 on Arja and the ancient copper mining settlements, the results of which were published by the Omani Ministry of National Heritage and Culture. The ziggurat, as well as ancient houses and furnaces found in the area, were dated by this study to the 10th century.

Getting there The journey from Sohar in search of the ziggurat takes you through some attractive mountain scenery and gives you the chance to see some of the more remote villages. From the main road inland to Buraimi, look out for the blue sign to the right signposted Arja (6km) which you reach some 23km from the *Falaj al Qubail* (Falaj of Tribes) roundabout (recognisable by its rocks, model goats and waterfalls), and just 1km or so before arriving at the massive modern smoke stack chimney of the copper smelting factory. Follow this graded track, which is easily drivable by saloon car as it winds through the foothills, to emerge into a valley after about 4km, then fork right along the edge of the wadi on the track signposted to Arja. This track leads in a straight line for 1–2km along a ridge until it arrives at the small northern settlement of Arja with its smart white mosque topped with a blue cone minaret, the most prominent building. Directly in line with this mosque, look to the left to catch a glimpse about 500m away of the stone terraces of the ziggurat. There is a track that leads round to the far side, where you can park in order to explore it properly.

Continuing on the track leading away from Arja village the road passes the old mine, now close up to your right, and comes to a dead end in a huge open cast mine ringed with a wire fence.

LUSAIL (AL ASAYL) COPPER MINE This is the most spectacular of the copper mines, mined as recently as 20 years ago, but now abandoned. It is about a 1½-hour detour off the main coastal highway. Here stands a famous rock arch – its date and origins unknown – beside the huge open cast mine. All around the foot of the arch are extraordinary rock colours showing the mineral wealth in reds, whites, purples and yellows.

Lusail is not marked or signposted off the main road. To reach it look out for the old tarmac road roughly 1km after the chimney stack of the modern copper smelting factory, running on the left, parallel to the main road. Get onto this road and turn right, then follow it over a wadi crossing, up and over a hill with a Pakistani mining settlement of Portakabins to the left. Then continue down over the second wadi crossing and arrive at a dead end with 'Danger: no entry' signs. This is where you park and walk on. The deepest ancient gallery at Lusail was 88m below ground and the length of the galleries was 20–30m with the roof supported by acacia wood and date palm. Food and water for workers was raised and lowered by winches, many parts of which have been unearthed. Tools and the mined ore were also transported this way. When functioning in the 1980s Lusail used to produce 2,500 tonnes of copper ore a day, while Bayda and Arja each produced 1,000 tonnes, and in total the factory produced 20,000 tonnes of refined copper a year. The Majis jetty, 17km north of Sohar, was specially constructed in 1983 for exporting the copper.

Crossing over the earth rampart on the way to the mining area many samples of turquoise/green copper can be found in the rocks, as well as some fool's gold. Correctly known as copper pyrites, fool's gold is made of copper, iron and sulphur. It looks bright and yellow when freshly unearthed, but tarnishes with exposure. The rock arch lies about a ten-minute walk further on, passing a few sealed-off mine shafts on the way.

Returning to the junction at the modern copper mine and its smoking chimney stack, fork to the right onto the track opposite the chimney and climb up leaving the bridge over the road to your left, then continue straight on over the crossroads. Follow this wide track for 2km along the ridge until you reach a small track forking to the right, then follow this for 500m to reach the edge of the ridge overlooking the Wadi Jizzi, with the remains of an ancient settlement and field systems. This makes a good picnic spot.

According to Sumerian texts there were 32 mining settlements built along the great wadis and foothills of these mountains. This copper mining area was referred to as Magan and there are at least 50 mentions of Magan in Mesopotamian texts of the 3rd century BC. From these texts we know that the farmers of Magan grew sorghum, wheat, barley and dates, and that they had herds of camels, cows, sheep and goats. The landscape was evidently much more heavily wooded and the climate wetter than now, but the necessity of chopping firewood for the furnaces resulted in the gradual deforestation of the region. The miners' houses were built of stones with imposing towers inside which were wells. Their circular graves now known as Umm Al Nar style were 5–13m in diameter with up to 200 skeletons inside. Besides copper, the other resource of this area that interested Mesopotamia was diorite. Mesopotamia lacked such stone, suitable for carving into statues, and here it was easily gathered as the rains washed it down from the mountains into the wadi beds and thence to the coast, where it was collected and loaded onto ships.

TO BURAIMI VIA WADI JIZZI It is about an hour's drive from the Falaj al Qubail roundabout on the coastal dual carriageway to the Wadi Jizzi Omani border post, which you have to pass in order to get to Buraimi (although Buraimi is in Oman!). The good tarmac road bends and weaves through low-level jebels and past old villages with their mosques, forts and watchtowers. As this is not dual carriageway, it requires alert and aware driving, as other vehicles may overtake in risky fashion. (For further information on Buraimi, see *Chapter 6, The Dhahirah*.)

THE RUSTAQ LOOP

Al Sawadi Beach Resort makes an excellent base for the inland circuit via Nakhl, Rustaq and Al Hazm, three of Oman's finest forts. Each fort takes at least an hour to visit so set aside a day, or ideally two, for the round trip. Alternatively, if time is not an issue, the locations on the loop can easily be visited in a series of outings from Muscat.

The more scenic approach of the two ways into the loop is opposite Barka, taking the inland route marked Nakhl and Rustaq. This brings you to Nakhl after

15 minutes and then on to the 40km stretch to Rustaq, which leads through some spectacular mountain scenery in the approaches to Jebel Akhdar, with many water-filled wadis and picnic spots. The stretch from Rustaq onwards via Al Hazm to the coast opposite Wudam is by contrast dull and flat, with no wadis and the mountains ever more distant; there's little to see here.

MUSLIMAT Just before Nakhl you will notice a turn-off to Muslimat. The modern town now engulfs the 300-year-old walled village, recognisable from a distance by the squat round tower rising above the date plantations. Drive round, following the walls, until you reach the point where you notice the arched gateway entrance beside an impressive two-storey mansion – built around 1900, but recently restored. The old *falaj* follows the edge of the walls, fast flowing and wide, but has lost much of its charm through modern concrete reparatory and maintenance works. Immediately to the right after entering the gateway, some steps lead up to the old mosque – still in use – with a deep well on the raised platform beside it. Inside it has round pillars with arches and a beautifully decorated plaster *mihrab* niche.

Many of the two-storey houses can be explored in the now deserted village, a fascinating testimony to the lifestyle lived just a few decades ago by many Omanis.

The other main feature of the town is the huge round defence tower set by itself in the centre of the village. Now locked, its rooftop was used in the past to signal to the fort at Nakhl.

NAKHL FORT قلعة نخل (*Roughly 120km from Muscat;* ↘ *26 781384; open Sat–Thu 09.00–16.00; admission free*) was built to protect the oasis and trade routes through Nizwa to the coast. Its construction seems to have been a rather piecemeal operation. It is believed to be pre-Islam, although it was restored in the 3rd and 10th centuries AD, during the reign of bani Kharous and Ya'aruba imams. It was then reportedly built upon further in 1649, by the Ya'arubi family, for whom it served as headquarters throughout the 18th century. The gate, fence and towers of the fort were built later, in 1834, during the reign of Imam Said bin Sultan. Final restoration works were completed in 1990, at which time rooms were labelled and furnished with crafts and antiquities.

From a distance it does not look anything very special, but the closer you get (once you fork off at the signposted turn), the more impressive it becomes. The fort has six towers, with walls that ingeniously follow the natural contours of the high rocky outcrop on which it sits. Labelled rooms, such as the *majlis,* the judge's room, and the jail, aid an understanding of past times. You can then progress upwards and inwards through a second gateway into the private family quarters. This is the most charming area furnished with cushions and ornaments and with the guest room boasting a painted ceiling. As in all forts, the layout ensures that the men's living areas get the best position to catch the prevailing wind through their windows, while the women's quarters get the less comfortable inland side. The wali still conducts weekly meetings in the public majlis room and there is an antique gun collection.

NAKHAL SPRINGS (AIN A'THOWARAH) These hot springs are probably the best known of all the springs in Oman and make a popular picnic spot. They are situated about 3km beyond Nakhl, accessible only via the tarmac road behind the fort. This road winds on through the date plantations, past old decaying houses (some still lived in, to judge by the washing lines and satellite dishes). The road then arrives at the flowing stream of the springs beside some shops and you park and walk on through the picnic area, laid out with tables and shades. You can walk

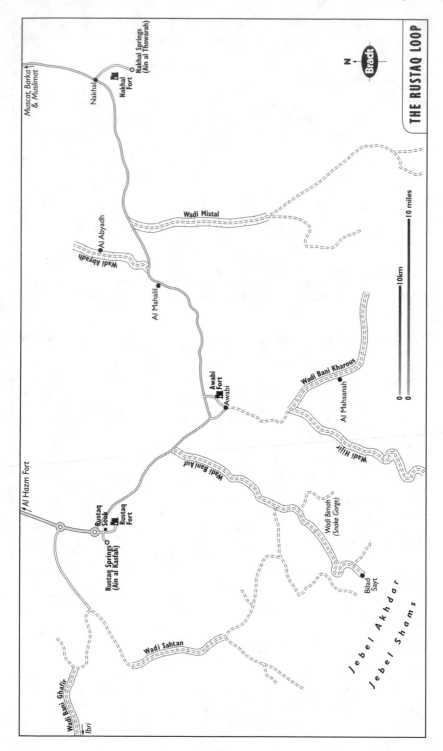

N

Bradt

Muscat, Barka & Muslimat

Nakhal

Nakhal Fort

Nakhal Springs (Ain al Thowarah)

Wadi Mistal

Al Abyadh

Wadi Abyadh

Al Mahalil

Wadi Bani Kharous

Awabi Fort
Awabi

Al Mahsanah

Wadi Hilir

Wadi Bani Auf

Al Hazm Fort

Rustaq Souk

Rustaq Fort

Rustaq Springs (Ain al Kasfah)

Wadi Bimah (Snake Gorge)

Bilad Sayt

Jebel Akhdar

Jebel Shams

Wadi Sahtan

Wadi Bani Ghafir

Ibri

10km

10 miles

0

0

further up to the actual source of the springs at the end of the picnic area. There are steps down to the stream which flows all year round, and little fish swim about in shoals.

These springs are an important water source for the residents of Nakhl, stemming from Wadi Hammam. In spring, white lilies grow among the green pastures in the shade of the palms. The waters are said to have medicinal and healing qualities. A notice beside the stream forbids cars from driving across but local vehicles tend to take no notice and drive over to the houses and village on the other side. The village women still come down to the stream to collect water, balancing the containers on their heads. Together they wash their clothes and dishes in the running water, chatting as they work to ease their chores.

WADI MISTAL With a 4x4 you can take a fork to the left after Nakhl to explore the natural phenomenon of the Ghubra Bowl (6.5km off the tarmac) surrounded by the high peaks of Jebel Akhdar. Beyond is **Wokan**, a mountain village known for its terracing, especially pretty in February when the almond and apricot trees are in blossom. The total distance to the end of the drivable track is about 30km from the tarmac.

WADI ABYADH وادي أبيض Some 6km beyond the turn for Wadi Mistal, a turn on the right signposts Al Mahaleel and leads into Wadi Abyadh (White Wadi). This wadi is famous for its blue pools, caused by the white calcite covering the pool bottoms that reflect the blue sky. Fork immediately right along the tarmac, then bear left after 1–2km into the gravel plain that leads to the narrow wadi. A 4x4 is essential and your speed must be kept up to avoid getting bogged down in the loose gravel. Water always flows here and is very plentiful in the winter rainy season. The pools themselves lie about 10km into the wadi from the main road and you can walk from that point for about 1½ hours to reach the village of Abyadh. There are many delightful picnic spots among the lush vegetation.

AWABI العوابي From the Mahaleel turn-off the road towards Rustaq now enters some of Oman's most spectacular scenery in the foothills of Jebel Akhdar. Geologists call these reddish-brown jagged rocks **ophiolite**, meaning ocean crust, now pushed above ground. The wadi you are crossing time and again is the Wadi bani Kharous, which starts high in the hills and flows out here to merge with the Wadi Abyadh.

The tarmac now sweeps round to Awabi, more or less at the centre of the inland loop from the coast. Having virtually passed the town, a tarmac road forks off to the left towards the old fort of Awabi, at the head of the gorge leading into the mountains. This fort is badly crumbling, its glass all smashed and the upper floor severely collapsed from heavy rainfall.

Beyond it the track leads into the gorge, the start of Wadi bani Kharous, and after 1.5km on the left, close beside a rusting black water gauge pipe, are a series of rock drawings on the cliff face and boulders, mainly of fighting men and animals. The drawings are thought to be 1,500 years old.

Awabi has been home to Omani scholars, poets and the literati, and was known as a place of eminent learning.

WADI BANI KHAROUS وادي بني خروص If you have a day to spare with a 4x4 you can continue up this spectacular wadi, dominated by high mountains, to explore the villages. The remotest of these villages, **Al Mahsanah**, has highly decorated castellated houses of a style unique in Oman, but reminiscent of Yemeni architecture. The distances are not great and Mahsanah is only about 30km off the tarmac from Awabi, but the drive is slow and takes 1½ hours. A further 20km off the tarmac is the village of **Al Hajar**, which has a famous old mosque called Al Ghamama. The rocks in this upper part of the wadi are some of the oldest found in Oman, ranging from 250–600 million years old.

As the road leaves Awabi, the next settlement you reach, on the very edge of Rustaq, has an attractive tower surrounded by a group of ruined two-storey houses, with the modern village then spreading out below.

WADI BANI AUF, BILAD SAYT AND WADI BIMAH (SNAKE GORGE) Beyond Awabi (by about 10km) is the signposted track to Far and the start of Wadi bani Auf, considered by many to be the most scenically spectacular of any of Oman's mountain drives. It culminates at Bilad Sayt, probably Oman's most picturesque mountain village, with extensive fertile terracing. A 4x4 is essential and the first 10km is along the bumpy gorge floor green with mango, lime and oleander. After rain the pools of water here can be tricky to negotiate. The sparkling white stones scattered about on the wadi floor are natural quartz. At 14km from the tarmac the track forks, with a right turn signposted to Al Jafa, leading (after 10km or so) to the Sahtan Bowl set directly at the foot of Jebel Shams (Oman's highest mountain at 3,048m), and making an interesting circuit via which to return to the Rustaq Loop and then Barka.

For Bilad Sayt, keep left and continue along Wadi bani Auf through splendid scenery till you come to the village of Zammah, 22km from the tarmac. A good shaded picnic spot is about 17km along the road before Zammah, where a deep ravine on the right appears to be blocked by boulders. In fact behind the boulders are a series of pools connected by waterfalls. You can park opposite at a little side road.

Bilad Sayt lies a steep 6km beyond Zammah requiring a 4x4 for the vertiginous winding track. Its name is said to be a corruption of 'the town I forgot' (*bilad nasaytuhu*) so called after a Moghul general sacked the villages of the wadi but overlooked this remote one.

The road is signposted to the right and after 26km (where the track drops into a dip) there is a parking area big enough for two or three vehicles. The narrow cleft in the dip is known as Snake Gorge because it twists and turns across pools, rocks and waterfalls. Snake Gorge can be tackled by trekkers and is a 3km-long walk, bringing you out at Zammah. The first 2km of this is very rough going with climbs and slippery rocks, unsuitable for young children. Even for grown-ups it is not to be undertaken lightly and a local guide is recommended. People have been drowned here in flash floods and it is difficult to monitor the weather when you can see only a tiny piece of sky above you. Speak to any tour operator about this, quite separate, adventure.

After Snake Gorge the graded track forks again with the left turn taking you 3km to Hat, the end of the wadi. The right fork leads you for 1km to reach Bilad Sayt, the view opening up in spectacular style as you round a bend.

Another way to enter the village, less intrusively and with a bit of exercise, is to continue on the Hat track for just a few hundred metres until on the right you notice the entrance to a slim shady defile. The 30-minute walk along the well-polished rock path here leads past deep pools where villagers do their washing and children play. It helps if you can speak Arabic here so that the villagers feel less like animals in a zoo that you have come to gawp at.

WADI SAHTAN If you wish to continue your loop round to Rustaq you should return to the fork marked Al Jafa. There are many villages in the vast natural Sahtan Bowl and some are known for their traditional beekeepers. Using date-log hives made into 1m-long hollowed-out palm-tree trunks, they stack the logs in threes and put a small piece of honeycomb inside. The ends are blocked up leaving only enough space for the bees to enter. From the time of nesting the bees take two months to produce the honey and the beekeeper repeats the process three times a year by opening the ends and smoking out the bees and then removing the honeycomb before starting all over again. It can be a profitable business with a single honeycomb fetching as much as RO60. One hive produces around 100 bottles of honey a year. A rapport seems to develop between bees and keeper and the beekeepers wear no protective clothing and say they never get stung – either that or they no longer notice.

The village of An Nid (the nest) can be used as the start of an ascent of **Jebel Shams**, using a guide and donkeymen from the village to carry water. Donkeys are essential on such a trip and the recommended number is one donkey per person to carry water, food and bedding for the two days.

There is at present nowhere to stay in Rustaq overnight so unless you camp the night before the ascent the best bet is probably to stay at the Sheikh's Lodge, which opened in 1997 offering simple accommodation in traditional Omani style and located at the entrance of Wadi bani Auf, between Awabi and Rustaq. This is still a two-hour drive from An Nid. From Rustaq, An Nid is a one-hour drive.

Leaving the Sahtan Bowl to complete your loop, you enter some 8km of a narrow ravine which follows the course of the Wadi Sahtan. It is a bumpy drive, with strewn boulders and running water at most times of year and the occasional piece of rock art etched onto the boulders.

Once out of the ravine another 2km along the track brings you to **Tabaqah**, a village with an impressive and photogenic fort on a cliff edge, guarding the entrance to the Wadi Sahtan. The women of the village are often found doing their laundry in the flowing stream beneath the fort. A steep descent takes you out of the wadi and onto the track that forks left via Wadi bani Ghafir to Ibri (a bumpy, challenging, three-hour drive away), or along the tarmac to Rustaq, 9km further on.

RUSTAQ الرستاق

Rustaq, which means 'market town', is about a two-hour drive from Seeb International Airport or about 1½ hours from Sawadi Beach Resort via Nakhl.

The town served as the Omani capital for some 150 years, first as the Ya'arubi imams' base from 1624, then in the early part of the Al Bu Said dynasty from 1744. In the late 18th century, Hamad bin Said established Muscat as the capital and it has never been contested since.

Today, Rustaq is still a major administrative centre. The town owes its importance to its strategic location at the exit of a wadi on the coastal side of the mountains, so it served as a commercial centre for trade between the jebel and the villages of the interior and the coastal Batinah towns. The people from the mountains and the foothills of Jebel Akhdar brought fruits such as grapes, peaches, pomegranates, plums, figs and apricots for sale here, while the coastal people brought fish, lemons and bananas. Pure Omani honey is most sought-after and of high quality. Beekeeping is one of the main occupations in Rustaq.

As a result of its political and commercial influence, various industries grew up in Rustaq, notably silversmiths famous for khanjars, ornaments, copperwork and other traditional crafts. Remnants of these crafts remain in Rustaq old souk opposite the fort. Wooden storage chests can be found and old weaponry on the antique stalls. Date packing has long been carried out here and today there is a proper date-processing factory. Omani *halwa* (see box above) from Rustaq is also famous.

Today the town of Rustaq is a shadow of its former self, though still easily the largest of the inland towns set on this side of the Jebel Akhdar. The presence of two or three roundabouts and sets of traffic lights seems rather incongruous. The approach is entirely modern with shops run by Indians lining the dual carriageway, as you follow the signposts to Rustaq Fort and town centre.

WHAT TO SEE

Rustaq Fort (*Open winter daily 08.00–17.00, summer daily 08.00–18.00, closed Fri 11.30–13.00 for prayers*) is said to have been built four centuries before the arrival of Islam in Oman and is one of the country's oldest. It sits at the foot of Jebel Akhdar. It is easy to miss the left turn at the traffic lights leading directly to the fort, tucked down the side of the wadi bed. However, you can just as easily follow the main road as it loops round to the left, giving you views of the fort before you drive down along the bumpy track through the wadi to reach the main entrance.

Heavy rains have meant frequent closures for repairs, including continuous closure from October 1997 to September 1998. Huge efforts have been made to improve the waterproofing of the flat roofs, as it is this that causes most damage. The rainwater from heavy sudden storms is unable to drain away, and brings the ceilings down with its weight, flooding the rooms below. You can park by the main entrance beside a telephone box that looks more like a summer gazebo under the shade of a tree, and this will then serve for visiting the old souk.

A tour of the fort, which is built on three levels, has four towers, and is furnished with old items, can take between one and two hours, depending on your level of interest. In addition to the fort itself there is a large courtyard area which you enter on stepping through the tiny entrance door. Strolling in a circuit right round will give you glimpses of wonderful butterfly life amongst the wild plants and the chance to use the old *falaj* system to refresh yourself. The water still flows strongly and is hot. The castle inhabitants used to collect this water in pottery jars and hang it in a shady place to cool, after which it could be drunk.

To the right as you first enter is the large 32-pillared mosque which used to be the Friday congregational mosque for the town before the large green-and-white one with twin minarets was built on the modern outskirts. Known as Bayadha Mosque, it was an institute with a fine reputation from which many eminent scholars graduated. To the left as you enter (after shedding your shoes) is a magnificent elaborately sculpted plaster *mihrab* marking the direction of prayer towards the holy city of Mecca. The mosque is still used sometimes on Fridays as the overspill for the new mosque.

To the right as you walk towards the main castle entrance, the building that is raised up and overlooked by the double towers (the Red Tower and the New Tower) is where the wali stays when he comes to town. The sultan has issued a new decree that once a month the wali and the judge (*qadi*) must come to the fort and hold an open *majlis* session for the townspeople and surrounding village people in the official suite of rooms within the fort, designed for this original purpose – a fine revival of the old tradition in its authentic setting.

Inside, the most splendid rooms with painted dark red-and-white ceilings are the imam's rooms, up on the second storey, to catch the prevailing wind. The central beam on the ceiling carries Koranic inscriptions listing some of the 99 attributes of God, ie: the king, the wise, the holy etc. Note too the women's tiny mosque, barely big enough for two to enter, with its minute *mihrab* to the left.

Continuing up as far as you can you come to the left (southeast) corner of the Tower of Winds, the largest of the four towers, with its British steel cannons guarding all directions set round the huge central pillar. The date of 1821 can still be seen on them, and one has its end blasted off where it was hit by the enemy cannons before it could fire. Through one of the window seats you will see the white domed tomb of Imam Saif Bin Sultan, raised up on a hill. The highest tower of all, to the right (northwest) corner, is the mysterious Devil's Tower (*Burj A'Shayateen*) which has no entrance and appears to serve no function whatsoever. You can walk up along the parapet round the courtyard to approach it, but nowhere can it be entered. The two graves in the courtyard belong to two previous imams and the big long windowless room along the back of the courtyard was a barracks for the guards.

Back down at the same height as the imam's rooms are the wali's offices, which are the only way through to approach the two more modern towers, the Red Tower and the New Tower. On the ground floor are prison cells, stores and an armoury.

The earliest castle on this site pre-dates Islam and was built around AD600 by the Persian governor who controlled the area at that time. A second fort was built on the ruins of the early Persian fort by a tribe called the Julandas in 1250, and then the first Ya'arubi imam moved his capital here from Bahla and rebuilt Rustaq Fort again in 1650. The Red Tower was added in 1744 by the Al Bu Saids and the New Tower in 1906. The fort also featured in the 1950s' Jebel War, when it served as home to the dissident Taalib Bin Ali. Its greatest heyday was in the 18th century under the Al Bu Saids, when Ahmad Bin Said, head of the Al Bu Said dynasty, used it as his capital from which he co-ordinated the expulsion of the Persians and restored independence to the country.

Rustaq Souk To reach the old souk, walk up the alleyway to the left of the fort entrance, following the wall of the fort until you reach an entrance on your right into the collapsing stalls and lanes. The best time to visit the souk is before 11.30 and Fridays are the busiest days. Many stalls have caved in completely after heavy rains, their earth and *barasti* roofs lying entangled on the floor. The area is not large, and it takes about half an hour to browse round, longer if you stop to buy a few items. Herbs and spices, walking canes, cheap shoes etc are on offer for a pittance, while the occasional *khanjar* and belt sells for RO60–100. Water bottles, colourful cow-tethering bands, mousetraps and tools are among the collection of eclectic items. The Omani stallholders are getting on in years, white-bearded with lined faces, but extremely friendly to visitors. When they pass on it is unlikely the younger generation will take their place.

AIN AL KASFAH SPRINGS These hot springs, not far from Rustaq Fort are less attractive than the springs at Nakhl, but nevertheless are said to have the same healing and medicinal properties for rheumatism and skin complaints (due to the sulphur content). They have been walled to create segregated bathing areas for men and women. A famous 15th-century doctor, Rashid bin Umeirah, lived nearby (the remains of his house and clinic can still be seen) and wrote his medicinal expositions on the illnesses of the day and how to cure them in the form of long descriptive poems, which could be memorised more easily.

The springs today are fetid and the attendant rest area is neglected and rubbish-strewn with a thriving hornet population.

FORTS

There are over 1,100 fortifications in Oman, an extensive network of forts, fortified castles and watchtowers built throughout all the regions to defend against foreign invaders like China, Persia, Europe and Africa, but also from other internal rival tribes.

Forts and fortified castles went beyond defence and also contained law courts, the wali's residence and office and Islamic schools. Watchtowers were used to raise alarms, collect taxes and protect the local water supply.

The design of forts was intended to delay and disorientate the enemy. The outer walls were the delaying method, where the enemy encountered the date honey poured through the slit over the entrance. If he did succeed in entering, he was confused by towers, spiral staircases and doors at all levels, ever-changing design features in each fort. It is often impossible to tell if one room is a new room or an extension of the previous one and without help it is difficult to find the way out. As the last resort there were also tunnels for the escape route, sometimes linking neighbouring forts, and sometimes so tall that soldiers on horseback could ride through them.

The sheer number of forts in Oman can lead after a time to 'fort fatigue', reminiscent of Freya Stark's 'tomb fatigue' in Lycian Turkey – 'The time came when D B and I looked at each other and said, "Do we really have to go and look at that tomb?"' The fact that so many exist is a reflection of the essentially warring nature of the Omani tribes. The fort was the centre of authority, headquarters of the main sheikh or the wali. Any pretender to authority had to control the fort, and anyone who had something to protect like a water source or fertile ground would build watchtowers and forts on prominent hilltops to ensure they stopped a neighbouring tribe from taking it. War was a way of life in order to survive in a country not overly blessed with natural resources. The *sur* (walled enclosure) was built as a refuge for the villagers.

Since the coming to power of Sultan Qaboos, the major forts of the country have undergone a gradual process of restoration. This process is continuing and being stepped up, in line with the country's relatively recent concentration on, and investment in, tourism.

Getting there To reach the springs, take the sign to the right marked Ibri off the main road into Rustaq and follow this as it loops round for 1.5km.

HAZM FORT (*Open Sat–Thu 08.00–14.00; admission free*) is located about 15 minutes' drive further along on the loop from Rustaq Fort (the loop leads you back to the main highway). Your first sight of Al Hazm Fort, squatting in the sandy plain set well forward of the mountains, gives no inkling of the architectural complexity within. Built by the Ya'arubi imam Sultan Bin Saif II in 1711, it is an example of Omani Islamic architecture, its exterior plain, even a little disappointing, though its scale once you are close up more than compensates. The Arabic Al Hazm means 'the vanquishing one' and when you have completed your tour you will understand why the fortress was itself never vanquished. An Arabic-speaking guardian greets you, in full Omani regalia complete with rifle and cartridge belt.

The roof is built on columns and the walls are at least 3m thick. In the courtyard is the first of the three wells, the other two lying within the impregnable walls, impossible for the enemy to cut off or poison. The fort also had its own running water supply throughout the ground floor, in the form of the *falaj* system (see box, *Chapter 7, The falaj system,* page 179) The restful sound of running water can be heard in many places on the ground floor. This too could not be cut off by the enemy, as it only appears within the castle. In the washing area the water has a faster flow.

Defence and secrecy have been the dominant factors influencing the remarkable labyrinth of corridors and rooms inside. Among the more amazing features of the castle is a series of prisons which you can still climb down inside. Prisoners were left here to die with no light, food or drink. The horses were kept upstairs on the roof and the water was pulled up by bucket to a trough. You will be shown the imam's intercom system leading from his private room to downstairs, enabling him to give instructions to his servants. The imam himself slept up on a raised platform where it was both cooler and safer. A secret passageway links the east and west towers. This passageway is the coolest place in the fort, as it is set between the first and ground floors, with massively thick walls, its only connection to the outside world being some small ventilation holes. There are also secret passages leading outside.

There are no refreshments available here, but there is a picnic area laid out behind the fort with tables and shades, unfortunately rather dilapidated. Thursdays and Fridays are the busiest times, when there may be several hundred visitors a day, but on other days ten–20 a day is more normal. There are two Omani guides, both speaking some English. The guided tour takes one hour.

The Batinah RUSTAQ

4

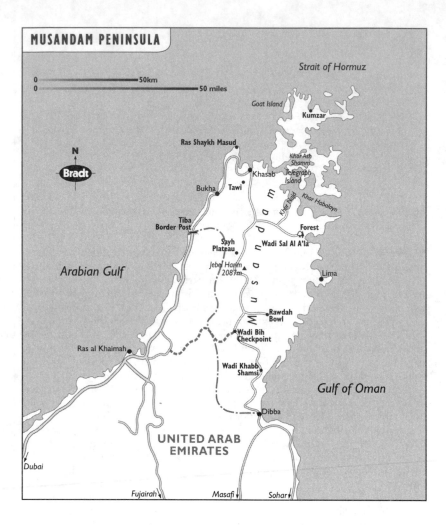

MUSANDAM PENINSULA

Strait of Hormuz

0 _____ 50km
0 _____ 50 miles

Goat Island

Kumzar

N

Bradt

Ras Shaykh Masud

Khor Ash Shamm

Khasab

Telegraph Island

Bukha   Tawi

Khor Najd

Khor Habalayn

Tiba Border Post

Forest

Sayh Plateau

Wadi Sal Al A'la

Jebel Harim 2087m

Lima

Arabian Gulf

Rawdah Bowl

Wadi Bih Checkpoint

Ras al Khaimah

Wadi Khabb Shamsi

Gulf of Oman

Dibba

UNITED ARAB EMIRATES

Dubai

Fujairah   Masafi   Sohar

5

Musandam مسندم

Musandam is a paradox. While it is Arabia's least-known and least-populated corner, it overlooks one of the world's busiest and most strategic waterways: the Strait of Hormuz. The strait is only 55–95km wide, but a large percentage of the world's crude oil trade passes through it.

Isolated from both Oman and the United Arab Emirates by its own rugged mountains which fall directly into the sea, the Musandam peninsula belongs geographically to neither. Only sparsely populated by the semi-nomadic Shihuh tribe, it did not much matter to whom it belonged until the late 1960s and early 1970s when the granting of oil concessions to foreign companies meant that allegiance had to be decided and borders drawn up accordingly. The Shihuh decided their allegiance lay with the Sultan of Oman and hence the border was drawn along the edge of Shihuh territory to separate it from the tribes whose allegiance lay with the Sheikh of Ras al Khaimah. Musandam is therefore cut off from the rest of Omani territory by a 70km tract of UAE land. Some of the old tribesmen have been heard to mutter that they now wish they had backed the UAE horse as it may have proved more beneficial to them through possible generous handouts from the UAE federal budget.

The origins of the Shihuh themselves are unclear, and with their separate and distinctive language and culture, it is tempting to speculate that they were the original inhabitants of the region, driven up into the barren mountains by successive waves of Yemeni Arabs arriving from the south. The Shihuh are the most populous of the three tribes of the Musandam, living in the mountains in the winter rainy season and down in the coastal settlements in the summer, where they own gardens and run small trades.

There are thought to be some 200 villages scattered about in the mountains, half on the UAE side and half on the Omani side of the border. Of the Omani ones some 20 are still inhabited, while on the UAE side there are perhaps around five. The numbers are always declining: the Sayh Plateau, for example, was well inhabited even in the late 1980s with busy, tended fields, whereas now just a handful of villagers remain.

The scenic fissures of the mountains, locally known as Ruus al Jebel, have been likened to the fjords of Norway, and, coupled with the diving of the region, are the main tourist draw.

Roads are a recent phenomenon in this peninsula; before 1980 precipitous footpaths were the only links between the mountains and the flat open plains of Fujairah and Ras al Khaimah. Even donkeys could not be used on such paths, and the Musandam towns of Khasab, Bukha, Limah and Bayah, with their small harbours, could be reached only by small boats.

Musandam has throughout history had no exploitable commodity – no copper diorite or chlorite in ancient times, no oil in modern times – so no incentive has existed to defy nature and blast routes through the barren limestone. There is no coastal plain, and the sheer cliffs plunge straight into the sea in all but a few coves and bays where the towns and fishing villages sit. These are in turn connected by steep paths to a handful of mountaintop plains and terraces where rainfall in winter is plentiful enough to allow for limited agriculture.

Thor Heyerdahl, sailing in his replica Sumerian boat *Tigris* in the 1970s down through the Gulf towards the Strait of Hormuz, could hardly believe his eyes at his first sight of Musandam:

> Above the cloud banks, raised above the earth was land, like another indistinct world of its own. Solid rock was sailing up there ... with rock walls dropping almost perpendicularly into the sea.

The currents carried these early boats round Musandam to land on the safe shores of the Batinah, where the plentiful water and fertile coastal plain made it by far the more attractive option. In addition, the commodities needed by Sumeria (irrespective of all the copper from Wadi Jizzi), could be far more easily loaded and collected from such open coasts, in preference to the narrow beaches of Musandam with their difficult hinterland routes.

The mountain villages represent a pragmatic adaptation to the semi-nomadic way of life. In the summer months, the villages are deserted while the people migrate to the coast to fish or to tend date plantations. The possessions left behind in the village therefore need to be secured and kept safe until the autumn, giving rise to the invention of the House of the Lock (*Bait Al Qufl*, in Arabic). Built of local limestone, whose strata lend themselves to easy splitting into tabular blocks, the foundations go 1½–2m below ground, giving the strength to withstand the torrential winter rains. The roof of stone and mud is supported by acacia trunks and needs frequent repair. Paolo Costa, contemporary Italian archaeologist and art historian, calls it 'the most extraordinary and unique building in the Arabian peninsula ... the result of local adaptation of the architecture to the semi-nomadic way of life'.

The Royal Geographical Society, which conducted a survey here in 1972–73, concluded that the Musandam peninsula has tilted into the sea by up to 60m over the last 10,000 years along a fault line from Sham in Ras al Khaimah to Dibba. Wells on the coast coincide with where the main settlements are and the water table is only a few feet above sea level. There is enough water to sustain date-palm and fruit-tree oases only at Dibba, Limah, Khasab, Qida and Bukha. In Khasab they had a particularly inventive method of fertilising crops via the water system by allowing *metoot* (the local sardine) to dry and rot in the sun for a few days in the empty well reservoir. Then they started the well and the stinking fecund water was released through the irrigation system. The rains that can occur intermittently and torrentially between November and April (peaking between December and February) mean that the only way to retain both topsoil and water is by building terraces. Silt is thereby trapped behind retaining walls, creating areas of potentially intensive cultivation. To protect the precious crops (barley, wheat and lucerne) against sheep and goats, the outer retaining walls are made high and topped with thorn bushes, while the inlets of water conduits are protected by tall vertical stones. The crops in such conditions never make a surplus, but goat breeding can produce a bit of extra income in the way that they can be sold or bartered for dates, cloth or other items.

At Khasab, a third of the date palms are owned by the Kamazirah, a secondary tribal group to the Shihuh, whose centre is at Kumzar (as their name suggests). Kumzar is a small fishing village in one of the northernmost bays of the peninsula. It is undoubtedly Oman's most remote settlement, so isolated that its only link to the outside world is by boat; its hinterland is too sheer to be crossed on foot to link with the mountain plateaux behind. As a result the Kamazirah are fishermen, boat

A whole range of crafts centred round basketry and palm-work survive in Musandam and are still used for functional purposes like mats for drying fish and dates, conical food covers, weighing baskets, fans and date sacks. The palm ribs were used until recently, and were soaked in water then sliced into strips, for domed fish traps and chicken coops. Nowadays they are made of wire. Chemical dyes from India are used in the decorative basket work as none of the requisite plants for natural dyes exists in the northern extremities of Musandam. The fibrous top part of the palm trunk was used by men for making rope and string, while the women used it for scouring pots and pans.

Traditional measurements are still used, based on distances from elbow to fingertip, or thumb to little finger when the hand is outstretched. A woman can make 100 fans as well as 20 mats and food covers a month, but today as more and more artefacts for the home are bought rather than made, a woman will not make them unless there is a commission. Women have more time than in the old days, with water and electricity making household chores easier, their children out at school, and men out fishing, so most would be willing to sew and braid each day if there was a demand. The crafts are no longer passed automatically from mother to daughter and father to son, as there seems little point and the children are away at school anyway.

builders and sailors. They even speak their own language (a kind of mix of Persian and Arabic but still distinct from either) and the women are veiled and wear black face masks. The tribal group has a limited number of goats, which they take by boat to seasonal grazing grounds on the islands, notably Jazirat Al Ghanim (Goat Island). There are ruins on Goat Island in which pottery finds have been dated to Sassanian times (3rd to 6th century AD).

The third and smallest tribal group of Musandam are the Zahuriyeen, found mainly in Khasab and Bukha. In summer they work as fishermen and as farmers in the palm gardens. Each tribe (*qabilah*) is divided into a number of clans or extended families (*ahl*). Each *ahl* breaks down into a family group (*batinah*) made up of single households (*bait*).

Administratively, Musandam is separated into four wilayats: Khasab, Bhuka, Dibba and Mudha.

GETTING THERE

Musandam is separated from the rest of Oman by 70km of United Arab Emirates territory and so the options are either to fly into Khasab, or drive in through one of two borders: at Thibat (from the emirates of Ras al Khaimah and Dubai) or Dibba (from the Batinah coast of Oman, after a stretch through the United Arab Emirate of Fujairah).

This chapter follows the route from Dubai, entering Musandam at the Thibat border post, just beyond Sham in northern Ras al Khaimah.

BY AIR There are currently only two flights each week on a 19-seater aircraft from Seeb International Airport in Muscat to Khasab, and two return flights. If you are restricted for time, this means that an overnight stay is likely to be all you will manage, because the days on which the flights fall allow you either one night or six. In terms of excursions offered by the tour companies in Khasab, one night is probably all you will need to get a flavour of this peninsula.

Muscat–Khasab Thursday dep: 08.55, arr: 10.00
Khasab–Muscat Friday dep: 16.05, arr: 17.10

Muscat–Khasab Friday dep: 14.30, arr: 15.35
Khasab–Muscat Thursday dep: 10.30, arr: 11.35

The return ticket costs RO49 and there is a 10kg luggage restriction.

As with Salalah in the south of the country, Oman Air operates package deals with the hotels which include a return economy flight, one night's accommodation with breakfast, and airport transfers. For RO68, this seems quite a good option (and you haven't got to concern yourself with arranging the short transfer from the taxi-less airport).

Seats on the right have the better view. If you are seated on the left, it appears as if the wing of the aircraft might just clip the mountains as you come in to land!

The departure lounge of this small airport is surprisingly modern and clean, complete with a flat-screen TV on the wall, and all signs in English. (For details of Oman Air offices, see *Chapter 2*, page 36.)

BY CAR From the Batinah coast of Oman, you enter Musandam at Dibba (Wadi Bih) border post. There are two border post crossings on the way up, which have to be crossed again on the way back down, travelling this route. As with entering and leaving Buraimi, there is considerable bureaucracy at the borders. Although it seems more progressive to be able to get visas and road permits on arrival at any border post between Oman and UAE (you used to have to apply in advance), visas still have to be closed down on exiting Oman and a UAE visa needs to be issued; then, on entering Omani territory at Musandam, another Omani visa needs to be purchased and the UAE visa closed. The whole process has to be reversed on the return leg.

The drive from Muscat takes about seven hours and is about 460km. The drive from Muscat to Dibba takes roughly four hours on tarmac (350km), then it is about another three hours to Khasab (110km) on steep tracks for which a 4x4 is essential.

From the Dubai/Ras al Khaimah end, you enter Musandam at the border post at Thibat.

It is now possible to do the whole Musandam loop, but the border-post rigmarole may just dissuade you. By flying, you avoid it all, but are car-less when you get there.

BY COACH To get to Musandam by coach you will need to travel from Dubai via Ras al Khaimah to Khasab.

BY SEA From the UAE it is possible to get to Musandam by sea. For further information contact tour operators in Dubai. A good starting point for information is Hormuz Line Tours (see opposite).

GETTING AROUND

BY TAXI Note there are no taxis in Khasab, or in Musandam! So it is advisable when you are making your booking with your Khasab hotel to confirm that you will be transferred from the airport. If you have booked one of Oman Air's packages then the transfer is included and should be arranged as a matter of course. If you haven't, then don't expect your hotel to prompt you to the fact that you will need to be collected from the airport – you have to do all the thinking for yourself.

BY HIRE CAR With Oman Air's flight schedule, you have the option of staying for one night or six nights. An overnight stay is fine and will give you a basic feel for the region; it is easily possible to take a half-day mountain safari trip and a half-day boat trip (arranged through your hotel or chosen tour operator) in this time. For the mountain safari you will be collected from your hotel by your guide in a 4x4, and for your boat trip, your hotel will transfer you to the harbour; therefore, for an overnight stay it will not be necessary to hire a car, unless you want to be strictly independent with the limited time you have between tours.

However, if you stay for six nights, and want to explore a little, a hire car is essential, and without a 4x4, you will be severely restricted.

The question of car hire met with fear and alarm in Khasab. On enquiry I met with wide-eyed, 'ums and ahs' from the few local tour operators and hotel receptionists. Finally, and after a real struggle, I was told there are no car-hire companies in Oman. Then I managed to find a number for Al Mawada Bridges car rental (c/o *Musandam Sea Adventure Tourism;* ↘ *99 552027*). Outside of this, Dolphin Tourism provided me with two names. These were Jassim (↘ *99 414600*) and Mohammed Sulaiman (↘ *99 449666*). You can try an unsolicited call to them if you haven't organised anything, but otherwise I recommend that you make specific arrangements in advance via your hotel in the region, and get these confirmed. Through the Khasab Hotel, and with no notice, a Toyota Echo saloon (model 2005) with manual drive was the only vehicle available (at a cost of RO10 per day). Overall, though, the Golden Tulip Resort is probably your best bet for arranging a vehicle, as language and communication can be difficult elsewhere.

Fuel Fuel stations are limited to the two in Khasab and one at Bukha. There is nothing between Khasab and Dibba.

TOUR OPERATORS

The few tour operators there are in the Musandam region are all located in Khasab. They offer the stock dhow cruises, mountain safaris and city tours. The most common attractions are Jebel Harim (seen on a mountain safari tour), Telegraph Island (seen on a dhow cruise), dolphin watching, snorkelling, fishing, diving, fjords, birdwatching and falcon towers.

Dolphin Tourism PO Box 111, PC 811; ↘ 26 730659, 92 423833; f 26731676; e dolphint@ omantel.net.om; www.dolphintourism.net. Offering the usual array of tours: the Khasab city tour, a mountain safari to Jebel Harim, and dhow cruises. Full-day safaris include lunch; half-day safaris include refreshments. RO20/15 full-day/half-day dhow cruise, 09.00–16.00/09.00–13.00 or 13.30–19.30; RO35/25 full-day/half-day mountain safari, 09.00–16.00/ 09.00–13.00 (under 12s half price; under 5s free). Dolphin Tourism works in association with Khasab Hotel and Qada Tourist Hotel (so ask at either).
Hormuz Line Tours PO Box 441, PC 811; ↘ 26 731616; f 26 731615; e faisal@hormuzlinetours.com or hormuzline@hotmail.com; www.hormuzlinetours.com. This company offers dhow cruises of all sorts, as well

as all the usual tours on offer in Musandam, including fishing, diving and camping. For travellers from Dubai, there is a Dubai office (↘ +971 4 2664541; f +971 4 2664542). Special packages include transportation from Dubai, visa fees at the border, accommodation and tours.
Khasab Travel & Tours PO Box 464, PC 811; ↘ 26 730464, 26 730464; f 26 730364; Muscat office; ↘ 24 706463; e khastour@omantel.net.om; www.khasabtours.com. They operate from Esra Apts (opposite Khasab Airport), and also have a desk in the Golden Tulip Resort in Khasab (↘ 26 831351; e omandisc@omantel.net.om), a branch in Muscat under the name of Oman Discovery, and a Dubai office (↘ +971 4 2669950; f +971 4 2686857; e khaztour@emirates.net.ae). Established in 1992, they offer excursions which include half-day dhow trips, 09.00–13.00 (RO15), full-day dhow trips

(RO25), full-day dhow cruise on the air-conditioned *Sindbad Dhow* (RO40), half-day 4x4 mountain safari, 13.30–16.30 (RO30), full-day mountain safari (RO40), and diving trips with tank and weights (RO28). In addition they also offer an overnight stay on the *Sindbad*. They also arrange camping safaris and full equipment, kayaking, trekking, fishing expeditions, and special 1-, 2- and 3-night packages, plus car hire, subject to availability. **Musandam Sea Adventure Tourism** ☎ 26 730069; f 26 730069; ☎ 99 346321; e adventure@omantel.net.om; www.msaoman.com. Offers mountain safaris and dhow excursions to the fjords of Musandam.

DIVE CENTRE The region's only dive centre is in Khasab, operating from the Golden Tulip Resort:

Extra Divers & Partners PO Box 498, PC 811; ☎ 26 730501, 99 877957; f 26 730501; e musandam@extra-divers.li; www.extra-divers.li, www.scubasailing.de. This German-owned dive centre is located in the Golden Tulip Resort, and is accessed via the hotel's pool terrace. They offer courses, dives, and live-aboard trips on a traditional dhow into the fjords of the Strait of Hormuz. They operate 2-tank dives by boat daily, 08.30–15.00. Guests are collected from any Khasab hotel.

WHERE TO STAY AND EAT

The only places to stay and eat in Musandam are in Khasab itself (see page 156).

OTHER PRACTICALITIES

USEFUL TELEPHONE NUMBERS
Police stations
Bukha ☎ 26 828399
Dibba ☎ 26 836999
Khasab ☎ 26 730148

Lima ☎ 26 735111
Kumzar ☎ 26 733001

Hospitals and health centres
Bukha Hospital ☎ 26 828562
Dibba Hospital ☎ 26 836443
Khasab Hospital ☎ 26 730187

Lima Health Centre ☎ 26 735147
Kumzar Health Centre ☎ 26 733047

WHAT TO SEE AND DO

BIRDWATCHING Many tourists visit Musandam for the purpose of birdwatching alone, although there are no birdwatching tours offered by the tour operators in Khasab. The most common large birds are the Egyptian vulture, Bonelli's eagle and the Barbary and sooty falcon, which can be spotted anywhere by the vigilant as you drive the mountain roads.

CAMPING You can camp on the beach, where shades, playground and water tanks are provided, but they are not very clean and rather close to the road. The best spots in the winter months are down in the **Rawdah Bowl** and the **Sal Al A'la Forest**. In the summer, the mountains are better, preferably without a tent as the terrain is rather rocky for tent pegs. For campfires, do not use local wood and palm fronds which will damage the fragile ecology; take your own. Camping tours are offered by the four main tour operators listed above.

Local fishermen can drop you off at Telegraph Island for the night and collect you the next day. Their boats tend to be simpler than those used for organised boat trips, and so not as well equipped with such things as shade awnings. Ask at the boatyards on your right after passing the harbour before Khasab Town as you enter from the Thibat (Ras al Khaimah) direction. This is fine if you aren't too concerned about exact timings and are prepared to devote some effort to making the arrangements. They won't rip you off.

CANOEING The calmness of the fjords offers ideal conditions for canoeing. Speak to the tour operators at the desk in the Golden Tulip Hotel in Khasab for details.

DHOW CRUISES/BOAT TRIPS From Khasab harbour the standard boat trips are half-day or full-day dhow cruises and cost around RO15 and RO20 respectively. Children under 12 go for half price and the under fives are free. Half-day cruises include light refreshments, whereas the full-day trips include lunch. The boats are equipped with life jackets as well as snorkelling equipment, if you haven't got your own. It is best to pre-book with a tour operator on arrival at your hotel to avoid any chance of disappointment, although it is possible to arrange one on the spot at the offices opposite the harbour.

Trips take you into **Khor Ash-Sham**, a giant fjord in which Telegraph Island sits along with a few other islands and where the water is calm and sheltered. You will spot the fishing villages of Nadifi, Qanaha, Maglab, Seebi and Sham along the route. You also have a good chance of spotting dolphins in the fjord, as they like the calm water, but are also attracted by the sound and wake of the engine, swimming with the boat as if it is a giant dolphin. Once the engine is turned off, they tend to lose interest.

The dhows anchor at Telegraph Island (see box, page 160), and you are given the opportunity to swim and snorkel. If you wish you can swim up to the island itself and climb the stone steps up to the top (it's not high).

There are various degrees in the quality of dhow cruises and it may be that you prefer to go on a larger two-storey dhow for the extra space and elevated views it allows. These are more popular with European families and visitors. The small dhows can become full and cramped and are generally popular with Asian visitors. It can make or break your enjoyment, and so you might like to enquire about the boat when booking your cruise.

Guests will be collected from their hotels and taken to the harbour to join the tour.

DIVING AND SNORKELLING Musandam is an excellent location for diving. As all divers will know, it is necessary to produce proof of your PADI Open Water qualification or equivalent, so remember to pack it.

Those wishing to gain their Open Water qualification can do so here. Extra Divers Partners operates from the Golden Tulip Resort with fully certified tutors (see above). So as not to waste time in the region to undergo the theoretical side of diving (unless you have the time to spare), you can gain your qualification for this

AROUND OMAN CHALLENGE

In 2004 and 2005, Mark Evans – a schoolteacher and geographer, who leads challenging expeditions around the world for young people – paddled a 5m kayak around the 1,700km or so of Omani coastline, a feat never attempted before. He carried a week's supply of food, tents, a GPS and a satellite phone, and was supported by a road-vehicle team. He began at Khasab and travelled all the way to the Yemeni border, coming ashore at night to camp. The Omani government supported the event, promoting Oman as an adventure-tourist destination. Funds raised went to support local and international charities (e *mevans@windlesham.com* or *adventurelectures@hotmail.com*).

aspect of the course back in your country of residence. You will then be free to concentrate fully on the practical side of diving when in Khasab.

The main dive sites are Lima Rock, Oakley Island, Umm Al Farrayan, PC Rock, Red Island and Ghubbat As Shabbus. Species include reef and whale sharks, barracuda, sunfish and turtles. Those new to diving are taken to the *khors* and bays of the area for their tuition.

For snorkelling, Sibi Island is perhaps the best location in the area, as the coral and marine life is good. If you are not a diver, you can opt for snorkelling as part of a dive-boat trip, or as a dhow cruise. The dhow-cruise trips make a stop at Telegraph Island to allow for snorkelling and swimming. Trips cost around RO15.

From October to February visibility is excellent, about 20–30km. From the end of February it drops to about 5km, which detracts somewhat from the overall experience.

DOLPHIN, WHALE AND SHARK WATCHING The hammerhead, nurse, reef and whale shark are found in the temperate waters of the Strait of Hormuz. Dolphin-watching trips are done as part of a dhow cruise (see *Dhow cruises* section above).

FISHING Fishing trips can be arranged through the tour operators or the dive centre, which depart from Khasab harbour.

MOUNTAIN SAFARI If you have flown to Khasab from Muscat and are staying in a hotel here, it is likely you will arrange a mountain safari (as you won't have a car to travel this independently). The route below (from Khasab, onwards) is the one your driver will take.

BUKHA بخة

Bukha is west of Khasab and borders the UAE at Ras al Khaimah. It is potentially large and thriving, but has suffered an exodus to the oil-rich emirates next door, leaving it struggling to maintain the remaining population. New capital investment by Oman may help it to revive its considerable agricultural resources. Numerous buildings are being constructed. In among the new houses are the decaying mud-brick ones, some on two storeys with courtyards, which you can see by turning off the main coast road and following a road inland that runs parallel to the coast.

GETTING THERE Starting from Sham take the right fork marked Al Jer at the final roundabout by the mountains. This leads round past endless shops selling car spares and hardware to reach the border post on the coast 1km later. Queue at the first counter on the left marked *Al Mughaadireen* (those departing) with your passport and pink form. The second counter is marked *Al Qaadimeen* (those coming) and is where you will queue on your return into Ras al Khaimah at the end of your Musandam trip. Allow 30 minutes for this UAE section of the border.

The Omani border post is 1km or so further on, and you should again allow 30 minutes for the paperwork followed by the vehicle search. Go to the first counter marked Al Qaadimeen with your passport and white form. The second counter is marked Al Mughaadireen and is where you will go on your departure with your yellow form. After this you will be waved on to the vehicle search. Beyond the border is a Shell petrol station in case you forgot to fill up in Ras al Khaimah. The relatively new tarmac road from now on clings to the edge of the sea and had to be blasted in places where the mountain came right down to the waves. It was only fully completed in 1998. Some beaches are equipped with *barasti* sunshades on iron frames (often with their *barasti* roofs missing), and sometimes have children's playgrounds and water tanks. They tend to be a bit close to the road for comfortable camping and anyway are heavily rubbish-strewn despite regular refuse collections. The first town you come to is Bukha.

WHAT TO SEE

Bukha Fort (*Open Sat–Thu 09.00–14.00, Fri 08.00–11.00*). The coastal fort of Bukha, built by the Portuguese in the 16th century and renovated in 1990, sits proudly on the new road, and is open and accessible only when the watchman is there – usually workday mornings until 14.00. Its shallow moat, especially visible at the back, used to fill with seawater before the coastline was pushed further away by the construction of the road. A square building of stone blocks faced with mud plaster, its most unusual feature is the round tower on the southwest corner which curves inwards, giving it a pear shape which reduced the impact of cannonballs. Inside, the tower has four cannon ports. The earliest parts are thought to date back to the 16th century and the recent restoration has retained the remains of rich plasterwork wall decorations and carved doors and shutters. The main gate has the *kuwwa* or *muscat* (literally place of falling), the slit found in all Omani defensive buildings, used for pouring hot date honey on the enemy or for water to quench any fire that threatened to burn down the door.

Beside the fort is a large crumbling structure built up on a raised terrace. This was the **Friday mosque**, surrounded on all sides by an extensive cemetery of headstones which have the effect of distancing the town buildings. At the back on the inland side a crumbling double set of steps leads down into the ablution area. Stairs also lead up onto the roof, in place of the minaret. Inside, the once grand mosque is in a sorry state of disrepair; most of its roof is missing and much of the delicate stucco plasterwork decorating its pillared arches is falling away, now that it is exposed to the elements. The motifs are alternate rosettes and arches. The *mihrab* niche itself is surprisingly plain and free from decoration, as are the *minbar* (pulpit) steps from where the imam would give the Friday sermon. A crude wooden *minbar* was found on these steps, but has now disappeared (probably used for firewood). The outer high walls of the mosque are pierced with elaborate decorative grilles displaying geometric and plant motifs carved in good-quality strong plaster. Despite its highly dilapidated state, this mosque is sure to be restored in the near future because old traditional congregational mosques such as these are extremely rare in Oman now; the only other remaining examples are at Rustaq (within the fort enclosure) and at Bahla (outside the fort).

Up on the hill behind Bukha stands a fine **hill fort**, a tower ringed with a defence wall. Those with the energy to climb up will be rewarded by an excellent view and a closer look at the unique domed cistern on the summit complete with pointed-arch door.

QIDA AND TAWI

Just 4km before Khasab the new road winds round to the fjord-like bay of Qida, with fishing boats lining the beach. Unusually lush and green for Musandam, the oasis of Qida sits in the narrow river valley with date palms and many fruit trees. Take the signposted track to Tawi off the tarmac here, leading in a northeasterly direction into the valley, following a riverbed lined with some interesting old houses. One in particular, raised up on the left side, has attractive plasterwork in semicircular arches above the grilled windows. Follow the track beyond the village until you come to a second small village, in the centre of which, opposite a well between a group of three trees to the right, is an enormous cluster of grey boulders to the right of the road, many covered in prehistoric rock art of ships, horsemen, ibex and camels. Their date and origin is unknown. Village women, attuned to visiting foreigners, may emerge from their houses to sell you their basketry weaving. You can continue up the wadi to explore more mountain villages, some uninhabited.

KHASAB خصب

Khasab is Musandam's main town (although only a small fishing port) and is the next town you reach. Of Musandam's approximate population of 27,000, Khasab is home to 18,000 and is the northernmost wilayat overlooking both the Arabian Gulf to the northwest and the Gulf of Oman to the east. It acts as the seat of the wali, whose influence extends in practice about as far as the limits of the town. Its mainstays are fishing and agriculture, *khasab* being the Arabic for 'fertile'. Khasab has traditionally been a community of fishermen, boat builders, craftsmen and traders. The population swells in summer as people come from Kumzar and the mountain villages to harvest dates and to fish, thereby retaining its old way of life. The name itself is thought to be a contraction of *khawr* (Arabic for 'bay' or 'creek') and *asaba* (the ancient name for the whole peninsula coined by the Roman scholar Pliny in the 1st century AD). Its large shallow bay turns to mud flats at low tide and the type of boat built here, called the *baatil*, was quite flat bottomed but big enough for regional trading even as far as India. The harbour today is still busy with small boats which do a roaring trade in goats from Iran, destined for Ras al Khaimah. The Iranian smugglers then buy televisions, washing machines and cigarettes with bags of cash, returning to Iran under cover of night when the coast is radioed clear by accomplices.

The big wide bay is the mouth of the large wadi that extends inland for several kilometres, and the alluvial silt that has been deposited near the mouth by torrential seasonal flooding has enabled the extensive oases of the date gardens to build up. The old *sur* (mud and stone wall enclosure) of the Kamazirah tribe on the eastern side of town seems to have disappeared, along with the picturesque old summerhouses built of *barasti* and raised up on six pillars that used to be grouped around it. Khasab Town used to have many houses with traditional wind towers, a style introduced from Persia. Few now remain in the age of the air-conditioning system.

Behind the town as you drive inland – past the fort, and deeper into Wadi Khasab – you will notice the wide low dam spanning the wadi floor. Such dams have been one of the priorities of the Musandam Development Committee, to minimise damage caused by violent torrential flooding. The Royal Geographic Society expedition of 1972 found a few pot shards in the alluvium of the wadi floor, which were dated to the 15th–19th centuries. Anything earlier, if it exists, is likely to be buried deep beneath the silt. Combined with that, the effect of the extreme subsidence of the last 10,000 years and the post-glacial rise in sea level would have meant any early coastal sites would now be either underwater or destroyed.

WHERE TO STAY
Upper range

Golden Tulip Resort (60 rooms) PO Box 434, PC 811, Khasab; 26 730777, 26 730789; f 26 730888; e info@goldentulipkhasab.com or packages@goldentulipkhasab.com; www.goldentulipkhasab.com. This is clearly the best hotel in Musandam. It has a fully licensed restaurant (indeed the only licensed venue in town) and a separate bar. There is internet access here too (500bzs for 15mins). The hotel offers special packages which include your stay and certain excursions, which seems a pretty good option, as this will eliminate any extra hassles of arranging an

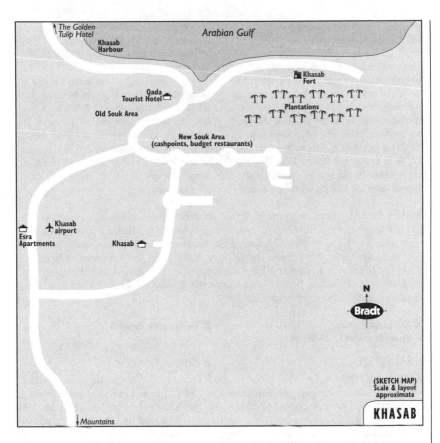

Within the map:

The Golden Tulip Hotel

Arabian Gulf

Khasab Harbour

Khasab Fort

Qada Tourist Hotel

Old Souk Area

Plantations

New Souk Area
(cashpoints, budget restaurants)

Esra Apartments

Khasab airport

Khasab

N

Bradt

(SKETCH MAP)
Scale & layout
approximate

KHASAB

Mountains

---

independent trip. The **Resort Package** (RO25 + taxes) includes a welcome drink, fruit basket, overnight stay in deluxe sea-view room, breakfast and dinner by the pool or at Dibba Restaurant, guided tour to the fort of Khasab and late check-out. The **Dhow Cruise Package** (RO40 + taxes) includes the same, but with a half-day dolphin-watching cruise taking in Telegraph Island. The **Fishing Package** includes the same, but with a fishing trip from 17.00 to 20.00, which includes cooking your catch, a bottle of house wine, T-shirt, photo and a certificate for catcher of the largest fish. The **Tour Package** (RO109 + taxes) includes the same

but with the addition of an extra night's stay, a full-day cruise and a mountain safari trip. You might like to check any updates on the tour packages offered. If you choose not to arrange one of these 'package' trips, this hotel has a **Khasab Travel & Tours** desk from which you can arrange dhow cruises, mountain safaris and trips to Kumzar independently. The tours operate all year round. This desk is helpful and informative and certainly the most efficient place at which to organise your trips as and when you require. Accepts credit cards. Confirm your complimentary airport transfer with them. *RO40/46 sgl/dbl,exc taxes.*

Budget

⌂ **Esra Apartments** (16 apts) ☎ 26 730562; f 26 730364. Virtually opposite Khasab Airport, and so are the furthest from the harbour. The self-catering apartments (all with their own kitchen and living room) are of good clean standard, and, as they are self-catering, there is no restaurant on the premises. *RO35/RO55 1-master bed (total 3*

beds)/2-master bed (total 4 beds) deluxe.

⌂ **Khasab Hotel** (15 rooms) PO Box 111, PC 811, Khasab; ☎ 26 730267; f 26 730989; e khoman@ omantel.net.om. This hotel is about 5mins' drive from Khasab Airport, and sits on the left almost opposite the Shell petrol station. The rooms are laid out round a courtyard with a swimming pool. There is a simple restaurant (unlicensed) and communal lounge area with a TV. This hotel was the first to be built in Khasab and the rooms, which are a little shabby and dated, reflect this. You may find you have to work a bit harder with communication here, although the staff are pleasant and do make the effort to accommodate your requirements. They are nearing the end of the construction of a new building adjacent to this old one, due to be finished around May 2006 (but do check!) and so it looks as if standards may improve. Still, this is a lot cheaper than the Golden Tulip and very convenient for boat trips and mountain safaris. They will collect you from the airport, but, so you're not left stranded, it is safest to confirm this with them. Accepts cash only. *RO20/34 sgl/dbl.*

🏠 **Qada Tourist Hotel** (22 rooms) PO Box 64, PC 811, Khasab; ☎ 26 731664, 26 731667; f 26 731676; e qdahotel@omantel.net.om. This hotel is located closer to the harbour than the Khasab Hotel (its partner). The main office of **Dolphin Tours** is here. They will collect you from the airport, but you will probably need to remember to instruct them to do so before you leave Muscat. There is a restaurant on the premises (*Dhabi al Yemen;* ☎ 26 731665). Accepts cash only. *RO15/20/35 sgl/dbl/3-bed apt, inc taxes, exc b/fast.*

✘ **WHERE TO EAT** There are quite basic restaurants inside the Khasab Hotel and the Qada Tourist Hotel. The Dibba Restaurant, in the Golden Tulip Resort, is the only upmarket and licensed one. Outside of the hotels, there are a few local restaurants (all budget range), all located in the vicinity of the bank and new souk. They serve an Indian, Arabic, Chinese and European menu and are well worth a try.

There are also a few budget restaurants where you are likely to get a meal for two, including drinks, for under RO5:

✘ **Alshamaliya Restaurant** ☎ 26 730477   ✘ **The Musandam Restaurant** ☎ 26 730569
✘ **Bashair Restaurant** ☎ 26 731164

WHAT TO SEE
Khasab Fort (*Open Sat–Thu 09.00–16.00, Fri 08.00–11.00*). An impressive square enclosure with towers at each corner and an old round tower in the courtyard are all that remain of the original 17th-century Portuguese fort at Khasab. The steps up to it are shaded by an enormous *Albizia lebbeck* or rain tree (sometimes known as mother's tongue because of the large flat pods which hang on the trees for months and appear to chatter in the wind). The two separate towers to the rear house the wali's private rooms for his two wives, and the front towers are the public rooms and gun-firing rooms.

The guide leads you round from tower to tower and along the parapet walls for the tour which takes about 30 minutes. You can climb up ladders to the roof. The fort has been built from a complete hotchpotch of wadi pebbles, stones, mud bricks and careful stonework, each from a different period of construction, the oldest parts of which date back to the late 1800s.

KUMZAR كمزار

Accessible only by boat, Kumzar – a cliffside village – is the northernmost settlement of Oman, crammed into the narrow valley of Wadi Marwan and ringed with bare precipitous mountains. It takes two hours to reach it by speedboat from Khasab, nearly four by motorised dhow. The houses are so closely packed that there is hardly space to walk between them. There are two small mosques, each with a small graveyard which were filled centuries ago. Recent burials have therefore been forced to take place under the floors of the houses. Kumzar *baatils* (fishing boats) were unique in the Gulf in having shell-decorated bows and zoomorphic sterns to secure the rigging. The village sheep and goats have to be taken regularly by boat to pastureland on Jazirat al Ghanim (Goat Island) or to other coastal bays where grazing is more plentiful. The government has now built a desalination plant, but before that everyone had to rely on a well at the back of the village. Visiting crews used to paint their ships' names on the cliffs behind the harbour, still clearly visible today.

Back on the mainland at Khasab harbour, the road (graded track) now heads inland past the Khasab Hotel, which is on the outskirts of the town. If you have arranged a mountain safari, this is the route your driver will take. The road continues beyond the airport and into the Wadi Khasab. Some 14km along this road (about ten minutes' drive from Khasab harbour) you come to a major junction with large signposts. The left takes you to both Khor A'Najd and Sal al A'la, potential camping spots within 30 minutes or so of Khasab. Keeping straight on leads to the military road up and over **Jebel Harim**, Musandam's highest peak, down to the checkpoint at Wadi Bih.

This checkpoint is only open to Omani passport holders or residents with a special road permit issued by the Royal Oman Police, so in practice very few people use it.

The drive over the mountain to the checkpoint takes a good two hours with no stops (approximately 60km), and relatively few make the journey right over the top and down as it tends to require another night's camping, usually in the Rawdah Bowl (see page 163).

KHOR A'NAJD

Turning left at the signpost towards Khor A'Najd you come after 6km (a further five minutes) to the fork off left again to Khor A'Najd, the only piece of fjord coastline reachable by road in the whole of Musandam. It passes a military firing range. The track is steep and snakes up to the brow of the hill from where there is a stunning view out to sea and over the fjord and down to the *khor* (cove) itself. The total drive takes 15–20 minutes from this turn-off and is suitable for 4x4 only, because of the gradient and some bumpy sections. Only those with a high tolerance of litter and hornets would enjoy camping on the muddy beach itself, although it is geared for campers, providing sunshades and water tanks. At busy times like Eid the litter bins overflow and the water tanks get empty. The swimming is not good, as the shoreline is muddy and tacky, with rocks further out, so most people who stay here use boats – either their own or those rented out by fishermen.

SAL AL A'LA

Back in the wadi floor the track continues straight on to Sal al A'la (not to be confused with Salalah, in Dhofar), a dead-end road finishing in a natural silt bowl ringed by mountains on three sides and with a few signs off to several villages on the way. The distance from here to the end of the bowl is 6km, and certainly this is the cleaner spot to camp and arguably the more beautiful. The name Sal al A'la means 'higher silt flat', reflecting its position at the head of the main valley of the largest drainage system of the Musandam Mountains, flowing into the sea at Khasab.

The silt plain at Sal al A'la supports an astonishing forest of acacia trees (*simr* and *salam*), as well as *Zizyphus spina-christi* (*sidr*) and *Prosopis cineraria* (*ghaf*). The forest covers an area of 35 hectares and the trees reach a height of 9m. In the spring months from January to April a thick carpet of green grass grows under the trees that contrasts sharply with the barrenness of the surrounding mountains.

Sheep and goats are in paradise here, and a few donkeys are also to be found. Cows, which one could easily imagine grazing happily here, do not exist in

In the mid 19th century the technological revolution in Europe and the invention of telegraphic communications via a cable began to change the face of worldwide communications. Britain's empire and its links with colonial India had been transformed too by the introduction of steam ships in 1840 and the British India Steam Navigation Company started a postal service first to Calcutta and Rangoon, then to Ceylon and Karachi. Subsequently it extended in 1862 into the Gulf where the postal service then connected Bombay, Karachi, Muscat and Basra (Iraq).

By 1858, a telegraphic landline had been laid between Baghdad and Scutari (Albania), and the proposal was subsequently made to connect this system to India via a landline to Basra, then via a submarine cable down the Gulf. After lengthy diplomatic discussions between Turkey (to which Iraq belonged at that time), Persia and Britain, the land stretch was finally completed in 1854 and the difficult submarine stretch was begun. At the Omani end there were difficulties about the placement of the telegraph terminal on the Musandam tip. This was because the local tribes, specifically the Zahuriyeen who lived on the Maqlab isthmus – the thin strip of land running between the two major fjord inlets of Elphinstone (Khor Ash-Sham) and Malcolm (Khor Habalayn) – disrupted progress for a month while they tried to establish what benefits there might be for them. It appeared that the British too had some doubts about jurisdiction over the area, but after further discussions the sultan reasserted his control over Musandam and the telegraph line was led into Elphinstone inlet and from there onto a small island to be known thereafter as Telegraph Island. The site was selected as it offered more security than the mainland against potentially hostile local tribes, and the telegraph station was built there in 1854 and maintained until 1869, the same year when the opening of the Suez Canal also brought Britain and India closer.

The terminus functioned for only five years since no-one wished to live in such an inhospitable place. Its strategic importance was felt by the British to be such, however, that in 1904 they decided to erect flags there, but could not agree what flag should fly – not the Union Jack since it was not British territory, and not the Blue Ensign of the Royal India Marine, for that would mean they might have to defend it. So the flagpoles were all taken down again, except one which was allowed to remain on Telegraph Island with no flag. None of the flagpoles was visible from the open sea anyway, but it is doubtful the decision makers in London ever realised. This tiny connection with modern technology had no effect on the lives of the Musandam tribes, needless to say, for whom life went on at subsistence level as before.

The tidal variation of two to three feet means that it is not always possible to land at Telegraph Island as the boat would damage itself on the rocks at low tide.

Musandam and are anathema to the Shihuh. Wild animals found in Musandam are leopards, wolves, foxes, hyenas and the Arabian *tahr* (a sturdy russet-haired type of mountain goat).

The spring of **Birkat al Khalidiya** (spring of eternity) lies beyond the playground, where the track ends. The name is rather ironic as the spring is no longer maintained and has more or less dried up. As the cistern runs low, heading into April, hornets are drawn by the remnants of the water. Rubbish is still a problem, but far less so than at Khor A'Najd and because the woodland is so large you can still find privacy even during religious holidays.

The village over in the left corner of the bowl (the opposite side to Birkat al Khalidiya), is **Limhas**, the largest settlement in the area. It has a large walled area that used to house a date plantation and fields of crops and fruit trees. The wall was specially constructed with the largest stones at the top to allow floods to pass through without resistance, keeping the strongest part at the top to prevent collapse. The settlement itself has stone *Bait al Qufl* houses (see box below) as well as modern houses. It used to take a day for the men of the village to reach Khasab, so they used to migrate there for the summer months, but now that it takes only 30 minutes, they commute on a daily basis.

JEBEL HARIM جبل حريم

Jebel Harim is the tallest peak in the region at 2,097m and lies between Khasab and Dibba.

Returning to the main signposted fork at Khasab, you can now (if you have a minimum of half a day or preferably a full day) continue on the main mountain road signposted for Dibba. Again, if you have arranged a mountain safari, this is where you will head. The road runs very flat along the wadi bed, well compacted and smooth for another few kilometres until signs warn you of the impending mountainous section which requires 4x4 low ratio, especially on the descent. The road, built by the Omani military, is tricky driving, probably more difficult than the drive up to the Saiq Plateau or up the Wadi Ghul–Jebel Shams road in the Jebel Akhdar Mountains, both of which are wider routes with better-compacted surfaces. You also require more of a head for heights, as some of the edges on the beginning stretch and just beyond the summit itself are extremely vertiginous.

The first section of the ascent is very steep but if you can wrench your eyes off the road for a moment, you can spot the Shihuh villages tucked into the mountainsides and perched on the edge of gorges. Old Bedouin houses (now disused) can also be spotted, at rather extraordinary heights. Look out too for the wispy bushes of the wild almond (*shu*) tree (*Amydalus arabica*) whose branches are used for the handles of the Shihuh small axe worn by Shihuh men instead of the traditional *khanjar* of Oman. This axe is unique to Musandam. It is called the *Jerz* and some villagers may even offer you theirs for sale to earn themselves a bit of welcome cash. At each settlement are the white water tanks at the roadside, regularly filled by blue water tankers. If you see the water tanks with no sign of a village, rest assured that there will be a village tucked away somewhere nearby but out of sight of the road. As you get higher it becomes easier to stop and admire the views.

SAYH PLATEAU Towards the upper part of the ascent you will suddenly arrive at the Sayh Plateau, an extremely attractive miniature lush plateau about 2km long and 500m wide.

In the winter months the plateau is delightfully green, but starts to go brown by mid April. The settlements, most of which are on the opposite side across grassy meadows, exist to tend the small palm groves and fields of wheat and alfalfa. Donkeys, sheep and goats frolic in the pastureland.

On the opposite side of the plateau is another small settlement with Bait al Qufl houses, some of them built into the mountainside like caves. The numbers of villagers are constantly on the decline as men leave for the coastal towns.

On the summit of Jebel Harim immediately above, you can spot the grey dome (like a golf ball) which is the radar station set at 2,097m.

A climb of another ten minutes brings you right up to the summit of the pass where the Omani air force in its austere grey-green buildings sits just below the pass. Half a kilometre before the final zigzags to the V-cut in the mountain pass

Today the Khasab municipality runs a system of water tankers that regularly go to each village or to the closest point on a drivable track to replenish large white roadside water tanks for the remaining inhabitants of the mountain villages. This system dates back only to the early 1980s. Before that the Shihuh tribespeople devised other ways of surviving on minimal water.

The *falaj* irrigation channels so common in the rest of Oman are absent in Musandam. The nature of the terrain is such here that there would never be enough water to keep them flowing, so the high mountain villages tried instead to trap as much as possible of the heavy winter rains. To achieve this they built water-deflecting walls (*musaylah*) – following the contours of slopes where they observed the water ran best and most frequently – then caught it in cisterns built of stone and lined with mud. These can still be seen in many mountain villages, where the wall is often mistaken for a defensive structure. One of the best examples is on the raised outcrop directly above the Islamic cemetery at the junction of Wadi Bih with the track into the Rawdah Bowl.

The other practice was the use of a *khayr* (Arabic for 'good'), a large clay water jar donated by a family for public use. The benevolent donor thereby increased his social standing in the village, and it was his responsibility to keep it full. These jars were generally placed under a tree beside a main track, to facilitate travelling, or sometimes among a group of village houses. A few can still be seen in the remoter villages, and tend to have their tops stuffed with thorn bushes to keep debris out when the village is abandoned for the summer months.

summit is a bumpy track to the right, leading along flat ground for 2km to reach a helicopter landing pad used for delivering supplies to the air force base. There are a few small walled gardens close by that appear largely disused, and this whole area makes a fine camping spot in the summer months, the altitude providing welcome coolness – though there is virtually no shade and of course no water.

Continuing to the summit, as you pass through the V-cut to the other side of the mountain range, the most staggering view presents itself and the faint-hearted will quiver at the sight of the road they must follow for the descent. It starts by clinging to the left precipitous side of the mountainside, then snakes off over a long thin ridge, before the final descent down to the wadi bed on the other side, a total of some 45 minutes' driving. The route is definitely at its most spectacular when seen from this direction – the climb back up again gives angles which are less dramatic and less vertiginous too.

The ridge Just at the start of the ridge as the road leaves the mountain massif there is a small settlement of stone houses to the left of the track. If you fork off into this village, following the track through and beyond it for a kilometre or so, you will reach a deserted village which you can explore at leisure, to examine the exact layout of the Bait al Qufl houses and the walled garden areas. You may also notice the occasional stone plinth, apparently in the middle of nowhere, thought to have been used for the call to prayer. Another unexpected sight is the occasional use of scarecrows in the fields to protect the precious crops. The walled field systems round the tiny village settlement are remarkably complicated, the walls positioned for maximum rainwater run-off collection in harmony with the contours of the ground. Once crops were growing, the tops of the walls were rammed with thorn bushes to prevent goats jumping in and helping themselves.

After the long ridge the final descent into the wadi floor can be very bumpy after rains have gouged out deep runnels in the steep track. Bulldozers and steamrollers try to repair the damage as soon as they can but occasionally it can take weeks rather than days if the rains have been very heavy.

RAWDAH BOWL At the foot of the mountain you come to a crossroads, the left of which takes you back along the gravel wadi floor to a minor settlement before reaching a dead end. The right takes you along Wadi Bih to the border checkpoint. Straight over leads you into the Rawdah Bowl – the best camping spot in the area.

From here into the Rawdah Bowl is a five-minute drive along a good track through a narrow defile which suddenly opens up into a large mountain-ringed bowl some 5km long by 2km wide. There are a few settlements in the bowl, and two interesting cemeteries. The area is large enough for you to find houses tucked away, often close to ruined stone homes, deserted in favour of newer buildings.

As you enter, your arrival will be noted by the police post on the left and if you stay the night a couple of men from the police post will almost certainly be sent out to check up on you after nightfall to make sure you are not causing trouble. A few friendly and polite words are all that is required, and even if you invite them to join you, they will respect your privacy and refuse.

The wildlife in the bowl is abundant, with owls, hedgehogs, birds of prey, numerous butterflies including tigers and blue pansies, and amazing cricket life, as well as the usual sheep and goats. February and March are the best for flowers and by April the grass is beginning to go brown. The bowl is heavily wooded with acacia, but is nothing like as lush as the forest at Sal al A'la.

Back out at the four-road junction at the foot of the mountain, you should fork left onto the Wadi Bih track, even if you do not intend to cross the border, for within just 1km is an extensive cemetery which deserves some attention. The **Islamic Cemetery** lies to the right of the road, just round the corner from a large bluff. Its headstones are unusually tall, often over 1m, a few of them with engravings etched onto the rock, like that of the man with a spear and shield. Extremely neat and well arranged, this cemetery is one of the most impressive in the quality of masonry anywhere in Oman. Two slabs marks a male, three slabs a female grave. This is the Sunni, Hanbali style of grave, quite different from the

BAIT AL QUFL (HOUSE OF THE LOCK)

The Bait al Qufl style of house is unique to Musandam, and its whole construction and design is geared round security. The name 'house of the lock' reflects this and a highly complex locking device was devised to ensure that no-one could enter the house during the summer months when it was left unattended.

These houses are built from local stone. The roof is made from acacia wood and covered with an earth and gravel mix, then edged with stone blocks. The walls never have windows. The floor level was usually 1m below ground level, and the door extended down to the sunken floor, with a deep recess, opening inwards, making it difficult to get in and out.

Inside, the inhabitants locked away all their essential items and possessions – such as storage jars, cooking utensils and tools used for crop growing. Sometimes the storage jars were so big they had to be put in the house before the roof was put on. Warmth was the secondary consideration, as the cold winter nights could reach close to freezing point. By preference, however, the Shihuh slept outdoors, only retiring to the Bait al Qufl in extreme cold. Outside there was generally a ledge or step running the length of the front of the house like a bench, where the owner would sit.

small random stones of the typical Ibadhi graveyard. One unusual structure is circular, reminiscent in style of the foundation of an Umm al Nar tomb, with pinkish regular blocks.

The only house that remains as part of this settlement is back at the foot of the bluff on the same side of the road, a remarkable building constructed of colossal stone blocks. Again this is a mystery building, undated and unique in the country, and so perfectly crafted it almost resembles a small rural temple.

On the sloping bluff above it is a carefully constructed low double wall for deflecting water, a *musaylah*, with a few circular tower-like structures which were probably cisterns for collecting the mountain run-off.

Beyond the Islamic Cemetery are a few very collapsed cairn tombs, but the better-preserved ones are on the other side of the track over towards the entrance to the Rawdah Bowl in the wadi plain. These cairn tombs, some 15 in all, are also a mystery here in Musandam, as yet undated and unexcavated. One has a long narrow chamber in the centre with roof slabs over the top. It is almost as if the loose stones have been added to cover this above-ground grave structure.

DIBBA

Dibba (or Daba) is located in the southeastern edge of Musandam and has the second-largest population in Musandam after Khasab. The town is divided into three parts, although the divisions aren't clear, and the signposts lacking. The southern part is Dibba Muhallah and is in the emirate of Fujairah; Dibba al Hisn is part of the emirate of Sharjah; and Dibba Bayah is the part belonging to Oman. In Dibba al Hisn there is an old fort, which is now used by the police. Excavations have shown that this area was already inhabited c1000BC.

It can be reached following the course of Wadi Bih until it reaches the mountain pass, again built by the Omani military and announced by the same warnings of steep gradients. This road is less vertiginous and steep than the earlier section over Jebel Harim, but nevertheless impressive. As you near the top you will notice to the left of the track a large settlement set about 500m off the road, with extensive terracing. It also has two stone-built towers, one round, one square. The round one – with three levels, and rather dilapidated – is thought to have belonged to the wealthiest inhabitant. The square tower is a granary (*yanz*) in which the agricultural produce was stored. There is an opening in the side which was kept sealed to keep animals out, or to keep it clean when empty.

The border post is here, for crossing into the UAE and onwards to enter Oman at the northernmost tip of the Batinah coast.

TOUR OPERATOR

Al Marsa PO Box 44, PC 813; ☎ 26 836550; f 26 836455; e info@musandamdiving.com; www.musandamdiving.com. Providing dhow charters, diving, live-aboard (12 persons max), cruising (35 persons max as non-divers, or 25 persons max with dive equipment as day dive boat, can be mixed); 75ft-long dhow, four AC twin-berth cabins, one 4-berth master cabin, electronic navigational aids, AC saloon, top sun deck, diving and swim platform, bar, sound system and home theatre, festive lighting.

WHAT TO SEE

Dibba Fort (*Open Sat–Wed 07.30–16.00, Thu–Fri 08.00–11.00*).

MADAH

Madah (or Mudha) is the small piece of land surrounded on all sides by UAE territory and roughly 3km inland. If you are approaching from the Oman end,

Madah is about 60km from Shinas. Ruins have been found here dating back to the Iron Age (1500–1000BC). There is rock art and calligraphy to be found at Jebel al Rukham (the Marble Mountain), and elsewhere in Madah, mostly dating to the 10th and 11th centuries, although some is believed to be pre-Islamic. New Madha is the new administrative part of the town with schools, health centres and government buildings.

Madah is one of Oman's least-known areas, with peaceful oasis villages, valleys, streams, springs, *falaj* and date-palm gardens; it is ideal for picnicking. The natural springs are said to have healing properties for skin disorders, as they contain sulphurous water. A local historian who is keen to preserve Oman's heritage, **Mohammed bin Salem al Mad'hani**, has filled his home with relics, handicrafts, antiques, curios, manuscripts and over 12,000 ancient weapons. We understand that it is possible to visit him, but you'll need to ask locally.

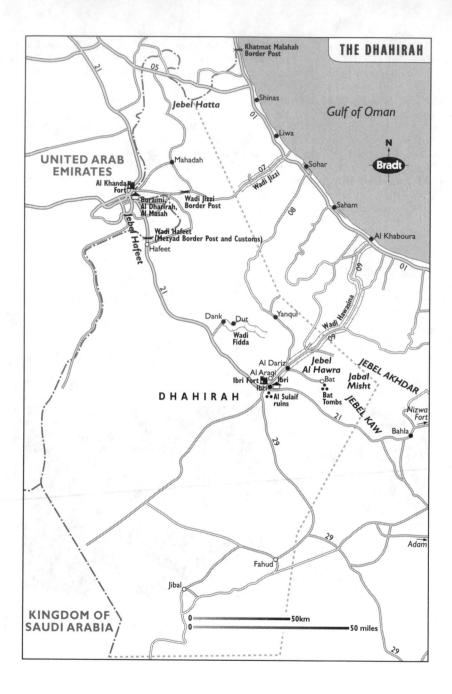

6

The Dhahirah الظاهرة

The Dhahirah region is the vast stretch of desert plain extending from the foot of the Hajar Mountains out west into the Rub'al Khali (the Empty Quarter), which crosses the border with Saudi Arabia, and north, up to the UAE. South and eastwards, it meets Al Wusta and Al Dakhiliyah regions of Oman.

The modern significance of the region lies in its oilfields, notably Fahud which produces a third of Oman's oil. The historical interest lies in the region of Bat. Tombs have been found here dating back to c4000BC and the area is now a UNESCO World Heritage Site. Ibri is one of the main towns of the Dhahirah.

Overall, the area hasn't too much to offer the tourist, but the wadis and oases make it perfect for the camping and outdoors enthusiast.

GETTING THERE

BY ROAD You can access this region via Nizwa from the southern and eastern regions, via Buraimi from the north, or via Wadi Jizzi from the Batinah coast.

BY COACH Coach services run from Muscat to Buraimi, via Sohar. For coach times and details see *Practical information*, page 49.

TOUR OPERATOR

Omani Travel and Tourism Bureau (OTTB) Buraimi; \ 25 655890; f 25 655889; e otboman@omantel.net.om

WHERE TO STAY

There is not much choice in terms of places to stay in this region. There is one mid-range hotel and a few budget hotels in Buraimi and one mid-range hotel in Ibri and that's about it.

Your only other option is to camp. One of the best options for camping is to head for Wadi Fidda (off the Yanqul road, see page 171), the wettest wadi in

---

DURU BEDOUIN TRIBE

Oman's major oilfields of Fahud, Natih and Yibal lie right in the middle of Duru territory. The three wadis of the Duru lands, Al Ain, Aswad and Amairi, disgorge into an area known as Umm As Samim ('Mother of Poison'), reputed to be an area of deadly quicksand. The Duru used to be nomadic, moving about with their livestock of camels and goats and utilising the trees as camps, by hanging tent material around them, or by building up *barasti* huts around them. Since the 1970s the Duru tribe have begun increasingly to settle in their date groves at Tanam, near Ibri.

Oman had to wait a long time for its oil to be discovered and the quantities are relatively small compared with Saudi Arabia's or Abu Dhabi's reserves. The first oil concession was obtained from Sultan Said bin Taimur, Qaboos's father, in 1937, by the Iraq Petroleum Company. World War II then intervened, and the poor communications in the hinterland slowed everything down enormously. Around £12 million was spent and in 1960 most of the partners gave up. Only Shell, supported by Gulbenkian interests, kept trying and in 1964 they succeeded in finding commercial quantities of oil in the fields of Fahud, Natih and Yibal. They spent a further £25 million and actual oil production and export began in 1967. A main pipeline runs from the oilfields through the Sumail Gap to reach the tanker terminal at the oil port – Mina Al Fahal – in Muscat.

northern Oman, where you are guaranteed water pools all year round. After rains in the winter the wadi may well be too wet to be drivable, but in April and May it is perfect, with stunning gorge scenery.

From the main Buraimi--Ibri road there are two interesting diversions: one via Dank to Yanqul, the other via Ad Dariz to Bat. These can be done as a loop tour (for which you will need a 4x4), although they are described in this chapter as two separate diversions, in which case a 4x4 is not strictly necessary.

The road is signposted left to Fidda, 11km off the Yanqul road. When the tarmac ends at the Oman Oil station you simply follow the track through the wadi. This first stretch is the most scenic anyway, so if camping, you need only allow 40 minutes from Al Dariz to find your camping spot. A 4x4 is necessary unless you camp on the very edge of the wadi.

IBRI عبري

Ibri, located 297km from Muscat, is the main town of Al Dhahirah. It is suggested that the name Ibri may come from the Arabic root 'a-b-r', which means 'crossing' or 'traversing'. It is renowned for its oilfields in addition to its ancient tombs at Bat.

Ibri had a reputation as a fanatically Ibadhi place with a hostile attitude to Christians. After the Imamate Revolt was suppressed in 1959 its wali was put in prison in Jalali Fort, where he died an old man in 1968. Today it has a thriving souk and benefits from its proximity to the oilfield at Fahud. You can therefore safely disregard the description of an early traveller in 1836 that 'to enter Ibri a man must go either armed to the teeth, or as a beggar with a cloth…'.

Ibri is also known for its distinctive black-and-red-striped goat-hair rugs, and for its traditional dancing. There used to be about four bands that performed regularly at celebrations like births, weddings and Eid holidays, but numbers are dwindling now. Dances were performed, as they are today throughout Oman at times of celebration, by men organised in rows and often carrying swords and sticks, who would enact a mock battle to the beat of the drums. In Ibri there was also a dance for women, and even for men and women performing together in rows facing each other.

For the future there are plans for a road and border crossing into Saudi Arabia, facilitating access to Mecca at times of the Hajj, and a road providing access to the Batinah coast. A good road already links this region with the United Arab Emirates, via Al Ain in Abu Dhabi.

GETTING THERE The drive from Bahla northwest towards Ibri takes approximately one hour. The summit of Jebel Kawr is 2,960m, only a little lower than Jebel

Shams (the highest peak in Oman). As you begin to leave this behind to your right, the terrain flattens out and becomes rather monotonous.

As you enter the sprawl of Ibri the first signpost off to the right avoids Ibri town centre completely and leads to Al Araqi, Bat (sometimes spelt 'Bath'), Yanqul and Dariz.

To see a little of Ibri itself, continue straight for another kilometre or so until Ibri is signposted off to the right. Follow the tarmac road on through the older houses, which spread up a rocky outcrop to the left with the ruins of a hilltop fort. The tarmac road then winds out through date gardens and across the wadi bed to rejoin the Al Araqi, Bat and Yanqul road that is heading east into the hills.

WHERE TO STAY

Ibri Hotel (27 rooms, 2 suites) PO Box 387, PC 516; ↘ 25 689955, 25 691626; f 25 692442; no email. This mid-range hotel, opened in 1999, has an international restaurant and bar. They will provide you with packed picnic lunches. They work closely with Mark Tours, United Tours and others. Accepts credit cards. RO21.80/29.50/40.40sgl/dbl/deluxe suite, inc taxes, exc b/fast.

WHERE TO EAT If you haven't brought a picnic with you to this region, then the best place to stop for a meal would probably be the restaurant inside the Ibri Hotel.

WHAT TO SEE

Al Sulaif ruins Your approach to Ibri is heralded by the sight on your left of the ruins of Al Sulaif across the wadi bed on a rocky outcrop. Abandoned some 20 years ago in favour of the new settlement beside it, this large walled village is well worth a detour of half an hour, to get a feel for a typical fortified Omani village. The road is signposted to the left and you can park in the new settlement close to the main gateway. A few old men are still to be found sitting near the entrance to the old souk and a small alleyway leads up to the covered main gateway, with several inscriptions carved into the rock beside it. The *falaj* still flows, if rather fetidly, and inside the walls you will find a mosque, fort, wells and many houses, some quite grand. The sloping rock up behind is ringed with watchtowers.

Forts The three main forts in Ibri are Ibri Fort, Jebel al Shahshah Fort and Al Aswad Fort. Of these, the most accessible is Ibri Fort, in the centre of the town, and over 400 years old. Within its walls is one of Oman's largest mosques to be found within a fortification, and can accommodate about 1,000 worshippers. This mosque – the Friday Mosque – has been restored and is still in use today.

WADI HAWASINA وادي الحواسنة

The road from Ibri through Wadi Hawasina to the coast at Khaboura will only ever be secondary because of its tortuous narrowness, no more than a twisting cut in the mountains carved by floodwaters and a dangerous place to be in rainstorms. The Hawasina tribe after whom the wadi is named are the most loyal and trusted tribe in Oman and for that reason the old Sultan Said bin Taimur always had them as his palace guards in Salalah. A tarmac road to the coast at Khaboura is planned, but the current track is bumpy, slow and difficult. About 3km from Al Araqi, those who have an hour or two to kill could attempt to find the **cave of Al Kittan**, said to have some of Oman's best and oldest cave decorations.

GETTING THERE You begin by forking off to the left to follow the left edge of an outcrop. This outcrop is the only one for about 7km and comes to an end at a gravel gap in the hills. Here, maintaining your speed to avoid getting stuck in the deep gravel, keep to the left and turn round the corner of the outcrop. Almost immediately the terrain hardens as you exit the wadi bed, and you pass a ruined village on your left called Uqabiyah with derelict field systems. Drive south from here for 3km, keeping to the right hand of the two tracks until you reach the mouth of a wadi. The cave opening is said to be a short walk on the right-hand side, but be prepared for a long and possibly futile search. If you do go looking for it, be sure to take plenty of water.

AL DARIZ الدارز

Back on the road to Al Dariz you will notice the impressive tall fort of **Al Ainayn** to your left rising from some date palms. The entrance has been blocked up, but the local sheikh has the key to the other door, if you have the time to spare.

At Al Dariz there is also an attractive sand-coloured fort beside a mosque and *falaj* in the centre of the village, still inhabited by the local sheikh.

BAT بات

The real reason for making the detour along this road is to visit the necropolis of Bat with over 100 burial sites, selected by UNESCO as a World Heritage Site. The whole area was heavily settled in the earliest times here, on the intersection of several major trade routes, and pottery finds and radiocarbon tests have dated the Bat beehive tombs to c3000BC. The site is extensive. In addition to the beehive tombs there is a circular fortress and several Umm Al Nar circular tombs. It covers an area of about 2km² in total, in largely shadeless terrain – so avoid any lunchtime visits, except in the winter months.

GETTING THERE The detour from Ibri to see Bat takes at least 2½ hours, which includes an hour to explore the site itself. The tarmac road leads as far as the modern village of Bat, and along the 14km you will frequently notice the remnants of beehive tombs along the tops of ridges beside the road. The track off to the side used to be signposted Medina Al Athar, City of Ruins, but there was no signpost at the time of writing. It forks off to the left just before the modern village of Bat and then winds round to the right. The fencing gives you a clue, erected to protect the site; but whole chunks are missing, which makes access straightforward.

To the right of the track you will come first to a substantial circular structure, once fenced, but the fence has been washed away by flash floods from the nearby wadi. This fortification has been identified as a tower and is dated to 2750BC. It is a complex structure and seems to have a well in its centre. Archaeologists have calculated the original height was around 10m and they have found traces of five other similar towers in the vicinity. They also uncovered constructed water channels leading to the site which would make these the earliest-known use of the *falaj* system for which Oman is so well known.

Opposite the round tower you can skirt the fence to drive past the old city walls over to the Umm Al Nar tombs, seven or eight circular communal graves with a diameter of about 11m, designed for up to 200 people. Only the beautifully crafted foundations remain and the group of fenced beehive tombs beyond. Anyone who saw these tombs 20 years ago would be shocked now to see the extent of the deterioration. Not one has an intact roof and only one has an intact arched doorway. A Danish team first excavated in 1976 and found the beehive tombs to contain two to five graves each. Up on the ridge above the site there are more. The Bat Tombs are one of the most complete collections of settlements and necropolises of the 3rd millennium BC.

DANK ضنك

From the main Buraimi–Ibri road take the turning off to Dank, clearly signposted. The tarmac road goes straight through Dank and curves to the right, built up on a high flyover above the wadi and date groves from the point where the tarmac ends (and Wadi Dank is signposted). After 16km the tarmac runs out and the road drops down to become a track through the Wadi Dank, a popular tourist attraction and a good picnic spot. There are a number of imam forts in Dank as well as the Dank caves. Signs at this point announce Yanqul (42km) and Fidda (24km). The first 5km through the wadi are very attractive and lush and the gravel road is fine for saloon cars at this point. There are many pools and the water flows freely to the left of the gorge, with the occasional settlement among the date gardens.

The next section opens out into a wide gravel plain, less scenic by far, and the track becomes bone rattling, permitting no more than 40km/h and requiring 4x4 transport.

WADI FIDDA وادي فضة

Once you arrive at Dut (or Dawt), the first village en route to Fidda from Dank, the gorge narrows again, and there are caves visible in the cliffs. Only when you reach Fidda, recognisable by its red flags and Red Crescent clinic, does the gorge become really scenic again with many pools and date gardens offering shade. After 5km the wadi opens out just before the modern unsignposted settlement where the tarmac road begins again.

Follow the tarmac on for 4–5km to reach the T-junction from which Yanqul is signposted 11km to the left. The terrain here is unusual, with pointed mountains, some conical, some jagged, some pyramid-shaped and some in giant table-top slabs.

YANQUL ينقل

Yanqul is considered a transit stop between the Dhahirah and Batinah regions, the most famous landmark being the mountain peak of **Jebel al Hawra**, which is used as the emblem for the wilayat. Goldsmithing, carpentry and weaving are the traditional crafts carried out here. Oman's only gold mine, producing 500kg of gold a year, opened near Yanqul in 1994.

The old Yanqul Fort and settlement, now abandoned, lie just 1km further on from the point where the tarmac ends (and Wadi Dank is signposted), tucked round the corner from the flagged government building just out of sight. Park by the old main gate and take some time to poke round inside this unrestored walled village. Abandoned some 20 years ago in favour of the modern housing provided by the government, the tall building to the right of the entrance has an impressive deep *falaj* within its walls and an attractive painted ceiling in one of its upper floors with Koranic inscriptions on the beams. There are three wells within the old village, and the building at the far end also has some attractively carved doors still *in situ*. Note too the mosque with four domed chambers.

The dirt track continues from here to loop round and rejoin the entrance of Wadi Fidda. Copper and silver have been found in the surrounding hills and gold has been produced from copper oxide deposits.

From Yanqul a difficult graded track continues through scenic gorges to Al Wuqbah (45km) on the edge of the Batinah coast, and the intrepid with total faith in their 4x4 vehicles can proceed this way to Sohar in three hours.

BURAIMI البريمي

Buraimi and Mahadah are the northernmost wilayats of the region. Both are known for their farming and agriculture. In Mahadah corn is the most common crop, along with dates and animal fodder. In Buraimi, agriculture is centred on the farming of limes, dates and alfalfa. Buraimi has a long history of conflict, and its many forts are testimony to this. Its two main forts are Al Khandaq and Al Hillah.

Buraimi is significant because of its strategic situation as an oasis on trade routes between Oman, Abu Dhabi, Saudi Arabia and the rest of the Arabian peninsula. The oasis is in fact a whole group of villages, mainly belonging to Abu Dhabi, and a handful belonging to Oman. Buraimi and Al Ain are tightly juxtaposed, and so, with British assistance, Abu Dhabi and Oman staked out a complex but agreed border, with the Omani part named Buraimi and the Abu Dhabi part named Al Ain, after the largest village in each case. Within the area itself there is no obvious indication where the border runs, and there is no border crossing within the city. Instead, the two border crossings (at Wadi Jizzi and at Wadi Hafeet) are both well in advance of it.

In the 1960s and 1970s the differences were far more marked, with Al Ain aspiring to grow and develop, with street lights, banks and Coca-Cola stores, while Buraimi remained exactly as ever – a collection of hovels and dust. The wali's fort remained unmodernised, while Sheikh Zayed's new guesthouse sported air conditioning. The contrasts were extraordinary, with the Omani dirt track meeting the immaculate tarmac road of the Abu Dhabi side. Now, in the 21st century, the differences are less obvious, and Buraimi, though not as affluent and buzzing as Al Ain, is nevertheless a thriving modern centre. Outside of Buraimi there is desert.

HISTORY In 1800, the Saudi Wahhabis marched into Buraimi, planted their governor there and began to dominate the surrounding territory. From its original back-to-basics beginnings, Wahhabi doctrine became single minded and intolerant in its attempts to propagate itself over the next 70 years through a series of raids and invasions from this southeastern Arabian base. Raids were profitable and in the name of *zakat,* the religious tax of Islam rather like a church tithe. If the British had not supported the sultan, the Wahhabis might well have conquered Oman. When the Saudis renewed their claim to Buraimi in 1952, it was because of suspected oil reserves in Abu Dhabi territory (which indeed proved to be correct), though they concocted an elaborate web of historical claims based on *zakat* payments and old documents. In 1955, the Saudis were driven out by the British and the Trucial Oman Scouts, and have never yet returned, though their claim has never been formally dropped. The Saudi presence in Buraimi between 1952 and 1955 was one of the main reasons for the Jebel War of 1957–59 in Oman, as the Saudis supported the rebelling Imamate of Ghalib and his brother Talib.

GETTING THERE AND AWAY Those wishing to travel the circuit of Oman will undoubtedly be frustrated by the bureaucracy and inconvenience of the border posts. They are huge trouble to those simply wishing to do a full tour of the country, stopping overnight at the Buriami Hotel (which is in Oman!) and continuing the following day on an Oman circuit tour down to Ibri (with no intention of visiting Abu Dhabi's city of Al Ain). Although Buraimi is Omani territory, your Omani tourist visa needs to be cancelled and a UAE one issued – and that's a real drag.

As entering Buraimi causes both extra expense (in terms of visa purchases) and hassle (in terms of paperwork and security checks), it seems skirting Buraimi would be a good option. But although the layout on the maps seems to indicate otherwise, it does not appear possible to simply go round Buraimi (and thus eliminate the border hassles), as the border post is located that much further away from Buraimi town itself; you have to go through Buraimi to access the road southwards to Ibri/Nizwa. For this reason, coupled with the fact that there is not too much for the tourist to see there, you may choose to avoid Buraimi altogether.

Entering Buraimi To enter Buraimi you can approach from two directions in Oman: first from Ibri to the south and second from Sohar to the east. Either way you have to cross the border and enter UAE territory, which means you will need to have your Omani visa cancelled and a UAE visa issued. This procedure is reversed on the return leg. The route from Ibri crosses at the Jebel Hafeet border post, and from Sohar at the Wadi Jizzi border. The Wadi Jizzi border is quicker, as it has no UAE checkpoint, so it only involves one stop and one set of forms to fill in.

Wadi Jizzi border post (from Omani side) This border post lies nearly 40km before Buraimi and roughly an hour's drive from the coastal dual carriageway. It consists of an Omani checkpoint with no UAE entry or exit post, taking an average of a mere 15 minutes – where, in theory, you will be issued with an exit ticket.

Once past the signs to Mahadah you will soon reach a roundabout which is signposted right towards Buraimi. The route to Buraimi from the Omani border side takes you through mountain scenery with occasional villages and terracing. It is a good new empty road, which crosses over the wadi many times with attractive views down into the wadi floor, with rivers and pools for much of the year. At one point just after Al Wasit, a long white bridge crosses the wadi and looking up to your right just after the bridge you will spot a natural rock arch which can be clambered up for fine views. A plateau with a few graves lies just below the arch.

Jebel Hafeet border post (from Omani side) This is a large border post stop, officially named the Mezyad Border Post and Customs, involving six stops and accessed via the long road from Nizwa through Ibri. About 20 minutes after this stop you will reach Buraimi.

Leaving Buraimi Finding your way out of Buraimi/Al Ain to continue your travels around Oman can be difficult the first time around. The two border posts are at Jebel Hafeet (leading to Ibri/Nizwa) and Wadi Jizzi (leading to the Batinah coast). There are no signposts from the main roads in the centre of town indicating directions south to Ibri/Nizwa, or east to Sohar, no signposts indicating directions to the Jebel Hafeet or Wadi Jizzi border posts, and no signposts simply indicating the direction for Oman. You may find yourself driving blindly around the busy city of Al Ain, praying for a recognisable signpost.

Wadi Jizzi border post (from Buraimi side) Approaching from Buraimi, leave the centre of Al Ain turning right at the horse roundabout in front of the wali's fort and then following signs to Sa'raa. At the next roundabout with model gazelles follow the signs to Al Khadra'a Al Jadida. At the third roundabout with the model oryx, known as Buraimi Hospital roundabout, you go straight on following Sohar and Al Jizzi.

As you leave the Buraimi sprawl behind you there are fine views of the Jebel Qattar escarpment to your left and the looming mass of Jebel Hafeet to your right.

You then pass through a dramatic V-cut in the rock and turn left at the roundabout following signs to Sohar. The road takes you through an open wadi with jagged mountains to each side, and there are traces of water in the wadis near the turn-off to Al Kitnah. The next turn-off right is to Al Malaqah and then within 1km you come to the Omani border post set astride the wadi.

Jebel Hafeet border post (from Buraimi side) This border crossing will lead you down to Ibri and Nizwa. From Buraimi/Al Ain you need to follow signs to Mezyad to reach it, some 15km south of Buraimi. It takes about 20 minutes to drive from the Hilton Hotel (which is in Al Ain) to reach the border. Expect formalities here to take approximately an hour, and incorporate around six separate police points. Your UAE tourist visa will now be cancelled and an Oman one re-issued (costing RO6). If you have the inclination, after this tedious process, you may notice the striated rock formation of Jebel Hafeet towering over the border post. Nizwa is roughly a three-hour drive from Buraimi.

WHERE TO STAY There are no upper-range hotels in Buraimi. If you are looking for something in this bracket then Al Ain (closely interweaved with Buraimi, and to which you are free to travel) offers the Hilton Al Ain (*www.hilton.co.uk*); Al Ain Rotana Hotel (*www.rotana.com*); the Intercontinental Hotel Al Ain (*www.ichotelsgroup.com*); and the Mercure Grand Jebel Hafeet Hotel (*www.mercure.com*).

Mid-range

Al Buraimi Hotel (30 rooms, 20 chalets, 10 villas) PO Box 330, PC 512; ℡ 25 642010; f 25 642011; e alburaimihotel@yahoo.com. Located on Oman's border with the UAE, this hotel is close to Al Ain (300km from Muscat). You need to 'exit' Oman and enter the UAE to stay here. The hotel is of good standard, with a licensed restaurant called Club Tropicana, and a bar. There are no internet facilities and the piped music can be loud. On the Club Tropicana menu (which is also served as room service) you have the option of grilled pigeons, stuffed pigeons and ox tongue, among the usual extensive list of pasta, 'international favourites' (steak, chicken etc), snacks, seafood and Arabic/Indian dishes. The hotel organises camel safaris and full-moon desert barbecues. *RO20/22/30/45 sgl/dbl/1-bed chalet/2-bed villa, inc taxes, exc b/fast; accepts credit cards.*

Al Dhahirah Hotel LLC (35 rooms) PO Box 169, PC 512; ℡ 25 652992; f 25 655408;

e Al_blushi79@hotmail.com or yasser_amrea@hotmail.com. Situated 2km from Al Ain and 270km from Seeb Airport. Al Dhahirah deal with a number of car-hire companies, including Fast Rent a Car. There is a Lebanese restaurant which serves all kinds of grilled food and fish. *RO12/13/24/34 sgl/dbl/2-bed suite/3-bed suite, inc taxes. B/fast RO2. Airport transfer RO12/25/35 from Al Ain/Dubai/Seeb airports.*

Al Masah Hotel (59 rooms) PO Box 490, PC 512, Buraimi; ℡ 25 653007; f 25 653008; no email. This is a 3-star hotel with a restaurant and coffee shop. Travelling past the Buraimi Hotel continue straight until you meet a roundabout. Go straight over this roundabout. At the second roundabout take the left. Continue straight until you meet another roundabout where you continue straight again. The hotel is about 500m past this on the right-hand side, behind the Toyota showroom. *RO 20/30, sgl/dbl (twin beds or kingsize), inc taxes, exc. b/fast. B/fast is RO2.50.*

Budget

Abha Hotel (12 rooms) PO Box 577, PC 512, Buraimi; ℡ 25 654700; fax 25 655454; no email. This hotel is located close to Buraimi hospital. It has a restaurant offering 24hr food and a friendly manager called Reza Mahmood Salim (Al Ain mobile 00 971 504720387). *RO 20/25 sgl/flat, inc tax, exc b/fast.*

Al Baraka Oasis Hotel Apartments (27 apts) PO

Box 17, PC 512, Buraimi; ℡ 25 650955; no fax. These self-catering apts and rooms are located about 200m further along from the Buraimi Hotel and on the opposite side. *RO15/25, sgl room/apt, inc tax.*

Hamasa Hotel (28 rooms) PO Box 490, PC 512, Buraimi; ℡ 25 651200; f 25 651210. There is no restaurant here, but they will bring food to your room for you from a local restaurant. This 1-star hotel is located about 2–3km from the Buraimi Hotel. With the Buraimi Hotel on the right-hand side, continue straight until you meet the first roundabout. Take a left here and continue straight over the second roundabout. *RO12, inc tax, exc b/fast.*

Nafahat Al Buraimi Hotel Flats (8 apts) PO Box 624, PC 512, Buraimi; \f 25 654777. These self-catering apts are opposite the Buraimi Hospital, which is about 500m from the Buraimi Hotel. *RO15/20/25, 1-bed/2-bed/3-bed, inc tax.*

OTHER PRACTICALITIES
Hospitals
Al Buraimi Hospital \ 25 652319

Ibri Hospital \ 25 691990

Police stations
Buraimi \ 25 650199
Al Dhahira \ 25 650099
Dank \ 25 676099

Ibri \ 25 489099
Wadi al Jizzi \ 25 659309

WHAT TO SEE Most of the sights of interest to visitors lie in the Abu Dhabi section of the oasis. The only historic monuments in the Omani Buraimi side are Al Khandaq Fort and Al Hillah Castle. Because of Buraimi's strategic position on the crossroads into the rest of the Arabian peninsula, the forts are steeped in the region's history of conflict.

Al Khandaq Fort This fort is located beside the 'horse' roundabout where the modern wali's fort stands. Recently restored, it is open to the public free of charge whenever the guardian is in attendance. It provides a good example of the ancient strategy of using a defensive trench or dry moat to protect and strengthen the stronghold. From its towers you can get a good view over towards the old Buraimi oasis with its picturesque, decaying houses. You can drive over and stroll in the winding alleyways between the date plantations, which are tended nowadays by Beluch and Pakistanis who live in huts on the edge of the oasis.

Al Hillah Castle This castle is situated in the centre of Buraimi and is notable for its plasterwork decorations and motifs. Like Al Khandaq Fort, this too has been restored.

The Dhahirah BURAIMI

6

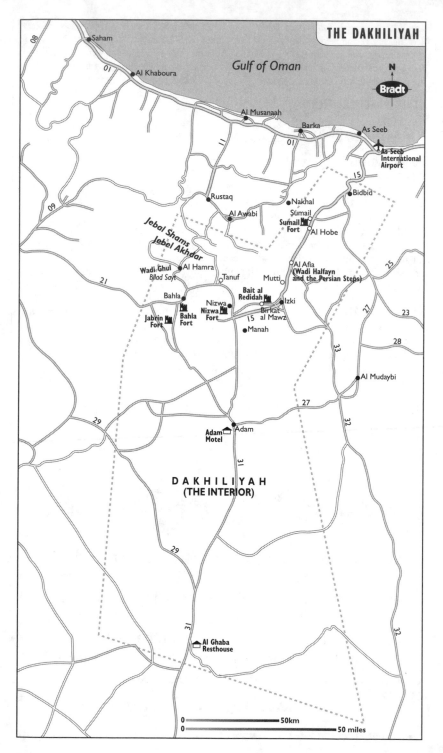

THE DAKHILIYAH

Gulf of Oman

N

Bradt

Saham

Al Khaboura

Al Musanaah

Barka

As Seeb

As Seeb
International
Airport

Rustaq

Nakhal

Bidbid

Al Awabi

Sumail

Sumail
Fort

Al Hobe

Jebal Shams
Jebel Akhdar

Al Afia
(Wadi Halfayn
and the Persian Steps)

Wadi Ghul

Al Hamra

Bilad Sayt

Tanuf

Mutti

Bahla

Nizwa

Bait al
Redidah

Izki

Jabrin
Fort

Bahla
Fort

Nizwa
Fort

Birkat
al Mawz

Manah

Al Mudaybi

Adam
Motel

Adam

D A K H I L I Y A H
(THE INTERIOR)

Al Ghaba
Resthouse

0   50km
0   50 miles

7

The Dakhiliyah الداخلية

The Dakhiliyah translates as 'the interior' and is the area that begins at Fanja and incorporates the western Hajar Mountains. It consists of the eight wilayats of Nizwa, Bahla, Bidbid, Sumail, Izki, Manah, Adam and Al Hamra.

The region is an important agricultural area, both historically and currently. The unique climate of the jebels facilitates growth of a wide range of fruit trees, plants and shrubs, which are a crucial part of the country's economy.

The interior is considered very different from coastal Oman, largely because it accepted the imam as leader. The imamate had always tended to be inward looking and detached from the activities of the coast. By contrast the coastal population had always had contact with the outside world through maritime trade. Historically then, the interior and coastal Oman were separate, so much so that the interior was referred to as Oman, and the coast as Muscat. When local people left the coast to go to the interior they would say 'I am going to Oman'.

The interior was the area which accepted the authority of the imam as spiritual and political leader. He was the elected head of the Ibadhi sect, an early sect of Islam which exists today only in Oman and in small pockets of north Africa, having been wiped out in all other parts of Arabia. Ibadhi are deeply conservative and traditional, and their beliefs are based on the earliest Islamic sources, the Koran and the *Hadith* (ways of the Prophet Muhammad). They believe the imam must be elected by the whole community and if he loses support or credibility, he may be removed or deposed. If no suitable imam can be found, then the office can remain unfilled until such time as the community agrees on a suitable candidate. Thus, the status of tribes and individual leaders was constantly changing. There was no imam for 60 years from 1810–70 and at one point three elected candidates in a row refused the position.

Problems began when the Al Bu Said dynasty in Muscat started to interfere with the traditional ways of the Omanis of the interior. These differences were not exclusively religious, for not all Omanis of the interior were Ibadhi; the problems were also tribal, and these tribal characteristics and traditions continue to exist even today.

Today, the region has eight wilayats and Nizwa is the administrative centre.

For an exploration of the region, Nizwa makes the perfect base, and a stay of two or possibly three nights will allow you to experience most of what the region has to offer while providing an interesting and marked contrast to the city of Muscat.

GETTING THERE

BY AIR There is no airport for civilians.

BY CAR To reach the interior, take the Muscat–Nizwa road (Route 15) just after Seeb Airport; the excellent dual carriageway speeds you along between the mountains, through the Sumail Gap. This gap has always been the major link corridor between Oman's coast and the interior, the chief trade route of old. The drive from Muscat to Nizwa takes two hours, and is dual carriageway as far as Firq, where it changes to single carriageway. It can be subject to flash floods.

Driving on the single carriageway roads can be a little hairy at times. Locals do have a tendency to want to overtake you even if you are doing the speed limit, and they can do so seemingly at the most inopportune moments, and at places where 'no overtaking' symbols are displayed. Don't be pressured to go faster if you are being tailgated; leave it up to them to get round you as soon as they can. For this reason the drive on single carriageways can be a lot less enjoyable. It is better to drive defensively.

BY COACH All coaches travelling to Salalah in the south go via the interior and drop-offs/pick-ups can be made at any of the designated coach stops.

GETTING AROUND

CAR RENTAL Currently, there are no car-rental companies operating in the Dakhiliyah, so you are advised to rent a car from Muscat. If a 4x4 is required for a specific trip, either up the jebels or off-road camping trips (see details under each location) you can arrange for the vehicle to be delivered to, and collected from, your hotel in the region. This means that you won't incur the additional expense of keeping hold of a 4x4 for the duration of your stay, when only a saloon is required (see *Chapter 2, Practical information*, page 47 for general rates).

TOUR OPERATORS

If you are not intending to travel the area independently, it is necessary to pre-arrange any tours through operators in Muscat to avoid any disappointment. They will either collect you from your hotel in the region (which is invariably in Nizwa), or transport you from Muscat, whichever suits your needs best. If you are travelling independently, do note that for the mountain trips (ie: Jebel Akhdar, Jebel Shams) you will need a 4x4 – this too is best organised in advance through car-rental companies in Muscat. Currently, there are no tour operators operating in Nizwa and its surrounds.

OTHER PRACTICALITIES

USEFUL TELEPHONE NUMBERS
Hospitals
Adam ` 25 434055
Bahla ` 25 419233, 25 420013
Izki ` 25 341755

Jebel Akhdar ` 25 429055
Nizwa ` 25 449155
Sumail ` 25 352236

Police stations
Adam ` 25 434099
Bahla ` 25 419099
Bidbid ` 25 360099
Dhahirah Police HQ ` 25 650099

Izki ` 25 340099
Nizwa ` 25 425099
Sumail ` 25 350099
Wadi al Jizzi ` 25 659309

Post offices
Nizwa ` 25 410302

All major tourist destinations into the jebels are signposted from the Nizwa–Bahla road with large brown tourist signposts. To access these destinations you will need a 4x4. For independent travellers arriving in saloon cars, it is recommended that you pre-book any tours into Jebel Akhdar, the Hota Caves or any other jebel trips with the tour operators based in Muscat, so that you are not disappointed. It may not be possible for you to arrange to join a tour group in a 4x4 or organise an individual 4x4 trip with driver/guide at short notice once in the region. So if you want to go it alone, you would be advised to rent a 4x4 from Muscat and travel to Nizwa in it, or arrange for it to be delivered to your hotel in Nizwa, if you want it only for a particular trip into the jebels.

Caving, rock climbing, trekking and wadi bashing are all possible in this region. For caving and climbing you will need to arrange your trip through a tour operator in Muscat.

ROCK CLIMBING Around 160 climbs have been pioneered in the region. Each is rated in terms of difficulty and they range from 120–500m. Jebel Misht, Jebel Ghul and Jebel Misfah are the three rock-climbing sites and they are all in the Jebel

THE FALAJ SYSTEM

Thought to have been introduced by the Persians in pre-Islamic times on account of its obvious resemblance to the Persian *qanat*, the *falaj* is a channel for water which leads from its source, usually an underground spring, to the fields where irrigation is required. The concept began in Persia and dates back to 1000BC. Some 20% are open channels direct from springs, while 80% are underground channels leading water from mother wells at the foot of the mountains where the water table is higher because of rainwater run-off. Some are said to originate 40ft underground, while some never go underground at all. Some run for miles while others are very short. Maintaining the *aflaj* (plural of *falaj*) requires much skill and money, and the state of them has therefore tended to be linked to the economic health of the community. During the prosperous Ya'arubi times (17th and 18th centuries) the *aflaj* were not surprisingly in excellent repair and many new ones were dug. One ingenious aspect of their construction was the way they crossed a wadi bed. They were dug down vertically on one bank until below the wadi floor, then continued horizontally until the wadi was crossed, then a vertical shaft was dug to a point fractionally lower than the upstream bank, thereby creating a siphon system.

The *falaj* tends to be the collective property of the village or group of landowners and a complex system then evolves where each landowner pays for a certain number of minutes or hours of water a day, depending on his need (for both agriculture and domestic use), and the water is channelled to his land accordingly. An elected worthy known as the *Arif* is appointed to monitor the fairness of this system, and he is also in charge of repairs, the cost of which is distributed according to the size of water share in the same way. In the recent past there were still *falaj* books with the title, sales and accounts of the *aflaj*, which would have been fascinating glimpses into the hierarchy of a rural community. In many village communities the *falaj* is still part of the essential way of life, and one of the standard exchanges for a visitor on arrival at a neighbouring village was 'And how are the *aflaj*?' 'Full, Inshallah.' It is estimated that 11,000 *aflaj* exist in Oman today, of which 4,000 are constantly flowing.

The Dakhiliyah WHAT TO SEE AND DO 7

Akhdar range in the Dakhiliyah. Climbs are arranged through most tour operators in Muscat (see pages 67–9). *Rock Climbing in Oman* published by Apex will certainly be of interest to you if climbing is your thing (see *Appendix 3, Further information*, page 276).

CAMPING AND PICNIC SPOTS Although the area is relatively heavily populated (compared with other regions) it is still possible to find places away from villages to camp and picnic, especially if you have a 4x4 and are prepared to drive off the tracks a little.

CAVING Al Hota Caves near Hamra is the caving destination of the interior (see page 198), but this is currently undergoing major development to facilitate tourism and is inaccessible. Check with any tour operator in Muscat for updates. For further caving opportunities in other regions of Oman, see page 116.

FANJA فنجاء

If you are heading out from Muscat on your first exploration of the interior, Fanja will be your first opportunity to explore an old walled town, now deserted but with a few houses at the very edge.

GETTING THERE On the Muscat–Nizwa road, after 32km, Fanja is signposted off to the right and you follow the approach road to the new villages set on the far bank of the wide wadi.

WHAT TO SEE
Fanja Tower Look carefully as you get closer to see the old town and its famous tower set up high on an escarpment above the modern village, built of the same rock as the cliff face and therefore surprisingly easy to miss. Head for the foot of the escarpment and park below near some shops now run by Indians, then walk on up the narrow tarmac road, past the running *falaj* at the roadside, to enter the old gateway into the village after a five-minute walk. Once inside you will notice one or two inhabited houses, quite smartly renovated and with TV aerials, but the houses beyond are empty. Most interesting though is the walk up the sloping escarpment past the 17th-century cannon to the fortification towers, especially the unusual oval-shaped one at the very summit. There is a kind of reservoir beside it, originally used by the inhabitants before the days of piped water, and the views out over the date gardens and the majestic sweep of the wadi are very impressive, especially at sunset when the rocks glow a deep red.

On the way to rejoin the main road there are a few shops near the bridge selling pottery and earthenware made at Bahla. With a 4x4 you can also drive down into the wadi bed before reaching the bridge to drive along the Wadi Fanja back towards the coast as far as Al Khoud. This is the site of a fine fortified and decorated castle and Sultan Qaboos University. There are many pools and good picnic spots along the way.

BIDBID بدبد

Just 2km beyond the Fanja turn-off (and about 30 minutes from Seeb roundabout) you come to the Bidbid exit, where you could make a half-hour stop to visit the fort, the first one in Oman to be restored using traditional methods from the original materials of mud, gypsum and straw.

Ranulph Fiennes, a British army officer (later explorer), was sent to Bidbid on arrival in Muscat in 1968 to train his men before being transferred to Dhofar to fight against the infiltrating Marxist rebels. The military camp was set on a cliff above the riverbed. He spent the first two days keeping close to the mess lavatory, as the Bidbid water played havoc with newcomers. There were no other lavatories in the camp 'for the soldiers were accustomed to using stones – not paper – and no European flushing system can cope with such jetsam'. He was reproached on his first night for killing an enormous spider which fell on him in the shower and was told by the Arab who brought tea: 'It is no good thing to crush such an insect for there is a chapter of the Holy Book given to its honour.'

Fiennes swam in a deep pool with reeds down in the valley and his companion told him: 'There were puff adders here and water snakes which made swimming a touch risky till we dropped some grenades in last month.'

WHAT TO SEE

Bidbid Fort To reach the fort, follow the tarmac road through the village, then fork off to the left just as the main tarmac through-road starts to drop down into the wadi. The fort lies 1km along this road, rising up above the date palms on the very edge of the wide wadi bed. It is now kept locked, but there is one point at the back where you can climb in with care. The rooms are all empty, with a cannon embedded in the tower, and the whole fort has a tumbledown air with a big tree in the centre of the courtyard. Outside, flowing past the main gate, is a very attractive *falaj* still in use by the village beside the fort.

AL FIRFAREH

After Bidbid the road returns to being normal two-way traffic, a bit of a shock to the system if hitherto you've been used to the dual carriageway of the capital area and the Batinah coast. There is no more dual carriageway in Oman from this point on, be it on to Nizwa, Ibri and Buraimi, on to Salalah or down to Sur. As a result your average speed now drops considerably.

At the point where the dual carriageway ends, the road forks left to Sur and the Sharqiya (eastern province) and nearby is a small village called Al Firfareh, known for a group of four religious hermits who once lived there, all women (as are many of the Omani adherents of the Sufis, the mystical sect of Islam). They were three sisters and their aunt, and the small mosque they built for their devotions outside the village in the early 1900s still stands in a renovated form, but now incorporated into the expanded village. Today there is no continuing tradition of Sufism in the village.

THE SUMAIL GAP

The Sumail Gap – the only natural pass through the northern jebels, and separating the Hajars into the western and eastern ranges – is 60km inland from the airport and coast, and forms the main access route from Oman's coast to the interior. It starts at Sumail and ends at Izki, and today it is the main road (Route 15) from Muscat to Nizwa. It is not totally flat, but in fact climbs about 2,000ft above sea level at its highest point. This was the ancient, strategic route for trade and communication between coastal and interior Oman. It was the frankincense route taken by caravans as well as the road travelled by explorers such as Marco Polo and Ibn Battuta.

In geological terms it is also the gap between the limestone range of the Jebel Akhdar and the lower jagged volcanic hills that head off into the Sharqiya. If you are venturing out of Muscat for the first time, it is the colossal massif of the Jebel Akhdar on your right that will draw your eye. The extraordinary tilt of the layers of rock is mesmerising even to the geological novice, with the occasional cleft snaking off into dark shadowy ravines. Its sharp lines and jagged layers make it immensely photogenic, especially in the early morning and late afternoon. Sometimes around the midday period the exceptional heat of the summer months can make it disappear from view altogether behind a haze, a most disconcerting experience when you know it is looming just there behind the shimmering blur.

SUMAIL Like many Omani towns, Sumail is divided into two parts, the lower (*Sufelat*) and the upper (*Aliyat*). Sumail Sufelat is Ghafiri and had the great fort (*Husn*) where the wali lived until the 1960s and which also housed a Koran school, judge's office and prison. Sumail Aliyat was Hinawi and the two parts of the settlement had many fights against each other, let alone against intruders. There are around 115 forts or towers defending the area – such was its importance as a trade route – and the many small villages of Wadi Sumail, with their farms and gardens, are watered by nearly 200 *falaj* channels stretching over 16km.

Some of the best dates come from Sumail. The first Omani to embrace Islam also came from here and was responsible for building one of the first mosques – named the Mosque of Mazin.

Getting there If you follow the signs to Sumail from the Muscat–Nizwa road, you will drive through the new town and out beyond for a few kilometres where the old town is heralded by two watchtowers on a hill rising above the date gardens. Follow the tarmac road to the right and over a narrow wadi to reach the old souk on a bend in the road. Once the third-largest souk of the interior after Nizwa and Bahla, it is now all but deserted. The fort of Sumail lies further along this road, perched up on a rocky hill by the main road. Just beyond the fort is a traditional old mosque with a corner dome, crumbling, but still with a well-decorated *mihrab*. Nearby, surrounded by a stone wall, is the grave of Oman's first Muslim, who is said to have built Oman's first mosque here after meeting the Prophet Muhammad in Medina back in the 7th century.

AL HOBE Still part of the Wadi Sumail fortifications but signposted separately, Al Hobe has a splendid ruined castle fort rising up on a hill above the date palms. There are five supplementary watchtowers on surrounding hills, and the castle fort itself still has a fine entrance door.

MUTTI Some 8–10km before you reach Izki is the village of Mutti, built of typical jebel dry stone walls, an interesting contrast to the mud-brick villages of the wadis. From here up the twisted wadi that lies behind the village is one of the routes up the jebel, with well-cut stone steps (for other routes see the box *Paths to the jebel*, page 184). The villagers here sheltered rebels in the Jebel War in the 1950s.

WADI HALFAYN AND THE PERSIAN STEPS About one hour's drive from Muscat (105km), you will reach this spectacular gorge. It makes a fine camping spot, as there are many large *sidr* trees for shade. A bumpy, rocky track leads for 2km to the mouth of the gorge where you can camp. A disused *falaj*, the Falaj Sahama, runs along the right-hand side of the wadi gorge. To reach it, take the turn-off to Al Afia some 30km beyond Sumail on the Nizwa road, then turn right onto the track 2.8km later, heading towards the nearby gorge. Park by the trees and continue on foot through the large boulders littering the wadi floor. One of them, on the left some 200m from the parking spot, has rock art etched into it.

The disused *falaj* on the right runs about 20ft (6m) above the wadi floor and the easiest option is to climb up to it and walk along it. Allow a full two hours for walking to the point where the *falaj* reaches the first of many deep pools. The scenery is attractive with palms and wild flowers.

Purple marks on the rocks show the trail onto the Persian Steps – 1,400 steps cut into the rock of the jebel to reach the high plateau at 6,000ft (see the box *Paths to the jebel*, page 184). The base of the steps is marked by a box canyon with three tall waterfalls. Look for the purple marks to the right of the waterfall-stained cliff. The climb up the zigzagging steps takes a minimum of four hours and requires a moderate degree of fitness. Locals who live in the mountain villages can do it in under two hours in flip-flops, using the technique of gliding effortlessly in one flowing movement from rock to rock. This technique is especially noticeable in their descent, where they appear virtually to run down the mountain with none of the jarring movements so wearing on the knees. Allow a whole day for this trip from Muscat and see how far you get.

IZKI إزكي The Sumail Gap ends at the inland town of Izki, which lies along the course of the Wadi Halfayn, one of Oman's great wadis. The wadi is normally dry, but after heavy rain a raging torrent runs off into the desert and often blocks the main road on to Nizwa.

Izki – once known as Jarnan in pre-Islamic times, and renamed Izki as a derivative of *zakah* (an Islamic alms tax) – is known for its tribal intrigues, as it is inhabited by both Hinawi (Yemeni from the south) and Ghafiri (Nizari from the Nejd in Saudi Arabia in the north). Intermarriage between the two was taboo until very recently, and their dialects retain separate characteristics.

Izki also has what is reputed to be Oman's oldest *falaj*, the Falaj Al Mulki, which originally, in its earliest Persian form, was known to have 370 separate channels. It is still well maintained and is a superb example of a stone-roofed tunnel, some 6ft (2m) high. Steps lead down to where it flows about 1ft deep at 10ft below ground level.

From the main road only the modern town is apparent, but Izki does have a 150-year-old fort, now ruined, which overlooks the walled town and dominates the head of the Sumail Gap.

In the cliffs above the wadi floor is an inaccessible cave called the Jarnan Cave, where local folklore has it that Jarnan, an idol in the shape of a golden calf, was hidden after the new faith of Islam spread with its condemnation of idol worship.

At Izki the main Nizwa road bears right to follow the line of the Jebel Akhdar, while straight on there is now a tarmac road to Sinaw, a market town on the edge of the Wahiba Sands (see *Chapter 8, The Sharqiya*, page 211). It takes about 20 minutes to drive from Izki to Nizwa.

BIRKAT AL MAWZ بركة الموز

Roughly an hour and ten minutes' drive from Muscat is Birkat al Mawz (translated as 'Pool of Bananas'). Like Tanuf, Birkat al Mawz was a town of the Beni Riyam whose sheikh, Suleyman Bin Himyar, was the rebel leader in the Jebel War.

GETTING THERE Birkat al Mawz is signposted off the main Nizwa road and is reached via a right turn some 10km after Izki (coming from Muscat) or a left turn (coming from Nizwa). The first turning takes you past the date and banana plantations and skirts the old town, while the second turn-off has a brown signpost for Bait al Redidah with Wadi Muaydin/Jebel Akhdar on the blue sign and which bypasses the town itself. The second turn-off bends steeply round and down. If you follow this road for three–four minutes you will see the fort on your right-hand side.

WHAT TO SEE

Bait al Redidah (*Open Sun–Thu 08.00–14.30, closed Fri and Sat; admission 500bzs. Currently closed for renovation for 15 months from Feb 2006–April 2007. For further information contact the Ministry of Tourism; e info@omantourism.gov.om; www.omantourism.gov.om*). The British RAF was invited by the sultan to destroy Suleyman's fine palace at Birkat al Mawz, which they did. It was restored and opened to the public in 1999 and today the serene two-storey fortified house (or castle) is known as Bait al Redidah. It guards the entrance to the Wadi Muaydin, another key route up into the mountains, and the point from where the military road up to the Saiq Plateau begins. Suleyman, whose base was at Tanuf, had a third private palace at Saiq which has today completely disappeared, bombed by the RAF at the sultan's request, and then utterly demolished to serve as a lesson to the Jebel Akhdar villagers. A modern white fort was subsequently built with a detachment of the SAF (Sultan's Armed Forces) permanently garrisoned up on the Saiq Plateau ever since. Even today there is certain sullenness among the inhabitants of Saiq, who do not welcome visitors in the normal Omani manner.

An impressive *falaj* – Falaj al Sharieh – built in the Ya'arubi era (1624–1741) in the same style as the original palace, runs out from behind Bait al Redidah, and an old mosque stands just before it, unusual in that it is built of stone and not clay.

WADI MUAYDIN

The road on to Wadi Muaydin (which leads up to Jebel Akhdar) runs straight ahead past Bait al Redidah, heading for the gorge beyond. About 3km past the fortified house the road splits and the right fork brings you, less than 1km later, to the military checkpoint with barrier, which is the start of the military route up to the Saiq Plateau.

Taking the left fork before the military checkpoint will lead you into Wadi Muaydin, a favourite area for walking and camping. In dry weather you can drive a few kilometres into the gorge before stopping in shade and exploring further on foot. In wet weather you may have to stop earlier and wade through running streams. If so, keep a sharp lookout for any signs of rain higher up in the jebel, which can suddenly rush down the gorge from the higher peaks without it ever actually raining where you are.

PATHS TO THE JEBEL

The main paths to the jebel are via Wadi Muaydin starting in Birkat al Mawz (see above); via Wadi Ghul up Jebel Shams (see page 198); the Qamr track from Nizwa (see page 260), which is longer but less steep; the track from Mutti near Izki (see page 211); from Wadi Halfayn up to Munaikhir (see page 182); and a couple of tracks from the Rustaq side, the most used of which starts from Al Awabi. Most of these ascents have stone steps cut into the rock, thought to have been the work of the Persians when they conquered the jebel in the 10th century. The amount of labour involved in such a task is so mind-boggling that one cannot help but wonder whether the summits were green and fertile at that time, to warrant the expenditure of so much effort, or whether slave labour was enlisted.

Before the construction of the military route, the ascent to the Saiq Plateau was a gruelling six-hour climb up a near-vertical path. A special kind of jebel donkey was used, tough and agile like a goat, as a normal donkey would not cope with such an ascent, let alone when loaded. The plateau itself is at 6,000ft with temperatures to match. Even during the day you will need thick clothing here in the winter months.

Follow the military road 33km to reach Saiq. After this the ascent takes one hour of extremely steep hairpin bends, especially at the beginning, where a 4x4 with low ratio is necessary. An excellent feat of engineering, it is well maintained and easily wide enough for two lorries to pass each other. Vehicles kick up huge quantities of dust. As you climb you often pass through wispy cloud for some way, before then rising above the clouds. Once higher the scenery and views are less dramatic and green than one might expect, certainly less dramatic than the road from Wadi Ghul up Jebel Shams on the far side of the jebel, described on page 199.

At 20km from the military checkpoint there is an unsignposted fork at which you turn left, and at 23km there is a signposted right fork to Menakhir (3.5km), at which you fork left.

At 24km there is another signposted fork to Hayl Yemen (2km) where you stay on the main track. At 26km the Jebel Akhdar Hotel is signposted, and at 27km you suddenly arrive at a strip of tarmac which leads you on to the village of Saiq. There is a seven-acre farm at Saiq, run by the Ministry of Agriculture and Fisheries which is worth a visit for its diversity of fruit trees, including plums, peaches, pomegranates, apricots, olives, almonds, pears, apples and figs.

Just before the tarmac a rough track leads right for a further 10km past the stone-built village of Dar Hajimta. You then come to an area generally referred to as the meadows, a popular picnicking spot where the scenery, relatively barren up to now, becomes a little more varied with more trees, bushes and grasses growing. The area is announced by a green sign to the right addressed to 'Brother Visitor and Brother Citizens', exhorting people to look after the trees, animals and birds here. Myriad tracks lead off from the main one, all ultimately ending in white water-connection blocks, suggesting some future development is planned here. For now though it is home only to wild donkeys, lizards and birds as well as a few ancient beehive cairn tombs found over in the far left corner of the meadow bowl.

JEBEL AKHDAR الجبل الأخضر

Jebel Akhdar, which translates as 'green mountain', refers to the mountain range whose highest peak is Jebel Shams (or 'mountain of the sun'), standing at 3,048m. The name Jebel Akhdar is misleading, as the greenery is confined to the terraces of a handful of villages on the Saiq Plateau, notably Shuraija, where grapes, peaches, pomegranates, apricots, figs, walnuts, almonds, lemons, apples, barley and desert roses grow, a large proportion of which are sold in the Nizwa souks.

Everything else is bare rock, predominantly grey with little or no vegetation. One convincing explanation of the name Akhdar, is that it does not mean 'green' but 'living', in the sense that it is living limestone rock, not dead volcanic rock as is found in the foothills round Nizwa and in the Sumail Gap.

Jebel Akhdar is the home of the Arabian *tahr*, a unique species of wild goat. It is with the preservation of this animal in mind that the sultan has designated part of the jebel a national park.

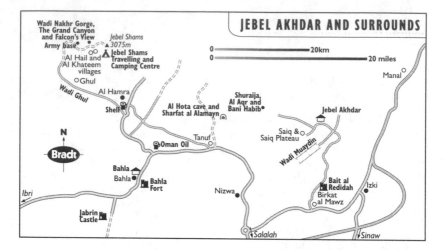

The jebel is home to around 58 separate villages and communities and about 300 wadis. Water from the springs flows through *aflaj* (ancient manmade channels) directing the flowing natural springs to these communities, who also receive regular deliveries of drinking water provided free by the government. The jebel has a hospital, some schools, a post office, and interconnecting roads are being slowly developed linking the larger villages.

The unique climate of the jebel allows for a diverse range of vegetation which cannot grow anywhere else in the region. Fruit trees and shrubs are a major part of the heritage of the jebel and all parts of the plants are utilised for culinary, perfumery, medicinal and beauty purposes. The pomegranate and walnut are the two most lucrative commodities to grow here. Saiq, bani Habib and Al Menakhar are the three main villages involved in the growing of such vegetation. Other Mediterranean fruit trees are being introduced to the region, the climate being ideal: pears are relatively new here. Honeybee breeding is also carried out in the jebel's plateaux.

The government is focusing on Jebel Akhdar as a major tourist destination and is slowly developing the area to accommodate visitors. A 36km road linking Birkat al Mawz to the Saiq Plateau will be a fundamental aspect of this phased development.

From the tarmac onwards to Saiq the extent of development is almost frightening. There are various government buildings including an agricultural development centre and a host of construction sites. In order to see any sign of terraced agriculture, take the turn-off to Shuraija.

The grapes grown here were said to have been imported by the Persians (along with many of the other exotic fruits) and were used to make wine. Suleyman's cellars in his Saiq palace were said to contain casks of wine rather than rifles and ammunition.

The village of **Al Aqr** is known for its roses, flowering mainly in April. The desert rose is unique to Jebel Akhdar. Traditionally, Omani rose-water was made here from the petals picked in April before dawn and distilled in traditional mud ovens by boiling for three to four hours. It was then used not only as a perfume but also in cooking desserts and in making flavoured coffee. Today, there is a demand for the product and perfumers can be seen at work here. Plans are said to be under way for a modern factory to be constructed, to enable rose-water to be produced in commercial quantities.

Beyond the modern development you pass the firing range with its red flags and military training centre. As the road drops down into a dip beyond this on the way to bani Habib, the village at the far edge of the plateau, you will see on the right the smashed remains of a British Venom aircraft shot down by the rebels in the Jebel War. Beside it is the grave of the pilot marked by a white marble headstone with a white cross.

You can now drive on to **Bani Habib** on the edge of the plateau and leave the car to walk a little and see the old village clinging to the cliff edge, its houses in terraced rows. Being such a popular spot from which to enjoy spectacular views, a sitting park has now been developed, providing benches and shaded areas. The village has now been largely deserted in favour of the new town on the top because of the lack of vehicular access.

On the drive back from bani Habib about halfway to Saiq, look out for three walled-up cave entrances in a wadi cliffside facing you, where the road does a deep bend and dips into a wadi. A new silver water pipeline is being laid in this wadi, which helps you identify it. You can park on the road opposite the caves and scramble down into the wadi gully and up the other side to the caves, used by Suleyman as his final hideout. The narrow entrance requires a small adult to get down on all fours with a torch, but once inside, it opens out to be quite spacious. You can even stand up when inside, though no light from outside can penetrate. Spending even one minute in this cave is enough to help you vividly imagine what it would have been like for Suleyman, waiting for weeks at a time while the furore of the pursuit outside died down.

The Bani Riyam, with Suleyman as their sheikh, was the leading Ghafiri tribe whose territory extended along the base of the mountains and right up into the summit area as well. The jebel itself had only once before been conquered by outside forces (in AD972), so Suleyman must have considered himself pretty safe up at Saiq in the third of his palaces. When the British SAS finally made an assault up the mountain in 1959, Suleyman was therefore not prepared for it. Although he had his caves to hide in, the SAS effectively put an end to the Jebel War, and Suleyman was exiled to Dammam, Saudi Arabia, to one of the flattest and dullest landscapes in Arabia.

WHERE TO STAY
Mid range
Al Jabal al Akhdar Hotel (24 rooms, 2 suites) PO Box 26, PC 621, Al Jabal al Akhdhar; 25 429009, 25 410500; f 25 429119; e jakhotel@omantel.net.om. This 3-star hotel has an international restaurant and there are plans for further development, including a swimming pool, children's park, chalets, a fitness centre, and facilities for live entertainment. RO21.80/29.50 sgl/dbl inc taxes.

NIZWA نزوى

Nizwa is about 1³/₄ hours' drive from Muscat (174km).

As the key settlement of the interior, Nizwa was a verdant oasis city, famous for its large, busy souk. It was the capital of Oman in the 6th and 7th centuries. When the traveller Ibn Battuta visited in the early 1300s, he described it as a city at the foot of the mountains surrounded by gardens and rivers with beautiful bazaars. He observed the men's habit of bringing their own food to dine together in the mosque courtyard and said of them: 'They are a bold and brave race and the tribes are perpetually at war with each other.' Even when it was not the capital itself, Nizwa was always a centre to be captured by anyone seeking to have power in Oman.

Nizwa represents an important crossroads at the base of the western Hajars linking Buraimi, Muscat and Dhofar, and was once a centre of education and art.

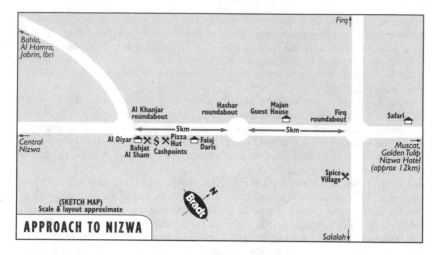

The Falaj Daris is the largest single *falaj* in the country. Forty different varieties of date palm grow in Nizwa; Khalas and Khunaizi are considered the top quality and most valuable varieties.

For an exploration of the region, Nizwa is the recommended base, offering some good hotels. Any of the old villages and places of interest listed under *What to see* below are easily reached from here. You will need a stay of two nights or so to fit it all in, but it will certainly provide you with a different feel of the country from that which you will have experienced in Muscat. However short your visit is to the country, I would highly recommend a trip to Nizwa and its close surrounds in order to gain a fuller and more rounded impression of the country.

GETTING THERE From Muscat, Nizwa is clearly signposted from Seeb Airport roundabout. This is Route 15 and is well known as the Muscat–Nizwa road. If you are intending to stay at the Golden Tulip Hotel in Nizwa, remember to keep a close eye out some 20km before Nizwa proper (as this hotel is closer to Birkat al Mawz than Nizwa). You will need to take a right-hand turn after emerging from the mountains (see below for further details). Built in 1996, it is the most luxurious base for exploration in the region.

At about 3km before Nizwa Old Town itself is the Falaj Daris Hotel, which sits on the left (see below). Passing the Falaj Daris Hotel, you now approach the heart of Nizwa itself, recognisable by the vast round tower of the fort beside the new bright cobalt-blue dome of the Sultan Qaboos Mosque (see the cover photograph of this guide). Before you reach it, there is a wide wadi bed, usually flowing either weakly or impassable after heavy rains, as Nizwa is at the confluence of two wadis – Wadi Abyadh and Wadi Kalbouh, one of the reasons for its location. Using this water, it has an extensive network of *falaj* channels irrigating its date gardens which extend for some 8km behind the town.

It is probably best to leave your car in the extensive parking areas in front of the modern sand-coloured souk façade that faces the wadi bed.

WHERE TO STAY
Upper range
⌂ **Falaj Daris Hotel** (55 rooms, 2 suites) PO Box 312, PC 611; ☏ 25 410500; f 25 410537; e fdhnizwa@omantel.net.om; www.falajdarishotel.com. This single-storey hotel is situated after the Golden Tulip Hotel as you approach from Muscat and is closer to the centre of

the town, about 4km before the fort. Irrespective of the end from which you approach the hotel, the signpost comes up on you at the turn into the entrance; there is no earlier indication. So don't worry if you miss the turning, as you can simply go to the next roundabout and come back on yourself. Try to get onto the slip road at the Shell garage (on the left past the Falaj Daris going towards Nizwa town centre) as the road is less hectic and you can drive more slowly. The hotel is set round two courtyards with a small pool in each. It has a licensed restaurant, a bar (Castle Bar), and a health club. In addition there is an Arabic bar (Sahara Lounge), the entrances for which are outside and to the left as you exit the front doors of the hotel. This has local entertainment with belly dancing from 21.00. Many Europeans stay at the Falaj Daris, which has an almost colonial feel about it. There is something special about its courtyard setting with

its mountain backdrop. It's a shame the rooms have showers only and no bath, but its proximity to the old town is a major plus point. *RO21.80/29.50 sgl/dbl, incl taxes.*

🏠 **Golden Tulip Nizwa Hotel** (120 rooms) PO Box 1000, PC 611; ☎ 25 431616; f 25 431619; e info@goldentulipnizwa.com; www.goldentulipnizwa.com. This hotel is the plushest base for exploring the interior. It is about 1hr's drive from Seeb International Airport, in its own grounds about 20km before Nizwa Town proper, which is about another half-hour's drive further on. The rooms are in a low-rise complex set round a large pool, business centre and 3 bars with live entertainment. There is a licensed, elegant restaurant, a poolside café, a lobby café, a large bar (Al Wasit) with a live band and a nightclub (Tanuf). *RO33/38 sgl/dbl exc taxes.*

Budget
🏠 **Al Diyar Hotel** (60 rooms) PO Box 1166, PC 611; ☎ 25 412402; f 25 412405; e al_diyarhotel@hotmail.com; www.aldiyarhotel.com. The rooms are fine and a little cheaper than the Falaj Daris, but it is unlicensed and so has no minibar in your room (although it does have a fridge). There is an unlicensed restaurant attached to it, called Bahjat Al Sham, offering a good cheap menu. It has a swimming pool. Hire cars can be arranged from here (10 days' advance notice), for RO40/65 saloon/4x4 (inc driver/guide). *RO18/22 sgl/dbl, inc taxes and b/fast.*

🏠 **Majan Guest House LLC** (21 rooms) PO Box 1262, PC 611; ☎ 25 431910, 25 431912, 25 431913, 99 453884; f 25 431911; www.majangh.com. This is located roughly 8km before the Falaj Daris Hotel, and just after the Firq (or Faraq) roundabout on

the right-hand side coming from Muscat. Considering this is near to and half the price of Falaj Daris and has good, clean rooms and friendly staff and management, this is certainly an alternative option if you simply want to get your head down after your tours. There is no restaurant as yet. *RO10/12 sgl/dbl incl taxes and b/fast.*

🏠 **Safari Hotel** (70 rooms) PO Box 202, PC 611; ☎ 25 432150; f 25 432151; e safarihn@omantel.net.om. This hotel lies just before the Firq (or Faraq) roundabout, on the right-hand side of the road, coming from Muscat. There is a restaurant and coffee shop, swimming pool and a residents' bar. Accepts credit cards. *RO15/20/25 sgl/dbl/suite, exc taxes, inc b/fast; RO3 for extra bed in room; children under 12 free, staying in parents' room.*

✖ WHERE TO EAT
Upmarket (RO20+ for a meal for two) The plushest restaurants of the interior are in the Golden Tulip and the Falaj Daris hotels, both of which are fully licensed.

✖ **Birkat al Mawz** Golden Tulip Hotel; ☎ 25 431616. With an international menu.
✖ **Pool Café** Golden Tulip Hotel; ☎ 25 431616. Serves poolside snacks and can be used by non-guests.

✖ **Al Fanar** Falaj Daris Hotel; ☎ 25 410500. Serves continental, Oriental, Chinese and Indian dishes.

Budget (under RO20 for a meal for two)
✖ **Bahjat Al Sham** ☎ 25 412409. This is an unlicensed restaurant with a good cheap international menu and is located immediately next to Al Diyar Hotel (and part of it) at the first

roundabout after the Falaj Daris Hotel, going towards the town centre.
✖ **Bin Ateeq** ☎ 25 410466. Bin Ateeq Restaurant lies a little way up the road on the right just after

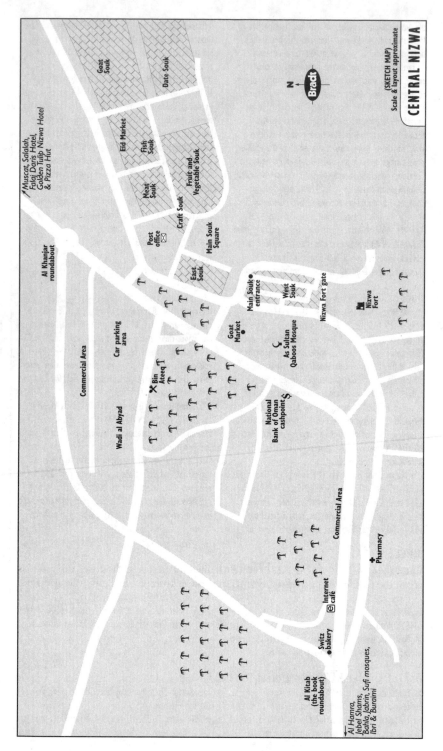

190

CENTRAL NIZWA

(SKETCH MAP)
Scale & layout approximate

Bradt

N

Goat Souk

Date Souk

Eid Market

Fish Souk

Muscat, Salalah,
Falaj Daris Hotel,
Golden Tulip Nizwa Hotel
& Pizza Hut

Meat Souk

Fruit and
Vegetable Souk

Al Khanjar
roundabout

Post office

Craft Souk

Main Souk Square

Commercial Area

East Souk

Car parking
area

Main Souk
entrance

West Souk

Nizwa Fort gate

Nizwa Fort

Goat Market

Wadi al Abyad

Bin Ateeq

As Sultan
Qaboos Mosque

National
Bank of Oman
cashpoint

Commercial Area

Pharmacy

Internet café

Switz bakery

Al Kitab
(the book
roundabout)

Al Hamra,
Jebel Shams,
Bahla, Jabrin, Sufi mosques,
Ibri & Buraimi

the vast car-parking area and is clearly signposted. It is the only traditional Omani restaurant in the area, and offers a great eating experience at ground level in the traditional Omani style. It is cheap and serves good food. You are taken to your own private room behind a sliding door, where you leave your shoes. You are served dates and coffee as a matter of course and they round off the meal perfectly as dessert. A meal for one consisting of salad, fried king fish with white rice and then coffee and dates comes to a little under RO2. Excellent for the true Omani experience. There are two more in the chain, in Salalah and Muscat.

✗ **Pizza Hut** ✆ 25 412096. If you are suffering from homesickness, this could be the place for you, situated about 200m beyond the Falaj Daris Hotel (going towards Nizwa Old Town centre). It is almost always empty and is open all day, offering a salad bar and the usual range of thin and deep-pan pizzas. It is unlicensed but has clean toilets. This is the only big-name fast-food outlet so far in Oman's interior.

✗ **Spice Village** ✆ 25 431694. Serving Thai, tandoori, Chinese, Arabic, south Indian, north Indian and Punjabi meals. This is located a little before Nizwa. Take the road left at the Firq roundabout (if you are coming from Muscat), in the direction of Salalah. It is just a little way down on the right side, close to the Oman International Bank.

WHAT TO SEE

Nizwa Fort (*Open Sat–Wed 09.00–16.00, Fri 08.00–11.00; admission 500 bzs*). As chief town of the interior and Oman's capital for many centuries, Nizwa is dominated by its vast circular tower. This colossal structure took around 12 years to build under the imam Sultan Bin Saif bin Malik al Ya'arubi, who repulsed the Portuguese (who were never to return) from Muscat. He is said to have financed the construction from the spoils of sacking the emirate of Ras al Khaimah.

One of the oldest and largest forts in Oman, it was completed in 1668, to protect its strategic position at the crossroads of the caravan routes. Before the massive restoration project (completed in 1990), the wali (district governor) lived in the tower and had to move out whenever parts of the roof collapsed following heavy rainstorms. On the roof of the tower itself the army guards lived among scattered iron bedsteads, draped with clothes.

The massive round tower is filled in with earth and stones for half of its 30m height and 36m diameter. This solid in-fill made a strong and solid platform for cannon to fire over the tops of the palm trees and made it impossible for rival cannon fire to breach the walls. An additional protective wall with three sets of steps to the top encircles the cannon platform with excellent vantage points over the town. The round tower is entered via a narrow zigzag flight of steps with three sets of doors to block off the enemy at each turn.

Entering through the main gateway to the left of the round tower, you come to the courtyard in which one of the outbuildings has an interesting display of figures showing the restoration process in action, with explanations of the techniques used. It helps to see these before your tour, so that you fully appreciate the labour involved.

Once inside, the sheer extent of the main fort comes as a surprise. From the outside, the round tower appears to be the entire structure, but the other areas are extensive, with prisons, storerooms, kitchens, washing areas, sleeping quarters, a mosque, a Koranic school, *majlis* rooms, a judge's room and living quarters for the wali. These rooms are spread at various levels, a veritable maze in which it is easy to lose all sense of direction. Back down on the ground floor within the fort itself is a small **Omani Heritage Gallery** (e *ohgmq@omantel.net.om; www.omaniheritage.com*), which is a shop selling handicrafts. The prices are a little inflated compared with those of the souk, but you may prefer to simply pay the tag price and be gone, rather than haggle over prices. Furthermore, it is a not-for-profit organisation which aims to support Omani artisans with a view to preserving their traditional crafts. There is also another Omani Heritage Gallery outlet next to the Intercontinental Hotel in Muscat at the Jawaharat al Shatti Complex.

By the 1950s there was much disaffection in the country about the fact that the sultan, Said bin Taimur, who had ruled since 1932, sat mainly in Salalah and refused to delegate any decision making, preferring instead to guard all affairs of state jealously to himself. This led to a state of sterility which the rebel leaders – Ghalib, who had been elected imam in 1954, Taalib his brother and two tribal leaders, Suleyman Bin Himyar and Salih Bin Issa – aimed to overthrow. At this time too the Wahhabi Saudis, who had seized Buraimi in 1952, were at the height of their attempts to spread Wahhabism through Oman, and they lent their support to the rebels, who were able to capture Ibri and other towns north of Nizwa. To repel them, Qaboos's father, Sultan Said bin Taimur, made his only trip from Salalah with a collection of cars and trucks to Nizwa, Buraimi and Sohar, before returning to Muscat. The rebels dispersed and the country was briefly unified. This was the first and last trip he ever made to the interior of Oman. Within a few years things had drifted back to where they started, with the rebel leaders active again, and the sultan called on the British to come and use their armed forces to crush the rebels, which they duly did. The British however did not wish this to become a precedent, at a time when the United Nations was vociferous on the subject of intervention, as it was only shortly after the Suez fiasco. In 1958, British Foreign Office Minister Julian Amery was sent out to negotiate an agreement as to the future security of Oman, which resulted in Britain paying £250,000 a year to the sultan, and the setting up of the SAF (Sultan's Armed Forces) and the SOAF (Sultan of Oman's Air Force) with Britain providing seconded officers to run them. The RAF was to continue to be allowed to use airbases at Salalah and Masirah.

Nizwa Mosque (Masjid Sultan Qaboos) The mosque, with its distinctive blue and gold dome (see cover picture), was built by Abdulla bin Mohammed al Ibadi and lies next to the Nizwa Fort. It was modernised and developed in the 1970s. Non-Muslims are not permitted to enter, but views of the mosque and the surrounds generally are superb from Nizwa Fort.

Nizwa souk The renovation programme of the 1990s extended beyond the fort itself into the whole surrounding area and the modern souk façade conceals renovated areas of pristine cleanliness, sanitised for tourists. If you want to see the old Nizwa however, this façade is just that, and a few more steps will take you beyond to the medieval mud streets ripe with the usual medieval smells. Spices, seeds, berries, herbs and all sorts of intriguing produce used in traditional medicinal remedies can be bought here.

Vehicles can drive in through the main gateway in the souk façade and there is some parking within. The central area has been imaginatively recreated with Omani craft shops selling antiques, silver jewellery, khanjars, swords, leather goods, copper, pottery, weaving and wooden artefacts. Artisans go about their craft in the small workshops. Prices in the souk are already cheap, so bargaining scope is limited.

In the area to the left, away from the round fort tower, are the refurbished fruit and vegetable souks, the fish souk and animal souk (where goat and cattle auctions take place on Thursday and Friday mornings and the eve of Eid).

The Sufi mosques Spare an extra half hour if you can to make this interesting short diversion to a walled graveyard on the outskirts of Nizwa, where the Sufi mystics built a series of little mosques on low hills as places where they could worship in seclusion away from the town.

Go out of Nizwa on the Bahla road and turn left by a high watchtower shortly after 'the book' roundabout. The graveyard is to both sides of the road and has some important tombs of imams and scholars. Some of the tombs have engraved stones with names and dates going back to the 7th century AD, the first century of Islam.

The road leads on through old Nizwa and its date gardens, giving an unusual contrast to the modern and renovated centre of town, until it leads back to the fort.

Falaj Daris, Mosque of the Rock and Al Shawadhna Mosque detour Approximately 10km after Nizwa on the Nizwa–Bahla road near Marfa, look out for the small green sign indicating Falaj Daris to the right, where you can make a detour of half an hour or so. There is now a park and picnic spot here and you can climb down inside this, one of Oman's largest *aflaj*. Beside the *aflaj*, there are two unusual ruined mosques tucked under the lee of the mountains. Once you have turned right off the main road from Falaj Daris, keep to the left passing the high school building and follow the route for 2km after the tarmac runs out. To the left of the road you will see the small square **Az al Qadim** Sufi Mosque

(Mosque of the Rock) on the edge of a hill with a large rock beside it. There is a legend associated with the rock and the mystic who used to pray here alone away from the town, whereby the 100kg rock disappeared and reappeared inside the mosque overnight.

A further 1km along the graded road to the left are three more abandoned mosques including **Al Shawadhna**, which has a beautifully carved *mihrab* and the unusual feature of two *qiblas* (a niche marking the direction of prayer), one facing Mecca, the other facing Jerusalem. It must therefore date back to the first Islamic century (7th century) when prayer in the early mosques faced Jerusalem, before the direction of prayer was changed to face Mecca some ten years later, still during the Prophet Muhammad's lifetime.

You can stay on this track, forking right to rejoin the main road.

SEIH AL BARAKAT

Before reaching Manah, some 7km from the Salalah turn-off, you will notice a high picnic spot on a hillock to your left. This is Seih al Barakat, where the sultan meets local people on his annual tour. There are a few little towers, an incense burner and some palm sunshades. The sunset views from here are very evocative. From this point also you will notice a tall sand-coloured structure standing proud of the date plantations – this is Fiqain Fort.

FIQAIN فقين

Take the turn-off marked Fiqain and follow the tarmac as it winds round behind the tall tower. Park here where the road narrows, under a tree, and walk back the short distance through the old town gate towards this amazing building. It is a remarkable fortified **tower house** (*open 08.30–14.30 or whenever the guardian is present*), almost Scottish baronial in its narrow proportions and restored in 1988. The guardian sits below and lets you take yourself on a tour, hardly surprising given the number of stairs involved, and may offer you coffee afterwards for your exertions. The ruined town of Fiqain lies crumbling to the right of the fort, now ringed by modern houses.

The design of Fiqain Fort is quite unique, with massive stone-built walls faced with *sarouj* plaster. The tall side tower to the left as you approach is a wind tower, designed to catch the breeze and funnel it down into the top two floors of living space. This section is approached by the stairs to the left side of the entrance door, leading up to the rooftop. Each floor has a perfectly aligned circular hole for the family to shout instructions down to the servants or for raising water or food up on a tray.

This section is totally separate from the second slightly larger section which is approached from the stairs at the back of the entrance hall. The rooms off the hall were for weaponry as well as cooking and storage, and the upper levels were used for the guards and soldiers defending the sheikh's family. The door through which you now enter was a secret entrance, not discovered until 1991 after an old man in the village told the authorities about it. Before that, entry was only by rope and pulley, still in place in the guard section, into the two high windows. All the restoration work was carried out through these high windows. Note also the two overhanging latrines on the top floor of the guard section.

MANAH منح

Probably Oman's most impressive ruined town, Manah is well worth the short drive (11km) south from Nizwa. To reach it take the major fork south to Salalah on the eastern outskirts of Nizwa, and after 1km take the signposted turn left to Manah. The modern town of Manah has tarmac running to it, and the old town lies just behind it and can easily be approached on dirt tracks, which are fine for saloon cars. Follow the tarmac to the end of town, passing an Oman Oil petrol station on your right, until you reach a small roundabout with a restored mosque to the left, raised on a terrace. This mosque dates back to 1534 and was renovated in 1991. It cannot be visited by non-Muslims. Turn right at the roundabout onto a gravel track past a large ruined building and drive skirting the edge of the walled town until you come to the tall square tower built into the stone walls. Park here and walk in through the gateway to see the remarkable covered street to your right, now covered with debris. Go straight along the main street and then into the first building on your left, up some steps to a terrace with a well still in use. This is the forecourt of a disused mosque, inside which you can still see a very elaborately detailed green painted *mihrab*, with a valuable blue-and-white Chinese plate as its centrepiece stuck onto the plasterwork. Wall niches still hold loose pages of the Koran.

Further down this main street are two more mosques, also with elaborately decorated *mihrabs*, one with all its Chinese plates painted over in green. The *mihrab* inscriptions show that they date to the early 16th century, and all three *mihrabs* were built by Oman's most famous mosque architect, Abdullah Al Hamaimy. The town is mainly built of mud brick, and though the houses still have many carved doors left, the walls are badly crumbled.

The overgrown *falaj* system at Manah is claimed by local folklore to have been dug by Malik Bin Fahm, leader of the Yemeni Azdite tribe who settled in Oman after the bursting of the famous Marib Dam in Yemen in the 2nd century AD. Yemeni civilisation was thereby terminated and Malik's tribe migrated east to Oman, driving out the Persians who were at that time dominant in Nizwa.

Coming upon it in the late 19th century, one English traveller wrote: 'Is this Arabia ... is this the country we have looked on heretofore as a desert?' Today these words are unfitting, as the *falaj*, broken and dusty, lies off in a field smothered with dead grass.

Neither part of the Sharqiya nor part of the true interior, the curious towns of Izz and Adam are both situated at the beginning of the road to Salalah. Izz was originally a Bedouin nomad settlement surprisingly close to the Jebel. As such it had little permanent housing but had a large date grove. Adam, a large settled town a long way into the desert from the jebel, was fed by *aflaj* led in from three surrounding hilly outcrops.

Izz lies some 10km south of the Manah turn-off and Adam about 25km beyond that. Adam is roughly 295km from Muscat and is the main entrance to the interior of the country from the south. It is the last green oasis before the featureless desert stretches all the way to Salalah. It has an old quarter called Harrat al Jamii (Mosque Quarter), birthplace of the founder of the Al Bu Said dynasty. The mosque named after him, Jamii Al Bu Said, has been restored and stands outside the walls with pillars and an ornate *mihrab*. Inside the walls is an unusual small domed mosque, now disused, with two small arched doorways leading in through the mud walls.

WHERE TO STAY

Al Ghaba Resthouse (10 rooms) ☎ 99 358639. This budget resthouse provides basic accommodation with an international restaurant. It is situated on the Salalah road at the southernmost point of the Dakhiliyah, 715km from Salalah. Accepts credit cards. *RO18/25 sgl/dbl.*

TANUF

About 15 minutes on from Nizwa on the Bahla road there is a brown sign marked Wadi Tanuf. The name of Tanuf is known today for the mineral water which is bottled from the springs at the nearby factory. A small modern settlement has grown up beside the bottling plant. But today Tanuf is visited more for the crumbling ruins, abandoned some 45 years ago, that sit at the mouth of the spectacular gorge. Follow the tarmac road in towards the mountains, keeping to the right, for about three minutes. You will see the old ruins easily as you approach. If you follow the road around immediately behind the ruins this takes you into the wadi. After parking in the shade by the gorge you can climb the steps to explore the old town.

This ghost town is a stark reminder of the savage and relatively recent civil war, called the Jebel War, fought in the 1950s. Tanuf was singled out for destruction as a reprisal against the Beni Riyam, whose sheikhs were known as Lords of the Green Mountain. From the wadi behind the town there were escape routes up into the mountains, which is how Suleyman Bin Himyar, the sheikh at the time of the Jebel War, used to slip away up to hideouts in caves high on the Saiq Plateau (see page 185). The town was bombed by the planes of the RAF at the request of the sultan (Said bin Taimur) and what remains today is a crumbling collection of houses set on the hillock above the wadi. The *falaj* still runs through it, offering a rare opportunity to explore a traditional Omani town without disturbing the inhabitants.

The pillared mosque beside the *falaj* is still quite well preserved. If you cross the wadi, usually flowing until May, you can picnic in the playground on the other side, often accompanied by goats. There are good views of the *falaj* channel built into the sheer mountain wall. After the rains it fills to overflowing and cascades down the wall like a waterfall to join the river. The track into the gorge is drivable for 8km, passing to the right of the Wadi Tanuf recharge dam (which was completed in 1989 with the intention of increasing the supply of subterranean water feeding the *aflaj* of Daris and Tanuf). The wadi at the end, called Wadi

Qashah, has good walking with pools deep enough for swimming. A whole day can easily be spent in this stunning scenery.

There is also a turn-off to Tanuf at a point further up the main road at Al Maha petrol station (the first sign you come to if you are coming from Ibri/Buraimi). Do not take this one; it is the Wadi Tanuf sign you need to look out for.

HAMRA الحمراء

One of Oman's most attractive and traditional towns, Hamra was founded in the Ya'arubi dynasty (1624–1741) and has Oman's most elegant collection of two- and three-storey mud-brick houses in the old part of town, many dating from the Ya'arubi era. You can reach them as you follow the tarmac road winding and twisting beside the date gardens, which are set down below street level so as to maximise rainwater collection. Unlike so many Omani towns, Hamra has no fort and no defensive walls. As a result it was never involved in tribal warfare and hence the houses are still very well preserved.

GETTING THERE AND WHAT TO SEE The road off to Hamra from the Nizwa–Bahla road is signposted (Hamra 17km) and heads straight for the foot of the Jebel Akhdar where the town nestles. Note the sections of *falaj*, built of stone and looking like a low wall, running along the side of hills to your right, with the occasional disused building nearby. As you approach the mountain you can see two roads snaking up the jebel behind Hamra. The one on the left leads to Misfah and the one on the right is a new track to the Hota Cave.

Continue straight on to the roundabout and follow the signs for Hamra East, straight on across the roundabout. This tarmac road runs through the new town, winds past the date gardens and on to the old part of town. The one-way system leads you up a ridge from where you have fine views over the old town and the greenery, and can see the watchtowers set on the surrounding ridges. What is unusual about Hamra is the large number of old houses still lived in, with air conditioning and TV aerials added, especially those on the edge which are easily accessible by vehicle. The least-inhabited parts are those up narrow alleys in the centre where no car can penetrate.

Dropping down from the bridge you come to a lush roundabout with a playground behind. The track to the right (not signposted) leads to Misfah, while straight on leads you back in a complete circuit to the original Hamra East/West signposts. Take the road to the left first, though, past the enormous stand-alone three-storey mud house with green shutters, and on into the heart of the old town. Park where the road bends and then walk in through the old gateway a little up to your left before dropping down to follow the fast-flowing *falaj* system within the walls.

The old houses here are fascinating. Some, near the edge, are still lived in with the *falaj* actually flowing through their entrance hall. Old men sit in the shaded alleyways drinking coffee and chatting about old times, and the youths hanging about may have difficulty pointing out to you which old house is **Bait al Safa**, House of Purity, where mystical Sufi women lived together like nuns. The 400-year-old house is now unoccupied and locked up, but is said to house old handicrafts. Opposite it is a small mosque built beside the *falaj*, originally for their use alone, now air conditioned with its porticoes glassed-in. Women in the Sufi tradition often chose to remain single and celibate, devoting their lives to prayer. Allow a minimum of 30 minutes for a stroll here, ending by the *falaj* at the *halwa* maker, his central freestanding stall piled round with wood for fires which he lights beneath the huge copper bowl.

Misfah is the ultimate medieval village, built into a rockface 10km up a winding dirt track from Hamra, suitable only for the most robust saloon car or 4x4s. The turn-off is signposted. If you want to walk through Misfah, leave your car at the end of the track and walk down the worn steps into the main alleyway. The lush date plantation lies directly below the village in a gully. Follow the narrow streets between the tall houses until you emerge at the other end in a green open area where the women come to wash their dishes and clothes in the *falaj* and water pools. The truly adventurous can arrange four six-hour walks from here over to Wajmah in the Sahtain Bowl and Bilad Sayt in Wadi bani Auf. Speak to any tourist operator in Muscat if you would like to arrange this as an accompanied trek.

AL HOTA CAVE AND SHARFAT AL ALAMAYN

Al Hota Cave (also Al Hoti) is one of the largest cave systems in the world with several lakes, which provide a home to a variety of different species of fauna. There is a wealth of stalactite and stalagmite formations in the chasms below, and the cave is also home to unusual species of pink-coloured blind fish which sense their way around the lake with feelers.

One of Oman's best-known caves, this used to be accessible only to serious cavers, requiring ropes and climbing gear to descend the 30ft into the sinkhole. But currently there is a major development project taking place, making the caves temporarily inaccessible to the visitor, so you will need to check the state of play when you arrive. The project involves the development of a visitors' centre, which is to include a restaurant, a ticket counter, a souvenir shop, a geological museum and a railway station with a 36-seater train which will travel along a tunnel for a distance of 2.7km into the cave. An illuminated walkway with stairs has been erected to view the cave, which has interesting offshoot chambers.

Sharfat Al Alamayn (Arabic for 'balcony of the two worlds') which, as its name suggests, is an excellent vantage point for views over Wadi bani Auf and Bilad Sayt to one side and the Sahtain Bowl to the other. The altitude here is 2,000m and the terrain is covered in bushes and juniper trees. Even in May and early June nights can be surprisingly cool, dropping to 10°C when the temperature at Nizwa may rise as high as 45°C.

GETTING THERE Take the right-hand turn off the Nizwa–Bahla road (following signs to Al Hamra), setting your mileometer to zero. As you approach the mountain you can see two roads snaking up the jebel behind Hamra. The one on the left leads to Misfah with the one on the right to the Hota Cave and Sharfat al Alamayn. After 3.7km take the right-hand turn, signposted to Qalaat al Masalha. Then at 8.3km turn right. At 8.5km turn right again, then bear left at 9.3km, and right again at 9.5km. This is where the track to the cave begins. At 14.8km you reach a fork. For the cave, take the left road and after a further 0.9km turn left. Following this road, you will reach the cave entrance at 16.7km. For Sharfat al Alamayn, take the right at the fork which leads you up a steep bumpy track.

WADI GHUL AND JEBEL SHAMS

WADI GHUL وادي غول The best time for an exploration of Ghul village, abandoned on its rocky outcrop, is late afternoon to dusk. The colour of the stone is brought to life by the red sunset, and the contrast as night approaches, between the eerily empty houses on one side of the valley and the noisily bustling modern village on the hilltop opposite, is all the more striking. The name *ghul* in Arabic (from which we get our word ghoul), means a kind of evil (*jinn*), usually female, that feeds on dead humans and appears in monstrous shapes, especially to travellers alone at night. This ties in with the reputation of nearby Bahla for witches and black magic.

Fork off the main track as you cross the wadi bed itself, heading towards the old village and the little mosque set at its foot just beside the *falaj* system. Leave the vehicle here, where a footpath leads past the mosque with steps down to a private ablution spot, and then forks to the left. After being a bit vague initially, the path soon turns into carefully made steps which zigzag up the rock to bring you within a minute or so into the main street of the village, heavily overgrown now, and full of collapsed stone walls from the adjacent houses.

Clambering about in and among the houses can take anything from 15 minutes to an hour depending on how exhaustive you wish to be. If you have the time it is well worth gradually making your way to the very top of the rocky outcrop, where the remains of an impressive fortification are to be found. At the entrance is a rock drawing showing a warrior with sword and shield. The views from the summit give a sense of strategic command.

Returning down through the main street, look out for the rock drawings of men on horseback chiselled into the flat grey rockfaces. There is a particular concentration of some 12–15 drawings about halfway down the street. Close by is a smooth worn hole in the rock, like a grinding mill in the grey stone, though quite why this is in the middle of the street remains unclear.

JEBEL SHAMS جبل شمس Jebel Shams ('mountain of the sun'), the tallest mountain in Oman at 3,048m above sea level, is a popular tourist destination because of its spectacular gorges, ravines and breathtaking heights. Trekking trips can be arranged through local tour operators. Its popularity has led to the construction of a modern camping site facility of five independent rooms with en-suite toilets and five open-style units, with plans to add a restaurant. Tourists are permitted to use the kitchen and cook their own meals. The water for this site is from Wadi Ghul. Summer camping up here can be surprisingly cool, so take thick clothes and blankets for the night. The contrast when you drive down to the plain again can be as much as a 30°C difference.

Tiny villages are signposted off the main track and occasionally visible clinging to the hillside with terracing. Children from these villages aged ten or over go by 4x4 down to Hamra to school daily. Boys and girls aged seven to nine are mixed in small village schools learning the basics of reading and writing.

WADI NAKHR GORGE (THE GRAND CANYON OF OMAN) En route to these villages is Wadi Nakhr, which, with its large water pool, is a major site of interest within Jebel Shams, and another popular camping area. Al Khateem village lies on the edge of a gorge with fantastic views, and this is where the trek to reach the cliff dwellings in the canyon begins. It is also the spot from where Bahla and Al Hamra can be seen in the distance – probably one of the best spots for an appreciation of Jebel Shams. **Falcon's View** is another outstanding spot in the mountains from which to take in spectacular panoramic views.

It rather goes without saying, but good care must be taken if camping with children on account of the precipitous location. Nights with a full moon are said to be the best. Do carry plenty of food, water and camping gear.

You may well encounter some of the children up on the plateau by the Wadi Nakhr rim, who can be over-enthusiastic in their desire for a sale of their handmade crafts. Remember not to stand too close to the edge as you back off from their zealous approach! Their skin is noticeably weathered and their eyes lined with *kohl*, which can be rather alarming. However, the cash they make from any sale of their little weaving creations, such as key-ring tassels in colourful patterns, I am sure makes a welcome contribution to their existence in this part of the desert.

Near the top Dar Sawda village is signposted 1km off to the left, while the main track continues straight on up to the restricted military zone. You must continue and turn right after 500m onto a track signposted Al Hail that brings you after another 4km to the plateau. The main track itself ends at Al Khateem, the tiny village on the edge of the rim, but smaller tracks fork off left before that to reach the edge of the rim. The Grand Canyon of Oman is truly spectacular, with near-vertical drops of 1,500m to the wadi bed below.

From Al Khateem village you can, if you have a good head for heights, follow the 'rim walk', which takes at least five hours to complete. It is a very narrow steep track and starts by leading down to a deserted village. Then it leads on across large boulders and along an old *falaj* channel to the other side of the canyon. The terraces over here are irrigated by a large natural bowl, Bir Dakhiliya (Arabic for 'interior well'), and are supported by a gigantic arch of rock.

The trees at this height are wild olive and juniper, while on the lower slopes in springtime you will see the delicate pink flowers of the *Moringa peregrina* (*shu*). For the rest of the year it is virtually leafless, but its seeds are crushed to make oil with medicinal properties, said to be beneficial for fevers, skin and stomach problems. Children will sometimes offer handfuls of wild juniper berries (*boo'ot*), delicious and full of vitamin C. The rock itself is often littered with shells and marine fossils, showing that it was once the floor of a warm shallow ocean aeons ago.

Getting there Shortly before Hamra, a new surfaced road runs through Wadi Ghul (10km) and Jebel Shams (37km) and is signposted to your left, by a petrol station. The road was built by desert line projects to enable military vehicles to gain access to the defence installations on the summit of Jebel Shams. The first 10km to Wadi Ghul itself is along a wide graded track, mainly flat and easy driving, until you reach the villages of Ghul, old and new, one each side of the wadi bed.

Once through Wadi Ghul, the road leading to Jebel Shams, which is surfaced for most of the way. However the final winding 7km is graded track until the turning to the villages of Al Hail and Al Khateem, and it is for this last leg that you require a 4x4. From Ghul, allow an hour for the steep 27km drive up Jebel Shams, as well as some time to stop and examine the goat-hair rugs woven and sold by the male villagers at Ghul and at several other points during the ascent. (Prices range from RO15–20, depending on size, and the striped geometric patterns can be very attractive. The predominant colours are red, black, brown, white, and occasionally grey, yellow and brown, using both vegetable and chemical dyes.)

At 2,000m, Jebel Shams is the highest drivable point anywhere in Oman. There are campsites located at 3km from this turn, and a further 2km will get you to the small modern camping resort.

Where to stay
Budget
Jebel Shams Travelling and Camping Centre (6 chalets and 6 tents) ↘ 24 635222, 99 228489. Said al Khatri is the co-ordinator of the camp, which is approximately an 80km drive from Nizwa. Modern AC and en-suite apts (but no fridges or towels in rooms). *RO15/10 pp chalets/tents, HB.*

BAHLA

A sense of the magnificence of Bahla can be gleaned from the extraordinarily extensive wall remnants that still surround the town for a distance of some 12km

The three mosques on little hills just before Bahla are also known as the Mosques of the Saints. In Orthodox Islam there are no saints, but to the Sufis, the mystical sect of Islam, saints' tombs are revered and often held to have miraculous powers such as healing the sick. The origins of Bahla's magical roots are not known, but it may simply be that these three mystics or religious hermits settled here and their reputations grew.

The prophet Muhammad was himself a sincere believer in the existence of good and evil *jinn* and the Koran has a *sura* (chapter) entitled Sura Al Jinn. In one of the Traditions of the Prophet it is said 'The *jinn* were created of a smokeless fire'. They were also meant to have a great fear of metal – hence the chains on the market tree – and someone who felt himself pursued by a *jinn* would shout 'Hadid, hadid!', ('iron, iron'), to protect himself. The existence of *jinn* in Islam is completely accepted and through the use of magic they have extended into folklore. A man who died by violence, for example, was commonly thought to become a *jinn* spirit and haunt the place of his death, just like our ghosts.

and which you cannot fail to notice as you approach from the direction of Nizwa. For the best view of Bahla Fort itself, rising majestically above the oasis palms, drive beyond the town and then double back on yourself to approach from the Jabrin side of town, crossing the wide, fertile wadi bed. If you have come from Buraimi, this will be the first view you get, and it is an impressive one as you approach via the winding road. The walls enclose not only the fort and the town itself, but also an extensive area of date gardens and irrigated fields. While Bahla was capital of Oman for four or five centuries (mid 12th to the 17th) under the Nabahina dynasty, a special group of slaves used to guard the walls during this period, when the Ya'arubi took over. The walls are said to have been designed by a woman named Ghaitha 600 years ago and have 15 gates and 132 watchtowers for sentries at regular intervals.

As you approach from Nizwa, the turn-off to the right immediately opposite the fort (clearly signposted) leads into the old souk area of town, which lies to your left as you advance slowly along the narrow road. You will notice the open area where animals and vegetables are traded, but immediately opposite to the right, just before where the one-way system begins, you will see a gateway into the old enclosed souk. At the centre of this gateway once stood a famous gnarled tree, said to be inhabited by *jinn*. The villagers were afraid the *jinn* might fly off with their tree, so they tied it down with chains. According to locals, when the tree was cut down, a spontaneous fire arose. A new tree has been planted in its place, surrounded by a low concrete wall. If you have the chance, visit this souk just before an Eid holiday, when a special traditional market called a *habta* is held. There are a few places here to park your car if you'd like a little walk around.

As an alternative approach from Nizwa you may like to slow down and take the track towards the three 'flying' mosques just 500m after the Shell petrol station on your left. The track leads through a vast cemetery of plain traditional graves, reflecting Ibadhi beliefs that graves should be as simple as possible. Clearly there was no question of revisiting a grave, as it was impossible to distinguish one from the other. Saint worship was strictly against Ibadhi and Orthodox Islamic beliefs, but in this part of Oman mystical Sufis held sway, with another Sufi fraternity or more accurately, sorority, dominant in Hamra. The three mosques are now in ruins, and have to be climbed up to from the track. You should allow 40 minutes to explore all three. They are said to have belonged to religious hermits and the highest one 'flew' here one night from Rustaq, hence the nickname.

In its colourful history Bahla was built and rebuilt many times, sometimes as a result of rainstorms, sometimes as a result of enemy attack. One such razing was in 1610, so most of the current fort was almost certainly rebuilt by the Ya'arubi, the same as in Nizwa, Jabrin, Rustaq and Al Hazm. Until the 1960s the wali used to live in the best-preserved part.

Bahla has long had a reputation for magic and sorcery, with witches, flying mosques, magic trees and a range of people who continue to claim extra-sensory experiences while in and around the town at night. The Bahla Motel has a domed and port-holed design, appearing just like something that flew in overnight from outer space.

Bahla is famous for its pottery and the ancient craft can be watched at the Aladawi pottery factory (see opposite page).

🏠 WHERE TO STAY
Budget

🏠 **Bahla Hotel** (6 rooms) PO Box 187, PC 612; ↘ 25 420211; f 25 420212. Set 2km before Bahla Town on the Nizwa side to the right of the road, 1km after the turn-off to Hamra, this hotel looks like a domed spaceship, circular with weird spherical windows. Each room can sleep a family of 4 comfortably. There is a very simple restaurant. *RO18/23 sgl/dbl.*

✖ WHERE TO EAT
As Bahla is so close to Nizwa, you might just as well move on there to eat, as there is nothing much to be found in the village, aside from cheap eats inside the local coffee shops and the simple restaurant at the Bahla Hotel.

WHAT TO SEE

Bahla Fort Inaccessible in January 2006 due to extensive renovation (*check with the Ministry of National Heritage and Culture, tel 24 602555, for the most recent information*). Bahla Fort rates in UNESCO's World Heritage Sites list as a 'monument of global importance'. It is considered Oman's most significant monument, closely followed by the archaeological site at Bat. It is the country's oldest fort, dating back to 1000BC. The UNESCO restoration project began in 1993 and is still continuing today, under the supervision of two Moroccan architects and a team of Indian and Pakistani labourers, with a handful of Omanis from the Ministry of National Heritage and Culture who are being trained to do management and restoration work. Their task is enormous and the state of disrepair so advanced that when they began work the first two years were spent clearing rubble to return to the original ground level. A dearth of old photos (pre-1960) has also meant that they are unsure of what the original looked like in some parts. The oldest-known photo was taken by a British colonel called S B Miles in 1885 which showed two incredibly tall wind towers, probably the tallest towers ever constructed in Oman. Today they have all but disappeared. The bulk of the work is concentrated on strengthening what already exists. It has not yet been decided how to present the fort once it is open to the public, whether to have it furnished or with craft shops inside or simply kept empty.

The internal mosque was the first building to be restored and is now in use. The main entrance is built of stone – the grey stones you can see are the originals, the orange ones newly put in. All materials used are local. In some places you can see a damp-proof course of stones about 1m up the walls, the natural height of rising damp. Maintenance is the big problem with these forts. If mud only is used it lasts a maximum of four to five years; *sarouj* plaster is much stronger. One of the high walls suffered bomb damage from the Jebel War, and the place where the hole was patched can be clearly seen. A deep well inside the main castle is divided into two with a washing area and wide pipe inside the wall.

Outside the walls on a raised terrace in the far southeastern corner stands the old mosque of **Ibn al Ass**. Its ceiling is collapsed, allowing glimpses from above down into the pillared interior with its beautiful moulded plasterwork *mihrab* and carved *minbar*.

The potters of Bahla To take a look at the pottery factory, continue driving through the narrow one-way system round to the right, passing the old village shops. The road then becomes two-way, but remains extremely narrow. Locals toot to warn you of their approach. Follow the tarmac road slowly all the way around behind the town (keeping to the turnings in the road furthest to your right). After 1–2km you will come to the area of potters, with the domed kilns on the edge of the date gardens. Continuing up the winding narrow road through more date plantations and sections of old and new housing, you reach the pottery factory. This is the **Aladawi Clay Pots Factory & Sale**, with men inside working the clay. The potters are happy for you to watch, even if you do not buy, although the pots here are far cheaper than the ones you will find in the shops and even inside the Nizwa Fort.

Continuing on this small road past the factory will take you back out to the main road (you will see more of the old Bahla town wall as you drive), where a left turn will lead you back to Nizwa, passing the Shell petrol station again. Turning right on this main road will take you along to Jabrin Castle.

Jabrin جبرين Castle (*Open Sat–Thu 09.00–16.00, Fri 08.00–11.00*). It is about a ten-minute drive from Bahla to the Jabrin Castle turn-off. It is clearly signposted left from the main road. Follow this turning for three minutes inland until you reach a roundabout at which you take a right. You can't miss it, as it stands by itself in a flat open plain beside some date gardens.

Jabrin (also Jibreen, Jabreen) is set apart from all other Omani forts through its elegance and elaborately decorated ceilings, which make it appear more like a palace than a fort. It was built by Bil'arub bin Sultan, an imam of the Ya'aruba dynasty, known for his interest in scholars and poets, initially as a home in 1670, and subsequently used as a sort of retreat by the Ya'aruba imams or ex-imams. It still retains a calm and peaceful feel. The restoration – which took seven years – was the first to be undertaken by the Ministry of National Heritage and Culture and was completed in 1983. The rooms were then furnished with antiques to give as close a flavour as possible of the original atmosphere.

It was not designed to have a defensive role – the two round gun towers at diagonally opposite corners were added later, as was the outer encircling wall. A small village used to nestle at its foot, but this was knocked down after the restoration and the government built a new settlement some 1km away back towards the main road and clearly visible from the palace roof. The large shady tamarisk tree by the gate is more permanent and has given shade for over 100 years.

Jabrin's builder, Imam Bil'arub bin Sultan, died here in 1692 after a siege by his brother. A later imam, Mohammed bin Nasir, then made Jabrin his headquarters, but after that it remained uninhabited from his death in 1728 until restoration began in the late 1970s. The imam is buried in the fort near the *falaj* that runs through its ramparts, said to be his favourite place in the building, to the left of the main fort door.

Inside, the three-storey structure is arranged round two separate courtyards, each with different floor levels. The main reception and guest rooms, known as the Sun Room and Moon Room, are the most elegant and elaborately furnished, with exquisitely painted ceilings. Some of the ceiling arches and passageways are decorated with Koranic inscriptions and geometric red-and-black patterns. A room on the second floor was specifically for the imam's favourite horse.

On the roof there was a Koranic school and Jabrin became an important centre for teaching Islamic law, medicine and astrology. The students were given bananas from the gardens below to keep them alert in their studies, according to an early source.

JEBEL KAWR AND AL GHAFAT

The settlement of Ghafat, signposted 6km to the right just 15km after the Jabrin turn-off, has a fine grouping of two- and three-storey mud-brick houses set in the centre of extensive date plantations. It is the capital of the bani Hina, from where the name Hinawi originates. There is plentiful water here, and much wheat is grown on the fertile plain beside it. Al Ghafat is set below Jebel Kawr (or Jebel Koor), the spiky rock known as an 'exotic' in geological terminology and reckoned to be one of the largest in the world. It is one of a cluster of peaks west of Jebel Shams known as 'the exotics', as the geomorphology of these peaks is somewhat different from the others' in Oman. Jebel Kawr is almost as high as Jebel Shams, but far less well known. The jebel is home to the third-longest cave in Oman, at 1.5km. The cave's gaping lower entrance is easily visible from the dirt tracks that enter the wadi from the signpost for Amla (53km – which is on the road that leads in a southerly direction from Ibri).

8

The Sharqiya الشرقية

The landscape of this eastern region contains a mixture of low-level mountains, which sit in the distance at the end of an extensive gravel plain. These eastern Hajar Mountains are far less concentrated than the harsh, dense massif of the Jebel Akhdar in the interior (part of the western Hajars). *Sharq* is Arabic for 'east', and so the Sharqiya translates literally as the 'east of Oman'.

The region can be split into three distinct areas: the Indian Ocean coastal stretch, the desert and the city of Sur. The coast is rather different from that of the Batinah; it is barren and cliff-bound in places, with few natural harbours. From Al Ashkhara all the way to Ras Nuss in Dhofar, the coast is desolate. The Wahiba Sands constitute the Sharqiya's southern edge.

The region has been dominated for many years by the Al Harithy tribe and its sheikhs, who are strongly Ibadhi. It is believed that the east African cities of Mogadishu and Barawa were founded by Omanis of Al Harithy descent in the 10th century, and so, after the Zanzibar revolution of 1963, many of the Zanzibaris who fled east Africa sought asylum in Oman and settled in the Sharqiya, considering it to be their ancestral homeland. Qabil, the Al Harithy capital of the Sharqiya, was on the route of the slave trade from the ports at Sur and Al Ashkhara. African goods used to be imported to Oman via the ports of Sur and Al Ashkhara, and dates were exported in exchange. But when Oman lost the Zanzibar connection in the late 19th century, the prosperity of this region, and indeed the whole of northern Oman, suffered a tremendous setback.

The Al Harithy people are Hinawis, yet the Hinawi tribes outside the Sharqiya do not pay allegiance to them; thus the Hinawi tribes of this region are quite distinct from those outside of it (see box *Ghafiri/Hinawi tribal split*, page 16).

GETTING THERE

BY AIR There is no airport open to civilians.

BY ROAD There are two ways to access this eastern region from the capital: the inland route or the coastal road. Whichever route you take, it would be a good idea to come back via the alternative, if you have the time, as the full circle provides an excellent tour of the Sharqiya. The towns and villages of interest have been placed in the order that you meet them travelling the inland route from Muscat first, followed by the coastal route from Muscat

BY COACH Coaches operate from Muscat to Sur. Request drop-offs/pick-ups can be made at any of the designated coach stops en route.

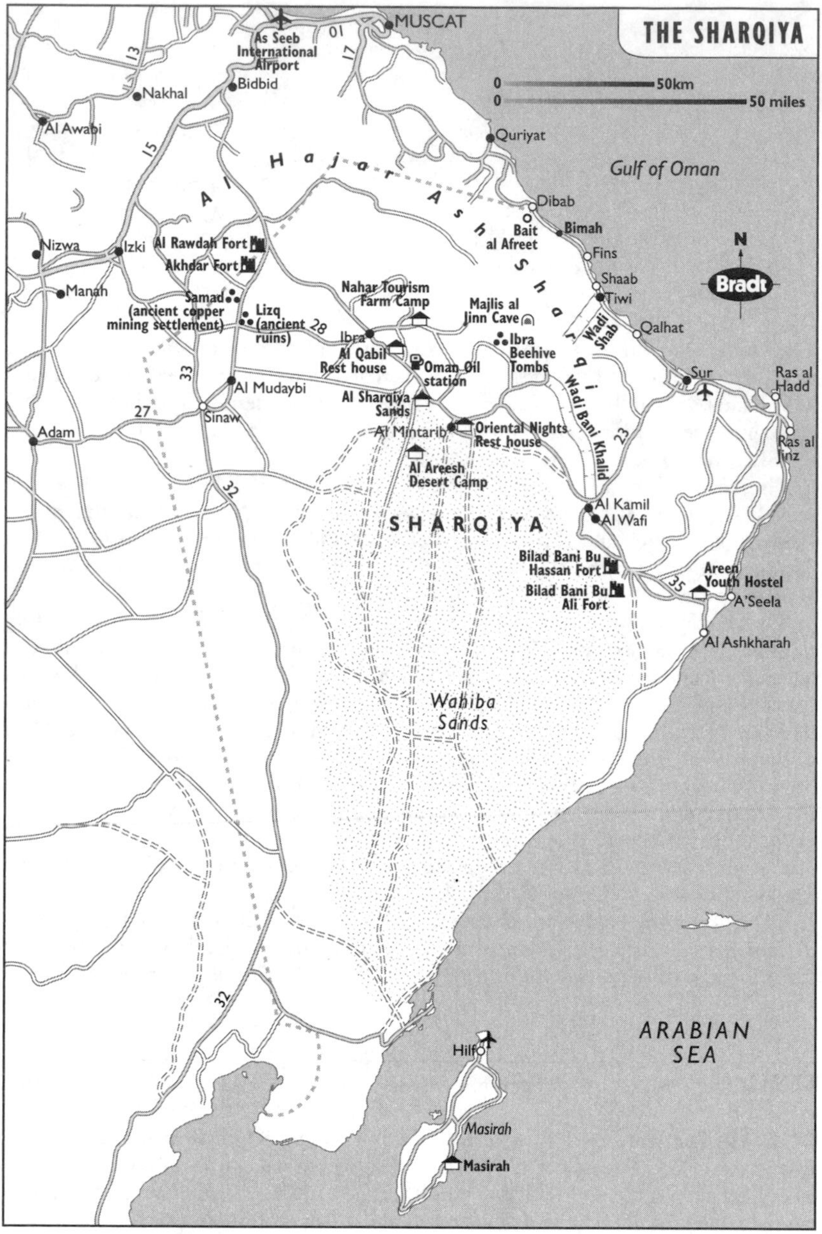
THE SHARQIYA
0 50km
0 50 miles
MUSCAT
As Seeb International Airport
Bidbid
Nakhal
Al Awabi
Quriyat
Gulf of Oman
Al Hajar Ash Sharqi
Dibab
Bait al Afreet
Bimah
Fins
Shaab
Tiwi
Wadi Shab
Qalhat
Sur
Ras al Hadd
Ras al Jinz
Nizwa
Izki
Al Rawdah Fort
Akhdar Fort
Manah
Samad (ancient copper mining settlement)
Lizq (ancient ruins)
Nahar Tourism Farm Camp
Majlis al Jinn Cave
Ibra Beehive Tombs
Ibra
Al Qabil Rest house
Oman Oil station
Al Mudaybi
Al Sharqiya Sands
Sinaw
Adam
Al Mintarib
Oriental Nights Rest house
Al Areesh Desert Camp
Wadi Bani Khalid
SHARQIYA
Al Kamil
Al Wafi
Bilad Bani Bu Hassan Fort
Bilad Bani Bu Ali Fort
Areen Youth Hostel
A'Seela
Al Ashkharah
Wahiba Sands
ARABIAN SEA
Hilf
Masirah
Masirah
N
Bradt
01
13
15
17
23
27
28
32
33
35

TOUR OPERATORS

The tour operators shown below are also included in *Chapter 3*, but are reproduced here as they operate camps and tours in the Sharqiya region.

Desert Discovery Tours PO Box 99, PC 115, Madinat Qaboos, Muscat; ☎ 24 493232, 99 328858, 99 317107; f 24 490144; e tours@omantel.net.om; www.desert-discovery.com. This tour company manages Al Areesh Desert Camp in the Wahiba Sands, Al Naseem Tourism Camp near Ras al Jinz turtle-nesting beach and Al Qabil Rest House. It also arranges mobile camping units for stays in the Wahiba and elsewhere They collect guests from Al Qabil Resthouse. Mobile camps are arranged to suit and include 4x4s, camping gear, cooking staff, food, water, drivers and guides. The units can be moved to anywhere in Oman, or can cross the Wahiba. Tourists have the option of driving themselves with a guide. For a camp booking 24hrs notice is fine, but for the mobile units, at least 4 days' advance notice is recommended. *RO17/8/4 adults/children aged 2–6/children under 6; inc dinner, b&b.*

Empty Quarter Tours PO Box 9, PC 115, Madinat Qaboos, Muscat; ☏ 99 387654; f 24 698292;

e emptyqtr@omantel.net.om; www.emptyquartertours.com. Operates the Nahar Tourism Farm Camp in the Sharqiya near Ibra, and specialises in tailor-made tours with Omani guides, focusing on Omani history, culture and wildlife. They offer all the Sharqiya trips: the Devil's Tower, Wadi bani Khalid, Ras al Jinz, a Wahiba trek (as a half-day trip, day trip, or 2 days and 1 night) and turtle beach tours, and treks through the Empty Quarter (following Wilfred Thesiger's route). They collect guests from their hotel in the region, if required. Wahiba is recommended in the winter months, and turtles can be seen all the time in the season from Jun–Aug. Owned and managed by Abdullah al Harthy, who is the guide for all tours in the sands.

WHERE TO STAY

There are a few guesthouses and budget hotels along the interior route to Sur. These are located at the larger villages, such as Ibra and Qabil, which lie on this ancient trading route. On the coastal route there is nowhere to stay until you get to Sur, unless you are camping. Once you have reached the vicinity of Sur on the eastern coast, you have a choice of a few hotels and a few camps at various nearby locations. If you are after a little adventure, do try one (or more) of the various camps in the region, like Al Areesh Desert Camp or Golden Sands Resort (in the Wahiba Desert), Al Nahar Tourism Camp (close to Ibra) and Al Naseem Tourism Camp (Ras al Jinz). Independent camping is best along the beaches of the coast road between Muscat and Sur, especially between Bimmah and Tiwi. You can take your own equipment or hire from a tour operator. You can camp in most places, whether mountain, beach or sandy desert, but Ras al Jinz and Ras al Hadd are designated camping areas. You can check with any tour operator about this. Desert Discovery Tours (see opposite for contact details), to name just one example, provides full camping equipment.

WHERE TO EAT

Your options for eating are largely limited to the restaurants within the hotels and the resthouses. **Al Qabil** serves good curries and an international menu at budget prices and is a great stop-off point about midway to Sur on the inland route. However, each village does have its share of basic coffee shop-type cafés catering to the local community. You might stumble on a gem, but otherwise keep in mind that these villages, thankfully, weren't designed to titillate the Western tourist. Having said that, there is a Pizza Hut in Sur!

OTHER PRACTICALITIES

USEFUL TELEPHONE NUMBERS
Hospitals

Al Ashkhara ☏ 25 566100		Ras al Hadd ☏ 92 177549	
Bidiyah ☏ 25 581167		Sinaw ☏ 25 524338	
Ibra ☏ 25 587100		Sur ☏ 25 561100	
Masirah ☏ 25 504363			

Police stations

Sur ☏ 25 542599
Sinaw ☏ 25 524999
Bidiyah ☏ 25 583099

Ibra ☏ 25 570099
Al Kamil/Al Wafi ☏ 25 557420
Jalaan bani Bu Hasan ☏ 25 550420

WHAT TO SEE AND DO

BIRDWATCHING Masirah Island in the winter is the home for greater flamingos, seagulls, terns and herons. There are no organised birding tours to this destination, and so it is very much an independent affair. Ayga Island is a 30-minute boat ride from the coast of Sur, and a good birdwatching spot. This can be visited independently (by enquiring at any of the boats on Sur harbour), or through a tour operator (if you would prefer being accompanied). For example, Bahwan Tours offers a day trip along the coast road to Sur from where you take a boat trip out to Ayga Island. The full-day trip costs RO150, which includes a 4x4 vehicle (accommodating four passengers), a driver/guide and the return boat trip to the island. The day starts at 07.30 and finishes back at your Muscat hotel at around 19.00. Water and soft drinks are provided. You have the option of taking a picnic along with you or using one of the basic local restaurants.

CAMEL RACING Camel racing events are held at tracks at Bidiya and Mudaybi and are announced in the local press. For more information, see page 21.

CAMPING The beaches along the Sharqiya coast are ideal for camping. Tiwi is a particularly popular spot. Masirah Island is deserted and so, perfect for camping. If your trip falls in the turtle-nesting season too, it will undoubtedly be a memorable island adventure.

CAVING The cave near Ibra called Majlis al Jinn (meeting place of the spirits) is the second-largest in the world (for further information, see page 213). It is for advanced cavers only and it is essential to arrange trips through a tour operator in Muscat (see pages 67–9).

There is also the Moqal Cave in Wadi bani Khalid, which you can visit independently. You will need flashlights and must be prepared to enter the cave on your hands and knees. For more information, see page 217.

GAME FISHING Sur and Masirah are especially good sites for this sport, with species such as marlin and tuna lurking in the waters. Tours can be arranged through operators in Muscat (see pages 67–9).

HIKING AND TREKKING Like the rest of Oman, the terrain is great for those with a penchant for trekking and hiking, and, as with the rest of the country, you're never far from a mountain, wadi or canyon.

Wadi Dayqah is a favourite in the Sharqiya.

CANYONING Canyoning is a special kind of trekking, and doesn't require specialist equipment. It usually involves a combination of narrow canyons with sheer rockfaces, natural water pools to swim in, caverns and grottos. Wadi Shab, on the coastal route to Sur (see Wadi Tiwi on the map) is excellent for this. If you travel to Wadi Shab independently, there are usually two local teenagers at the entrance who will guide you through. Their guidance is invaluable, but it is probably best to agree a small fee with them beforehand. The *pièce de résistance* is swimming in the cavernous water pool at the end, reached by swimming through a head-width opening in the rock.

DHOW CRUISE Dhow cruises around Sur Bay can easily be arranged through the Muscat tour operators (see pages 67–9).

SURFING Oman offers excellent windsurfing at all levels from beginner to advanced. Lessons are given by Al Bustan Palace Hotel (which offers a good sheltered bay for beginners), the Sawadi Forum Resort and the Intercontinental Hotel. Once you know the basics you can progress to Ras al Hadd 4½ hours from Muscat, a good location for intermediate-standard surfing, with higher waves but a good sheltered bay and no dangerous currents. A slightly trickier site is Asylah on the east coast near Al Ashkhara, 3½ hours' drive from Muscat. For the real experts the ultimate windsurfing destination is Masirah Island, 6–7 hours' drive from Muscat, best reached from Sinaw on the new surfaced road to Al Hij just north of Barr Al Hikman. It is at its best during the monsoon winds that blow from mid June to late August. From Al Hij a graded road runs to Shana'a from which a ferry (RO15 each way) goes to Hilf on Masirah Island, taking 1½ hours. The best beaches are then reachable via graded roads some 40 minutes south of Hilf.

TURTLE WATCHING The three main turtle-watching sites are Ras al Hadd, Ras al Jinz and Masirah. Green turtles, loggerheads, hawksbills and leatherbacks come to nest and lay their eggs in the sand on these beaches every year. Turtles can be seen at virtually any time of year at Ras al Jinz, though the best times to see large numbers are June–November. In January only a few females nest per night. In July and August the number is in the hundreds, anything from 100–600 per night. August is a good month as the strong monsoon winds make it reasonably cool for camping. There are huts, which are currently being renovated, on the site at Ras al Jinz and it is possible to arrange an overnight stay in them (see *Where to stay*, page 230). The beach itself is about three-quarters of a mile long, with cliffs at the back and a high sandbank. The nearest village is about 1–2km away, but is not visible from the campsite.

A permit is required to visit the sites, as these are endangered species. These are easy to come by, either through a tour operator or through any of the hotels in Sur, which all offer visitation packages.

DESERT SAFARI Of the Sharqiya region's offerings, a desert safari trip into the Wahiba Sands (otherwise known as 'dune bashing') is one of the best. It provides the 'real' sandy desert experience. It is vital in terms of safety that you have an accompanying guide – someone with demonstrable desert driving experience and logistical knowledge. A minimum of two 4x4s is also recommended, again for safety. It is advisable to arrange a trip into the Wahiba a few days in advance with a tour operator, as you may be disappointed if you are unable to arrange anything while in the vicinity. See *Tour operators*, page 206, for details. You can opt for a day trip or an overnighter, which includes a barbecue and sleeping in *harasti* huts. Either trip includes a visit to a genuine Bedouin camp, dune bashing and camel riding if you want it.

ALONG THE INLAND ROUTE FROM MUSCAT TO SUR

The inland road, as opposed to its coastal alternative, is the smoothest option for getting to Sur. In all, the inland journey from Muscat to the east coast (Sur) is 335km (approximately a four-hour journey, including a short rest stop for petrol/refreshments). A good tarmac road takes you initially toward the interior (on the main Nizwa road) passing through the Sumail Gap. The Sumail Gap is the natural divide between the eastern and western Hajar mountain range. It takes about an hour from Muscat to reach this fork. At this point there are signposts to Sur, 263km away, and the road forks off just beyond Bidbid. From this point there is no more dual carriageway for the whole distance to Sur.

The initial part of this single carriageway is attractive, winding through wadis and gorges with low hills all around. After roughly 60km the road leaves the hills and wadis behind and you reach a clearly signposted major fork at which the right turn takes you to Al Mudaybi, Sinaw and Samad. This route to Sinaw is now an excellent tarmac road; it is fast driving on dead flat terrain, and is of interest for the archaeological sites of Samad and Maysar, the hill fort of Lizq and the old market town of Sinaw on the edge of the desert. There is also now a tarmac link eastwards across to Ibra from Sinaw, so it can be an interesting variation in the route to Sur. Also, there is a tarmac road from Sinaw leading south to reach the coast (after 218km) at Barr al Hikman, close to where the ferry to Masirah operates (at Ras an Najdah).

AL RAWDAH From the Sinaw turn-off, the first signpost you see marks a right turn to Al Rawdah (also spelt Al Rowdah). A short detour can be made here to drive the 2km over to the fertile date plantation, where a fine restored fort, built at the end of the Nabhani dynasty, sits on a hilltop commanding the village. The approach to the tiny oasis village is along a gravel wadi with shallow water, fine for a 4x4. Further in, and away from the main road is another fort, this one a ruin. The whole spot is very attractive, and an hour could easily be spent here strolling about exploring the forts and other old buildings.

AKHDAR أخضر Beyond Al Rawdah, a sign turns off to Akhdar, whose brown stone-built tower can be seen from the road. The village, with its picturesque fort in ruin, is rich in history but particularly noted for its pit-weavers (all of whom are men). If you spend half an hour here strolling in the old part of town, you can still see the weavers at work, under *barasti* shades, sitting in the sunken pits where their wooden hand looms are erected. There is a range of weaved items including wall hangings, bedspreads and shawls. Prices start from RO40, the high price reflecting the labour-intensiveness and skill required to produce a beautiful item. You can buy direct here if they have any spare produce. There are several fine old houses around the tower, some of which were lived in until the late 1990s.

SAMAD South of Akhdar, the road continues through low rocky mountains until you see the signs for Samad and Al Meyasar (also spelt Maysar). Samad is steeped in history with several fine forts and archaeological sites. One area of archaeological interest in the town is the copper-mining settlement from the Umm al Nar period in the 3rd millennium BC. Within the settlement are ruins of copper smelting kilns 40cm wide by 50cm high, and the foundations of a hill fort. Copper implements were found in the old houses, such as chisels, axes, needles and rings. Also at Samad is a deserted old walled town and ruined fort which can be explored rather more easily. The fort at Hozam bin Falah also lies in ruins. Date palm groves, fruit orchards, full-flowing *falaj* and tranquil gardens surround it.

LIZQ Continuing through the landscape of gentle hills you come next to a blue signpost marked Al Lizq. A detour of some 45 minutes is recommended here for those interested in ancient ruins, for on a hill to the southwest of the modern village is an impressive stone staircase dated to the Iron Age. This is the only one of its kind yet found in Oman. A staircase leads on to a fortified citadel on the summit: the final 30m or so of the ascent is tricky for all but the sure-footed and agile. Good footwear should be worn, as the rocky terrain can be loose and slippery.

A low wall lines both sides of the stone steps and at the point where the stairs end and the ground flattens out a little, there used to be a well and two small towers guarding the entry point. From here you simply have to pick whichever way across the boulders to the summit you find easiest, as there is no clear path. The total ascent takes about 15 minutes, and less if you are fit. The view from the summit is magnificent, the hilltop commanding the land in all directions. A few scant remains of stone-built rooms and fortifications are left mainly over towards the far side of the summit, where the ground starts to dip a little. The whole area of small, almost volcanic-looking hills is attractive, and the area at the foot of the hill makes a good picnic or even camping spot. The old village, of which no trace remains, used to be situated here just at the edge of the date-palm trees.

Getting there To reach the hill drive straight through the centre of the modern village, over the tiny roundabout, veering a little left; you pass over a small humped bridge, and need to keep to the right when presented with two tracks. The dirt road wriggles through the plantations between high mud walls, passing a small round watchtower raised up on a group of rocks to the left; you then need to turn right and continue straight on and out of the village. Once you are on the outskirts of the village sprawl you need to fork left and head towards the hill that stands by itself immediately to the left of the large date plantation, a total distance of about 1km from the edge of the modern village. There are many tracks, all of which are can be driven in a saloon car and it does not matter which you take as long as you focus on the hill itself. Once you arrive at the obvious parking area at the foot, the stone staircase is clearly visible rising straight up the middle of the hill.

AL MUDAYBI Al Mudaybi is now a large modern town on the edge of the desert, but until the 1970s it was still a traditional walled mud-brick town. The town would be at its busiest in the summer, when the Bedouin would come in from the desert for the date harvest, and live in *barasti* huts by the date plantations until August. The old town can still be explored on foot by forking left for 1km just before the Shell petrol station.

At Al Musalla, the road south to Barr Al Hikman (Route 32) on the coast begins, but if you keep to the main road, it bends round and heads north again to reach Sinaw shortly after.

SINAW سناو Sinaw is famous for its colourful souk and cattle market, but is also visited for its attractive old town. It is signposted and sits just off the main road from Al Mudaybi to the left. Drive through the new town for about 1km to the final roundabout where you fork right to reach the market and the old part of town. The market area itself lies on your right after leaving the roundabout; it consists of a rectangle of shops each facing into the centre, where there is a roofed but open pillared area for selling fruit and vegetables. There is a one-way system in and out at each end for vehicles, through large green metal gates. The souk is at its busiest on Thursday and Friday mornings. Some of the shops sell traditional silver jewellery as well as the more modern gold jewellery which has become popular with local women. Unusually, women sell produce in this market alongside the men. A rather unusual (and rather frightening) souvenir is the *burka* mask still worn today by Bedouin women in Oman. Leaving the souk on your right, you can walk or drive along the dirt track to reach the old crumbling parts of town, consisting of two separate walled villages. These are now deserted, but still contain remnants of an old way of life in the abandoned houses, such as cooking pots, kettles and plates. From Sinaw the new tarmac road takes you along flat, unexciting scenery to Izki some 60km to the north and from where you can join the motorway back to Muscat or on towards Nizwa.

IBRA إبرا Ibra is about 150km from Muscat on the main Sharqiya road from Bidbid to Sur (Route 23), past the turn-off to Samad. It is a relatively large sprawling town, with several wadis. Ibra is the chief town of the inland Sharqiya, and used to have close trading links with Zanzibar and east Africa. It is known as the gateway to the eastern region, and is famous for its fine horses and horsemen, situated as it is, on the ancient caravan route from the interior to the port at Sur. The houses of wealthy merchants still stand crumbling among the palm gardens, evidence of the town's more prosperous days. Ibra is the home of the Al Harithy tribe, Ibadhi Muslims of aristocratic descent who have featured large in the country's history.

On occasions of celebration, camel racing takes place here as well as in Barka on the Batinah coast.

Where to stay
Budget

Nahar Tourism Farm Camp PO Box 9, PC 115, Madinat Qaboos; ☏ 99 387654; f 24 698292; e emptyqtr@omantel.net.om; www.emptyquartertours.com. This is run by Abdullah al Harthy of Empty Quarter Tours (see page 207). Here is a charming collection of 6 *barasti* huts, near Ibra, complete with furnishings and electricity. Each of the huts has 2 sgl beds, with sheets, blankets and mosquito nets. In winter it is chilly and the wind howls through the palm frond walls, but it is perfect in the summer. If it rains they have some plastic sheeting they can quickly pull over the hut to stop the roof leaking. Each pair of huts shares a basic shower/WC block with an open basin on the side. An evening meal is included in the price, consisting of kebabs, hummus, bread, salad and soft drinks. They have no objection if you bring your own alcohol. The food is cooked for you on a barbecue, or in a traditional underground oven, beside an open-plan seating area where you relax on carpets and cushions in the traditional Omani way. There are generators to produce lighting and a plug where an anti-mosquito device can be plugged in but the generator is turned off as soon as everyone is in bed, so do take anti-mosquito spray (to cope with the occasional hole in the mosquito netting). Towels and soap are also provided. For breakfast you stroll across to an attractive covered area where there are bamboo tables and chairs colourfully painted in blue and yellow. You can stroll about in the melon-filled fields and pat the horses. Sometimes the rooftop irrigation pool beside the breakfast area is filled with water for a quick dip. The farm is reached by turning left towards Wadi Nam (signposted) after the Oman Oil station as you enter Ibra. Three kilometres along the road, look for the sign on the right for Nahar Farm Camp and follow the track off to the low buildings. *RO40/50 sgl/dbl inc taxes, b/fast and dinner.*

Where to eat
There are local coffee shops (budget range) dotted about on the main road here which serve Indian, Chinese and Arabic food.

What to see
Ibra souk On Wednesday mornings, from 07.30–11.00, modern Ibra has a souk for women only (the only one of its kind in Oman). The women do the selling as well as the buying, mainly of items like perfumes, cosmetics, clothing, lotions, powders and textiles, as well as fruit and vegetables. It was started in 1986 and its popularity is increasing year by year as women enjoy shopping away from the pressures of men's impatience. 'Men do not enjoy shopping like we do,' says Fatima, a regular visitor. 'We like to take our time and chat while buying, but they want to get it over with. This arrangement frees them from the need to do the family household shopping.' Traditionally the household shopping was the man's role, so that his wife was not seen in public. The modern souk is off the main road

to the right by the Oman Oil petrol station, then a further 3km along the road, past the wali's office.

Ibra beehive tombs Further along the road to Wadi Naam is the difficult and tortuous route to the Ibra beehive tombs, set to the east in the mountains of Jebel bani Jabir on a high ridge 2,000m above sea level. There are roughly 90 in all, dating to the 3rd millennium BC, and many have survived remarkably well, still standing to three-quarters of their original 5m height. They are carefully built of stone blocks, tapering in towards the top and with a double wall. In 1994, archaeologists opened one to find skeletons, beads and pottery, which enabled accurate dating to take place. The tombs are visible from below, where the tarmac road to Wadi Naam ends. To reach them you follow the sign for Al Dammah, forking left along the main graded road where a date plantation wall ends. From this point the tombs are a gruelling 67km drive into the hills through several villages, which takes roughly two hours. You would need to devote a whole day to visiting the tombs and a 4x4 vehicle is needed for the steep ascent in the final stages.

Majlis al Jinn Cave The other reason for enthusiasts to come this far is for access to the Majlis al Jinn Cave (place of the genie), in Wadi bani Jabir, the second-largest cave chamber yet discovered in the world at 310m long and 225m wide, about the size of seven aircraft hangars. The cave was 'discovered' in 1983 by an American employee of the Ministry of Water Resources.

Inside the cave – correctly known as **Khosilat Maqandeli** – you can see colourful stalactites and stalagmites. Since it is a two-hour trek from the nearest village (Karan) and then a 160m rope descent through a sinkhole to the floor of the cave, it is clearly not going to be undertaken by the average visitor to the Sharqiya. Experienced climbing guides will need to accompany you and these climbing tours can be arranged through the tour operators in Muscat. Close to this cave there is another cave system with over 5km of passages to be explored, again with accompanying guides. Camping up on the high plateau here is possible, but chilly and exposed.

Old quarters of Ibra There are two old quarters of Ibra: Al Kanaatir and Al Minzfah. They are reached by forking to the right off the main inland road where the signpost says Ibra Sufelat (lower Ibra). After 1.5km turn right towards Kanaatir and follow the track down into the wadi bed, which is usually flowing with water in places. The hills lining the wadi are topped with watchtowers. You come almost immediately to two grand ruined houses, one on either side of the wadi; both merit an exploration, especially the one set on higher ground to the right-hand side.

Some 500m further along the wadi you will see an arched gateway to your left, set on the edge of the palm plantations lining the wadi. This is the entrance to

---

CONTROLLED DEVELOPMENT

Under the previous sultan (before 1970) it was forbidden to replace your house with anything except what it was already built from. So if your *barasti* hut burnt down it had to be replaced by a *barasti* hut unless you could obtain special dispensation, normally only available from the sultan. All controls tended to be negative in those early days and the municipality existed primarily to tell you what you could not do. This was good in the sense that it prevented the unbridled development boom which has been gripping Dubai for years, but bad in that it hindered much progress.

Kanaatir, and you can park here below a shady tree and walk into the old quarter, following the main alleyway. A few houses at the edge, where vehicle access is possible, are still lived in. Further into the middle the entire area is deserted, with a very evocative derelict souk set in a pillared courtyard on the right.

At the far edge of the village take the left fork and continue walking through the lush plantations for another ten–15 minutes to reach the other old quarter in the lower part of Ibra known as Al Minzfah.

You enter through a fine gateway. You will find some of Oman's grandest old merchants' houses here, a few of them four storeys high and built of stone faced with mud plaster (*sarouj*) like that used on the old forts. They are in varying states of repair, one or two are locked and inaccessible, while others no longer have doors and can be wandered in freely. A few modern houses have also been built now, their concrete hulks scattered incongruously among these magnificent ruins.

In the 1980s many of these houses still had blue-and-white Chinese plates embedded in the walls and ceilings, but all have now mysteriously disappeared.

AL MUDAYRIB المضيرب Al Mudayrib is 20km beyond Ibra on the road to Sur. This small town is worth a detour, especially towards the end of the day when the colour of the distant Wahiba Sands reflects a gentle redness. Don't visit at midday, as it is stiflingly hot with the full glare of the desert and little shade.

The attraction here is the fine old buildings built by wealthy merchants often resident in Africa, but intended for public use as an endowment for the town. They are known as *sablas*, and only ten remain. The public reception areas are used for meetings, wedding celebrations or halls of mourning. Each prominent family would have a *sabla* for use by its extended relations, which was like a social club for that family. Unfortunately it is not possible to enter any of these *sablas,* some of which are even fortified and on two storeys. There are also 20 small mosques scattered about the town, and it is worth climbing the hill to the crumbling 18th-century fort built on flaky black rock.

The town lies 1km off the main road to the left, and you can follow the road into the centre and park under a shady tree in the old town square, encircled by the stalls of the old souk. The old *falaj* channel runs through here by a stone bridge, making it a popular place for villagers to sit and children to play.

One of the most impressive *sablas* is raised up and overlooks the souk, and by climbing up on a little path for just a few metres you will reach its magnificently carved door, imported from east Africa in the 19th century. The locked door conceals a finely decorated room with painted ceiling beams.

Al Mudayrib is at its most evocative just before the Eid holidays, when the souk comes alive and everyone, man and woman alike, is dressed in their finest clothing and jewellery.

Where to stay
Budget
⌂ **Al Qabil Resthouse** (10 rooms) PO Box 53, PC 419; ☏ 25 581243; f 25 581119. This is one of four hotels in the Arab Oryx Rest House group (the other three are on the Muscat Salalah Highway — see *Chapter 10, Dhofar*). Just a few kilometres beyond Al Mudayrib is the little village of Al Qabil, with a simple resthouse of the same name. The resthouse is on the main road (Route 23) and is signposted. It is close to the Wahiba Sands and provides a great stop-off for lunch, if you have opted for the Muscat to Sur inland route. The unlicensed international restaurant sells good food, which is very cheap. The rooms are simple but comfortable with fridge, TV, AC and 24hr room service. Children's beds can be added. Alcohol is served in the bar for guests only. Accepts credit cards. RO13.10/17.50/24 sgl/dbl/dbl king size, inc taxes and b/fast.

In Islamic architecture the door or gateway to a building is often the most elaborately decorated feature. All the effort is concentrated on the façade of the door; from the inside it is often quite plain. Oman does not have the right kind of indigenous tree for carving, so the wood was usually imported teak or rosewood from India or sometimes from Zanzibar. Omani carpenters then carved their favourite motifs, often the traditional floral patterns of roses, Oman's favourite flower. These days, alas, there are few Omani carpenters left and most wood is carved by Indians imitating local designs. Omani doors have become popular now with expatriates and tourists who like to turn them into coffee tables. To tell the difference between an old door and a new one there are two things to look for: colour and texture. Old rosewood or teak (200 years old) is dark with a deep redness to it. Young wood looks more orange. Some dealers stain the doors darker to disguise their age, but this masks the grain of the wood. Newly carved doors also have a sharp feel to their carving and edges, while old doors will have gained the smoother finish that comes from wear and exposure. Today in new houses metal doors, often brightly coloured reflecting the east African link, are increasingly replacing the old carved doors.

AL MINTIRIB المنتيرب Bidiya and Al Mintirib are set on the banks of Wadi Batha which heads from Qabil for 97km deep into the Wahiba Sands. Heavy rains in this area can cause floodwaters from Wadi Batha to form a huge lake, dramatically set among the dunes. The tribe here is Hijriyeen, who had their moment of glory in the early 19th century when they were the only Omani tribe to successfully ward off the invading Wahhabis from central Arabia. Today they have been largely absorbed by Al Harithys.

Al Mintirib today still has a surprisingly grand main street and a very solid fort. Up until the 1960s the *qadi* (judge) could regularly be seen sitting in the sand in front of it, holding his *majlis* to decide on legal matters of dispute. The senior sheikh of the Hijriyeen at that time was a deaf old man who had a delightful garden filled with shady vines and papaya facing onto the dunes. His successors have no doubt swapped it for a concrete air-conditioned block.

The brown signpost off the main road announces **Bidiyah Castle**. This strong and square defensive fort, with no towers, sits by itself 2km off the main road, and is generally kept locked. Nearby to the right of the fort your eye will be drawn by a tall tower house which, on closer examination, has painted green crenellations. It is still lived in, with a TV aerial attached and a very fine carved entrance gateway.

⌂ Where to stay

⌂ **Oriental Nights Rest House** (19 rooms) PO Box 84, PC 421, Bidiya; ☎ 99 354816, 99 006215; f 24 493836; e onrh@onrh.net; www.onrh.net. This small hotel, with gardens of mango and orange trees, offers tours into the Wahiba Sands and into Wadi bani Khalid (*2-day tour RO20 pp*), including food and accommodation. If you have 4 people in your group then no notice is required. Starting at around 16.00 a tour guide fluent in Italian, English and Arabic will accompany you on your trip into the desert where you can watch the sunset and have dinner under a canopy. You return to the guesthouse for an overnight stay. The following morning, after breakfast, you take a trip into Wadi bani Khalid to see the waterfalls. At 14.00 you return to the guesthouse for lunch. You can eat in the restaurant or have food delivered to your room. Very friendly manager. Many European visitors pass through this hotel. *RO15/18 sgl/dbl inc taxes and b/fast.*

WAHIBA SANDS رمال وهيبة The sands are about three hours' drive from Muscat. Bidiyah Castle is probably the best of the many entrances to the Wahiba Sands, which are Oman's mini-version of the Rub'al Khali (the Empty Quarter – which is the largest desert expanse in the Middle East, and borders the western edge of Oman). The Wahiba is a true rolling-sand desert measuring 180km from north to south, 80km from east to west, and with dunes 100–150m high. Bedouin camps can be found along trails and tracks in the Wahiba. The petrol station on the main road to Sur is the last place to fill up if you are intending a full crossing of the sands, which almost certainly requires an overnight camp. Any mechanic at one of the plentiful auto tyre-repair shops will take some of the air out of your tyres to a recommended level for the desert terrain.

The most spectacular of the dunes are along the northern end of the Wahiba, and they progressively flatten out as you get closer to the coast in the south. The dunes flow in corridors north to south, making orientation relatively simple as long as you continue to drive in straight lines. An east–west crossing is very tricky, and there are almost no tracks in that direction.

If you want a less gruelling sensation of the Wahiba, there are other options. One is to drive 7km further east from Bidiyah Castle to Al Huwayah, which is a large oasis on the very edge of the Wahiba with extensive dates and banana plantations. The high dunes completely encircle the oasis, giving a real sense of the encroaching desert. There is a *falaj* and narrow one-way road running through the plantation and you can picnic in the shade here, watching the awesome dunes pressing in, or camp just outside the plantation on the very edge of the desert.

In the high summer months from June to September the Wahiba Bedouin families come to the oasis, complete with livestock, and live in the *barasti* huts on the edge of the town, harvesting their dates. A gravel road leaves from here for 24km into the desert before becoming a sand track.

The sands were the subject of an expedition by the Royal Geographical Society in 1986, the results of which aroused international scientific interest. The project director wrote:

> No body of sand in the world contains such a full range of study terrains, nor has so much to offer desert scientists urgently trying to piece together the complex jigsaw of arid zone areas. Its isolation and size lend itself to field research simply because it can be studied as a complete unit. It can be circumnavigated by Land Rover in three days.

The 35 scientists involved discovered 150 species of plant, 200 species of mammals, birds, reptiles and amphibians, and 16,000 invertebrate specimens.

If you are interested in learning more, there are two titles you might wish to track down. The first is *The Scientific Results of the Royal Geographical Society Oman Wahiba Sands Project 1985–1987* ; the second, N Winser's *The Sea of Sands and Mists: Story of the Royal Geographical Society Oman Wahiba Sands Project* (see *Appendix 3, Further information,* for more details).

Along the eastern edge of the Wahiba are extensive woodlands of prosopis (*ghaf*) and acacia (which have been shown to live on dew), with many Bedouin shanty towns scattered among them. The best way to reach this part of the Wahiba, quite different in character from the high dunes, is to take the tarmac road to Al Ashkhara on the coast, where you can fill up with petrol at the Shell station. Fork right in the village; soon after, the tarmac stops and becomes a graded track. This track leads all the way to Khuwaymah, 78km away on the coast. The woodlands can be reached by turning right, almost back on yourself, after 61km by a makeshift petrol stop, thereby completing a loop as the woodland track emerges onto tarmac by Bilad bani Bu Ali. There is a shipwreck on the beach 15km from the start of the track, but the sand all round is too soft for easy driving.

The easiest and safest option with the Wahiba is to set up an organised trip through an experienced company like Empty Quarter Tours or Desert Discovery Tours (see pages 206–7 for contact details). Both use knowledgeable guides, so that the navigation and logistics responsibility falls to someone else. Alternatively, you can contact a desert camp direct.

Where to stay

Al Sharqiya Sands Hotel (24 rooms) PO Box 585, PC 413, Ibra; 99 205112, 99 205113; f 99 207012. This is a good hotel about halfway between Muscat and Sur (at 180km) on the inland route, and is a welcome find after a monotonous drive with only rubbly desert plain to look at. The rooms are of a good standard and pleasant décor, positioned around a garden courtyard area and swimming pool. It is peaceful and serene here and a major plus factor is that you can buy a cold beer (and there are not many places in the Sharqiya where you can). There is a licensed restaurant and a separate pub. Members of staff here are pleasant, professional and assisting. It advertises itself as 'an oasis by the desert' and it truly is. However, the hotel does not arrange desert tours. Tours should therefore be arranged in advance through tour operators in Muscat to avoid disappointment. This aside, this is a great hotel to stop off at either for refreshments or an overnight stay if you plan to tour the Sharqiya, the sands, or take a trip south to Masirah Island. *Rooms are available on a b&b, HB or FB basis ranging from RO19 for a sgl occupancy b&b to RO54 for 2 persons FB in a suite, exclusive of taxes.*

Al Areesh Desert Camp (43 tents) 24 493232, 99 317107; e tours@omantel.net.om; www.desert-discovery.com. This is another camp run by Desert Discovery Tours and located a few kilometres south of Al Mudayrib (which is on the inland Muscat–Sur road). The tent bungalows are covered with palm fronds in the traditional Bedu

style, equipped with electric lighting and bedding. Showers, hand basins and flush toilets are also available on site. Guests who are more adventurous can sleep on raised platforms out in the open. There is a reception/entertainment area with cushions and carpets, where you are offered Omani dates and Arabic coffee. The camp has shower and toilet facilities. You can experience dune driving (with experienced Bedu drivers), sand skiing, camel rides or a visit to local Bedu homes. There is an evening campfire and entertainment from traditional musicians, dancers and singers. *RO20/16 pp, with/without en-suite toilet, inc dinner, B&B. Short camel ride RO2 pp; long ride (2–3hrs) RO10 pp. Visit to Bedouin settlement or short dune bashing (1hr) RO5 pp if Desert Discovery vehicles used, RO1 pp in own vehicle. Long desert trip (3–4hrs) RO20 per vehicle in DD vehicle, RO10 per vehicle in own vehicle.*

Golden Sands Camp (20 en-suite chalets and large furnished Bedouin tents) 99 445092. The Golden Sands Resort office is at Al Wasil. This is where you park to join a vehicle to transport you to camp. It offers a great place inside the Wahiba Desert. The dining and entertainment area is called The Oasis and there is even a small shop for essential items. Quad bikes can be hired, there is a children's adventure playground and beach volleyball, soccer, archery and golf are all available. Or you can 'star gaze' in a tent away from the camp, or take a camel ride. Large groups are welcome.

WADI BANI KHALID وادي بني خالد Continuing from Al Mintirib on the main Sur road you see a sign pointing left (after 15km) towards the mountains to Wadi bani Khalid. The graded track leads over the sandy plain for 24km before reaching the start of the wadi and its numerous villages. As one of the wettest wadis in Oman the area is lush and heavily populated – a real oasis. One of its specialities, found only here, is the red-skinned banana, which you can buy in the local shops. The end village is Moqal, from where a path leads along the wadi floor for about half an hour's walk to the entrance of the **Moqal Cave**, accessible without special gear, but with a very narrow entrance only 1m high, from which several passages lead off. A strong torch is essential and the climb to the cave becomes steep after the bridge and is difficult for younger children.

Camping in the area and swimming in the wadi pools is made difficult by the density of the local population. The journey to Sur for the villagers is now a two-hour drive, but before 1970 it was a gruelling seven-hour trek by donkey.

Just 2km beyond the turn-off to Wadi bani Khalid look out for some tracks to the right towards an outcrop of Wahiba dunes close to the road and easy to scale for a view or picnic stop.

At Al Kamil, 60km beyond Al Mintirib, the main tarmac road bends left towards Sur, and a secondary tarmac road continues straight on towards the coast at Al Ashkhara. The final approach to Sur (see page 224) from Al Kamil takes about 20–30 minutes and leads across a series of wadis.

AS SALEEL NATIONAL PARK

This sanctuary is signposted from the main road that bends round to Sur just after Kamil – a red sign in Arabic with pictures of oryx. The park was proclaimed as a national park in 1997 and its aim is to protect and conserve the variety of wildlife in its natural habitat. It is a plain covered with acacia woodland, home to Arabian gazelles, the rare Gordon's wild cat, wolves, red fox and Egyptian vultures. Animals such as the Arabian oryx and sand gazelle will be reintroduced when the vegetation has recovered. The park used to be a site of poaching, with unlimited access. This conservation project plans to educate as well as conduct environmental studies and research.

JALAAN BANI BU HASSAN بلاد بني بو حسن

Taking the road to Al Ashkhara (Route 35), you will meet the twin towns of Bilad bani Bu Hassan and Bilad bani Bu Ali (7km apart along the main road). They have a certain curiosity value for their forts and splendid fortified houses.

The first town, bani Bu Hassan, has a neat four-towered renovated **fort** (*open Sun–Thu 08.00–14.00*) on the edge of the sands, signposted from the main road. One of the fortified houses in the old town, called Awlad Mushed, is 25m high with five storeys, and was lived in until 1986.

JALAAN BANI BU ALI بلاد بني بو علي

The town of Bani Bu Ali has an uneasy history of war. In the first quarter of the 19th century, the Bani Bu Ali tribe (see box below) accepted the new Wahhabi creed, becoming a fundamentalist Muslim sect. They were the only tribe in Oman to do so.

When, in 1820, the bani Bu Ali tribe renounced the rule of the sultan, matters escalated until the sultan called on the assistance of the British to carry out an attack. They did so, destroying the town of Bilad bani Bu Ali in 1821. Prisoners who were not killed were shipped off to Bombay, but were shipped back again only two years later with large grants to rebuild their destroyed homes and *aflaj*. The bani Bu Ali remain nominal Wahabis and although some say they remain unreceptive to Europeans, this does not appear to be true today. The BBC World Service arm was set up in a house in bani Bu Ali as a temporary base while constructing the site at Asylah (from approximately 2000–02), and the lone Scottish employee, who oversaw the project, used to cycle daily through the village, to waves and greetings from the locals.

At the back of the village there is a tall 11th-century fort, which encloses a simple white mini-domed mosque in its courtyard, reminiscent of that at Al Badiyah in the emirate of Fujairah (United Arab Emirates). Restored in 1990, the mosque also has an ablution *falaj* running close by in the courtyard.

THE WAHHABI CREED

The Wahhabi creed is a puritanical reform movement begun by the conservative Syrian jurist Muhammad ibn Abd al Wahhab (1703–92). It rejects any innovations that occurred after the 3rd century of Islam. Arabia's history, from around 1750 to the present day, is largely centred on the history of the Wahhabis.

AL ASHKHARA Al Ashkhara is a quiet, coastal fishing town where you can see traditional dhows (no longer in use) preserved on the beach as a reminder of its prestigious past. In addition, many fishing boats line the beach, these days made of fibreglass. Al Ashkhara was the landing point for merchant ships from India, Yemen and Iran from the 11th century onwards.

Where to stay
Budget
Areen Youth Hostel ☎ 25 566266; f 25 566179. This youth hostel is a good, clean, modern hotel at which to stay in the region. Although it seems in the middle of nowhere (with the sea on your left-hand side, it is just past the BBC World Service site. It is set back on the right-hand side of the road); if you want to get your head down at a clean, quiet place with a good restaurant, then this place is fine. RO25/29.40 sgl/dbl inc tax, exc b/fast. Cash only.

AS SEELAH Also spelt 'Asaylah', this is another quiet coastal fishing village. Close by is the relatively new BBC World Service Relay Station – the replacement for the closed site on Masirah Island.

ALONG THE COASTAL ROUTE FROM MUSCAT TO SUR

The most scenic route through the Sharqiya is the coastal road to Sur, which at this stage requires a 4x4 at the stretch of road between Dibab and Tiwi – it is still dirt track. The journey from Muscat to Sur via this route takes about 3½–4 hours (240km), which of course various widely depending on the amount of stops you may wish to make – and you undoubtedly will. There is fabulous coastal scenery here, with mountains and gorges extending down to the sea, rock pools and good walks into the mountains. The stretch of coastline is a series of rocky inlets stretching all the way down to Sur (roughly 210km away). Whole stretches are reachable by boat only, and some of the villages are linked only by graded tracks.

In a couple of coves hidden from land between Muscat and Sidab are 19th-century Christian graves, including that of the first missionary, Bishop French, who came to Muscat aged 65 from Lahore, rather than settle for old age in England. He would go to the coffee houses and preach on street corners to whomever would listen. 'I cannot say,' he admitted, 'that I have met with many thoughtful and encouraging hearers or people who want Bibles and Testaments.' He died three months later of ill health.

The Muscat to Sur return drive is quite tiring if taken as a day trip, and you will miss out on a lot. However, if you are pushed for time, you could, with an early start around 08.00, set off through Qurivat, Dibab and Fins to have a picnic lunch in the Tiwi/Wadi Shab area, then complete the circuit by returning to Muscat on the inland tarmac road (four hours' drive from Sur) arriving back in Muscat at about 20.00, having made a couple of further brief stops along the way; a good 12-hour stint. So, if you can, try to stay overnight in the area. Two or three nights here would be ideal. One night could be spent in Sur or Ras al Hadd, the next at the turtle camp in Ras al Jinz, and the final night in the desert camp in the Wahiba Sands. Each of these stays offers its own unique and memorable experience.

The starting point within Muscat is the Wadi Adai roundabout just before Ruwi. Follow signs to the right in the direction of Quriyat, Hatat and Watayah.

WADI DAYQAH وادي ضيقة Wadi Dayqah is one of the most famous wadis in Oman, and links the Sharqiya with the Muscat governorate. Its name means 'narrow wadi'. Wadi Dayqah is an old pack-animal route from the coast to the interior and was still used as such until about 1980. It is the largest perennially flowing wadi in

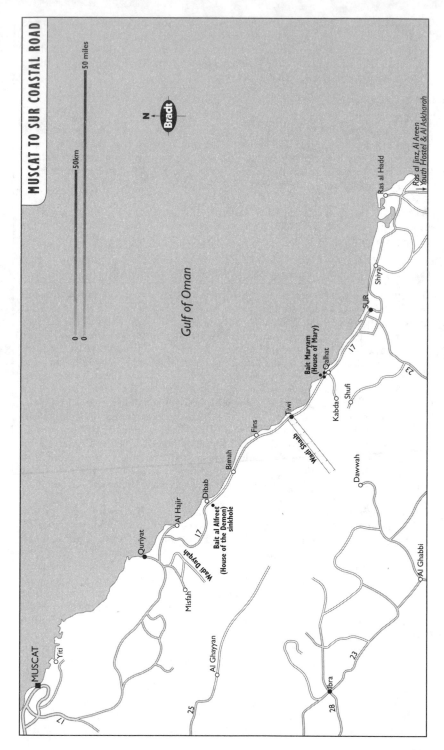

MUSCAT TO SUR COASTAL ROAD

Gulf of Oman

MUSCAT

Yiti

Quriyat

Al Hajir

Dibab

Bimah

Fins

Tiwi

Qalhat

Bait Maryam
(House of Mary)

SUR

Shya

Ras al Hadd

Ras al Jinz, Al Areen
Youth Hostel & Al Askharah

Kabda

Shufi

Wadi Shaab

Dawwah

Bait al Alfreet
(House of the Demon)
sinkhole

Wadi Dayqah

Misfah

Al Ghayyan

Al Ghabbi

Ibra

N

Bradt

50km

50 miles

0

0

17

17

25

23

28

23

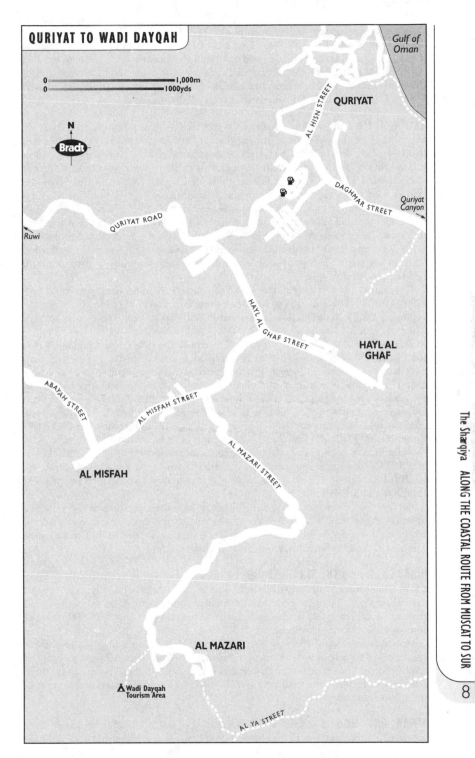

QURIYAT TO WADI DAYQAH

Gulf of Oman

0 ————— 1,000m
0 ————— 1000yds

N

Bradt

QURIYAT

AL HISN STREET

DAGHMAR STREET

Quriyat Canyon

QURIYAT ROAD

Ruwi

HAYL AL GHAF STREET

HAYL AL GHAF

ABAYAH STREET

AL MISFAH STREET

AL MAZARI STREET

AL MISFAH

AL MAZARI

Wadi Dayqah
Tourism Area

AL YA STREET

Oman, 14km long, with many deep pools. The head of the wadi, where it meets Wadi Tayin, is called Devil's Gap. The walls here are 1,700m high and the gap as narrow as 12m. The best scenery is this stretch to **Mazara**, which can be reached only on foot. There are spectacular cliffs and a fast-flowing river. The summit of the surrounding mountains reaches 1,885m here. Tour operators arrange trips to Devil's Gap: it is one of Oman's best canyon excursions.

Getting there Following the road to Quriyat from Muscat, and having dropped to sea level on the plain, look out for the Oman Oil station on the right (85km from Muscat, 9km before Quriyat). For the coastal road to Sur you will need to go straight on, but to reach Wadi Dayqah, this is the turn-off you must follow. It is signposted Hayl al Ghaf, a village in Wadi Dayqah. After another 4km the tarmac road turns right to Misfah, a small mountain village with a fine *falaj* that crosses the wadi via an aqueduct. About 3km prior to reaching Misfah is a left fork – a graded road. Follow this graded road left for 5km, then left again for 1km following the sign to Al Hayl (8km). You will reach the wadi at a point where there are many lovely pools and shaded picnic spots among the rocks and trees. You can complete the loop from here by driving the remaining 7km up the wadi bed back to Hayl Al Ghaf.

Alternatively, if you have all day ahead of you and are in no rush, you could fork right at the previous junction to Mazara, to the dam from where the six-hour walk begins up the Dayqah Gorge inland towards Wadi Tayin, with spectacular scenery and many pools.

To continue along the coast towards Sur, ignore the turn-off to Hayl al Ghaf at the Oman Oil station and instead continue straight, taking the right-hand turn 5km later, 4km before Quriyat Town. The road is tarmac and is signposted for Daghmar. At the next roundabout, 6.5km further on, take the right fork to Tiwi on the graded track. After a further 3km the track to the right enters the gorge of Wadi Dayqah and climbs up the hills for another 3km. Straight on at the mouth of the gorge would lead you to Daghmar on the coast, through which Wadi Dayqah flows; however, there is no coastal road between Daghmar and Dibab, and so you have no option but to head inland via the mouth of Wadi Dayqah. Around 8km after leaving the gorge you come to a junction at which the right takes you to the small fishing village of Dibab, 15km away. From here the road keeps to the coast for the remaining 90km to Sur.

For a scenic diversion, those with time can take the right turn at the previous junction, signposted Wadi al Arbiyeen, which leads for some 15km of steep track requiring low ratio 4x4 to Wadi Suwayh, reckoned as one of Oman's most scenic wadis, with steep mountains, pools and lush vegetation.

DIBAB ضباب **AND THE SINKHOLE** The beaches around Dibab are particularly good for beachcombing, with unusual shells and birdlife. Approximately 5km beyond the village along the main graded track, a cairn on the right-hand side of the road marks a small track that leads towards the mountains for just 400–500m where some wooden shades have been erected.

Concrete steps have recently been built here down into a huge natural water sinkhole – 40m across and 20m deep – known locally as Bait al Afreet ('House of the Demon'). The water is clear, green and slightly salty and can be swum in; there are tiny fish visible in the shallower part. If you have a snorkel you can use it to spot the colourful sponge-life.

BIMAH AND UMQ Ten kilometres beyond the sinkhole, after a drive along spectacular bays and coves rich in birdlife, you come to the village of Bimah. Bimah is unremarkable in itself, but 1km beyond the village is the start of the graded track (a dead end) that leads inland 10km to the village of Umq. This village is unusual for its mud houses built into the side of the mountain. The drive is scenically stunning and there is much wildlife in the area including wolves, foxes and gazelles. From Umq there is a difficult six-hour climb up the 800m cliff face up onto the Jebel bani Jabir Plateau where the Ibra tombs are located (see page 213). The climb is not to be attempted without a guide.

FINS TO TIWI طيوي From Bimah it is another 10km to Fins – the halfway point to Sur. The stretch of coastline from Fins to Tiwi has both long white-sand beaches and tiny gravel bays with rock pools. Litter can be a problem, especially on the popular sand beaches like Tiwi (known as White Beach, 6km beyond Fins). At weekends especially the beaches can become crowded.

SHAB AND TIWI شاب وطيوي These two settlements are both at the mouth of gorges which share their name. Shab comes first, and is approached by a road that has been cemented because of the steepness of the descent and ascent from the cliffs.

If there is one wadi you must visit in your trip to Oman it is Wadi Shab. It is a place of outstanding natural beauty and peace. The wadi itself is not drivable, but there is a footbridge that lead into the wadi. It is probable that a couple of teenage boys will be hanging around on the start of the walk into the gorge, who will offer to guide you in (for a small fee, of course). It's worth taking them up on their offer: these boys know which parts of the route can be climbed easily, as well as where it's safe to swim. The walk into the wadi is beautiful, leading through the steep ravine and past pools, waterfalls and lush plantations. There are several villages higher up, accessible only on foot. The *pièce de résistance* is the mountain pool at the end of the walk, deep in the mouth of the gorge. Here you can swim through a tight, neck-width gap and narrow tunnel, which opens up into a cavernous mountain pool area. At Tiwi, which almost runs into Shab village, the wadi gorge is wider and drivable for 10km or so before you come to a footpath leading on to the nine villages of the wadi. At the last roundabout through Tiwi, having climbed the steep hill into the village and wound through the houses, you turn right onto a narrow track that leads to the wadi. The vegetation here, including banana, mango and fig, is very lush and the water flows all year round.

As you begin the drive from Tiwi towards Qalhat and Sur, you will notice black signs marking archaeological sites, which have revealed a large settlement.

QALHAT From Sur, Qalhat used to be an hour by Land Rover then an hour on foot when the terrain became impassable, but it can now be reached by graded track from Tiwi. Marco Polo wrote:

> This city has a very good port, much frequented by merchant ships from India, and they find a ready market here for their wares, since it is a centre from which spices and other goods are carried to various inland cities and towns. Many fine war horses are exported from here to India, to the great gain of the merchants.

Ibn Battuta, the Moroccan traveller is said to have visited Qalhat in about 1330. He wrote:

> The city of Qalhat is on the coast. It has good markets, and one of the most beautiful mosques in the world. The walls of the mosque are covered with blue ceramic tiles. It stands on a hill beside the harbour. This mosque was built by an important woman named Bibi Maryam. The people here are merchants, and they bring many goods from India. When a ship arrives the people are very happy.

It is hard to see today why Qalhat was chosen as the site of such an important port, when Sur, just 20km down the coast, seems to have such a superior natural location, with an obvious route to the interior. But until the end of the 14th century, Qalhat had a *falaj* system leading down the wadi from the hills, with many wells to supplement it. And whilst the *khor* (lagoon) today is just a stagnant tongue of water by the modern village, it was, centuries ago, a deep anchorage reaching right up to the north of the wadi. For the route to the interior, merchants must have used the donkey path through Wadi Hilm, which leads eventually to Wadi bani Khalid.

Qalhat was affected by two disastrous events. Firstly, an earthquake destroyed many of the city's fine buildings at the end of the 14th century. Then in 1507, the Portuguese arrived in Oman and ransacked Quriyat and Muscat. The following year they attacked Qalhat, killing many of the local population and burning all the ships and buildings. Qalhat was completely devastated and the survivors fled the city. The earthquake of the 14th century had put an end to the *falaj* and the harbour, and the city never recovered.

Today it is difficult to picture the great city of Qalhat. **Bait Maryam** (the House of Mary) is the only major building to survive and is in remarkably good condition, especially considering the devastation of the buildings surrounding it, most of which appear at first glance to be little more than rubble. Inside there is a brown-grey resin wax built up from the candles over the years of offerings by visitors. It was originally said to have been covered in glazed tiles. The site is now much visited by tour groups, most of which stop briefly for a quick look before continuing their trip along the coast in convoys of 4x4s.

If you are not part of such a convoy, the site does merit a much longer stop. Take the trouble to cross the road and explore some of the rooms, walking on little paths towards the sea. You will be rewarded by the discovery of much interesting pottery, butterflies and plantlife, to say nothing of the atmosphere of the destroyed rubble town. After a 20-minute stroll you will reach the sea, where a small harbour is still recognisable. The semicircular arched tunnels are cisterns built by the princes of Hormuz in the 13th century.

SUR صور

Sur is a quiet coastal town that played a central role in overseas trade with east Africa. It occupies a position on a large lagoon, which is still the port today.

Along with Sohar, it has been said that Sur was the home of the legendary sailor Sindbad. The town shares its name with the coastal port of Sur in Lebanon, known to Westerners as Tyre, and one attractive theory, based on Herodotus's account that the Phoenicians came from the Gulf area, is that the Phoenicians originally hailed from here, then moved on to Lebanon, reusing the same name as their home town. Archaeological evidence to prove this theory is lacking, but certainly the rocky spit by Sur creek bears a resemblance to that of Tyre, and the origins of the Phoenicians are still disputed by experts. The reputation of the inhabitants to this day is that they are difficult and independent-minded.

The coastal town itself never had fresh water, but Bilad Sur, the large village amid the date palms a few kilometres inland, supplied all the necessary water from its wells, and water is still piped in today from the same source.

Sur has long been famous for dhow building and is still the centre for dhow and *sambuk* (fishing boat) building in Oman today. A large dhow (200 tonnes) will take five to six months to build, and only one or two are built in a year. In the 19th century some eight dhows a year were built and launched. The workers today are all Indian.

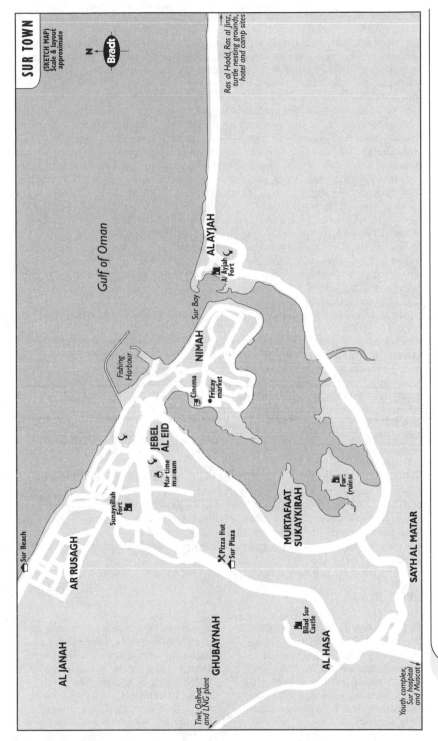

SUR TOWN

(SKETCH MAP)
Scale & layout
approximate

Bradt

N

Gulf of Oman

Sur Bay

ALAYJAH

Al Ayjah
Fort

Ras al Hadd, Ras al Jinz,
turtle nesting grounds,
hotel and camp sites

Fishing
Harbour

NIMAH

Cinema

Friday
market

JEBEL
AL EID

Maritime
museum

Sunaysillah
Fort

MURTAFAAT
SUKAYKIRAH

Fort
(ruins)

AR RUSAGH

Sur Beach

AL JANAH

Pizza Hut
Sur Plaza

SAYH AL MATAR

GHUBAYNAH

Bilad Sur
Castle

AL HASA

Tiwi, Qalhat
and LNG plant

Youth complex,
Sur hospital
and Muscat

The Sharqiya SUR

8

225

Many natives of Sur – some 3,000 in the early 1960s – had worked abroad in India, east Africa and the rest of the Arabian Gulf, reflecting a marked contrast to the inwardness of the natives of the interior. Amongst their particular interests abroad were the slave trade and arms trafficking – perfectly normal forms of trade at that stage and not tainted or associated with any moral wrong. The British attempts to eliminate these trades were always met with a certain incomprehension, and Sur was viewed with great disdain by Britain for its chosen activity. Even after the sultan in Muscat signed anti-slavery treaties with the British, implementing them in Sur was nigh impossible; the established routes inland to Saudi Arabia did not involve Muscat. The first anti-slave trade treaty was signed with the British in 1822, when it was recorded that some 4,000 slaves were imported into Sur. Later, the British began to control shipping more strictly.

When Zanzibar and Oman split into two separate sultanates in 1861, Sur had over 100 ocean-going dhows in its trading fleet. Trade declined after the split, hastened by the arrival in the Gulf of the British India Steamer Navigation Company, which also took trade away from Sur. Shipbuilding gradually declined as Sur became a less prosperous port.

The modern town of Sur today has a sprawl that extends many kilometres inland and it is difficult to establish when you have reached the centre of town. The Sur Beach Hotel is signposted off to the left from one of the first roundabouts (*see Where to stay* below), which is also the turn-off you take for the ruined city of Qalhat, passing the LNG plant.

Sur is renowned for its horses, hence the model horse statues that flank the road. The passion for pure Arab thoroughbreds survives here in the form of a few trainers who excel in 'mastering' their horses. One, a resident of Bilad bani Bu Hassan, trains 23 horses and has instilled his passion into his 22 children; the youngest son when aged nine could stand on a galloping horse.

If you follow the main tarmac road into the centre of town, this eventually does a big loop round the lagoon, on the edge of which are the boatyards, still in operation on a reduced scale and easily visited. You can park outside and wander in through any of the gates. The keels and hulls are made from teak imported from India, while the ribs are made from local acacia wood. No plans are ever used. The boats are built by eye, from the outside in, not the Western convention of inside out with ribs first.

Further on from the boatyards, the road loops round to pass the restored dhow, *Fatah al Khair*, thought to be 70 years old, and one of the last ocean-going vessels built in Sur. The boat was found in Yemen and a local retired captain was delegated to buy it with money raised from Sur inhabitants to keep it here as a symbol of the town's maritime heritage. It weighs about 300 tonnes and is over 20m long. At low tide here the lagoon water disappears and the dhows are beached on an expanse of wet mud.

From Sur there is a tarmac road to Ras al Hadd and Ras al Jinz.

WHERE TO STAY
Mid range

⌂ **Sur Plaza Hotel** (102 rooms) PO Box 908, PC 411; ℄ 25 543777; f 25 542626; e resvnsur@ omanhotels.com or gmsur@omanhotels.com; www.omanhotels.com/sur.htm. This hotel is part of a chain of hotels that includes Al Falaj Hotel and Ruwi Hotel in Muscat and Al Wadi Hotel in Sohar. It is a large hotel, set inland, with a licensed restaurant (Oyster Restaurant) and 2 bars, both with live entertainment. Captain's Bar has easy-listening music played by the resident duo; and the Sambuq and Al Shabaka Bar has Arabic/Indian bands. There is a Budget Rent-a-Car desk, but no tour operator here. *RO36/43 sgl/dbl, exc taxes and b/fast.*

⌂ **Sur Beach Hotel** (118 rooms) PO Box 400, PC 411; ℄ 25 542031; f 25542228; e surbhtl@ omantel.net.om; www.sigoh.com.om. This hotel is en

route to the beaches of Ras al Hadd. Al Rasag is
the restaurant serving international cuisine, and Al
Bahar is the coffee shop. Sur Bar has live music.

There is a swimming pool. Accepts credit cards.
*RO25/30/50 sgl/dbl/suite, exc taxes, inc b/fast;
RO5/3.50 plus taxes pp for picnic lunch.*

✖ **WHERE TO EAT** Your best option for eating is within either of the two Sur hotels.
Alternatively, local coffee shops are dotted around the town and are easy to find.

OTHER PRACTICALITIES There are several cashpoints in Sur Town.

WHAT TO SEE
Sur Maritime Museum (✆ *24 541466 (call in advance); open Sat–Thu 09.00–16.00;
admission free*) Situated opposite Sunaysillah Fort, and identified by the ship's wheel
on the wall.

Sunaysillah Fort (*Open Sun–Thu 08.00–14.00*).

AL AYJAH

There are very few elegant 18th-century merchants' houses in Sur today and
you will get a better picture of old prosperous merchant housing in Al Ayjah, a
small traditional fishing village. A road loops right round from Sur skirting the
edge of the lagoon past mangrove swamps to reach Al Ayjah, making the ferry
trips across the narrow *khor* unnecessary and therefore now obsolete. The
citizens of Al Ayjah, who belong to the bani Bu Ali tribe, have tended to relish
this separation and earlier this century set up their own customs post and flag
independent of the customs post in Sur. It then took the sultan two years to get
the flag down and back over to the Sur side, even enlisting the help of the
British then resident in the Gulf.

Late afternoon and early evening are the best times to see Al Ayjah, when the
sun sets over the lagoon and casts a reddish-purple tinge over the water. The new
lighthouse overlooks the bay where the road ends, and the town's youth play
football on the sands below. The road winds into the town, passing the **old fort**
(*open Sat–Wed 07.30–12.30*) and you can simply follow the tarmac road slowly
through the old houses and park somewhere near the lighthouse.

Take the time to stroll about among the houses, especially those that face directly
out to sea away from the sheltered lagoon. Some of these are imaginatively
decorated with maritime memorabilia like old anchors and nets.

RAS AL HADD رأس الحد

Ras al Hadd is Arabic for 'headland'. Scenically unprepossessing, this is the
point where the turbulent Indian Ocean meets the calmer Gulf of Oman; it is
not a dramatic promontory but a flat sandy spit at the end of a monotonous
plain.

An RAF staging post was built here in World War II and the remains of the
airstrip are still in evidence. Nearby was a collection of *barasti* huts where simple
fishermen lived, with a **fort** (*open Sun–Thu 08.00–14.00; a guide gives tours*) above
them. This fort, now painted white, still stands, worth visiting for the views from
the towers. It is open from Sun–Thu, 08.00–14.00.

The beaches of Ras al Hadd and Ras al Jinz provide nesting grounds for an
estimated 20,000 turtles each year which migrate from as far as the Red Sea and the
east African coast. Turtles can be seen virtually year round, but June to September
is the best time for observing them.

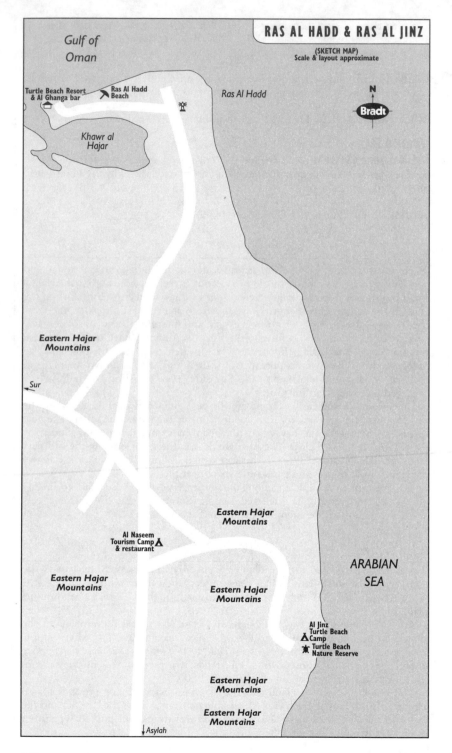

- Do not make any noise or disturb their peace.
- Do not use flash photography, as the lights unsettle the nesting turtles.
- Do not touch the turtles or their eggs.
- Do not stay overnight on the beach.
- Do not leave any litter.

WHERE TO STAY
Mid range

Ras Al Hadd Beach Hotel (50 rooms) PO Box 400, PC 411, Sur; ✆ 99 376989; f 99 314002; e surbhtl@omantel.om. This is one of 6 hotels in the Sur International Hotels Group, with welcoming staff who will greet you with dates and coffee in the tradition of Omani hospitality. The rooms are good sizes and decorated pleasantly. There is a licensed restaurant and separate bar. Turtle tours to Ras al Hadd turtle reserve can be arranged by the hotel and they will provide you with a visitor's permit. The permit costs RO1 for adults and 100bzs for children, and if you want to stay over at the camp this is an extra RO3 for adults and RO1 for children. It is always best to confirm in advance to avoid any disappointment, although you might be lucky to turn up and arrange something for the same day. Alternatively you can book directly though the camp. You will leave the hotel at 21.00 for a short drive along to the camp at Ras al Jinz for a 2hr round trip. A 4x4 is not necessary. Accepts credit cards. *RO21/27 sgl/dbl, inc tax and b/fast.*

Budget

Turtle Beach Resort (22 traditional beach huts) PO Box 303, PC 411, Sur; ✆ 25 540068; reservations: 25 543400; f 25 543900; e surtour@omantel.net.om; www.surtoursonline.com/resort.htm. This resort, established and run by Sur Tours and Marine Services, is located 8km to the left of Ras al Hadd Town. The furnished beach huts occupy a spot on the private beach, and there is a dhow-shaped restaurant (resembling its 16th-century predecessor) and bar (Al Ghanga) on the beach serving Asian and continental food. Dhow and speedboat trips can be arranged for dolphin watching. There is a lagoon for snorkelling, fishing and swimming. Khor al Grama Island (a peaceful location) is near to the resort. The resort works closely with tour operators such as Mark Tours, Nomadic Explorer and Bahwan Tours. The habitat for turtles is close to the resort. *RO12/16 pp off-season/high-season, inc dinner and b/fast.*

RAS AL JINZ رأس الجنيز

Ras al Jinz (also spelt Junaiz, or Junayz) is about 17km southeast of Ras al Hadd. The Turtle Beach Nature Reserve has been established here, complete with a campsite that provides simple *barasti* huts, water, toilet blocks and rubbish bins. It is staffed by guides who escort you to the nesting beach at dusk to watch the large female turtles come ashore and lay their eggs. The evening tour lasts until about 21.00, and the guide drives onto the beach with no headlights to find the best places, then summons you over. Just before dawn, you are allowed unescorted to watch the eggs hatching and the baby turtles scurrying to the sea before the hungry gulls or crabs have a chance to eat them. Many do not make it. The wardens have to keep records of the numbers nesting each night but in the morning for the hatching process there is no need to record anything, which is why you may go unescorted. No torch or camera is allowed.

A little further back from Turtle Beach Nature Reserve is Al Naseem Camp which is run by Desert Discovery Tours (see page 206).

There is an intended construction project for a Scientific Centre and Museum to be established by the Ministry of Tourism at Ras al Jinz within the next five years. A 12,000m² plot has been reserved for the project, at the entrance of the turtle sanctuary, which will be constructed in phases.

The facility will be designed to showcase both the turtles and the unique marine ecology of the eastern coast of Sharqiya region and will be housed in a modern complex with a museum, an indoor turtle pond, a café, information desk, ticketing counter, research and study rooms. The exhibits will provide visitors with comprehensive insights into the ecosystems that sustain turtles, charting the complete life-cycle stages of the turtle from hatchling, to nesting, to migration. In addition, antiquities uncovered during ongoing excavation work in the area will be preserved in the museum.

Italian and French archaeological teams were at work at a site behind the turtle beach camp here in 1998. A brick building divided into several elongated chambers was found, together with some burial sites. Items included a necklace and seals dating back to the Egyptian civilisations, c2200BC. The seals have letters in an unknown language but the finds indicate trading links between Egypt and Oman at that time.

⌂ WHERE TO STAY

⌂ **Al Naseem Tourism Camp** (20 standard tents) ☏ 24 493232, 99 328858; f 24 490144; e tours@omantel.net.om; www.desert-discovery.com. Run by Desert Discovery Tours and located at Ras Al Jinz, 4km from the Turtle Beach Nature Reserve. RO16/8/free adult/child/under 6 years, inc dinner, B&B. Turtle beach permit RO2.

⌂ **Al Jinz Turtle Beach Camp** ☏ 24 440068. This is located right on the beach at Ras al Jinz in an excellent location from which to view and appreciate the turtles. Rasheed manages the camp, which has a flagged entrance and an entry/exit barrier. 12 new huts have been constructed, and there are good, clean communal toilets and washing facilities. It is a short stroll down to the sea's edge to observe the turtle-nesting area. You will need to bring your own food, as there are no café/restaurant facilities. The allocated time to visit the turtles is at 21.30–23.00. The camp is open all year, although the best time to see the turtles is from Jun–Sep. RO1 to visit, RO3 to stay on the camp.

MASIRAH ISLAND مصيرة

Masirah is Oman's largest island, about 70km long, sitting 20km off the mainland, just south of the Wahiba. It is accessed by a ferry from Ras an Najdah on the mainland, which transports both vehicles and foot passengers. The ferry trip takes an hour and costs RO10. There are usually four trips each day, although these are dependent on the tides.

Masirah was said to have been visited by Alexander the Great, who referred to it as 'Serepsis'. The main occupation of the locals on the island today is weaving and making fishing nets.

This island remains largely untouched, and with many isolated beaches would make a fantastic complete getaway destination. The only hotel on the island is Masirah Hotel. Camping here would be excellent.

The eastern side of the island is good for surfing and windsurfing; 4–6ft waves are the norm, and surfing is particularly good in the *khareef* (June to September). Camping is good on the beaches and there are small shops from which to buy your essentials. Turtles come to nest here.

There was an RAF base here which played a central role in both the Jebel War of the late 1950s and the Dhofar War of the 1960s and 1970s. The BBC World Service had a relay station here – the British Eastern Relay Station (BERS), which no longer exists. Its modern replacement has been constructed and is fully operational at As Seelah, close to Al Ashkhara.

There is a book by Colin Richardson called *Masirah: Tales from a Desert Island* which reports the history of the island, enlivening it for the visitor (see *Appendix* 3, *Further information* for more details). An excellent source of further information on the island is www.globalsecurity.org/military/facility/masirah.

GETTING THERE To get to the island you need to take a 1½-hour ferry trip from the ferry station at Shennas, in Ras an Nakdah. It costs RO10 for a vehicle and its passengers to be ferried. There are no fixed timings, as the journey is dependent upon the tide – it cannot get off the ground in low tide. You simply need to turn up and queue at the ferry stop.

GETTING AROUND There are no taxis in Masirah and no car-hire firms. You will need your own transport.

WHERE TO STAY

Masirah Motel LLC (18 rooms, 6 chalets) ⤵ 25 504401; f 25 504411. This is the only hotel on the island and was opened for business in Dec 2005. There is a restaurant here (licensed). The rooms have several different bed-size arrangements (dbl bed/king-size bed/dbl bed with sgls (for a family), so it is probably best to state exactly what you require and then get your quote and needs satisfied accordingly. *RO10/12/15 sgl/dbl/family, inc taxes, exc b/fast. B/fast is approx RO1.*

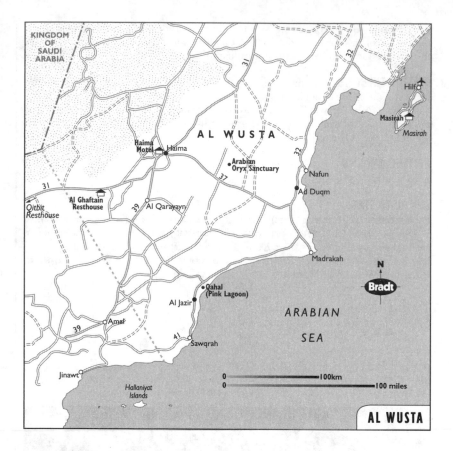

KINGDOM
OF
SAUDI
ARABIA

AL WUSTA

Hilf

Masirah
Masirah

Haima
Motel ● Haima

Arabian
Oryx Sanctuary

Nafun

Ad Duqm

Al Ghaftain
Resthouse

Qitbit
Resthouse

39   Al Qarayayn

Madrakah

N

Bradt

Qahal
(Pink Lagoon)

Al Jazir

ARABIAN

SEA

39   Amal

41

Sawqrah

Jinawt

Hallaniyat
Islands

0 ————————— 100km
0 ————————— 100 miles

AL WUSTA

Nubian ibex

9

Al Wusta الوسطى

The Arabic name Al Wusta means the 'central area' and that accurately describes this chunk of central Oman which is neither north nor south. It is Oman's least-populated province – most people simply drive through at speed on the long, central, inland road from Muscat to Salalah, longing for a sight of something other than gravel and featureless desert. In fact the only area of interest is the coast, undoubtedly Oman's most dramatic and unspoilt, on account of its sheer inaccessibility. The sights of the Wusta region are all natural; there are no forts or buildings of historic significance. There are no tarmac roads beyond the main through road, only graded tracks, and many of them difficult. The pace of travel is correspondingly slow with limited petrol, often sold from oil drums in the villages. Along with the Dhahirah, this region is home to Oman's oil installations.

To do justice to this part of Oman you are probably looking at a week of self-sufficient camping, definitely in the cooler winter months as there is no shade to be found at all – there is no vegetation to speak of. Birdlife, however, especially gulls and flamingos, exists in abundance along the coast – to date 130 different species of bird have been recorded. The beaches are rich in shells, and dolphins and turtles are also frequently spotted. Arabian gazelle and oryx roam freely in the gravel desert of the Jiddat Al Harasis, reintroduced by the sultan in 1974, having been hunted to near extinction. Perfectly adapted to the desert, the oryx can go without water for 22 months as long as it has plants to graze on with high water content. The region is also home to Nubian Ibex, caracal, and lynx desert rabbits.

The beaches of Ras Madrakah are dramatic, with stretches of white sand interspersed with black volcanic rocks and cliffs. Several shipwrecks still stand, rusting quietly on the beaches where they were washed up. Near Qahal (or Kahil) are the unique pink lagoons caused by algae, and at Shuwaymiyah is a box canyon quite unlike any other in Oman, with sheer white cliffs.

GETTING THERE This region is accessed via the long Muscat to Salalah road.

WHERE TO STAY AND EAT

On the drive from Muscat to Salalah there are five simple resthouses, with basic restaurants which are unlicensed. In the order that you meet them on the drive from Muscat, these are: Al Ghaba (Dakhiliyah, page 196), Haima (Al Wusta), Al Ghaftain (Al Wusta), Qitbit (Dhofar) and Thumrayt (Dhofar, both page 262), mostly owned by the Arab Oryx group. Two of them are in this region.

BUDGET
Haima Motel (15 rooms) ✆ 23 297103. This is a small hotel offering cheap rooms if you need a break from the unending Muscat–Salalah road. Note that there is no restaurant, so if you need to eat you'll need to travel a little bit further to Al Ghaftain Resthouse (page 234). RO15 inc tax.

🏠 **Al Ghaftain Resthouse** (10 rooms) ☏ 99 485881; f 593106. This is another one of the basic resthouses that sit on the main Muscat–Salalah road, 408km from Salalah. There is an international restaurant. Accepts credit cards. *RO15/25 sgl/dbl.*

MUSCAT–SALALAH (ROUTE 31)

The 1,000km tarmac road from Muscat to Salalah can be done in just over eight hours' solid driving if you keep your speed at 120km/h. Most people find this too strenuous and deadly dull, and therefore take typically ten–12 hours, allowing for stops at the rather uninspiring series of resthouses along the way – each of which has petrol and a small service garage. Note that this route covers three of Oman's regions, and four if we include the early part of the route (route 15) from Muscat. It therefore could have been included in any of these other regional chapters.

Of the resthouses you meet along this seemingly endless road, **Ghaba Resthouse** (see page 196) is the first. It is 319km from Muscat, near which a small diversion can be made to see the **Qarat Kibrit saltdome** with its salt stalactites. For centuries the Bedouin used to mine salt and sulphur here, which they then carried by camel to Nizwa for trading. It is a 45-minute diversion from the main road and to reach it you fork right before the resthouse on a graded road signposted for the oilfield at Ghaba North. You follow the track for 22km until you reach a roundabout where the Qarat Kibrit is signposted.

Follow the road south of Ghaba Resthouse for 207km and you will reach Haima. The small settlement here has petrol, shops, a motel and even a hospital.

From Haima, one option is to head for the coast towards Duqm, to camp at Ras Madrakah, taking in a visit to the Arabian Oryx Sanctuary en route. A second option is to take the road (a little beyond Haima), signposted Marmul, which leads to Qahal (or Kahil) of the pink lagoons and then Shuwaymiyah.

Continuing on the main Muscat–Salalah road south, 86km beyond Haima you reach the **Al Ghaftain Resthouse** (see above), from which point onwards you are skirting the edge of the Empty Quarter with open sand landscapes. The high dunes, reaching over 100m, are much deeper into the desert and therefore more difficult to reach.

Qitbit Resthouse (see above) lies 130km further on. Both the Ghaftain and Qitbit resthouses serve the oilfields of the area. A further 196km through uneventful scenery brings you to **Thumrayt**, with its small hotel and restaurant. From here the easy-graded track is signposted to Shisr (described in *Chapter 10, Dhofar*, page 262).

From Thumrayt it is 82km to Salalah, the final 32km of which is the reward: the much longed-for and interesting descent of the Qara Mountains to Salalah on the coastal plain. This is especially beautiful during the *khareef* season when the landscape is verdant. On the descent, views over the Salalah plain are spectacular and hold their promise of company, activity and respite after the protracted drudgery of the long desert road from the north.

Much of the Omani desert between Nizwa and Salalah is not rolling sands at all, but flat dark gravel plain, black or occasionally purplish green. The stretch from Adam to Haima is the most tedious. Curiously in the mornings there can be dense fog around Haima, caused by just the right combination of sea breeze and desert heat. After exceptional rainfall lakes form in the desert which can linger for months and extend to several kilometres, still deep enough to swim in. Reptiles whose eggs have lain dormant for up to ten years then hatch out, newt-like, and live in the lakes. The number of flint arrowheads, axe heads and other tools suggests that maybe the wetter climate here in earlier times meant that human settlements were possible.

The three major Bedouin tribes of southern Oman are the Jenaba, the Wahhabi and the Harasis. Since they are all nomads, their tribal areas are never entirely clear cut, but as a rule the Jenaba live along the coast from Bar Al Hikman (the mainland opposite Masirah Island) to the Dhofar border, the Wahhabi live in the Wahiba Sands and eastwards to the coast, while the Harasis live in the tedious expanse of desert known as the Jiddat Al Harasis, northeast of Salalah. The Harasis have always been the purest nomads in Oman, with no date groves to return to, just the inhospitable Jiddat lowland where they move about with their camels, speaking a south Arabian dialect incomprehensible to any other Arab. They are noted for their excellent sense of direction.

The **Nejd** is the desolate area to the north of the Dhofar Mountains, on the southern fringe of the Empty Quarter. Ranulph Fiennes wrote of this area: 'The Nejd looked both harmless and lifeless. In reality it was neither: every crack in the crumbling surface concealed something that crawled or slithered.'

If you camp anywhere on this desolate stretch, the kind of wildlife you may encounter in the evening includes fennec foxes with their gigantic ears, jerboa, desert hares and lizards. The dhubb lizard is a great delicacy for the Bedouin, for whom it used to constitute a rare source of free meat, and they had many ingenious methods of catching it. Another type of larger lizard is called Abu Ruwwal, with a scaly tail that it swings about aggressively, and an intimidating snake-like hiss. The Harasis tribe treats the fennec fox as a kind of private mascot and so would never kill it; instead they leave food out for it (scraps from their own meals). The Jenaba tribe along the coast of the desert do the same thing for the turtle.

ARABIAN ORYX SANCTUARY

The Jiddat al Harasis lies equidistant from Muscat and Salalah, in the wilayat of Haima (or Hayma). A sanctuary was established here in 1994 and covers approximately 27,500km². Its purpose is to conserve the desert habitat and protect the oryx from extinction. It is a UNESCO World Heritage Site, and the headquarters are at Jaaluni, which is roughly halfway between Haima and Duqm.

The sanctuary lies on bird migratory routes between Africa, Europe and central Asia and provides good opportunities for birdwatching. The Jiddat al Harasis attracts a fog which sustains life within the area, whose inhabitants include Arabian oryx, Nubian ibex, caracel, Arabian gazelle, sand gazelle, sand cat, houbara bustard, lizards, snakes, spiders, birds and endemic plant species.

Oryx are extremely hard to spot as they have a keen sense of smell and tend to disappear over the horizon, leaving their tracks and droppings as the only clue that they were there. Local tribesmen say they can be approached from upwind by lying flat on a camel's back, as oryx have no fear of camels. Gazelle are also shy and nimble-footed. It can therefore take a long time driving through the sanctuary before you spot either. For further information you might like to visit the Arabian Oryx Project website (*www.oryxoman.com*).

For the people of the sanctuary, the oil companies and the Arabian Oryx Project are the two largest employers. Prior to 1974 camels were their only means of transport, but by 1980 each household had a truck. Prior to 1956 they relied on fog water to sustain them; now water is available at the desalination plants within the sanctuary. The first school in the area was built in 1982.

The Bedouin of the south in the 1960s had a lifestyle so harsh it is hard to conceive. They owned nothing save their camels, goats and a few leather bags. The children would sleep squashed among the goats. Their close dependence on nature, where they could die if a well dried out or a camel died, gave them a deep sense of the will of Allah, and the Koran was their only education. Even though they had so little, the rule of the desert was to share with guests and unexpected visitors, even if this meant their own family going without. No Bedu would eat or drink until their companions had all reached the well; no-one would take more than their share. Petty theft within a tribe was despised as dishonourable, yet it was acceptable, even manly to raid another tribe's camels and kill their tribespeople in order to steal for your own. Freya Stark in her book *The Southern Gates of Arabia* observed: 'Crime is practically unknown in the Hadramaut; such things as robbery and murder, being done according to established rules, come rather under the heading of legitimate warfare.'

Blood feuds are also a question of honour; they are not crimes. The camel – the lifeblood of the Bedouin – does not normally sweat until its body temperature exceeds 104°F, thereby conserving its water for long periods even in excessive heat. So the Bedouin relied on her milk in the desert long after his own water ran out. A Bedouin was said to be able to tell from the footprint of a camel who its owner was, when and where it had drunk last by the amount and frequency of the droppings, and in which wadis it had last eaten, from the texture. If one Bedouin owned she-camels, he would arrange a meeting with a he-camel belonging to another man and borrow his services in exchange for milk or food.

GETTING TO THE SANCTUARY To get here, take the Muscat to Salalah road. At Haima, turn left towards Ad Duqm. After 80km on this road take the signposted left to Matar Hab Hab or Hab Hab Airport. Continue for 15km along this stretch, which is lined by oil drums. Jaaluni (or Yaloony) is on the right-hand side (not signposted). You will need a guide to help you follow the tracks to Jaaluni. After 15km along these tracks, you will reach the camp at the Oryx Sanctuary. Maps and GPS are needed to tour the reserve and at least two vehicles should travel together, for safety reasons.

Frankincense tree

10

Dhofar ظفار

Dhofar is Oman's southernmost province and covers roughly a third of the country. It is famed for its frankincense, and was the trading centre of this aromatic gum resin with Rome, Greece, Egypt, India and China. Its presence here kept southern Arabia wealthy into the 6th century AD.

Dhofar itself has its own dramatic regional variances of weather and terrain; it contains one of the largest expanses of sandy desert in the world – the Empty Quarter or Rub'al Khali – extensive gravel desert plains, lush green coastal plains and the Qara Mountains, with their gushing waterfalls and streams.

Salalah, on the southern coast, is Dhofar's administrative capital, and has quite a different feel to it from the rest of Oman, extending from Dhofar's mountain plateaux northwards. This is largely due to its monsoon climate, which can last from June through to September and results in the narrow band of land from the

THE KHAREEF AND ITS FESTIVAL

Through a quirk of nature, the mountains of Dhofar and the Salalah Plain are exposed to a monsoon climate, with daily rains from mid June to mid September blowing in from Africa. As the rain-filled winds brush past the island of Socotra off the southern coast of Yemen, the vacuum created by the vast searing deserts beyond sucks the winds against the Qara Mountains. Known as the *khareef* (meaning 'winds of plenty'), the clouds shed 15 inches of rain over those three months, causing the wadi beds to flow with deep rivers and spectacular waterfalls which plunge over sheer cliffs. The area becomes filled with mist and fog. Camels are forced to leave the mountains, which become slippery and dangerous, and have to be kept in the plains until the rains abate. When the camels return to the mountains in September, after the rains, the pasture is rich and plentiful. This is the season in which the region is most popular with Omanis from the northern provinces as well as other Arabs of the Gulf, who seek to escape their own hot dry summers, and enjoy the lush green landscape here.

Each year, at this time, there is a six-week-long carnival, much like that of the Muscat Festival, but organised by the Dhofar municipality. The festival, like its Muscat counterpart, is a showpiece for Omani customs and traditions, and hotels and flights can get booked to capacity. The Baladiya Entertainment Centre is one of the principal centres where festivities take place. It was purpose built, with a heritage village, two theatres (one open air) and a fairground. Al Marooj Amphitheatre, which can hold 7,000 people, was opened in 2005 and is located in the east of Salalah, in the Ateen plain. The festivities include folk bands, song and dance, art exhibitions, handicraft demonstrations, information on conservation projects of the region, as well as other exhibits displaying and promoting the culture and heritage of the region and country.

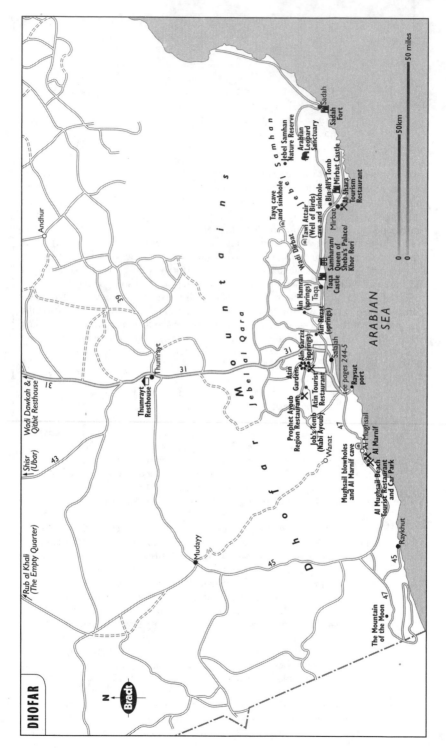

DHOFAR

N

Bradt

ARABIAN SEA

Jebel Samhan

Sadah
Sadah Fort

Arabian Leopard Sanctuary

Jebel Samhan Nature Reserve

Bin Ali's Tomb

Mirbat Castle

Al-Shara Tourism Restaurant

Mirbat

Tayq cave and sinkhole

Tawi Attair (Well of Birds) cave and sinkhole

Samharam/ Queen of Sheba's Palace/ Khor Rori

Taqa Castle

Taqa

Ain Hamran (springs)

Wadi Dirbat

Ain Razat (springs)

Ain Garziz (springs)

Salalah

Ain Tourist Gardens

see pages 244–5

Raysut port

Prophet Ayoub Region Restaurant

Job's Tomb (Nabi Ayoub)

Atin Tourist Restaurant

Wanat

Al Mughsail

Al Marnif

Mughsail blowholes and Al Marnif cave

Al Mughsail Beach Tourist Restaurant and Car Park

Raykhut

The Mountain of the Moon

Thumrayt Resthouse

Thumrayt

Andhur

Wadi Dawkah & Qitbit Resthouse

Shisr (Ubar)

Rub al Khali (The Empty Quarter)

Mudayy

Dhofar   *Jebel al Qara*   *Mountains*

43

39

31

31

31

45

45

47

47

0   50km
0   50 miles
50km
50 miles

238

Qara Mountains to the flat coastal plain becoming green and lush, giving rise to the name 'the green city'. The greenness of the September hills contrasts dramatically with the camel-coloured aridness of the rest of the country, yet by late October all traces of greenery from the monsoon have disappeared.

Unlike the rest of Oman, the temperature of this narrow band rarely exceeds 30°C. From October to February the temperature is guaranteed warm (28°C), sunny and dry, and therefore attracts European and North American visitors seeking to escape their cold winters. January and December are the coolest months, with temperatures averaging 25°C. From March onwards until the monsoon begins in mid June, the climate becomes muggy and unpleasantly humid and there are fewer visitors. The waves can reach a dramatic 8m during the monsoon season and the sea is then too dangerous for swimming. The average wave height outside the monsoon season is just 1m, but swimming can still be tricky because of undertows. Notices at the few beach hotels warn of the danger and absolve themselves of any responsibility in the event of an accident.

Agriculture and fishing are the key industries of Dhofar, followed by traditional crafts and tourism. In addition to its plentiful fruits, sweet potatoes, corn and wheat are grown in the region. Sardines, prawns, abalone and lobster are common catches in the waters off the Salalah coast.

Dhofar is now being promoted as a stand-alone holiday destination. For today's visitors Dhofar offers the three archaeological sites of Al Balid (Old Salalah), Sumharam (east of Salalah) and Ubar, which, collectively, are UNESCO-listed (together with the little-known ruins of Andhur, another frankincense-gathering city) as the 'Land of Frankincense'. Apart from the souks of Salalah, the other sites of the region are mainly natural and scenic, like the Mughsail blowholes, the dramatic road to Yemen and the lush Wadi Dirbat with its cave paintings. Of Salalah's 12 coastal creeks, nine are designated nature reserves.

HISTORY

Dhofar is in many respects a separate country to Oman – different in climate, people, customs and currency. Its only link to Oman was that the sultan, Said bin Taimur (Sultan Qaboos's father), chose to live here off and on for 35 years.

The sultan's presence in Dhofar meant that a contingent of the Sultan's Armed Forces (SAF) was based there to protect him. Said bin Taimur regarded Dhofar as a sort of personal property of his – a favourite retreat – taking responsibility for it from 1879. He spent the last ten years of his reign continuously at Salalah, together with the young Qaboos whom he restricted to the palace under a form of arrest. This was to ensure that Qaboos was not corrupted by outside influences after he returned from his Sandhurst military training in England. The ageing sultan's army consisted of about 1,000 fighting men, of whom half were Beluchi mercenaries and led by a handful of British volunteers.

Sultan Qaboos has always had a special affection for Dhofar: he was born there and his mother was a Dhofari from Wadi Dirbat. His mother and sister lived in the Mamura Palace just east of Salalah until his mother's death, and his sister lives there still. His mother is now buried in the cemetery at nearby Taqa. He spent much of his childhood there, as well as the period of near house-arrest as a young man after his return from Sandhurst. Now he comes every *khareef* season, staying in Al Husn Palace – the original stone-built residence of his father, now hidden from view by a huge wall. The newer Robat Palace is a smaller building, though its grounds are extensive; it tends to be used by his senior staff.

Although nominally under the rule of the Muscat sultans since the late 1800s, the sultans' authority only extended over the Salalah Plain itself, a fertile stretch

15km wide by 48km long. The Qara Mountains tended to be a law unto themselves, with the tribes frequently at war.

The sultan had an arrangement with the British that any British army officer could volunteer for a two-year attachment to the sultan's army and continue to be paid by Her Majesty's government. The British explorer and writer Ranulph Fiennes first came to Oman this way. In return the British were allowed to use the island of Masirah as an RAF base and a listening/transmitting post. One of the conditions set by the sultan was that the RAF had to maintain the airstrip and base at Salalah. The British did not require this base while they had Masirah, but the sultan insisted on its maintenance for his own personal safety.

From 1969, child recruits from among Dhofari villages were sought, first with parental consent, then without, after the first method yielded limited results. When one mother protested to the soldiers and tried to help her boy escape, she was stripped and flogged, then picked up by her ankles and swung round and round, faster and faster, moving ever closer to a cluster of rocks, until on the final swing her head was cracked open like a watermelon. After that there were no more rebellious parents.

The young teenagers who were sent off to be trained in Russia or China returned with beards shaven and preaching against God, strangers to their own families. The methods of the Russian and Chinese revolutionaries were also barbaric. The village elders often tried to preach against this assault on Islam, but all such insurrection ceased after two respected sheikhs had their eyes put out. The revolutionary who performed the blinding, remembered by the villagers as an idle boy who shirked his duties with the cattle, was nephew to one of the men, and used a pocket knife heated in the fire. The men died only a few days later. Of the grimness of war Ranulph Fiennes wrote, after killing his first enemy soldier:

> I found sleep elusive. I had often shot at people hundreds of yards away; vague shapes behind rocks who were firing back; but never before had I seen a man's soul in his eyes, sensed his vitality as a fellow human, and then watched his body ripped apart at the pressure of my finger. I tried to force away the image of his destruction

THE COUP

On 23 July 1970, in the afternoon when the old sultan was resting, a group of ten Omani soldiers led by the wali's son, Bareik, entered the palace in Salalah unopposed. Winding through a labyrinth of dark passages they came in the end to the sultan's private quarters. The startled royal bodyguard opened fire, and a ricocheting bullet hit Bareik in the stomach. Next Captain Tom Greening, Qaboos's young intelligence officer, appeared with more Omani soldiers and all but two of the slave bodyguards surrendered. The old sultan was wounded and refused to leave without the local British colonel. The colonel came and comforted the sultan while his wounds were dressed and he then agreed to sign the letter of abdication in favour of Qaboos, his son. An RAF plane then flew him to London with three of his palace staff where he lived in a private suite in the Dorchester Hotel until he died in 1972. Bareik later became Wali of Dhofar.

The younger Qaboos's first act was to withdraw all troops from the Qara Mountains and to declare an amnesty for all the guerrillas. This led to a steady stream of deserters from the Dhofar Liberation Front (reaching 1,000 within the next three years), and included many who had received their training in Russia or China. Over half the oil revenues had been spent on the war (£50 million a year) but Qaboos joined the Arab League and the United Nations and soon became creditworthy. World oil prices rocketed and in 1975 Oman's oil revenue was £300 million.

but his scarred face stayed watching me from my subconscious and a part of me that was still young and uncynical died with him and his comrade the commissar, spread-eagled on a thornbush with his red badge glinting in the hot Qara sun.

THE DHOFARIS

Dhofar's people are closer to the Hadramaut tribes (Yemen) than to the northern Omanis, linked by centuries of shared interest in the frankincense trade routes. They are said to descend from a mountain tribe that arrived with the Queen of Sheba when she colonised the frankincense orchards before her legendary journey to King Solomon. Numbering around 10,000–15,000, the Dhofaris speak four different languages – Mahra, Shahra, Kharous Harusi and Botahari, all linguistically different from Arabic.

The Qara Mountains were inhabited until very recently by hostile tribesmen. The Qara people lived for their cattle, like the Dinka tribes of the Upper Nile. They often named their eldest son after their favourite cow, and no healthy cow would be killed even when the owner's children were dying of malnutrition. After the death of a Qara tribesman, up to half his herd was slaughtered as a kind of death duty to save his soul. If a cow slowed down its milk production, they believed the cure was to blow as hard as possible up the cow's vagina, an act only permitted to Qara males.

An illuminating comparison between the society of northern and southern Omani provinces was made by Ranulph Fiennes. A British army officer and explorer, who revisited Dhofar in 1985, his first visit since leaving in 1970, Fiennes commented: 'If the northern Omanis had leapt in a single generation from the Middle Ages into the 1980s, then the Dhofaris had bounded from the Old Testament into the 1950s and were straining at the leash to close the remaining gap.'

GETTING THERE

BY AIR Oman Air operates daily flights from Seeb International Airport to Salalah Airport in Dhofar. The price for a return ticket is around RO73. Oman Air usually offer good package deals, and so it may be worth enquiring at the time of your visit as to what is available. A package deal, which includes accommodation, costs around RO96 (five star) and RO76 (three star), based on a return economy flight,

If the Russian and Chinese revolutionaries controlling the 2,000-strong PFLOAG (People's Front for the Liberation of the Occupied Arabian Gulf) had succeeded in overthrowing the British-led Sultan's Armed Forces in Dhofar and imposing their law, they would have soon encountered another problem – for the Arab mentality is totally at odds with the communist ideal. A regime that evens out all differences between rich and poor was irrelevant in this part of Arabia, where these differences were small anyway. Animals, land, and even water were already owned collectively by whole families. Sheikhs had power only for as long as the tribe collectively permitted them. And as Ranulph Fiennes observed after several months in Oman: 'Arabs are highly individualist people, with keenly developed ideas about religion, morals, and the inferiority of other beings in general and women in particular.' In 1968, Fiennes was on the point of resigning and returning to Britain because he felt Britain was supporting the corrupt and stifling regime of the old sultan. But his Omani staff sergeant persuaded him to stay, by talking of the importance of fighting communism:

I myself have met the communists from abroad, here in Oman. They are more often than not sly men with silken tongues but their souls are empty and all their talk of revolution is without sound base. You see they try to turn us from our God and that must never be. Communism must not come here, Sahb. You must not think the British do wrong here, Sahb. They do not meddle with our way of life or our religion. If you British leave before the sultan's son Qaboos can rule, then the communists will take over without a doubt. They will force us to leave Islam or kill us. With the oil money that now pours into Oman, thanks be to God, he (Qaboos) will give us all those things which the communists promise, without changing our religion.

two nights' stay with breakfast and airport transfers. Travelling independently, a transfer to any hotel in Salalah Town will cost roughly RO3 by taxi, although some hotels offer a free transfer.

The departure lounge of Salalah Airport is small but comfortable, and you can get yourself a cup of tea, coffee or a cold drink, plus light snacks at the counter at the back. There are only a couple of small shops inside the lounge, selling postcards, papers, cigarettes and phonecards, but nothing much else. The toilets are clean, and payphones are situated next to them at the back of the lounge. The seating area has a family corner with padded comfortable chairs.

Announcements are made in Arabic and English (although the English is indecipherable). The staff on the coffee counter at the back speak good English and will be able to clarify the message.

BY ROAD Route 31 runs from Nizwa all the way south to Salalah. The distance from Muscat is approximately 1,000km. The road runs virtually parallel to the Empty Quarter (or Rub'al Khali) and is a long 12-hour journey by coach (including stops). Travelling by coach is your cheapest option, but if you have others in your party who could perhaps share the driving, then a hire car would be a good alternative.

GETTING AROUND

CAR HIRE You can hire a car from the airport, if you intend to drive yourself around and explore, or pre-book one from the Muscat car rental offices (see *Chapter 2*, page 47). In Salalah itself, Sumharam Watersports and Diving provide a car rental service (RO14/40 saloon/4x4, per day). Do note that if you plan on taking excursions with tour operators, it is not altogether necessary to hire a car, as tour companies collect you from your hotel and return you afterwards.

TAXIS Taxis are reasonably priced and easily the best way of getting from your hotel to the city centre souks and budget restaurants. You won't be ripped off.

TOUR OPERATORS

Tour operators, which can be found inside the Salalah hotels as well as in the streets of the city centre (in Salalah), offer the stock tours of the area, albeit to varying degrees of quality and price. They may vary slightly in the sites they include in each tour. Tours can easily be arranged through your hotel, if you prefer someone else to do the organising. Alternatively you may prefer to hire a car and travel independently.

Arabian Tours Salalah; ☎ 23 290088; f 23 290088. Offering a full range of tours including dhow cruises, scuba diving and 4x4 safaris. Also offers car hire.
Bahwan Travel Agencies LLC Salalah; ☎ 23 294665, 23 290908; f 23 294213 e topclass@ omantel.net.om or lakshmy@bahwantravels.com; www.bahwantravelgroup.com. This is one of the biggest tour operators in the country, established for 25 years and offering the full range of tours. It's best to arrange Salalah tours through the Muscat office.
Sumharam Watersports and Diving Centre Crowne Plaza; ☎ 23 235333; m 99 099002 (Yousuf al Mahrooqi); f 23 235137; or The Hilton; ☎ 23 211234; m 95 205750 (Said al Mahrooqi); e sumharam@hotmail.com. The company also operates as Samahram Falcon Trading and Service. In business since 1994 and located in both the 5-star hotels in Salalah, this tour operator is the best

choice to organise your dive tours; it also offers a full array of tours. Car hire (☎ 23 297985; m 99 289991, 99 496707; fax: 23 297983). Around RO14 per day for a 2x4, and RO40 for a 4x4.
United Tours Salalah; ☎ 23 297948; f 23 297958; e utours@omantel.net.om or utours@unitedoman.com. Large firm with 40 4x4 vehicles and a fleet of buses offering the full range of tours, including comprehensive 8–12-day tours of Oman including camping, safari and culture.
Zahara Tours ☎ 23 202581, 23 202582; f 24 692950; e miscoman@omantel.net.om or harsh@zaharatours.com; www.zaharatours.com. Offers tours throughout the whole country. In the Dhofar region it offers three tours called 'frankincense', 'fabled castles' and 'serene Salalah', which incorporate most of what the region has to offer. See website for details.

WHERE TO STAY

Apart from the odd few, the hotels are all in Salalah Town. During the monsoon season they can get full and so advance booking will probably be necessary. Car-rental firms too are stretched to meet demand during the *khareef*.

WHERE TO EAT

The plushest restaurants are in the two 5-star hotels in Salalah – the Crowne Plaza and the Hilton – and these are licensed. All other eating places are simple and unlicensed. Outside of Salalah city centre, places to eat are few and so packing a picnic is always a good idea (unless you're visiting the blowholes at Mughsail, west of Salalah, where there are two good beach restaurants for tourists).

OTHER PRACTICALITIES

USEFUL TELEPHONE NUMBERS
Dhofar Police HQ ☎ 23 234599
Salalah Police ☎ 23 290099
Salalah Post Office ☎ 23 292933

Sultan Qaboos Hospital Salalah; ☎ 23 211555
Taqa Police ☎ 23 258199
Thumrayt Police ☎ 23 277099

Dhofar OTHER PRACTICALITIES

10

CURRENCY EXCHANGE Money exchangers are located in Salalah along Al Nahda Street (*open Sat–Thu 08.30–13.00 and 16.00–20.00, Fri 08.30–11.00*). Their rates are better than at the big hotels. There are cashpoints throughout the town.

SALALAH صلالة

Salalah, the capital of the Dhofar region, is considered Oman's second city, despite having a population of only 100,000. In reality, it is just a small town. And where northern Oman has its dates, southern Oman has its coconuts. The route from the airport (just 2km north of Salalah city centre) to the Crowne Plaza Hotel winds through lush plantations of coconut, papaya, banana and mango, and the fruit stalls which line the streets give the place an African feel (eg: only 150bzs for a fresh cold coconut prepared for you to drink!). There are no high-rise buildings here. The name *salalah* means 'shining one' in the Jebali language.

WHERE TO STAY
Luxury

Crowne Plaza Resort Salalah (153 rooms, 7 suites, 19 family villas) PO Box 870, PC 211; ✆ 23 235333; f 23 235137; e cpsll@omantel.net.om; www.crowneplaza.com/salalah. From Salalah Airport turn left at the first roundabout, right at the second and then left at the third, then follow signs to the Crowne Plaza Resort. This hotel, part of the Intercontinental Hotels Group, has undergone a reconstruction and refurbishment project. The sandy beach is public but the hotel has put out its own sunshades. There is a large pool, tennis, minigolf and health club with sauna, jacuzzi and gym. There are 3 fully licensed restaurants: Darbat Restaurant on Dolphin Beach, Al Luban Restaurant and an Al Khareef (an English/Irish pub). There is also a 3-bar complex located just outside

the hotel, a tea lobby lounge (Bird's Lounge), 9-hole green golf course (the first green course in Oman) and driving range, squash and children's playground. *RO80/90 sgl/dbl, exc tax and b/fast.*

Hilton Salalah Resort (150 rooms) PO Box 699, PC 211; ✆ 23 211234; f 23 210084; e salalah@hilton.com; www.salalah.hilton.com. Completed in 1999, it is Salalah's newest addition, and is located on the beach on the way out to Raysut, not far from the 'fish' roundabout. It is well placed to catch the business trade from Raysut Port. There is a complimentary airport shuttle service to the hotel. There are 2 restaurants: Al Maha, offering international, Italian and Arabic cuisine, and Palm Grove, which is an outdoor restaurant situated by the beach, which

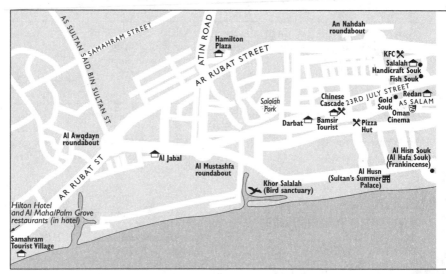

offers fresh fish in the evening and light snacks during the day. The hotel has an English pub called The Mayfair, complete with Nepalese barman. There is the Whispers Night Club and an Indian bar called Chequers. Internet access is not cheap in the hotel (RO3 for 15mins), but there are internet cafés in the street shops at approx 400bzs for an hour's usage – a cheap alternative. *RO90 for rooms (sgl or dbl occupancy) exc taxes and b/fast.*

Budget All of the hotels in the budget range provide comfortable accommodation at affordable prices. Even the cheapest have good clean rooms, and after your tours and all that fresh air, you can get your head down for a very reasonable price. The prices in summer, which for most hotels is from 1 July to 31 August, are higher, but only marginally so. Some prices include taxes and breakfast, some don't, so you might like to get this confirmed before you go. These budget hotels seem genuinely happy to accommodate you, so if there is anything you need, or would like to change, just ask. Also check whether there is a free airport transfer service provided.

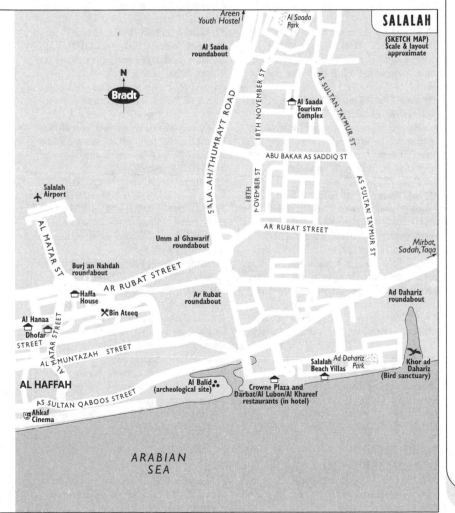

⌂ **Al Hanaa Hotel** (25 rooms) PO Box 194, PC 211; ☎ 23 298305, 23 298306; f 23 291894; e msarawas@omantel.net.om. This is situated in 23rd July St. *RO11/16 sgl/dbl inc b/fast and taxes.*

⌂ **Al Jebel Hotel** (90 rooms) PO Box 1284, PC 211, Salalah; ☎ 23 210611, 23 214020; f 23 210191, 23 214021; e jabalhot@omantel.net.om. This hotel is situated on Sultan Qaboos Road, which is in the centre of Salalah, close to Sultan Qaboos Hospital. In the Shahrzad lounge, there is live music and entertainment, including Arabian belly dancers. There is a 24hr restaurant. *RO20/25 1 person/ 2 people, inc taxes and free airport transfer.*

⌂ **Bamsir Tourist Hotel** (35 rooms) PO Box 2851, PC 211, Salalah; ☎ 23 202556, 23 202091; f 23202093. There is no restaurant here. *RO20/25, exc taxes.*

⌂ **Darbat Hotel** (53 rooms) PO Box 18532, PC 211; ☎ 23 295877, 23 295878; f 23 289281; e darbathotel@hotmail.com. This 6-storey hotel has rooms of various sizes. *RO15/25 exc taxes and b/fast.*

⌂ **Dhofar Hotel** (86 rooms) PO Box 2539, PC 211; ☎ 23 292300, 23 282300; f 23 294358; e dhfhotel@omantel.net.om. Located in Salalah city centre, with a restaurant serving international, Arabic, Indian and Chinese cuisine. Does not accept credit cards. *RO20/35 sgl/dbl (high season) inc tax and b/fast.*

⌂ **Haffa House Hotel** (63 rooms) PO Box 427, PC 211, Salalah; ☎ 23 295444, 23 294755; f 23 294873; e house@omantel.net.om. Located at the airport roundabout, this has a choice of either 1-bed, 2-bed or 3-bed apts and has a health club, pool and tennis courts. It is popular with families and long-stay guests. The on-site Al Haffa Restaurant serves Indian, Chinese, continental and Arabic food, and there is an English tearoom. *RO25/28/35/ 45/55 sgl/dbl/1-bed flat/2-bed flat/3-bed flat.*

⌂ **Hamilton Plaza Hotel** (185 rooms) PO Box 2498; ☎ 23 211025/6/7, 23 210000; f 23 211187. Set along Al Roba St in the city centre, about 5 mins from the airport, this 4-star hotel has a host of amenities, including Al Lou-Lou'a Restaurant (serving Arabic, Indian, Far Eastern and Continental food), a coffee lounge, internet café and supermarket. *RO35/55/85 (high season), 25/35/55 (low season),*

sgl/dbl/2-bedroom family room with sitting area, inc tax and b/fast.

⌂ **Oryx Hotel and Apartment** (56 rooms) PO Box 408, PC 211, Salalah city centre, close to Al Nahdah roundabout; ☎ 23 296262; f 23 297212; e oryxsll@omantel.net.om. *RO 20/30 sgl/dbl inc tax and b/fast.*

⌂ **Redan Hotel** (27 rooms) PO Box 957 PC 211, Salalah; ☎ 23 292266, 23 288032; f 23 290491; e redan@omantel.net.om. Situated on Al Salam St; also has 2- and 3-bedroom flats available. *RO14/ 17/23 sgl/dbl/suite inc taxes, RO15/22/28 in summer.*

⌂ **Al Saada Tourism Complex** (15 villas) ☎ 23 225250, 99 484205; fax 23 225251. Self-catering villas, located 8km from airport. *RO65/75 3-bed/ 4-bed, exc 10% tax.*

⌂ **Salalah Beach Villas** (8 villas, 10 apts, 25 rooms) PO Box 20, Dahariz, PC 214; ☎ 23 235999; f 23 235599; e beachspa@omantel.net.om. Located in southern Dahariz, close to the Crowne Plaza Hotel, this small resort offers sea views from most of its beach villas. There is a pool and candle-lit dinners can be arranged. They also offer tours: a 4x4 for the day with driver/guide and picnic costs RO100. *RO15/20 no view; 18/24 with sea view and balcony, sgl/dbl, exc 9% tax (winter season rates). RO5 buffet dinner, RO3.50 lunch, RO2.50 picnic.*

⌂ **Salalah Hotel** (24 rooms) PO Box 823, PC 211, Salalah; ☎ 23 295332, 23 295626; f 23 292145. This 2-star hotel is situated on A'Suq St close to the central market, and opposite the Oman National Transport Company (ONTC) bus station. *RO20 for sgl and dbl, exc tax and b/fast.*

⌂ **Samharam Tourist Village** (46 villas, 16 chalets) PO Box 427, PC 211; ☎ 23 295444, 23 211420; f 23 211267. This 5-star hotel is located on the same side as the Hilton and close to it (about 10km from Salalah Airport). To access it, and indeed the Hilton, you need to continue driving past until you meet the next roundabout where you can turn around and come back on yourself. Affiliated to the Shanfari Group, this is a peaceful beachfront resort with chalets that can be let from one night to a medium- or long-term stay. Restaurant, coffee shop, large pool and health facilities. *RO35/100, sgl and dbl/3-bed villas, exc tax.*

✖ WHERE TO EAT
Upmarket (RO20+ for a meal for two)

✖ **Al Maha** ☎ 23 211234. Located inside the Hilton Hotel, this restaurant serves international and Arabian cuisine.

✖ **Palm Grove** ☎ 23 211234. This is located on the seafront at the Hilton Hotel, serving international cuisine and fresh fish.

✗ **Darbat** ☎ 23 235333. Located inside the Crowne Plaza Hotel, serving breakfast, lunch and dinner, buffet or à la carte, with the option of eating on the terrace overlooking the sea.

✗ **Al Luban** ☎ 23 235333. Another of the Crowne Plaza's offerings, this restaurant is also a nightclub with live entertainment.

✗ **Al Khareef** ☎ 23 235333. This is the pub of the Crowne Plaza Hotel, which serves hot and cold bar food and snacks.

Budget (under RO10 for a meal for two)

✗ **Bin Ateeq** 23rd July St; ☎ 23 292384; e binateeq@omantel.net.om. Traditional Omani food served at ground level in private rooms. Worth a visit for its excellent food and the cultural experience. Take your shoes off at the entrance to your private room.

✗ **Chinese Cascade** 23rd July St (next to the National Bank of Oman); ☎ 23 289844. The food here is good and very well priced. Main dishes are around RO1.

Fast food KFC, Penguin, Chick Hut and Pizza Hut can easily be found dotted around Salalah.

WHAT TO SEE AND DO IN SALALAH AND THE SOUTHERN COAST Places of interest in the Dhofar region are largely based around the southern coastal areas. The stock tours offered by the tour operators include the 'City Tour', 'East Salalah', 'West Salalah' and 'Ubar and the Empty Quarter'. These may vary a little from one tour operator to another, but they all take in the stock tourist sites. For example, one tour to the east of Salalah is called 'Fabled Castles', but incorporates all the standard sites, including Taqa, the ruined city of Sumharam, Mirbat and Ayn Razat. Another tour to the west is called 'Frankincense Trail' and includes Job's Tomb, a visit to see frankincense trees, and Mughsail Beach. Each set tour lasts for roughly half a day (irrespective of operator), with the option for a full-day tour to Ubar (recommended).

So, if you want to tour the area, three nights will generally be enough time; however, if you are planning to include a visit to Ubar (which is a little further out), four nights is recommended, and will give you a little time to relax and spend at leisure. There are plenty of deserted picnic spots in spectacular surroundings both east and west of Salalah.

Birdwatching The birds of southern Oman are more African in character. They include the African silverbill, Verreaux's eagle, Ruppell's weaver, African scops owl, Bruce's green pigeon, Didric cuckoo, grey-headed kingfisher, African rock bunting, singing bush lark, African paradise flycatcher, shining sunbird and Palestine sunbird. Broadly, the three best sites for birdwatching in the south are the Mughsail Lagoon (west of Salalah), Dirbat (including Khor Rori Lagoon) and A'Dahariz (about 1km east of Salalah). Ain Rezat and Ain Hamran offer good spots too. Mirbat, Raysut and Mughsail are good for observing seabirds in the autumn. It is easy to travel to these sites independently, but if you would like an accompanied tour, speak to Sumharam Tours in the Crowne Plaza or Hilton hotels. For further information on birdlife, visit www.birdsofoman.com or purchase one of Hanne and Jens Eriksen's books, available in most bookshops in Oman.

Boat trips Sumharam Watersports and Diving Centre (see page 243) offers full- and half-day boat trips along the southern coast, where it is likely you will spot dolphins and whales. An afternoon trip means you have the additional pleasure of watching the sunset from the boat. Tours leave from both Salalah Port (west of Salalah) and Mirbat Harbour (east of Salalah). You will be collected from your hotel. A half-day trip costs RO200 for the boat, which takes ten people, and includes refreshments. The cost doubles for a full-day trip, which includes lunch and refreshments.

Canoeing/kayaking Canoeing can also be experienced outside of the *khareef* season off the Salalah coast. It costs RO20 for a full day and RO15 for half a day, from Saturday through to Thursday. On Fridays there is a special full-day canoeing trip around the lagoon of Khor Rori for RO45 including lunch. Guests will be collected from their hotels. It doesn't matter if you are no Mark Evans (see page 153) – all levels are welcome. Call Sumharam Watersports on 23 235333.

Caving Teyq Cave is situated between Taqa and Mirbat and is one of the largest in the world (see page 257 for further details on how to visit).

Desert tours and camping Overnight trips to the desert camp in Shisr (Ubar) are offered by Sumharam Falcon Diving and Watersports, costing RO250 for the 4x4 vehicle, the driver/guide, lunch, dinner and breakfast. A day trip costs RO120 per car, which includes the driver/guide and lunch, and allows for a maximum of four people in the vehicle.

Diving Diving is permitted in the waters of the southern coast of Oman at any time outside of the *khareef* season. Sumharam Falcon Watersports Centre (inside both the Hilton and Crowne Plaza hotels) is the sole arranger of dive trips at the moment. The knowledgeable and tremendously helpful Yousuf (who speaks excellent English and is based in the Crowne Plaza) will assist you. Two other companies, Aquadivers and Extradivers, are to operate in Dhofar come October 2006 season, but there are no details as yet.

There are three private dive clubs in Dhofar – Dhofar Divers, Thumrayt Divers and Salalah Subaqua – which are organised and operated by expats working with the air force and British army in Oman. You might be lucky enough to be invited along.

There are several dive sites off the Dhofar coast. The best are at Mirbat and Hasik (east of Mirbat), along with the Halaniyat Islands. The Aquarium, which is located 8km east of Mirbat, is a good, easy shore dive, for divers of all levels, and makes a great site for training new divers and snorkellers. Lion fish, sting rays, clown fish, scorpion fish, puffer fish, lobsters, rays and turtles are often spotted. The Eagles Retreat dive site is 10km east of Mirbat. A shore dive is offered from Mirbat to Habeen Hasik (an ancient small village whose shores offer some of the best diving in Dhofar). Close to the Halaniyat Islands there is a British wreck, which sank in 1914 on the return leg of its journey to Calcutta, carrying a cargo of tea. The *City of Winchester* lies at 30m depth (for the interesting history, see www.divernet.com/wrecks/winchester). Sumharam Watersports offer a two-night camping trip to the Halaniyat Islands, which incorporates ten dives and costs RO450 per person inclusive of everything (transport from your hotel, gear, food, camping kits), with a minimum of five people required. This has been very popular to date with British tourists.

For one-two dives, including tanks and weights, it costs RO35 per person. Snorkelling costs around RO20 per person.

Fishing Sport fishing trips can be easily arranged through Sumharam Falcon Diving and Watersports. The boat takes a maximum of six people and departs from either Salalah port (west of Salalah) or Mirbat harbour (east of Salalah). Hiring the boat for half a day costs RO360, while the full day costs RO600.

The delicacies of lobster and abalone are plentiful in the waters off Oman, especially in the Dhofar region and around Masirah Island in the Sharqiya. Their high commercial value has been steadily exploited, which has led to conservation regulations being established which now restrict the fishing of these species to the months of December and January.

Shark fishing is a lucrative business in Dhofar, and the season between October and April brings hundreds of fishermen in their dhows from Sur and Masirah to fish the waters along the Dhofar coast. The sharks, hunted primarily for their fins and tail, are snapped up by agents on the jetties along the coast. Shark fin soup is an exotic dish with a strong consumer market, especially in Far Eastern countries. Sharks here are often 5–6ft in length and fetch around RO50–55 each. A single overnight shark fish hunt would probably yield around 12–18 sharks, so it is big business for local fishermen.

Although the warm tropical waters of the Dhofar coast offer rich pickings, and draw the fishermen in from Masirah, Sur and Al Ashkhara for a two-month season, it is in the Sharquiya where the biggest ones are caught. Eighty different species of shark are known to exist in Oman's waters.

Al Hafa Souk (*Open Sat–Thu 08.00–11.00 and 16.00–19.00, closed Fri*). Salalah's oldest souk, named after the Al Hafa district of town, is close to Al Husn, the sultan's fort, between Qaboos Street and the corniche. It is a sprawling maze of little alleys where some of Salalah's few remaining old houses can still be seen, now lived in by Pakistanis and Bangladeshis; the Omanis have moved out to more modern suburbs. Here you can bargain for frankincense of three qualities – the most expensive white variety, followed by the mixed white and brown, and then brown, the least expensive. Perfumed oils, *bokhur* (see box, *Frankincense*, pages 254–5) and incense burners are also for sale here.

There are a few shops in the souk selling old silver jewellery like Omani *khanjars*, women's anklets, bracelets and headdresses, though these are diminishing year by year. Among the new items for sale in the souk are traditional Dhofari women's robes, usually made of velvet or polyester decorated with sequins or glass beads. The typical design is slightly shorter in the front, with a small train at the back. Colourfully dressed Dhofari women are often themselves the sellers, rings through their noses, bartering without inhibition. From the souk it is a short stroll to the corniche, its coconut palms leaning at amazing angles in line with the prevailing wind.

The other town souks are more modern – the new souk selling fish (mornings only), fruit and vegetables, and the old souk packed with tiny shops selling the gold trinkets which are favoured today. The traditional old silver Dhofari jewellery is increasingly rare, most of it having been melted down to make new items before the value of the old pieces was fully appreciated.

Al Balid Archaeological Park (*Open Sat–Thur 08.00–20.00, closed Fri, entrance RO1.*) Al Balid is the site of ancient Salalah, known as Zufar, from which the province of Dhofar gets its name. Descriptions by early visitors like Ibn Battuta (the Arab geographer) and Marco Polo referred to this ancient Salalah as 'a great and noble and fine city'. Today it is an extensive site on the Khor Salalah (Salalah Creek), a short walk west of the Crowne Plaza. It is 2km long and 600m wide.

A five-year project led by a German team from Aachen University began an archaeological dig here in 1996, discovering that many of the blocks of this ancient Salalah were pilfered to build the modern city, adding to the puzzle.

The extant ruins are from the 10th to 15th centuries, when the city was settled as a port for exporting frankincense and Arab horses, although archaeological finds date the origins of this ancient city to the early Islamic period, and even earlier. The city began to decline in the 16th century as the Portuguese took over the export trade to India.

The remains of the ruler's palace are still visible today, as are the remains of the Great Mosque, the Koran school, the cemetery and a large enclosing wall with towers. The site has an exhibition centre, which includes two museums (one historical, the other natural). The original Dhofar Museum has now been moved and incorporated into this park. The historical and archaeological exhibits from Sumharam and Al Balid and other areas in the region, include rock art, pre-Islamic pottery, coins dating back to the 11th century, manuscripts and photographs, plus a natural history section on plants and animals of the region.

There is a gift shop, restaurant and snack bar. There is also a botanical garden with indigenous plant species, which can be visited as part of the Salalah 'city tour'.

TOURS IN AND AROUND SALALAH

Salalah city tour The half-day Salalah city tour is likely to include Al Balid archaeological site, the frankincense souk, the gold souk, the Arabian fish market, Dhofar Museum and Al Husn, the sultan's summer palace. If you prefer to be independent, take a taxi to the gold or frankincense souk, where you can stroll about at leisure. Distances are a little far for walking if you are based at one of the beach hotels. On the coast at the edge of town is the Al Balid archaeological site, easy walking distance from the Crowne Plaza, but a taxi ride from the Hilton.

East Salalah tour The East Salalah tour lasts half a day and includes sites such as Taqa, Wadi Darbat, Sumharam and the Queen of Sheba's Palace, Khor Rori, Tawi Attair, the Anti-Gravity Spot and Mirbat.

At each old village there is a small collection of grocers, Automatic Bakery stores and pharmacies, so you will always be able to grab a drink, snack or painkiller if needed. There was even a candy-floss stall (*sharr banat*, meaning 'girl's hair') at an Al Maha petrol station along the route. Tour operators usually provide soft drinks for half-day tours, and snacks and soft drinks for full-day tours, so you might like to check this when you book.

In a full day, driving about 250km, you can complete a tour of most sites to the east of Salalah. The forts at Taqa and Mirbat have brief opening hours (*open Sat–Wed 08.00–14.00, closed Thu and Fri*), and the same applies to the ruins of Sumharam, so it is best to time your visit accordingly, leaving Bin Ali's tomb (*open all the time*) and the natural wonders of the baobab forest, Wadi Dirbat and Tawi Attair to the afternoon. To reach the baobab forest and the upper reaches of Wadi Dirbat you will need a 4x4, but for all else a saloon car is fine.

Leaving Salalah by the Taqa road it soon changes to a fine wide dual carriageway, the reason for which becomes clear when you realise it doubles as the approach to the Mamura Palace, residence of Qaboos's elder sister. Flanking this stretch of landscaped dual carriageway are large fodder farms and the Royal Farm, which grows grass, cereals and exotic fruits, and houses large stud farms of pedigree Arab horses as well as dairy herds of local cattle. Next door to the Royal Farm is the extensive Southern Oman Regiment which has been stationed here on the Salalah Plain since the Dhofar War and is now positioned to guard the palace.

West Salalah tour The West Salalah tour offered by the operators is likely to include Job's Tomb (also known as Nabi Ayoub), frankincense trees and the Mughsail blowholes and will take roughly half a day, allowing for a picnic and refreshment stops. At the point furthest west, as far as you are permitted to go towards the Yemeni border, you meet a military checkpoint and barrier. It is not permitted to cross over into Yemen. There are no sites of historical importance on this west side of Salalah, but the natural sites and landscape make up for it. The total circuit is approximately 240km.

As you head out west from Al Husn Palace along Qaboos Street you pass the bird sanctuary to your left among the marshes of Khor Salalah. It is not possible to visit the sanctuary, which is private to the grounds of the palace.

If you still have a couple of hours of daylight left (it gets dark at 18.00 all year around) on return from your trip west of Salalah, you can continue straight on up to Job's Tomb to enjoy the sunset over the mountains, looking down towards the sea. Otherwise a full-day trip can be done to the north of Salalah by heading direct to legendary Ubar (modern Shisr), T E Lawrence's Atlantis of the Sands. The site lies northwest of Thumrayt, 180km from Salalah, so after exploring it you can have a picnic lunch in the desert, and return via the Pools of Ayun and Job's Tomb. By reaching the tomb in time for sunset, you can enjoy a drink on the terrace of the adjacent restaurant overlooking the Salalah Plain from on high.

Ubar tour North of Salalah, the tour offered by all the operators is the 'Ubar Tour' and the 'Empty Quarter'. It lasts a full day. You will be taken to the archaeological site and small museum (for details see *Shisr*, page 262), after which you will be taken for a drive over the dunes of the Empty Quarter.

An early start is usually made, and although a 4x4 is not strictly necessary to reach it, the journey over the gravel track will take you rather a long time, and is not advisable by saloon car. Most organised trips to Ubar include a short spell in the desert beyond, to give the visitor a taste of the Empty Quarter and to experience the sensation, however briefly, of being surrounded by silence and sand. Sumharam Watersports and Diving Centre (in the Hilton and Crowne Plaza hotels) has a camp here, if you want an overnighter. You may find that camels lurk at a particular point beyond Ubar, the young owner ever hopeful that a party of tourists will want to experience a ride.

AIN REZAT

The turn-off to Ain Rezat, the spring from which the Royal Farm is irrigated, is at the Mamura roundabout, where the dual carriageway ends. A private road leads to the Mamura Palace itself. This is just five minutes from Salalah and a further few minutes leads you the 7km on tarmac road to the spring, where the gardens are opened at the weekend to picnicking families. A notice warns of bilharzia snails and forbids swimming or washing in the water. Set within ten minutes' drive of Salalah, the spot is inevitably popular but the crowds can be escaped to some extent if you park and walk through the gorge following the *falaj* systems which extend for 17km with some interesting remnants of old *aflaj* in places. The spot was the scene of heavy fighting during the 1963–75 Dhofar War. Birdwatching is good here.

AIN HAMRAN عين حمران

Just 12km outside Salalah a sign points inland to another spring, Ain Hamran, 7km away. The straight road takes you to the bottom of the cliffs, where there is no settlement as such, though during the *khareef* season a large tented encampment pitches here. The road leads round to a public area with parking, pretty and lush with trees, ending in a circular pool with steps down. Women and children can be found sitting by the pool at weekends, their washing hanging out to dry on the railings, the children splashing and swimming in the pool. Further tracks lead off among the trees with the *falaj* running through. As you leave, look out for the pre-Islamic citadel on top of a hillock that guards access to the spring, just where the vegetation stops. A little path leads up to the top – a five- or ten-minute scramble depending on age and agility. This is also an excellent birdwatching spot.

Taqa is the first town you come to east of Salalah, an easy 20-minute drive (30km), and was once a prosperous port. There are three tarmac roads turning off to Taqa and it is best to take the first one, signposted Taqa Castle (1.5km). This leads past the picturesque Khor Edge, through the town to the little fort set in the centre (*open Sun–Fri 08.00–14.00, closed Sat*), with a handful of older Dhofari houses facing it. The stone used in these houses is quarried locally and starts off as white, but then goes black when exposed to the sun and air over a period of years.

On the small hill behind Taqa are four small forts guarding the town, one of which can be reached via a gravel track. Sultan Qaboos's mother is buried in the graveyard of Taqa. The road from the fort in the centre of town loops on round in a semicircle to exit the town and rejoin the main road at the crossroads with Madinat Al Haqq, a town up in Jebel Qara.

WADI DIRBAT وادي دربات

A five-minute drive beyond Taqa sees you crossing a bridge over the Wadi Dirbat, one of Dhofar's lushest wadis and a beautiful place for a picnic. During and immediately after the monsoon rain, the wadi is a riot of water, with lakes, pools and waterfalls and lush pasture. Even for the rest of the year it is well worth a visit for its caves and their paintings, as well as the dramatic gorge scenery.

To get to the upper reaches of the wadi you need a 4x4 to cope with the steep gradient and rough surface. With a saloon car, the most you can do is take one of the easy graded tracks after the bridge that leads up towards the vertical cliff face. During the monsoon season, the water comes crashing over here from the upper wadi in a dramatic waterfall, much photographed for Dhofar publicity material. In practice it looks like this only for about two weeks of the year, in late August/early September.

The approach to the upper wadi is from the Wadi Attair tarmac road, signposted up the hill just to the east of the wadi. Halfway up the climb to the plateau a graded track forks left, signposted Dirbat, easy at first, but soon with gradients too steep for the average saloon car. In a 4x4 you can continue 2–3km from the start of the graded track until you reach a group of huts. Above them to the right you can climb 30m to a natural rock arch, which has cave chambers with stalagmites and

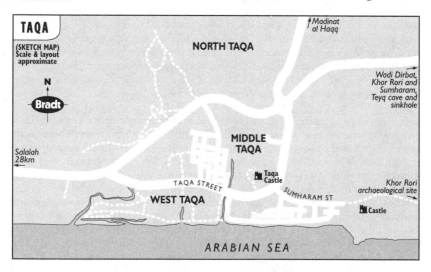

stalactites as well as stunning views over the lower wadi as it runs to the sea. A short distance beyond this on the track (1.5km) is a second cave on the right of the road just above wadi level. Though small, the cave has drawings of animals, coloured with pigments from iron, coal and ochre.

From hereon the track is rough and steep and ends at a limestone wall 4.7km later, to the left of which is Oman's largest natural cave. The area is full of trees and especially lush in the monsoon, when the track becomes very muddy. These caves are the most accessible in Oman.

TAWI ATTAIR

The tarmac road ends after a delightful 20-minute drive through the village of Tawi Attair, at the start of which is a track to the left signposted Khisais Adeen. Less than half a kilometre along this track is a group of small huts to the left. Turn right here along a faint track that follows the line of the water pipes heading for the village. Stop after roughly 200m when you get close to some corrugated huts, park and continue on foot for 200–300m towards the village looking out for a metal tripod sticking up in the boulder-strewn scrubby ground. This marks the edge of the gigantic and very impressive sinkhole, said to be one of the largest in the world. It is roughly 150m in diameter and 211m deep. There is water at the bottom, the same water that is pumped up through pipelines to supply the village. Pakistani labourers in the fields may help you if you cannot locate it yourself.

Also tricky to locate is the small path leading down to a platform overlooking an 80m drop to the bottom. Finding this and climbing down to it will double the time needed for your visit from half an hour to one hour. The purpose of this descent is to hear the birdsong which gives this sinkhole its name Tawi Attair, or 'well of the birds'. It is a wonderful experience in the total silence of the surroundings. The sinkhole is the start of an extensive cave system that can be entered only by experienced divers.

Beans, cucumbers, corn and mangoes are the main agricultural crops of the region of Tawi Attair. The region has many natural springs and caves. Honey production, livestock breeding and the craft of making *majmars*, which are the Dhofari-style incense burners, are all popular in this area. Diving for oysters is also practised here.

BAOBAB FOREST

From Tawi Attair, if you return to the tarmac and follow the line of the graded track, this will lead you for some 16km along the plateau through sprawling meadows. You gradually climb to 1,450m, the summit of Jebel Samhan (see page 257 for details), with stunning views to the coast. The descent of the range is extremely steep in parts, suitable for 4x4 only. To reach the baobab forest (70km from Salalah) it is preferable, if you only have one day, to approach from the tarmac coast road near Mirbat, where it is only 3km up the graded track, signposted Tawi Attair. This too requires a 4x4 because of the steepness. After 3km from the tarmac take the small track to the right that stops after 50m. Park here on the ledge overlooking the valley and you will find two paths, one leading up, one leading down. The one leading down takes you to a small wadi with a *falaj* deep in the forest. The other leads up through some rocks and reaches a small forest of huge baobab trees, some 30–40 in all. The largest, near the centre, has a diameter of 30ft and is thought to be over 2,000 years old. There is also a stream and the area is a splendid picnic spot with boulders and shade. The remaining ascent reaches Wadi Attair after 14km.

In ancient geography the southern area of Arabia was named Arabia Felix. Compared with the dry interior and the barren mountainous north of the region, the south was richly fertile, and home to the frankincense tree, the valuable gum from which allowed the region to flourish, giving rise to the name 'felix', meaning 'happy' or 'flourishing'.

Frankincense was used in religious rites and for medicinal purposes in most civilisations throughout the ancient world. Used in temples and at funerals, and as tribute to be paid by the Arabs to Darius the Persian king, it was a much-sought-after substance and, as with myrrh, more valuable than gold at the time of Christ. In the famous words of the Song of Solomon: 'I will get me to the mountain of myrrh, and to the hill of frankincense.'

Ancient Greek and Roman writers such as Herodotus, Ptolemy, Pliny, Strabo and Diodorus, relate that frankincense from Dhofar was taken by sea to all parts of the world. It was suggested that frankincense was the first commodity to lead to the whole idea of international trade routes and that the Queen of Sheba, for whom Dhofar was a colony, visited King Solomon in Jerusalem purely in order to agree a safe caravan route for the frankincense. Roman armies under Augustus went south in 24BC to try to conquer the frankincense-bearing countries, but either died or were forced back by thirst when attempting to cross the Empty Quarter. In the 1st century AD, the countries of southeast Arabia were the richest in the world as a result of the frankincense of Dhofar. At the height of the trade in the 2nd century AD, roughly 3,000 tonnes was being shipped from southern Arabia to Rome, Greece, Egypt, China, India and the Mediterranean world. Khor Rori was the centre.

Two thousand years later, frankincense is still at the centre of Dhofar's heritage. It is produced only in southern Oman, in Wadi Hadramaut in Yemen, and in Somalia, but the Arabian type is acknowledged to be the best. The best of the best comes from Sawdah, Hadhbarm and Mirbat, the worst from Qushm. The Arabs divide the trees into four types, of which Hoja'i produces the highest quality. The medium-quality frankincense comes from the slopes and hill summits, while the inferior type is collected near the coast.

KHOR RORI AND SUMHARAM خور روري. وسمهرم

Back on the main road almost immediately after the Wadi Attair signpost at Wadi Dirbat is a sign to the right to Khor Rori. A good graded track leads you down towards the sea. At a fork after some 3km, turn right to reach the hillock on which the fenced-in ruins of the ancient city of Sumharam stand, the fine limestone walls overlooking the silted-up harbour of Khor Rori (about 35km from Salalah). To the left the track continues for another 4km or so to reach the headland right on the sea. Rockfalls and silt blocked its harbour mouth, but before that it was a safe harbour for ships from the Red Sea, Mesopotamia and the Far East. The whole area is totally deserted, with no settlement or habitation, making an excellent spot to camp in magnificent surroundings. The creek is now fresh water, having been separated from the sea by a sandy bank, and is favoured by many migratory seabirds including flamingos, waders, herons, gulls and terns.

THE QUEEN OF SHEBA'S PALACE The archaeological site at Khor Rori is also known as the Queen of Sheba's Palace. There is a small hut manned by a guardian (*Sat–Wed only 07.30–14.30*) but there are holes in the fence, so even when the gates are closed there is access for the curious. Unsupervised entry has led to problems, however, and wanton damage has been caused by smashing the glass cases that have been erected over the inscriptions to protect them from the elements. The

Between March and August small incisions are cut into the *Boswellia* tree bark to allow the milky sap to seep out, taking three to five days to dry into semi-opaque lumps. In ancient times, according to Pliny the historian, only a small number of privileged families were permitted to carry out the harvesting and tending of the trees. He explained:

> These persons are called sacred, and are not allowed, while pruning the trees or gathering the harvest, to receive any pollution, either by intercourse with women or contact with the dead; by these religious observances it is that the price of the commodity is so enhanced.

Frankincense burns well on account of its natural oil content and is used throughout Oman today largely in this capacity, burnt on coals to fragrance a room as a gesture of hospitality and in fumigators to fragrance clothing. Travelling round Oman, you will soon become accustomed to the aroma of frankincense in souks, in the shopping malls, in hotel lobbies, and on the clothes of Omanis. It is also a component of a fragrance called Amouage, the most valuable perfume in the world (see www.amouage.com and *Chapter 3, Muscat*, page 113).

The burning of frankincense is an essential part of wedding and Eid festivities and at births. An exotic version of frankincense which is mixed with other aromatic materials is *bakhoor* (or *bukhour, bokhur*). The ingredients vary and can include *oudh* (scented wood from India and the Far East), rose-water, sandalwood, attar, myrrh, other perfume oils, aromatic resins and extracts. These are blended in their varying quantities, cooked, then ground down into a powder for burning on coals.

Salalah's frankincense souk is dedicated to the sale of incense and various perfumes, and is run by Omanis. The traditional hand-painted pottery frankincense burner (*mejmarr*) has had a revival after being used as packaging for Amouage's new perfume *Salalah*. Dhofari women make the pottery and then hand-paint it, thereby helping to supplement their family incomes. Frankincense and a frankincense burner make the ideal souvenir of your travels here.

site was first excavated in 1952 by the American Wendell Phillips, the first person to carry out archaeological work in Dhofar.

The only site in Dhofar that dates to before Christ, Sumharam was, in 1000BC, the greatest city of southeast Arabia. It was also a powerful port, which controlled the frankincense trade route inland through Arabia to Jerusalem, Alexandria and even Rome. The temple of the moon god 'Sin' here guarded the frankincense stores. The routes themselves, zigzagging across Arabia from watering place to watering place, were agreed on by the Queen of Sheba in consultation with King Solomon, her neighbour in the north. Wendell Phillips found evidence of an impregnable fortress city dedicated to a pagan god. The Romans sent an expedition in 24BC to Arabia to find the lands where the frankincense trees were grown, but they died in their thousands before reaching southern Arabia in the deserts north of Yemen.

Sumharam was the easternmost of the cities on the frankincense route, ruled by the kings and queens of Sheba and Yemen who controlled the myrrh of Yemen and the frankincense of Dhofar. From Sumharam, thought to be the greatest spice centre on earth, the bags full of frankincense would go to India and even China, or over the deserts by camel to Damascus and Alexandria. Archaeologists have now dated the site to 100BC from finds of bronze coins, amphorae and sculptures. The whole city is built from well-crafted limestone blocks. Known in ancient times as Moscha, the city was the major port for the incense trade, gateway to the inland route to Petra and Gaza, thence to Mesopotamia, and the sea route to Qana in the

Hadramaut, Yemen. The inscriptions in the broken glass cases are the only two remaining of the eight original ones on the main gate of the city. They are written in the old southern Arabian language Himyaritic, and explain the construction of the city, built under the orders of a Sabean king for the express purpose of controlling the frankincense trade and collecting it for export. The Sabean capital was at Shabwa in the Hadramaut (from where the Queen of Sheba is thought to have got her name).

The central temple area, approached by a ramp of steps, contains a well 30m deep, now covered with protective bars, with walls 2.5m thick in places. There are also many incense storage rooms which were unearthed with incense still in them. Further on towards the seaward of the site is an excavated sunken area with three sacrificial altars. On one of the altars is a relief carving of a bull, one of the forms in which the Sabeans worshipped their lunar god. Sacrificial remains of chicken, fish and bird bones were found round the altars, together with incense residue. The other significant find was a small statue in bronze of an Indian girl playing the flute (*nai*). Dated to the 2nd century AD, the statue proves a trade link between Arabia and India at that point.

From now the road heads east a little inland until, just after the graded track left to Tawi Attair which you take to reach the baobab forest after 3km, the main road does a sudden drop down to a long sandy beach. On the far headland of this beach lies the little fishing town of Mirbat. A recently built tourist complex with restaurant and playground stands right at the beginning of the beach and sunshades are spaced at regular intervals along the sand all the way to the Mirbat end.

BIN ALI'S TOMB At the end of the beach, as the road bears round to the right, is a little unsignposted tarmac street called Bin Ali Street that leads some 300m to the tomb of Muhammad Bin Ali, a local 14th-century prophet and scholar.

A mosque, still used for burial preparations, has been built beside the large car park and a path leads beyond it to the medieval twin onion-domed shrine or tomb of the saint. The tomb has a perennial water source in front under its own baby onion dome. Non-Muslims are permitted to enter the simple incense-filled room; all must remove shoes before entry. Surrounding the tomb is an extensive cemetery, some of the graves really very elaborate. Those with three headstones are for women and those with two are for men.

SADAH

Just after the turn-off to Bin Ali's Tomb is a graded track to the left along the coast, signposted for Sadah (Suduh). This little fishing village, about 135km from Salalah, was another trading port for the export of frankincense. It has a small fort (*open Tue–Fri 08.00–14.00, closed Sat*), and is a 1½-hour drive along a rough track through monotonous landscape far from the sea. Beyond Sadah the track is closer to the sea and the sandy bays have sheer cliffs making them good protected camping spots for those with a 4x4. The ancient city of Hasek is here, and coupled with the scenery of Jebel Nous, makes this place worth a trip. Livestock breeding, honey production and diving for oysters are all popular here.

The particular speciality of the sea here is abalone, a kind of sea snail (known locally as *sufailah),* whose firm white flesh the locals call 'the food of the gods'. It is also thought to be an aphrodisiac. Most of the catch is dried and shipped to the Far East where it fetches high prices. Since 1991, abalone fishing has been limited to two months a year. Excessive fishing had driven it to the verge of extinction, decreasing from a typical daily catch of over 400 in the early 1980s to barely 30 a day, prior to the law of 1991 being enforced.

Burial in the Islamic world is a quick affair, always within 24 hours of death, and in a fairly simple grave, often with no coffin, but with the corpse just wrapped in a white shroud. The Prophet Muhammad said that if the deceased were a good man, the sooner he is buried the sooner he will reach heaven; and if a bad man, he should also be speedily buried so that his unhappy lot might not fall on the others in the house. The actual funeral service is not recited at the grave, this being thought too polluted a place for such a sacred ceremony, so it is usually held in a mosque or in an open space near the house of the deceased, either by the family imam or the *qadi* (judge). The corpse is buried with its head to the north and feet to the south, and as it is lowered all present speak the sentence: 'We commit thee to earth in the name of God and in the religion of the Prophet.' Cremation of the dead is strictly forbidden under Islam, for a dead body was considered as fully conscious of pain as a living body, and Muhammad said: 'It is not fit for anyone to punish with fire but God.'

✗ WHERE TO EAT If you want to stop off for some food, take the first right after Mirbat Castle, then second right where there is a sign for Shaba Restaurant. This is actually Al Shara Tourism Restaurant (see page 258), and although basic, offers a good menu for a very low price, with a friendly staff.

BETWEEN TAQA AND MIRBAT

TEYQ CAVE The Teyq sinkhole, located between Taqa and Mirbat to the east of Salalah and about 15km north of the coast, is one of the largest sinkholes in the world. It is 250m deep and 75 times as big as Oman's Majlis al Jinn chamber (in the Sharqiya region). There is currently no conducted tour to the cave, but tourists can visit the outside of it independently. Alternatively, Sumharam Watersports, or any other tour operator in Salalah, will drive you there on request.

JEBEL SAMHAN NATURE RESERVE Proclaimed a nature reserve in 1997 and covering an area of 4,500km² the reserve extends down to the coastal plain between Marbat and Sadah, called Thalawt. The aim is to protect the wildlife in their natural habitat. The Arabian wolf, Arabian leopard, Nubian ibex, stripped hyena, Arabian gazelle, Blanford's fox and wild cats can be found here. Both green and loggerhead turtles nest here on the sandy beaches between Hadbin and Shuwaymiyah.

In a saloon car you can drive easily up the interesting climb to the plateau around Jebel Samhan, the highest point in Dhofar at 1,450m. On top, the scenery is lush and rolling and still quite green, even in late October and early November. Herds of cattle are everywhere, all over the fields and the road, interspersed with camels. Jebali villages dot the area, their simple dwellings showing the simplicity of their lifestyle. Many of their stone circular huts are still in evidence, but thatched roofs have now been superseded by plastic sheeting weighted down with old tyres. In the fields you can also see their stone-walled enclosures used for pasturing the herds.

MIRBAT مرباط

The tarmac road continues out on the headland to Mirbat (about 70km from Salalah) and at the approach, a sign points you off right to reach Mirbat Castle (*open Sun–Fri 08.30–14.00*). The castle overlooks the harbour with fine views from the towers and its trio of cannons, intact on a raised platform, remain as evidence of its defence against invaders from the sea.

Today, the fishing village is not large but still has some fine old merchants' houses with carved doors and windows. In earlier times it too was a port for the export of frankincense, as well as a breeding centre for Arabian horses which were also exported – the name Mirbat is said to have come from *marabat al khail* which means 'place of tethering' in Arabic. There is a statue of horses at the beginning of the village which indicates that this was what the area was known for. The old houses are now decaying fast, but two hotels, 20 bungalows and a diving club will be built here by 2008.

The waters at Mirbat, and to the east of Mirbat to Hasik, offer excellent diving (see *Diving*, page 248, for further details) and are the best places for spotting dolphins. Sports fishing tours begin here at the harbour.

✖ WHERE TO EAT If you want to stop off for some food, take the first right after Mirbat Castle, then second right where there is a sign for Shaba Restaurant. This is actually Al Shara Tourism Restaurant, and although basic in appearance, offers an extensive international menu for a very low price, with a friendly staff and views out to sea.

HALANIYAT ISLANDS

These five islands lie 200km east of Salalah, just off the coast of Shalim and Shuwaymiyah. They used to be called the Kuria Maria Islands, but now are known as the *Juzor al Halaaniyaal* or the Halaniyat Islands, and the intention is to make them a protected zone and reserve. They are a haven for migratory birds and marine life; turtles breed here and there are large dolphin populations. Diving trips can be arranged through Sumharam Watersports and Diving Centre in the Hilton and Crowne Plaza hotels (see page 243), and camping is possible on the islands.

The history of the islands is rather curious. They were once home to a handful of fishermen, and in 1854 the sultan gave them to the British Crown for nothing, after Lord Clarendon, the foreign secretary of the time, approached him with a scheme to extract guano (excrement of sea fowl used as manure) from the islands,

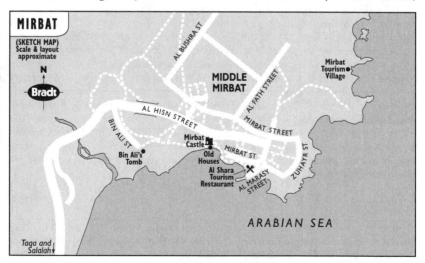

As their name implies, the Jebali are a mountain people of southern Oman (*jebel* is Arabic for mountain). They lived, until recently, largely on the milk and meat of cattle, goats and camels and were dependent on these livestock for their survival and livelihood.

Omani Jebali is a different language to Arabic, and the Jebali from the Qara, the Mahra and the Shahara tribes each have a language distinctive from each other (as well as distinct from the Dhofaris themselves), originating from the ancient languages of southern Arabia. Their traditional clothing is an indigo-dyed piece of material, wrapped up and over the shoulder and around the waist, forming a skirt, and the older Jebalis can be seen today dressed in this way. The younger ones have tended towards both the diet and attire of the people of Salalah town. Generally, the Jebali have been able to take advantage of the improved situation of their surrounds, in terms of education, medical care, employment, access to a wider range of foodstuffs, etc, since Sultan Qaboos took control.

The Jebali formerly lived in traditional round-stone windowless houses with earth and grass roofs, built slightly sunken into the ground; relatively few of these remain today. Instead they occupy concrete and corrugated iron structures.

a valuable commodity in those days. The scheme had been the brainchild of a British merchant called Ord, who, having spotted the guano while sailing by, duly enlisted the help of the Foreign Office, the India Office, the Colonial Office, the Admiralty and the Bombay government and a whole assortment of solicitors and MPs. The sultan refused to take any money for the islands, so Lord Clarendon felt obliged to send a snuffbox as a thank-you.

The guano project, run by Ord and Company, did extract many tonnes of guano but then had its licence terminated in 1861 for failing to make royalty payments. Britain still owned the islands, however, and they were officially administered from Aden. When Aden became independent in 1967, Britain was in the embarrassing position of feeling obliged to hand over the Halaniyat Islands to Aden. The sultan of course would have been furious if Britain were to give to a third party (let alone to the People's Democratic Republic of Yemen with whom it was at war at the time) a piece of sultanate territory which had been given as a generous gift to Queen Victoria. The only way out of the embarrassment was for Britain to return the islands to the sultan, which it duly did in 1967.

WEST OF SALALAH

PORT OF SALALAH Located at Raysut in the industrial zone, 15km west of Salalah (out past the Hilton Hotel), this used to be referred to as Port Raysut. It began its operations in 1998 and is now one of the world's busiest harbours. Before it was built, ships could come in to berth for only six months of the year, prevented for the rest of the year by the high monsoon tides. The facility today is a world-class transhipment and container terminal, competing with the container ports of Jebel Ali and Port Rashid in Dubai, Khor Fakan on the UAE east coast, and Aden. It is undergoing expansion this year.

MUGHSAIL مغسيل Once beyond the Raysut turn-off the road narrows and is very light in traffic. Scattered frankincense trees can be seen in the wadis at the roadsides. Take the right signposted to Al Mughsail, which is the road that leads to

Dhofar WEST OF SALALAH

10

Yemen (although the border cannot be crossed). The next landmark is Mughsail Beach, a comfortable half-hour drive from Salalah (roughly 45km). It is a magnificent 4km stretch of white sand with high cliffs at either end. The first area you can drive onto has substantial shaded shelters built of breeze block, though the quantity of rubbish littering the area is depressing, especially in view of the numerous green government notices in Arabic exhorting brother citizens to look after the environment and avoid pollution. Picnic shades stretch the length of the beach, at the far end of which is the attractively green and large Khor Mughsail, usually covered in grazing camels and cattle, with many seabirds, including flamingos, pelicans and storks. Directly opposite the khor is the sign to Kahf Al Marnaf (Al Marnif Cave), now complete with two tourist restaurants and car park – Al Mughsail Beach Tourist Restaurant and car park and the new Al Marnif Restaurant. The food at these restaurants is good and cheap, but you might prefer to simply stop off for an ice cream or a soft drink. At Al Marnif Restaurant there are disabled toilet facilities. It is from this car park that you need to walk to reach the Mughsail blowholes. Not visible from the road, the blowholes are clustered a short walk past the imposing rocky outcrop and cave and down some steps. They are at their most impressive during the monsoon season when the sea is at its most forceful, and water can shoot up to 30m high through the limestone rock. At other times of year the blowholes are still active at high tide, but at low tide you will mainly just hear the sea slopping about under the rocks, with the occasional soft roar and gentle spray forcing its way up through the metal grids which have been put over the holes to prevent accidents. Even a gentle spray can completely soak you so be careful what you wear, as watches, leather or cameras could be damaged. It is fun to watch people posing for photos beside the blowholes, tentatively awaiting the arrival of the huge forceful spray of sea water so that it can be captured on camera, before they hurriedly dart away to avoid getting soaked.

✗ **Where to eat** Just before the blowholes, at the place you park your car, are the two tourist seafront restaurants (budget range). Each has a good cheap menu and sells ice creams and soft drinks.

✗ **Al Mughsail Beach Tourist Restaurant** Serving international food, such as fish, steaks, omelettes, soups, salads etc.

✗ **Al Marnif Restaurant** Serving international food. There are disabled toilet facilities here.

JEBEL QAMR After Mughsail, the road westwards begins its impressive one-hour climb up to the plateau of the Jebel Qamr, the Mountains of the Moon. The hairpin bends wind their way up and down the first chain of mountains, the hillsides covered in frankincense trees, before the ascent proper begins leading up to the plateau. There are occasional stopping places from which to admire the views, but the best one is near the summit where a series of little tracks lead off the road towards the coast with tremendous views down over the sea. Camels, cows and donkeys are in abundance and the ground is teeming with wild flowers and butterflies. The countryside here is not as empty as it seems at first, and you can find a spot, sit down for lunch quite alone, then be startled by a Jebali herdsman striding past as if from nowhere.

The landscape of the plateau is very different again, with extensive rolling plains covered in grass, browning by late October, trees and the occasional settlement of cow farmers. There is one checkpoint which you can pass through with no documentation, but the second checkpoint 125km from Salalah, where there is a barrier, requires a permit to continue beyond to Sarfait 40km away on the Yemeni border. A signpost points to a place beyond called Furious.

RAYKUT رخيوت The tarmac road up on the plateau and the ascent itself are virtually traffic free with whole stretches where you do not pass another vehicle. If you take the graded road to Raykhut, a small fishing settlement and old sea port, 23km away on the coast, you come very soon to a whole succession of settlements of green corrugated-iron huts, and the amount of traffic on the road quadruples, making it feel positively crowded. The track deteriorates the further it gets towards the sea, and the long dusty drive along the busy track is not really warranted by the reward on arrival at Raykhut. Children have also been known to throw stones at foreigners' cars here, adding to the disincentive to persevere to the end of the track.

On the return drive as you approach the other checkpoint with the flags, look out for the fortification on the top of the hill to your left. It is built of well-crafted stone blocks and is very extensive. Cows are often to be found grazing in it.

✕ Where to eat
✕ **Al Muhit** This is located 5km west of Salalah on the way to Raysut, with beach-side patios. It offers Arabian, Chinese and Indian cuisine.

NORTH OF SALALAH

Travelling northwards up and out of Salalah, by the good main Muscat road, the flat coastal plain is soon crossed (within about ten minutes) and the road starts to ascend and bend as it climbs up through the clouds into the Qara Mountains, with fantastic views back down to the sea. In the *khareef* (monsoon season), this plain becomes a large camping area for locals, and home to the Khareef festival for three months. This is the busiest stretch of road in the Salalah region, carrying all the Muscat traffic. It is becoming busier all the time as the overland traffic carrying goods from Raysut Port begins to increase. Once past Ghadr, you can take the left to Job's Tomb or keep straight on the road to Shisr.

Cows and camels on the road are a normal feature of the climb up the mountains. They appear to wander freely with no sign of their owners, camels unhobbled, taking themselves in search of pasture. At dusk they are something of a hazard, and cows especially, being a darker colour and less easy to spot at night, can occasionally be found knocked over at the roadside, guts heaving in a mass of flies.

Once on the summit of the plateau, the landscape changes very quickly into featureless gravel desert. Signs to a tourist information centre may excite you, but the building looks as if it has been unoccupied for months. There is a police stop on the left that may or may not flag you down. Shortly after the police stop there is a sign left to a Frankincense Park. Continuing straight, you reach Thumrayt (about 50 minutes' drive from Salalah), and a major crossroads from which roads head east into the oilfields around Marmul.

THUMRAYT ثمريت Thumrayt links Dhofar to the rest of Oman and therefore, throughout history, has acted as an important juncture on the ancient caravan routes. Much of Dhofar's frankincense was grown here. The town has a camel racecourse, and races are held here just twice a year, in November and January. A camel providing milk sells for RO500 but a racing camel can sell for a great deal more, even over RO1,000. With changing lifestyles fewer people wish to own camels as they are not profitable and the status that used to go with owning a large herd is fast evaporating.

Many lifestyle elements have changed in recent years. Until 1991 it was a favourite pastime for men to go into the mountains for several days at a stretch and hunt oryx, enjoying the camaraderie of the camping lifestyle and the thrill of the hunt. Now that hunting oryx is banned, there is nothing to substitute for this type of hunting. A few leopards still survive in the hills. The crafts of palm-frond weaving, spinning and weaving wool and tent making are still carried out here.

The graded track to Shisr is clearly signposted 72km to the left, which takes 45–55 minutes from here, depending on your preferred speed over the gravel.

Where to stay

Thumrayt Resthouse \ 23 279371. The Thumrayt Hotel (with its missing 'H') and restaurant stands over to the right on the road to Shisr and Ubar, and is the first in the series of three resthouses on the long Salalah–Muscat road (for details of the others see *Chapter 9, Al Wusta*, page 234 and *Chapter 7, The Dakhiliyah*, page 196). Run entirely by Indians, it is a simple set-up despite its lavish marble entrance. The restaurant is not licensed and serves Indian or international cuisine. The resthouse at Thumrayt is a welcome stop if you are visiting the Empty Quarter and Ubar. *RO18/25 sgl/dbl, exc taxes.*

Qitbit Resthouse (10 rooms) \ 99 085686; f 593106. North of Thumrayt, continuing on the main Muscat–Salalah road, this is the next hotel stop you will reach. This is another basic resthouse with an international restaurant situated 275km from Salalah, but provides a welcome stop if you need it. Accepts credit cards. *RO15/25 sgl/dbl.*

Where to eat
By the petrol garage (close to the resthouse) there are a few coffee shop restaurants and fruit juice stalls. If you haven't brought a picnic, you might like to eat here or inside the Thumrayt Resthouse.

SHISR (THE SITE OF UBAR) الشصر وأرم القديمة It takes about two hours to drive from Salalah to Shisr and a 4x4 is needed. Your arrival at Shisr is heralded by a sudden appearance of trees and buildings in the midst of the bleak landscape. You will need to drive between the two model watchtowers at either side of the entrance road to Shisr itself.

The settlement here is on slightly raised ground. The permanent water source enables year-round irrigation so there are crops growing round the spring in a fenced area. A guardian keeps the key to the fenced site, beside which stands the housing estate built in 1970 by the sultan, with a school and mosque to encourage surrounding nomads to settle. Ranulph Fiennes rented two of these houses for the archaeological team that at the time was using Shisr as a base for digs in the area, never suspecting the site of Ubar was right beside them.

A small shop selling refreshments and occasional simple lunches of omelettes, rice and chicken has been set up by the guardian and his wife at the entrance to the site. There is also a wooden hut, which is the Ubar Museum. An official comes over from a government building opposite to unlock the museum for you. If no-one is around, then enquire at the small shop. The same official gives a brief talk on the history of the site.

Inside is a collection of photographic material, including the American satellite photos which claimed to pinpoint Ubar as the genuine site alluded to in the Koran, together with photos of pretty girls shipped in to ensure volunteers from the

Thumrayt army bases would come forward to boost manpower at the excavation site. Photocopies of the sensationalised international press articles are also pinned up on the walls. The articles at the time (in 1992) caused Oman much grief as the world press made many unscientifically proven claims, the most embarrassing of which was that Ubar was identified with 'Irem of the lofty pillars', as mentioned in the Koran. Outraged Muslim countries chastised Oman and the sultan for making such blasphemous claims. How could foreign infidels dare to say that they had found the holy city of the Koran?

Historical references to a city in the sands of great wealth, wickedness and idolatry begin around AD200 with Pliny and Arab geographers, who referred to Oman emporium, a market set on the crossroads of the lucrative frankincense trade at the southern edge of the Empty Quarter. Pliny called its inhabitants the Ubarites. The city of 'Irem of the lofty pillars' mentioned in the Koran is known from many other historical references to have been an ancient capital of the 'Ad people of southern Arabia. It was said to have been built by King Shaddad Bin 'Ad in the image of paradise. It grew to become rich and then corrupt, so that Allah saw fit to punish it and its people by total destruction – Islam's Sodom. The story of the destruction of a mythical city is recounted in the *Arabian Nights* and it is thought to allude to Ubar and to have occurred towards the end of the Roman period.

In 1991, Ranulph Fiennes published a book entitled *Ubar: Atlantis of the Sands*, the culmination of a search that began 24 years earlier while on secondment to the Sultan's Armed Forces during the war in Dhofar against the communist-inspired insurrection. Having read T E Lawrence's account of previous attempts to locate Ubar (sometimes called Wabar) and knowing that Lawrence suffered his fatal motorcycle accident before he had the chance to seek it for himself, Fiennes became obsessed with the idea of the legendary frankincense city. He used to take his platoon out on exploratory forays, using any opportunity to question Bedu tribesmen, often by his own admission in effect deserting for periods of a day or two to further his quest, before returning to base at Thumrayt.

Before him, others to search for Ubar included Bertram Thomas, author of *Arabia Felix*, who worked for the Sultan of Muscat as personal financial adviser in 1925, having been an administrator in Palestine. In 1930, he became the first non-Arab to make the 1,450km crossing of the Empty Quarter by camel. Next came H St J B Philby, father of Kim Philby the spy, at that time adviser to King Abdul Aziz of Saudi Arabia. He made the crossing a year later from east to west by a more difficult route. Each one claimed to have found evidence of Ubar.

They were followed 14 years later by Wilfred Thesiger, born in Ethiopia in 1910, who joined the Middle East Anti-Locust Unit as an excuse to be in the Empty Quarter, having been inspired while a student at Oxford by the accounts of Bertram Thomas and T E Lawrence. In spite of many journeys across the Empty Quarter, more than any other non-Arab, Thesiger never found the city, but saw many clearly defined camel trails, especially visible in rocky areas, from many directions, all of which, according to the Bedouin guides, converged on the one same site – a city buried in the sand.

When Fiennes had first begun his search for Ubar while still a soldier, he took a big risk – he knew that the sultan would be angry if he discovered his unauthorised expeditions while on the sultan's payroll. The sultan had previously ordered the American archaeologist, Wendell Phillips, originally authorised to go in search of Ubar, never to return to Oman.

Fiennes enlisted the help of NASA to provide satellite images that show up swellings of only a few feet in a flat desert setting, which, to an experienced archaeologist, can show manmade foundations. With the help of these, Fiennes eventually persuaded the sultan to fund the expedition and personally took on the logistic organisation of the project.

The other key players in the expedition were Nicolas Clapp, a Los Angeles freelance documentary film-maker who had worked with Fiennes before on a polar expedition and who had long shared his obsession with the quest for Ubar. It was he who had the idea to persuade NASA to take satellite images from the space shuttle *Challenger*, which he had heard would enable a trained eye to spot buried ruins under the dunes.

The expert eye, the archaeologist on the expedition, was Dr Juris Zarins, an American from South West Missouri State University who had been involved in digs in Arabia over the previous 20 years.

At the start, when the expedition was about to begin in mid July 1990, Fiennes wryly remarked:

> My polar expeditions normally start in dark, freezing shacks with a handful of comrades who know each other well and understand the minutiae of the straightforward aim to get to the Pole. The Ubar reconnaissance expedition began in Muscat's plush Al Bustan Palace Hotel and involved a group who were mostly strangers to each other, none of whom knew how best to set about searching for their goal, and each of whom had a different motive for being there.

The satellite photos were highly appealing to the sponsors of the expedition and Nicholas Clapp was entirely responsible for the film, which the Omanis had agreed was to be a film shot in Dhofar with the central theme being the archaeological search for Ubar. The desire to involve these satellite photos led to some frictions after the expedition was complete, when the American media began to claim that these satellite images had led to the discovery of Ubar by revealing ancient tracks of caravan routes that ran for hundreds of kilometres, disappearing under the dunes and then emerging again. The media claimed that these caravan trails converged on Shisr, which is why the expedition dug there. Fiennes and Juris knew this to be untrue, but Juris did not object, saying it was good for publicity anyhow. He admitted to Fiennes, 'I never thought Ubar was Shisr even when we started digging.' In fact the discovery was achieved, in Fiennes's words, through 'a large slice of luck, a lot of hard work and the experience-honed instincts of Juris together with the support of good vehicles and generous sponsors.'

Saudi reaction to the discovery of Ubar was to belittle it, annoyed at any suggestion that Ubar or Irem was not within Saudi territory. They claimed that the Omani Ubar was nothing special and that in Saudi Arabia similar sites had been found over the past 15 years, notably Jabreen. Juris, having been involved in these excavations was adamant however: 'Shisr is unique. There is nowhere like it in the desert for 900 kilometres.' He felt that Jabreen represented the northern end of the incense road connecting Mesopotamia with Dhofar, since it was already marked on the Ptolemy map as Labrus and was 900km away (or seven weeks' journey by camel) from the incense-gathering area. In between the two are well-spaced waterholes, but only at Jabreen and Shisr were large quantities of Roman pottery found, proving that when Ptolemy drew his map in AD150 (the height of the incense trade with Rome), trade was being carried on between Rome and Dhofar.

While speculation on the name will continue as long as no inscription is found on the site, the fact remains that the archaeological finds there were highly significant for southern Arabia. As one British professor wrote on behalf of UNESCO after visiting the site: 'The archaeological integrity of the site should not be allowed to be affected by possible disputes regarding its name.'

You approach the site today from above. Your first view is of the tallest tower, still standing some 8ft high, built of well-crafted blocks with the first steps of the internal staircase still intact. The original height is estimated at 30ft. Around the tower are storage rooms and hearths, one blackened by wood smoke. From this tower is the spectacular plunge into the collapsed sinkhole, which is probably the most interesting feature of the site. The Arabic name for the site, *shisr,* means 'rock cleft', named after this collapsed section in the very heart of the city. Juris thought it was caused by a decline in the water-table level, leading to a collapse of the immediate surroundings into the 12m-deep limestone cavern, or even by an earthquake, and estimated the timing as somewhere between AD100–300. This natural disaster tied in well with the Koranic description of Ubar, city of the 'Ad people as described in the Sura of the Star:

> It is He who makes men laugh and weep, it is He who kills and makes alive. He is
> the Lord of the Dark Star, He who destroyed 'Ad of yore, and Thamud, and left none
> of them, and the people of Noah before them. Their cities, He threw them down,
> and there covered them what did cover them.

As you descend the path round the rim of the crater, you pass some of the other eight watchtowers which encircled the waterhole and which archaeologists hypothesise are the 'lofty pillars' of Irem which, rising high on this raised land, would have been visible for up to 30km in all directions. Water pipes today run into the cavern itself. The source is fresh water, unlike the usual brackish springs of the desert. Scanners detected the outline of a 4m² well-head buried 28ft under the sand. Fiennes had a Dhofari guide who, on testing the water at Ubar, recognised it as the water from the Pools of Ayun, and another local story runs that a woman dropped her comb into the Pools of Ayun and it was later found in the well at Ubar.

At the time that excavation began here, the crater was filled in with blown sand and the bulk of the early work was in clearing the hole to reveal the original collapsed stonework around the water source. The ruins at Shisr had been written off by all previous seekers for Ubar as being only about 300 years old. Even local Omanis thought of the site as a relatively recent one, not realising what was buried underneath it.

Before digging at Ubar, the expedition which began in December 1991 dug at many other sites, but always to no avail. The local Bedouin had a habit of referring to ruins as 'rubbish piles', which is what many of them had become. In one ancient well-shaft, described by Ptolemy in his early map as the Oracle of Diana, the foul smell of modern garbage and animal bones defeated their attempts to find earlier debris below it. Once digging at Ubar began, they found within weeks 60% of the remains of the citadel walls and nine towers. Many artefacts (some 13,000) were found, including a 1,000-year-old soapstone chess set, the only one ever found in southern Arabia. The king was called 'Shah', for modern chess is based on a Persian war game, and when the king was cornered, the opponent would shout '*Shah Maat',* meaning 'The king is dead', a sound remarkably similar to 'checkmate'. Pottery was also found from Mesopotamia, Rome, Greece and Syria, as well as celadon and Ming plates from China and glass bracelets from Aden. Many of the artefacts date from Shisr's trading heyday from 500–300BC, the Roman, Greek and south Arabian period. There was a decline in materials between 300BC and AD300, and the name Ubar is thought to have declined in use then also. The artefacts showed a renewal of trade during the early Islamic period from AD650–1200, a period when Ubar was known also to be active.

Though the site today is small, the archaeologists speculated that this was the walled and towered caravanserai built round the strategically sited waterhole. They also hypothesised that vast tented encampments covered the hillsides around, to cope with caravans of camels carrying the incense on its route north to Alexandria and Rome and to the ancient Sumerian civilisation in southern Iraq. Speculation is that at its zenith around 3,000BC maybe 100,000 people would have been camped around its walls. Juris identified some 30 campsites on the outskirts of Ubar where caravans would have grouped and waited to enter the city. Until an inscription is found bearing the name Ubar, controversy will always surround the identification of the site, and sceptics doubt that camels were domesticated as early as 2800BC. But the evidence is compelling. Juris said defiantly:

> Historians and archaeologists the world over have always had the opinion that there's nothing of value in Arabia, that nothing will ever come out of Arabia…Only in the last 20 years have we begun to discover that Arabia is an integral part of the human experience of Mesopotamia, Palestine and Egypt.

Where to stay and eat There are no obvious places to stay or eat in Shisr.

WADI DAYQAH This wadi is known as the 'Devil's Gap' as it runs through a steep narrow canyon wih heights of 1,700m. When it rains, water rushes through the wadi, which makes it picturesque, but potentially dangerous. It is located east of Shisr running almost parallel to route 31.

WADI ANDHUR In eastern Dhofar, rarely marked on any map, lies an oasis of great beauty called Andhur, the site of a further frankincense-collecting centre. It is a difficult four-hour drive from Thumrayt requiring 4x4 and guide, and because of the distance and the terrain you would have to camp for a night. The ruins here, set in a remote valley on a hillock above the date palms, were superficially excavated by the American Wendell Phillips in 1952. They consist of a small fort with just a few rooms and a temple with a cut-stone storage tank lined with mortar. The basin and slabs in the temple are associated with Dhofari sun and moon worship that involved primitive sacrifice, possibly even human. There are rumours of girls buried alive, forcible circumcisions, trial by ordeal before the gods, and incestuous marriage.

The location overlooked water and the frankincense trails north of Mirbat. Andhur is in the region of the Mahra tribesmen and they believe the area is holy and do not take kindly to people camping or lighting fires near it.

On the return journey from Ubar or Andhur you can vary the route by turning right towards Ayun at the crest of the ridge of the Qara Mountains to find the Pools of Ayun, which are said to be the source of the spring at Ubar. The small tarmac road runs along the top of the ridge just on the edge of the area reached by the monsoon, so the scenery is a strange mix of desert bleakness to one side, and suggestions of fertility and greenness to the other. The frankincense trees shown here on old maps have mainly died in recent years, through incorrect harvesting of the incense. After about 20 minutes you reach the signposted right turn to Ayun (6km), but almost immediately you fork left onto a graded track, bearing right when there is a choice. This leads across barren hillsides for some 3–4km and ends at a parking area on the edge of a gorge, with no settlement in sight. Though a little bumpy in places, a saloon car can cope.

The pools themselves lie at the foot of the gorge and can only be seen by getting out of your vehicle, walking to the edge of the gorge and looking down. The perennial pools are a lovely sight, cool and green in the barren landscape, and the only sound is reeds blowing gently in the breeze. On Fridays there may be some youths from the village, which perches out of sight on an escarpment above, but on other days you should find the spot beautifully peaceful and deserted. The climb down to the pools is more of a clamber than a walk and takes ten–15 minutes depending on your level of agility in boulder hopping. Up by the parking area are several clusters of frankincense trees, often to be found with their gum oozing from inept cuts. These days, sadly, very few Omanis know how to harvest frankincense correctly. Instead Somalis are imported to do the work, disappearing into the hillsides for weeks at a time. They are used to the work from their own country's incense trade.

Job's Tomb Continuing on the same road you begin the descent of the mountains and some 20 minutes further on from Ayun you will come to the fork right to Job's Tomb (or Nabi Ayoub, as it is known locally). The little dead-end tarmac road leads 1km and forks left up to the walled enclosure for the tomb, now with several other outbuildings grouped together in a garden of trees. Admission is free and the path leads round past the toilets and mosque to the tomb at the far end. Before you enter the guardian may show you a footprint, reportedly that of the Prophet Ayoub. Both the footprint and the tomb are considerably large and giant-like. The guardian issues women with a green diaphanous scarf to cover their heads, and shoes must be removed by all before entering the heavily incensed single room where the large tomb lies covered in drapes. The Muslim prophet buried here is identified with Job of the Old Testament, well known for his boils.

Beyond the tomb complex, the tarmac road runs on to end at a restaurant and café with a parking area. This restaurant is well sited on the ridge with stunning views from its terrace down towards the Salalah Plain and the sea in the distance, but unfortunately this appeared closed down when visited in late 2005. It may be reopened by the time of your visit.

There is also a small collection of shops. In one of the foodstuffs stores you can buy anything from Red Bull to cigarettes, light bulbs to blenders, crisps to batteries, biscuits to ice cream. Even footballs are for sale here.

RETURN TO SALALAH

From this point back on the main road, the descent begins, winding through the extraordinary landscape of ravines and plateaux, with some excellent spots for photography. Just before reaching the outskirts of Salalah a sign points left to Ain Garziz – *ain* is Arabic for 'springs' – and a little restaurant complex sits on the edge of a garden called Ittine Natural Park. This restaurant, called Ateen Tourist Restaurant, serves full meals and has has a separate family eating area ('family division'), men's eating area ('gents' division') and attractive eating areas in their tranquil flower-filled gardens. Do take time to stop here, if just for a drink. Bees are kept here and fresh honey is available. There is a *shisha* counter for those that fancy a smoke in the traditional style.

The tarmac road continues to the Ain Garziz spring at the base of the mountains, an area of lush fertility with a running *falaj* through the trees. Again, it is a beautiful peaceful area, with not many other people about, although it is a popular picnic area at weekends (Thu–Fri). Continuing along this road, keep an eye open for the fascinating meat stalls cooking and selling fresh meat on stone mounds on the ground. From here you rejoining the Ateen Road which is signposted back to Salalah.

Appendix I

LANGUAGE

Like Hebrew, Arabic is a Semitic language with a root system. The root of an idea or concept is represented by a simple verb, usually consisting of three consonants. These verbs are the very basis of the Arabic language, and all variations of meaning around the root idea are expressed by imposing different patterns on the basic root. Hence, in the simplest of examples, from the root K T B (*kataba* when vowelled) which means 'he wrote', you can make *maktab* meaning 'office', *maktaba* meaning 'library' and *kitaab* meaning 'book'. The vowels are fully conjugated, so *katabnaa* is 'we wrote' and *yatabuuna* is 'they are writing'. Arabic dictionaries list words under their root, so if you cannot identify the root, you cannot look up the word. Hunting for words in the dictionary is something the beginner spends a long time doing.

Arabic script is arguably the easiest thing about the language. Many are daunted by the script and the right to left flow of text, yet the alphabet contains only 29 characters and there are strict rules to determine which characters join on to which. The characters change their shape according to their position within the word but always following the same strict rules. The process of learning the characters and their shapes is therefore purely a memory exercise which can be done easily in three days and thereafter just requires practice. As for the right to left flow of text, it just takes a little time to adjust, rather like driving on the right instead of the left of the road.

Having mastered the script the task begins in earnest. The first conceptually difficult thing you now encounter is that only the consonants are written – you have to supply the vowels yourself. In that case, how do you know which vowels to put where? The answer is that you do not, or at least not until you have a thorough grasp of the intricacies of Arabic grammar and word structure, which takes a good three or four months' study. For this reason all beginners' texts and children's school books are fully annotated with vowel signs added in the form of dashes and dots above and below the line. Getting students to read an unvowelled text aloud is always an excellent way of assessing their level, as it instantly reveals the depth of their understanding of Arabic grammar.

Pronunciation is another area which is not as daunting as it may seem. Of the 29 consonants, 18 have direct phonetic equivalents in English such as b, d, t, l, s. The rest have no direct equivalent and range from emphatic versions of d, s, and t, usually transliterated as D, S and T, to a small handful of sounds which are genuinely difficult for Westerners to pronounce. The guttural stop or '*ayn*' as it is called in Arabic, usually represented in transliteration as a reversed comma, is probably the one that gives most trouble, sounding like a vibrating constriction of the larynx.

THE ARABIC ALPHABET

Final	Medial	Initial	Alone	Transliteration	Pronunciation
ـا			ا	aa	as in 'after'
ـب	ـبـ	بـ	ب	b	as in 'but'

ﺖ	ﺘ	ﺗ	ﺕ	t	as in 'tin'
ﺚ	ﺜ	ﺛ	ﺙ	th	as in 'think'
ﺞ	ﺠ	ﺟ	ﺝ	j	as in 'jam'
ﺢ	ﺤ	ﺣ	ﺡ	H	emphatic, breathy 'h'
ﺦ	ﺨ	ﺧ	ﺥ	kh	as in the Scottish 'loch'
ﺪ			ﺩ	d	as in 'den'
ﺬ			ﺫ	dh	as in 'that'
ﺮ			ﺭ	r	as in 'red'
ﺰ			ﺯ	z	as in 'zero'
ﺲ	ﺴ	ﺳ	ﺱ	s	as in 'sit', hard 's'
ﺶ	ﺸ	ﺷ	ﺵ	sh	as in 'shut'
ﺺ	ﺼ	ﺻ	ﺹ	S	emphatic, strong 's'
ﺾ	ﻀ	ﺿ	ﺽ	D	emphatic, strong 'd'
ﻂ	ﻄ	ﻃ	ﻁ	T	emphatic, strong 't'
ﻆ	ﻈ	ﻇ	ﻅ	Z	emphatic, strong 'z'
ﻊ	ﻌ	ﻋ	ﻉ	'	guttural stop, hardest sound for non-Arabs to make, called 'ayn'.
ﻎ	ﻐ	ﻏ	ﻍ	gh	like a gargling sound
ﻒ	ﻔ	ﻓ	ﻑ	f	as in 'fire'
ﻖ	ﻘ	ﻗ	ﻕ	q	like a guttural 'k'
ﻚ	ﻜ	ﻛ	ﻙ	k	as in 'king'
ﻞ	ﻠ	ﻟ	ﻝ	l	as in 'lady'
ﻢ	ﻤ	ﻣ	ﻡ	m	as in 'mat'
ﻦ	ﻨ	ﻧ	ﻥ	n	as in 'not'
ﻪ	ﻬ	ﻫ	ﻩ	h	as in 'hat'
ﻮ			ﻭ	w	as in 'will', or 'oo' as in 'food'
ﻲ	ﻴ	ﺍ	ﻯ	y	as in 'yet', or 'ee' as in 'clean'

Arabic is, by the very nature of its structure, an extremely rich language, capable of expressing fine shades of meaning, and this is reflected in the wealth of Arabic literature, especially poetry. The average English tabloid reader is said to have a working vocabulary of 3,000 words, while the Arab equivalent is said to have about 10,000

There are also many interesting features of the language which hint at the nature and attitudes of the Arab mind, notably the existence of only two tenses, perfect and imperfect. There is no future tense. In the Arabic concept of time there is only one distinction that matters: has something been finished or is it still going on? Another curiosity is that the plural of inanimate objects is treated grammatically as feminine singular.

GREETINGS On first meeting when travelling generally outside the cities the respectful greeting to older people is: *As-salaamu 'alaykum*, meaning literally 'May peace be upon you.' The standard reply is: *Wa 'alaykum as-salaam*, meaning 'And on you the peace.'

There are three common phrases you will hear incessantly. *In sha Allah*, meaning 'If God wills it', is used all the time in the sense of 'hopefully', because nothing is certain to happen unless God wills it. So if you say to an Arab 'See you tomorrow', he will reply '*In sha Allah*', meaning, 'Yes, if God permits it and nothing happens in the meantime to prevent it.' It can also be a polite way of avoiding commitment, conveying 'Let us hope so …'

The second phrase is *Al Hamdou lillah*, meaning 'Thanks be to God'. This is said every time something works out the way it should have done. It also expresses relief, along the lines of 'Thank God for that!'

The third phrase is *TafaDDal*, meaning 'Please go ahead' or 'Come in' or 'After you'. It is always said by your host when you arrive and on entering the house or room and before eating. Literally it means 'Please be so good as to …'

Other greetings

Hello, welcome	*marHaba, ahlan*
Goodbye	*ma'a as-salaama* (literally, with the peace)

USEFUL ARABIC WORDS AND PHRASES
The basics

Yes	*aiwa, na'am*
No	*laa*
Please	*min faDlak*
Thank you	*shukran*
Thank you very much	*shukran jazeelan*
You're welcome	*afwan*
Sorry, excuse me	*'afwan, muta'assif*
Hurry up, let's go	*yallah*
More, again, also	*kamaan*
Is it possible? May I?	*mumkin?*
My name is …	*Ana ismee …*
What is your name?	*Shu ismak?*
I don't understand	*Ana maa bafham*
Where are you from?	*Min wayn anta?*
There is …	*Fii …*
There is not …	*Maa fii …*
What?	*shu?*

Getting around

airport	*maTaar*
bus	*baas*
car	*sayyaara*
suitcase, bag	*shanTa*
taxi	*taksee*
ticket	*tadhkira*
petrol	*benzeen*
diesel	*maazout*
far	*ba'eed*
left	*yasaar*
right	*yameen*
near, close by	*qareeb*
straight on	*dhughri, 'alaa aT-Toul*
where?	*wayn?*
Where is the museum, please?	*Wayn Al matHaf min faDlak?*
How far is it to …?	*Kam kiiloometre ila …?*

Hotels and restaurants

hotel	*funduq, ootel*
room	*ghurfa*
soap	*Saaboun*
toilet, bathroom	*Hammam, bait mai*
towel	*manshafa*
the bill	*Al faaToura, Al Hisaab*
restaurant	*maT'am*
breakfast	*fuTour*
lunch	*ghadaa*
dinner	*'ashaa*

Open	*maftouH*	مفتوح
Shut	*mughlag*	مغلق
Forbidden	*mamnou*	ممنوع
Police	*shurTa, boulees*	شرطة
Gents	*rijaal*	رجال
Ladies	*sayyidaat*	سيدات
Hospital	*mustashfaa*	مستشفى

glass	*finjaan*
I don't eat meat	*ana ma baakul laHm*

Food and drink

bread	*khubz*
butter	*zibdeh*
cheese	*jibneh*
eggs	*bayD*
fish	*samak*
fruit	*fawaakeh*
honey	*'asl*
jam	*murabbeh*
meat	*laHm*
sugar	*sukkar*
vegetables	*khuDar*
yoghurt	*laban*
half kilo	*nuSS kiiloo*
beer	*beera*
coffee	*qahwa*
mineral water	*mai ma'daniya*
red	*al Imar*
tea	*shay*
white	*abyaD*
wine	*nabeedh*

Shopping

cheap	*rakhees*
expensive	*ghaalee*
money	*fuluus*
a lot, much, very	*kateer*
no problem	*mish mishkila*
never mind	*ma'a laysh*
shop	*dukkaan*
market	*souk*
How much (does it cost)?	*bikaam? Addaysh?*

Health

chemist	*Saydaliyeh*
dentist	*Tabeeb asnaan*
doctor	*doktoor, Tabeeb*
diarrhoea	*ishaal*
ill, sick	*mareeD*

Days and time

Monday	*Yawn Al Ithnayn*
Tuesday	*Yawm ath-Thalaatha*
Wednesday	*Yawn Al Arba'a*
Thursday	*Yawm Al Khamees*
Friday	*Yawm Al Jum'a*
Saturday	*Yawm as-Sabt*
Sunday	*Yawm Al AHad*
today	*Al yawm*
tomorrow	*bukra*

Numbers

1	*waaHad*	١
2	*ithnayn*	٢
3	*thalaatha*	٣
4	*arba'a*	٤
5	*khamsa*	٥
6	*sitta*	٦
7	*sab'a*	٧
8	*thamaaniya*	٨
9	*tis'a*	٩
10	*'ashara*	١٠
20	*'ishreen*	٢٠
30	*thalaatheen*	٣٠
40	*arba'een*	٤٠
50	*khamseen*	٥٠
60	*sitteen*	٦٠
70	*sab'een*	٧٠
80	*thamaaneen*	٨٠
90	*tis'een*	٩٠
100	*mi'a*	١٠٠
150	*mi'a wa khamseen*	١٥٠
200	*mi'atayn*	٢٠٠
500	*khams-mi'a*	٥٠٠
1,000	*alf*	١٠٠٠
2,000	*alfayn*	٢٠٠٠

Other vocabulary

bank	*bank, maSraf*
museum	*matHaf*
post office	*maktab bareed*
good	*kwayyis, Tayyib*
bad	*mish kwayyis, zift*
hot	*Haar*
cold	*baarid*

Appendix 2

GLOSSARY

Ablution	ritual washing laid down by the Koran before prayer
Ain	springs
Bab	gate
Bahri	sea
Bait	house
Bander	anchorage
bani	tribal prefix meaning 'son of...' in Arabic
Barasti	made from the branches of palm trees
Bedouin	desert nomads
Bustan	garden
Dhow	traditional Arab wooden sailing boat
Eid	religious holiday
Falaj	irrigation channel running from a spring or water source to water crops or date gardens
Ghafiri	one of the main tribes of Oman, usually in conflict with the Hinawi tribe
Hadith	collection of anecdotes from the Prophet Muhammad's lifetime
Halwa	Omani sticky brown sweet often served to guests with coffee, eaten with the fingers
Hinawi	one of the main tribes of Oman, usually in conflict with the Ghafiri tribe
Ibadhi	sect of Islam followed in Oman (one of Islam's earliest), very traditional and orthodox
Imam	spiritual and secular leader who is chosen by consensus among the sheikhs
Jebel	mountain
Jerz	simple axe with wooden handle carried only by men in Musandam, instead of the *khanjar* dagger.
Jinn	spirit which can be good or evil like our 'genie'
Juzor/jazirah	island
Kabir	big
Kahwa	Arabic coffee
Khanjar	Omani silver dagger worn on the belt, with a distinctive curved blade. The more elaborate the *khanjar*, the higher the status of the owner.
Khor	creek or inlet from the sea; also *khwar*
Madinat	town
Majlis	literally 'place of sitting', meaning a meeting of an important person with others who have come to ask for something; the room where guests are received
Mihrab	prayer niche in a mosque indicating the direction of Mecca for prayer
Mina	port
Minbar	pulpit in a mosque from where the imam addresses the congregation

Oryx	creature (related to antelope) with two straight long horns, well adapted to desert life
PDO	Petroleum Development Oman, the main oil company in Oman, a subsidiary of Shell
Qadi	Islamic judge
Ramadan	Muslim month of fasting, which in 2000 happened to coincide with Christmas
Ramlat	sandy area
Ras	headland
Resthouse	simple hotel generally used for transit and found on a main road
Sable	fortified house used for communal activities like weddings and funerals, belonging to one family group
Sagbir	small
Sambuk	small fishing boat
Sarouj	mud plaster
Shatti	shore/beach
Sheikh	tribal leader
Shari'a	Islamic law, according to the Koran and the Hadith
Shi'a	offshoot of Islam from the Orthodox Sunni Muslims, following a hereditary principle of succession after Muhammad rather than an elected or consensus method. Mainly found today in Iran.
Sunni	Orthodox Islam, following the principle of consensus selection of the next caliph or imam.
Souk	Arab market
Sur	fortified walled enclosure
Sura	verse of the Koran
Wadi	valley, natural water course
Wahhabi	a highly conservative Islamic group
Wali	local governor
Wilayat	district/area

Green sea turtles

Appendix 3

HISTORY

Aguis, D A *In the Wake of the Dhow: The Arabian Gulf and Oman* Ithaca Press, 2002. Documents the history of the Arabian dhow.

Allen, C H, Rigsbee, W L, and Rigsbee II, W L *Oman Under Qaboos: From Coup to Constitution 1970–1996* Frank Cass Publishers, 2002. Examines the political, economic and social development of Oman since Qaboos.

Clements, F A *Oman: The Reborn Land* Longman ELT, 1980. An appreciation of Oman's past glories and traditions.

Dinteman, W *Forts of Oman* Motivate Publishing, 1993. Oman's history of battles and inter-tribal conflicts.

Eickelman, C *Women and Community in Oman* New York University Press, 1989. Christine Eickelman lived in Hamra on the western edge of Jebel Akhdar in 1979, and writes of her explorations into the culture of Omani women through the life she shared with them. She sheds light on their concepts of family, privacy, propriety, status and sociability.

Frifelt, K *The Island of Umm-an-Nar: Third Millennium Settlement* Aarhus University Press, 1995. Presents the results and the material found at the settlement of Umm-an-Nar. The Umm-an-Nar culture was the most conspicuous culture in the Oman Peninsula in the Bronze Age.

Gwynne-James, D *Letters from Oman: A Snapshot of Feudal Times as Oil Signals Change* Gwynne-James, 2001.

Hawley, Sir D *Oman and its Renaissance* Stacey International, 2005. An immense work on the history, geography and culture of Oman, and a beautiful book to boot.

Jeapes, T and Drury, I *SAS Secret War: Operation Storm in the Middle East* Flamingo, 1996. The ten-year Dhofar War lasted until 1976, taking place under conditions of secrecy. This is a first-hand account of the SAS's secret campaign in Oman, written by General Tony Jeapes.

Joyce, M *The Sultanate of Oman: A Twentieth Century History* Greenwood Press, 2005.

Peyton, W D *Old Oman* Stacey International, 1983. A fascinating and valuable album of photographs of a bygone age, with accompanying description, taken from around 1900 up to 1970.

Philby, Harry St J *The Queen of Sheba* Quartet Books, 1981. Harry St John Philby was a great Arabian traveller, scholar and writer. He examines the mixture of fable, history, magic and mystery surrounding the visit of the Queen of Sheba to King Solomon, from its origins in the Old Testament and the Qu'ran.

Phillips, W *Qataban and Sheba* Harcourt, Brace and Company, 1955. Wendell Phillips is an explorer, adventurer and archaeologist who explored the ancient treasures of the exotic civilisations of southern Arabia. In this book he unveils the history of Sheba territory in Oman.

Raban, J *Arabia through the Looking Glass* The Harvill Press, 1979.

Al-Rawas, I *Oman in Early Islamic History* Ithaca Press, 2000. An in-depth study of the history of Oman from the advent of Islam until the fall of the second Ibadi Imamate in AD893.

Richardson, C *Masirah: Tales from a Desert Island* The Pentland Press, 2001. This is a well–researched book which recounts a wealth of first–hand stories of RAF history by those who have known Masirah since the 1930s. Illustrated with photographs.

Salil Ibn Razik, *History of the Imams & Seyyids of Oman* Kessinger Publishing Company, 2004.

Severin, T *The Voyage of Sindbad* Putnam Publishing Group, 1983. The reconstruction of an ancient trade route mentioned in the legend of Sindbad; an experiment to see if a sewn wooden boat could reach China using only primitive navigational instruments.

Ward, P *Travels in Oman* Oleander Press, 1986.

Wikan, U *Behind the Veil in Arabia: Women in Oman* The University of Chicago Press, 1982. Unni Wikan explores the segregation of women, the wearing of the *burka* mask, nuptial rituals, and place of women in Omani society.

NATURAL HISTORY

Natural history books are available in the UK from NHBS Environment Bookstore, 2–3 Wills Rd, Totnes, Devon TQ9 5XN; ☎ 01803 865913; www.nhbs.com/info/address.html

Baldwin, Robert *Wales and Dolphins of Arabia* Bowlish Somerset, 2003.

Batty, P D *Bluewater Fishing in Oman* Muscat Game Fishing Association, Oman 2002.

Bosch, D and Bosch, E *Sea Shells of Oman* Longman Group, 1982.

Eriksen, H and J *Birdlife in Oman* Al Roya Publishing, Muscat, Oman 1999.

Eriksen, H and J *Common Birds in Oman* Al Roya Publishing, Muscat, Oman 2005.

Hanna, Dr Samir and al Baloushi, Mohammed *Caves of Oman* Sultan Qaboos University

Larson, T B and Larson, K *Butterflies of Oman* Bartholomew, London, 1980

Macgregor, M *Wilderness Oman* Ptarmigan Publishing Ltd, 2002.

Mandaville Jr, J *Wild Flowers of Northern Oman* Bartholomew Books, 1978.

Miller, A G and Morris, M *Plants of Dhofar, the Southern Region of Oman: Traditional Economic & Medicinal Uses* Office of the Adviser for Conservation of the Environment, Diwan of Royal Court, Sultanate of Oman, 1988.

Randall, J E *Coastal Fishes of Oman* University of Hawaii Press, 1996.

Salm, R and Salm, S *Sea Turtles in the Sultanate of Oman* Historical Association of Oman, 2001

Al Zubair M, *Landscapes of Dhofar* Bait al Zubair, Oman 2003.

ADVENTURE TOURISM

Dale, A and Hadwind, J *Adventure Trekking in Oman* Cordee, 2001.

Mackenzie, A *Oman Trekking Guide* Explorer Publishing, 2005.

Salm, R and Baldwin, R *Snorkelling and Diving in Oman* Motivate Publishing, 1992.

Mcdonald, R A *Rock Climbing in Oman* Verulam Publishing Ltd, 1994.

CULTURE AND TRADITION

Kendrick, I *The Bands and Orchestras of Oman* Diwan of the Royal Court, Oman 1995.

Newcombe, O *The Heritage of Oman: A Celebration in Photographs* Garnet Publishing Ltd, 1996.

Richardson, N and Dorr, M *The Craft Heritage of Oman* Motivate Publishing, 2004.

Vine, P *The Heritage of Oman* Immel Publishing, 1995.

BIOGRAPHY AND AUTOBIOGRAPHY

Beasant, J and Ling, C *Sultan in Arabia: A Private Life* Mainstream Publishing, 2004. A biography providing insight into the character of Qaboos bin Said.

Brown, M *Lawrence of Arabia: The Selected Letters* Little Books Ltd, 2005. This is Malcolm Brown's selection of the letters of T E Lawrence – a traveller, scholar, soldier, writer, critic, politician, and a fascinating and enigmatic figure of the 20th century who played a part in the Arab Revolt.

Burrowes, J *Sultan: The Remarkable Story of a Man and a Nation* Mainstream Publishing, 2005. Biography of Sultan Qaboos.

Monroe, E *Philby of Arabia* Ithaca Press, 1998 edition. Explores the life of Harry St John Philby – one of the great Arabian desert travellers.

Taylor, A *God's Fugitive: The Life of C M Doughty* HarperCollins Publisher, 1999. Charles Montagu Doughty, an explorer, scholar, scientist, travel writer and poet, was the foremost Arabian explorer, who started a tradition of British exploration and discovery in that region. He spent two years wandering with the Bedu through oases and deserts, and returned to England to write one of the greatest and most original travel books: *Arabia Deserta*. Andrew Taylor brings Doughty to life in this biography.

Thesiger, W *My Life and Travels* Flamingo, 2003. A chronicle, spanning the 20th century, of Wilfred Thesiger's life and travel writing.

TRAVEL WRITING

Barnett, D *Dust and Fury: A Novel Set in Oman* Woodfield Publishing, 2003.

Clapp, N *The Road to Ubar* First Mariner Books,1999. Nicholas Clapp, a noted documentary film–maker, arranged two expeditions to Oman with a team of archaeologists and NASA space scientists to search for Ubar, the city that had become known as the Atlantis of the Sands. This book is part travel journal, part archaeological history.

Doughty, C M *Arabia Deserta* Peter Smith Publishing, 1960. A classic account of two years spent with Arabian nomads in the late 19th century.

Fiennes, R *Atlantis of the Sands* Bloomsbury, 1992. Ranulph Fiennes – a leader of major travel expeditions around the globe – relates his search for the legendary Ubar in Oman.

Holden, W M *Dhow of the Monsoon: From Zanzibar to Oman in the Wake of Sindbad* PublishAmerica, 2005. William Holden follows Sindbad's journey by dhow relying on the monsoon winds.

Morris, J *Sultan in Oman*, Sickle Moon Books, 2003. A fascinating read from one of the world's great travel writers, who experienced Muscat prior to its development.

Owen, T *Beyond the Empty Quarter* Serendipity, 2003. Tim Owen's light-hearted memoir of his experiences in 1960s Oman.

Rollins, J *Sandstorm* HarperCollins Publishers, 2004. James Rollins's fiction based around the lost city of Ubar, in the desert of Oman.

Stark, F *The Southern Gates of Arabia* John Murray, 1936. Freya Stark – a travelling Englishwoman – relates her journey to explore the Frankincense Road, catching the spirit of people and place in this travel classic.

Thesiger, W *Arabian Sands* 1959.

Thesiger, W *Desert, Marsh and Mountain* Flamingo, 1995. Thesiger's writings are an absolute must for those interested in the accounts of previous explorers and travellers to Oman. Beautifully written. Thesiger recreates his five-year journey with the Bedu at the time before oil and the West transformed them.

INFORMATION ON OMAN

www.nizwa.net A useful site for information about Oman generally but especially the city of Nizwa and its heritage.

www.omanaccess.com Listings, tourist information and community forums.

www.omanet.om The Ministry of Information's website covering all aspects of the country.

www.omaninfo.com Classifieds and news and tourism features.

www.oman.org/tourism.htm General travel info, health advice, guidance for off-road routes, plus listings for hotels, tour operators and agencies.

www.omantourism.gov.om The Ministry of Tourism's website.

www.soukofoman.com An online market for books, clothes, incense, silver and cosmetics.

Index

Page numbers in italics indicate maps; page numbers in bold indicate major entries

280